Vancouver

written and researched by

Tim Jepson

D0113617

ROUGH
GUIDES

NEW YORK • LONDON • DELHI

www.roughguides.com

Introduction to
Vancouver

One of the world's most beautiful cities, Vancouver is centred on a glitzy Downtown, fringed by water and set against a spectacular backdrop of mountain peaks. Its setting and surroundings make it an outdoor-lover's paradise, and locals barely have to move to take advantage of the countless recreational opportunities afforded all year round – whether it's sailing or swimming in crystal-clear English Bay, biking or rollerblading in vast Stanley Park, skiing or boarding on the mountains, or wandering through the forests and canyons on the city's northern shore.

Vancouver's nearly two million residents exploit this spectacular natural setting to the hilt, and when they tire of the immediate region can travel a short distance to the unimaginably vast wilderness of the British Columbia interior. No wonder, given its superb natural heritage and outdoor facilities, that in 2003 the city completed a successful bid to stage the 2010 Winter Olympics.

Vancouver also has plenty that contributes to a cultured atmosphere: top-notch museums, superb restaurants – arguably the best in North America after New York and San Francisco – countless cafés, great parks and gardens, and any number of hip bars and clubs. Summer and winter it's all hedonism and healthy living, typically West Coast obsessions that

The Great Outdoors

"Spectacular by Nature" runs the tag line across much of Vancouver's official visitor material, emphasizing (as if emphasis were needed) the city's key attraction: the stunning mixture of cityscape and natural environment. Even if you only walk or cycle around the city, you'll experience some of the thrill of the great outdoors, from glimpses of snow-capped mountains at the end of Downtown streets to the centuries-old forest and ocean views of Stanley Park.

Meanwhile, the string of parks of North Vancouver offers super hiking for all levels, as well as tremendous skiing, snowboarding and other winter activities, all just twenty minutes' drive from the city centre.

Just because the parks are close, don't be fooled into thinking they're tame; most contain areas of real wilderness for which you should be properly equipped. Don't think either that Vancouver's great outdoors stops with the mountains. The ocean provides sailing, kayaking, canoeing and diving, among other activities, some of which, such as kayaking, you can pursue from the city itself.

spill over into its sophisticated arts and culture. Vancouver claims a world-class symphony orchestra, as well as opera, theatre and dance companies at the cutting edge of contemporary arts. Festivals proliferate throughout its mild, if occasionally rain-soaked summer, and numerous music venues provide a hotbed for up-and-coming rock bands and a burgeoning jazz scene.

Some idea of the city's outlook can be gleaned from a slew of lifestyle surveys which show that, per capita, its inhabitants read more, drink more wine, smoke less, spend more on outdoor gear and support more bars and restaurants than any other Canadian city.

Not all is devoted to pleasure here, however. Business growth continues apace in Canada's third largest city, much of its prosperity stemming from a **port** that handles more dry tonnage than the West Coast ports of Seattle, Tacoma, Portland, San Francisco and San Diego put together. The port in turn owes its prominence to Vancouver's much-trumpeted position as a **gateway to the Far East**, and its increasingly pivotal role in the new global market of the Pacific Rim.

Links across the Pacific, however, are nothing new. After all, the city is closer to China and Japan than it is to Britain, its old colonial master and source of many of its twentieth-century immigrants. And much of the city's earliest immigration focused on Vancouver's extraordinary **Chinatown**, just one of a number of ethnic enclaves – Italian, Greek, Indian and Japanese in particular – which lend the city a refreshingly down-to-earth quality that belies its sleek, modern reputation. So, too, do the city's semi-derelict eastern districts, whose down-and-out population is shockingly at odds with those pursuing pleasant lifestyles in the lush residential neighbourhoods. Low rents and Vancouver's cosmopolitan young have nurtured an unexpected **counterculture**, distinguished by second-hand shops, avant-garde galleries, and hip bars and clubs.

The city's vibrant feel is catching, its growth and energy almost palpable as you walk the streets. In just five years, between 1996 and 2001, the date of the last census, the city's population increased by an extraordinary fourteen percent, and it remains **Canada's fastest-growing city**: over the next few years it's expected to grow by as much as fifty percent. In response, the Downtown area is spreading, and the older, run-down districts on its southern and eastern fringes – the areas of Yaletown and False Creek in particular – are feeling gentrification's effect. On the whole, real estate in Vancouver is now more expensive than Toronto. In addition to

new residents, film and TV production companies have discovered the
city's riches, making it North America's largest production centre after Los
Angeles and New York. Yet, in the peculiar way that seems second nature
to Canadians, the changes are being handled in a manner that enhances
rather than compromises all the city has to offer.

Although there's plenty to occupy you here, you should also aim to visit
Victoria, easily reached by ferry or seaplane. An eminently charming old
town – albeit one that slightly overplays its ersatz Englishness – it has
enough sights and interest to merit an overnight stay. En route to the city
by air or sea you'll pass the **Gulf Islands**, an archipelago scattered across
the Strait of Georgia between the mainland and Vancouver Island. All the
islands make peaceful and bucolic retreats, with plenty of laid-back accommodation, good restaurants, sleepy villages and pleasant (and easy) hiking,
cycling and other outdoor opportunities. Like Victoria, they also offer
tremendous opportunities for whale-watching, increasingly one of the
region's most popular visitor activities.

If you hanker for more demanding outdoor pursuits, Vancouver is perfectly placed for excursions into the Coast Mountains to the north, notably

the peaks near the year-round ski and activities-laden resort of **Whistler**, and for trips along the mainland **Sunshine Coast** facing Vancouver Island known, above all, for some of the world's best diving.

What to see

Cradled between the Pacific and snowcapped peaks, Vancouver's dazzling Downtown district fills a narrow peninsula bounded by Burrard Inlet to the north, English Bay to the west and False Creek to the south, with greater Vancouver sprawling south to the Fraser River. Edged around Downtown's idyllic waterfront are fine beaches, a dynamic port and a magnificent swath of green – Stanley Park – not to mention the mirror-fronted ranks of skyscrapers that look across Burrard Inlet and its busy harbour to the residential districts of North and West Vancouver (or North Shore). Beyond these comfortable suburbs, the Coast Mountains rise in steep, forested slopes to form a dramatic counterpoint to the Downtown skyline and the most stunning of the city's many outdoor playgrounds.

You'll inevitably spend a good deal of time in **Downtown Vancouver**, which is where you'll find the city's most visited sights: **Canada Place**, an impressive waterfront complex; the **Harbour Centre** and its panoramic

Film and TV

The X Files wasn't the first major TV series or film shot mostly in and around Vancouver – Louis B Mayer was using local Mounties in his movies in the 1930s – but it was the one that made the world sit up and take notice of the city's emergence as a major player in the realm of film and TV production. Today, it ranks third behind Los Angeles and New York in terms of revenue, having emerged from almost nothing in 1980 to a business that is worth $650 million a year.

The reason for its success is simple: money. It costs less to make films here than it does in Hollywood. Labour is cheaper (and, on the whole, less unionized); the city and its mixture of sleek high rises and grittier suburban margins easily double for US and other cities; and there is tremendous and varied scenery on its doorstep for productions that require out-of-town locations. Furthermore – and no small consideration – it's also an easy hop up the coast for LA-based actors and executives.

Don't be surprised, therefore, if you pass several shoots as you walk around the city. Don't, however, expect to see too many stars – one or two honourable productions aside, most of the material shot here is B-grade.

Viewpoints

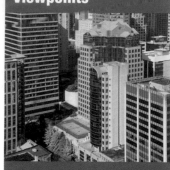

A city with a majestic setting demands viewpoints from which it can be admired, and in Vancouver you are spoiled for choice. If you fly here, then you'll enjoy one of the world's great aerial approaches, whether you come in over the ocean or over the mountains. Either way, you'll see the water-fringed skyscrapers of Downtown, the peaks of the Coast Mountains and the great expanse of the Fraser Delta. At some point, budget allowing, you should repeat this experience by taking a float-plane from the city's harbour (see p.31), either as a tour or as means of travelling to Victoria or the Gulf Islands.

Less expensive but only marginally less dramatic aerial views can be enjoyed from the Harbour Centre (see p.49) or Grouse Mountain (see p.112), and from some of the approach roads to protected areas on the city's North Shore such as Mount Seymour and Cypress provincial parks.

At water level the views can be equally captivating, notably on the SeaBus ferry (see p.29) between Downtown and Lonsdale Quay in North Vancouver. This crossing offers a wonderful close-up look at the city's port, as well as a stunning panorama of the Downtown skyline.

Other views can be more unexpected. Kitsilano Beach, for example, provides a different perspective on Downtown, as do trips over the Lions Gate and Granville Street bridges. See p.50 for a more detailed breakdown of the city's great viewpoints.

views, and the Neoclassical grandeur of the **Vancouver Art Gallery**, home to the works of celebrated Canadian painter Emily Carr. The Downtown core spills southward into **Yaletown**, a revitalized former warehouse district that's full of cafés, restaurants, galleries and interesting shops.

East of Downtown is its Victorian-era neighbour, **Gastown**, now a renovated and less-than-convincing pastiche of its past. Moving eastward, Gastown blends into edgy **Chinatown**, which could easily absorb a morning, and contains more than its share of interesting shops and restaurants along its busy streets, plus the area's main attraction, **Dr Sun Yat-Sen Garden**. At the northern tip of the Downtown peninsula, you'll find abundant recreational pleasures in **Stanley Park**, a huge area of semi-wild parkland and beaches.

Beyond the Downtown peninsula in the southern portion of the city are other worthwhile destinations, notably **Granville Island**, by far the city's most tempting spot for wandering and people-watching, situated in the waters of False Creek. Neighbouring **Kitsilano** to the west is home to the **Vancouver Museum** and the other museums of the **Vanier Park** complex, all easily accessible from Granville Island. West of Kitsilano and at the westernmost point of Vancouver lies the sprawling **University of British Columbia** and its formidable **Museum of Anthropology**, flanked by the protected area of **Pacific Spirit Regional Park**.

At a push, you could cram the city's essentials into around three days. If you're here for a longer stay, though, you'll want to venture further from Downtown. Trips across Burrard Inlet to **North Vancouver** are worth making for the views from the SeaBus ferry alone (see p.29) – they also provide a different panoramic perspective on the peninsula, and take you into the mountains and forests that provide Vancouver with its tremendous setting. The most popular trips here are to the Capilano Suspension Bridge, something of a triumph of public relations over substance, and to the more worthwhile cable-car trip up **Grouse Mountain** for some staggering views of the city.

The area of Vancouver east of Chinatown is a vast collection of suburbs, lacking in specific attractions and therefore not covered in the Guide.

When to go

Vancouver has a reputation for **rain**. About 46 inches, or 117cm (23 inches, or 59cm in Victoria) falls per year, a fair amount to be sure; however, only about ten percent of the year's total falls in the summer months of June, July and August. And unlike the rest of the country, Vancouver's generally benign climate means it can be considered a year-round destination.

Average temperatures and rainfall

	MIN °C/°F	MAX °C/°F	NO OF RAINY DAYS	TOTAL IN CM/INCHES
Jan	2/36	5/41	20	21.8/8.6
Feb	4/40	7/44	15	14.7/5.8
March	6/43	10/50	16	12.7/5
April	9/48	14/58	13	8.4/3.3
May	12/54	18/64	10	7.1/2.8
June	15/59	21/69	6	3.1/1.2
July	17/63	23/74	6	3.1/1.2
Aug	17/63	23/73	8	4.3/1.7
Sept	14/58	18/65	9	9.1/3.6
Oct	10/50	14/57	16	14.7/5.8
Nov	6/43	9/48	18	8.3/3.3
Dec	4/39	6/43	20	22.4/8.8

The best time to visit is in **summer** – July and August – when you're likely to enjoy plenty of hot sunny days. "Indian summers" are also common, often prolonging the good weather into September and/or October. Still, the city can also have a sunny June and wet July. The busiest months in terms of visitor numbers are July and August, but the city rarely feels overcrowded. Accommodation prices are highest between June and early September, though many hotels divide the year into four seasons, with appreciably lower rates in even the grandest hotels from December to February.

Winters are mild and damp, but there is little snow in the city. Snow is present on the Coast Mountains, however, allowing you to ski or snowboard just minutes from Downtown. Whistler, one of North America's finest winter-sports resorts, is around two hours' drive away. The winter season here extends to around April, but summer glacier skiing means you can take to the slopes here year-round.

Spring and **autumn** – roughly May to June and late September and October – are temperate, which is to say you can have great days and grim days. Note that the ocean and mountains mean Vancouver has several microclimates. The nearer you are to the mountains, the wetter you'll be: Grouse Mountain has an annual precipitation of 3500mm (140 inches), Downtown receives 1400mm (55 inches) of rain, and Richmond (near the Fraser River) just 1000mm (40 inches).

things not to miss

It's not possible to see everything that Vancouver has to offer in one trip – and we don't suggest you try. What follows is a selective taste of the city's highlights: outstanding museums, stunning vistas and vibrant nightlife. They're arranged in five colour-coded categories, which you can browse through to find the very best things to see and experience. All highlights have a page reference to take you straight into the guide, where you can find out more.

01 **Canada Place** Page **48** • Stroll by day or night around the walkways of this striking convention centre, hotel and cruise-ship terminal for wonderful views of Vancouver's port.

02 **The SeaBus** Page **109** • The city's principal ferry links Downtown with Lonsdale Quay in North Vancouver, offering superlative vistas of the city skyline and Burrard Inlet.

03 **Marine Building** Page **50** • The city's maritime heritage is celebrated in the motifs adorning Vancouver's only surviving Art Deco skyscraper.

04 **Vancouver Art Gallery** Page **53** • See the imaginative, aboriginal-influenced works of Victoria-born Emily Carr, the highlight of Vancouver's principal gallery.

05 **Yaletown** Page **57** • This former warehouse district is now a dynamic mixture of funky stores, bars and excellent restaurants.

06 Dr Sun Yat-Sen Garden Page **69** • Chinatown's cultural showpiece is the only full-scale classical Chinese garden in the Western Hemisphere.

07 Granville Island Page **73** • Fabulous food shops and teeming market stalls are the main attractions of this hugely popular enclave, easily accessible from Downtown.

08 Stanley Park Page **83** • North America's largest urban park is a green oasis of woodland, ancient forest, marshes, beaches and peaceful trails.

09 Sea-plane Page **31** • Leaving from the Downtown waterfront, the seaplane affords glorious panoramas of the city and its surroundings.

10 Kitsilano Beach Page **92** • While away a summer afternoon at this popular Southern Vancouver beach.

11 Museum of Anthropology Page **101** • Bill Reid's *The Raven and the First Men* is one of countless outstanding pieces of aboriginal art in Vancouver's most compelling museum.

12 The Skyride to Grouse Mountain Page **112** • The largest cable cars in North America offer a breathtaking way to reach the top of Grouse Mountain, the city's finest viewpoint.

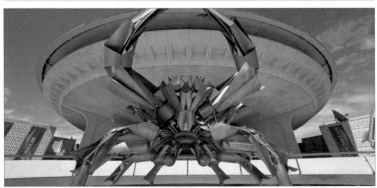

13 Vancouver Museum Page **93** • Fronted by an eye-catching fountain, this eclectic civic museum presents a lively account of the city's history, from its earliest aboriginal inhabitants to the burgeoning city of today.

14 Beacon Hill Park Page **228** • The views from Victoria's lovely city park extend across the Juan de Fuca Strait to the mountains of Washington State.

15 Butchart Gardens Page **231** • Over a million plants and 700 different species are spread across British Columbia's most celebrated gardens.

16 The Royal British Columbia Museum Page **225** • Victoria's showcase museum mixes fascinating historical displays with stunning natural history dioramas.

17 Whale watching Page **232** • The waters between Vancouver and Vancouver Island teem with whales, easily visible either on tours or kayaking.

18 Whistler Mountain Page 256 • Whistler is best known for its skiing and other winter activities, but there is also plenty to do in the summer too.

19 Pacific Rim cuisine Page 144 • Sample the inspired fusion of Far-Eastern, Italian and West Coast cooking, a mainstay of *CinCin* (pictured) and many other Vancouver restaurants.

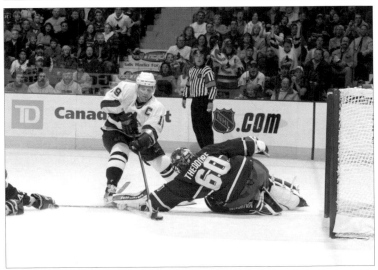

20 Ice hockey Page 205 • Excitement, finesse and high-speed action are guaranteed at a Vancouver Canucks hockey game.

Contents

Using this
Rough Guide

We've tried to make this Rough Guide a good read and easy to use. The book is divided into seven main sections, and you should be able to find whatever you want in one of them.

Front section

The front **colour section** offers a quick tour of Vancouver. The introduction aims to give you a feel for the city and tells you the best times to visit. Next, we round up our favourite aspects of Vancouver in the **Things Not to Miss** section – whether it's a bustling market, enthralling nightlife or a stimulating museum. Right after this comes the Rough Guide's full **contents** list.

Basics

The **Basics** section covers all the **pre-departure** nitty-gritty to help you plan your trip, and the practicalities you'll want to know once you're there. This is where to find out about money and costs, city transportation and local media – in fact just about every piece of **general practical information** you might need.

The City

This is the heart of the Rough Guide, divided into user-friendly chapters, each of which covers a major portion of Vancouver. Every chapter begins with an **introduction** that helps you decide where to go, followed by a chapter map and an extensive tour of the sights.

Listings

Listings contains all the consumer information you need to make the most of your stay in Vancouver, with chapters on **accommodation**, places

to **eat** and **drink**, **music** venues, **performing arts** and **festivals**. Specialized information for families travelling with children, as well as for gay visitors, is also provided.

Out of the City

Here we detail the sights and attractions of the city's surrounding areas, from the architecture of **Victoria** to the ski trails of **Whistler Mountain**.

Contexts

Read contexts to get a deeper understanding of Vancouver's engaging **history**, its historical and influential **aboriginal traditions**, and a survey of some of the best **books** concerning or set in Vancouver.

Index + small print

Apart from a **full index**, which includes maps as well as places and people, this section covers publishing information, credits and acknowledgements and also has our contact details, in case you want to send in updates, corrections or suggestions for improving the guide.

Colour maps

The back-of-book colour section has five **detailed maps** to help you get around and explore Vancouver easily, locate every sight discussed in the guide and make your way around the adjoining British Columbia area.

Chapter list

Contents

Out of the City

215–257

Contexts

258–272

Rough Guides Advertiser

273–294

Index and small print

295–304

Colour maps

Vancouver & Southern
  British Columbia
Greater Vancouver
Central Vancouver

Downtown & Gastown
Kitsilano, Granville Island & Yaletown
Southern Vancouver

Basics

Basics

Getting there

As one of Canada's gateway cities, Vancouver is well served by direct air links from all over the world. **Flying** is the most popular, time-effective option, unless you're already somewhat close by the city, in which case there are plenty of road and rail links to get you there. From outside of North America, flying is of course your only option, and indeed there is only one direct train service from the US a day, from Seattle. The main airport is Vancouver International, 14 miles south of the city centre (see "Arrival" for more).

Airfares from the UK, Australia and New Zealand to Vancouver depend on the **season**, with the highest prices applying from around mid-June to early September, the peak tourist season. You'll get the best prices during the low season, mid-November through to April (excluding Christmas and New Year, when seats are at a premium and prices are hiked up). Note also that flying at the weekend is generally more expensive. If you're flying from the US or from anywhere else in Canada, the same general strictures apply, though the market is more unpredictable, with airlines constantly moving their prices up and down.

Airfare costs can often be cut by going through a **specialist flight agent** rather than an airline. These agents come in two main flavours: there are **consolidators**, who buy up blocks of tickets from the airlines and sell them at a discount, and **discount agents**, who in addition to dealing with discounted flights may also offer special student and youth fares, plus a range of other travel-related services such as travel insurance, car rentals and the like. Some agents specialize in **charter flights**, which may be cheaper than anything available on a scheduled flight – though be aware that departure dates are fixed and withdrawal penalties high.

The city's linked **train and bus terminal** is the terminus for transcontinental Canadian VIA Rail services from Vancouver through Edmonton and Jasper in the Canadian Rockies, as well as for Amtrak train services from Seattle and Greyhound and other bus services from Seattle, Whistler, Victoria (on Vancouver Island), Calgary, Edmonton, the Rockies and other Canadian towns and cities. A smaller **BC Rail station** in North Vancouver that used to handle BC Rail services from Whistler, Prince George and other British Columbia destinations, has been suspended indefinitely.

Ferries from Vancouver Island arrive at either Tsawwassen, about 45 minutes' drive south of the city, or Horseshoe Bay, an equivalent distance to the north. Cruise ships arrive at Canada Place in Downtown or the Ballentyne Pier about five blocks east of Main Street. **Float planes** from the Gulf Islands and other points in British Columbia disembark at the float plane terminal close to the international airport or, in the case of planes from Victoria's Inner Harbour, at a terminal close to Canada Place in Downtown.

Booking flights online

Many discount travel websites offer you the opportunity to book flight tickets and holiday packages **online**, cutting out the costs of agents and middlemen; these are worth going for, as long as you don't mind the inflexibility of non-refundable, non-changeable deals. There are some bargains to be had on auction sites too, if you're prepared to bid keenly. Almost all airlines have their own websites, offering flight tickets that can sometimes be just as cheap, and are often more flexible.

Online booking agents and general travel sites

ⓦwww.cheapflights.com (in US), ⓦwww.cheapflights.ca (in Canada), ⓦwww.cheapflights.co.uk (in UK and Ireland), ⓦwww.cheapflights.com.au (in Australia). Flight deals, travel agents, plus links to other travel sites.
ⓦwww.cheaptickets.com Discount flight

specialists (US only). **Also at** ☏1-888/922-8849.

@**www.ebookers.com** Efficient, easy-to-use flight finder, with competitive fares.

@**www.etn.nl/discount** A hub of consolidator and discount agent links, maintained by the nonprofit European Travel Network.

@**www.expedia.com (in US),** @**www.expedia. ca (in Canada),** @**www.expedia.co.uk (in UK).** Discount airfares, all-airline search engine and daily deals.

@**www.flyaow.com** "Airlines of the Web" – online air travel info and reservations.

@**www.gaytravel.com** US gay travel agent, offering accommodation, cruises, tours and more. **Also at** ☏1-800/GAY-TRAVEL.

@**www.geocities.com/thavery2000** An extensive list of airline websites and US toll-free numbers.

@**www.kelkoo.co.uk** Useful UK-only price-comparison site, checking several sources of low-cost flights (and other goods and services) according to specific criteria.

@**www.lastminute.com (in UK),** @**www. lastminute.com.au (in Australia),** @**www. lastminute.co.nz (in New Zealand).** Good last-minute holiday package and flight-only deals.

@**www.opodo.co.uk** Popular and reliable source of low UK airfares. Owned by, and run in conjunction with, nine major European airlines.

@**www.priceline.co.uk (in UK),** @**www. priceline.com (in US).** Name-your-own-price website that has deals at around forty percent off standard fares.

@**www.site59.com (in US).** US sister site to lastminute.com, with good deals on last-minute holiday packages and flights.

@**www.skyauction.com** Bookings from the US only. Auctions tickets and travel packages to destinations worldwide.

@**www.travelocity.com (in US),** @**www.travelocity.ca (in Canada),** @**www.travelocity.co.uk (in UK),** @**www.travelshop.com.au** Australian site offering discounted flights, packages, insurance, and online bookings. **Also on** ☏1-800/108 108.

@**travel.yahoo.com** Incorporates some Rough Guides material in its coverage of destination countries and cities across the world, with information about places to eat and sleep.

@**www.zuji.com.au (in Australia).** Destination guides, hot fares and great deals for car rental, accommodation and lodging.

From elsewhere in North America

From most of the US and Canada, the easiest and often cheapest way to get to Vancouver is to **fly**; there are direct flights from larger Canadian cities and from most major US hubs. However, those in the northwestern US and western Canada may find that driving or taking the train or bus can be faster, cheaper and more convenient. Amtrak has a **train** service from Seattle, Washington, to Vancouver's main bus and train terminals, with the reasonably priced journey taking just under four hours. If money is more important than comfort and speed, **buses** will eventually get you to Vancouver from most of Canada and once a day from Seattle. Finally, there's the old standby, the **car** – flexible, just as fast for shorter journeys and cheaper if there's a group of you.

By air

Vancouver International Airport handles all flights into the city. It is a major entryway and thus served by most airlines, with **Air Canada** providing by far the most comprehensive service, reaching all parts of the country through its flagship brand and regional **Air Canada Jazz**. It has also launched an independent low-fare airline, **Zip**, as well as no-frills **Tango**, to fend off increasing competition from **WestJet** in western Canada and **Jetsgo**, which cherry-picks the busiest routes across the country. For the time being, Air Canada's higher published fares are somewhat irrelevant in the face of their almost weekly seat sales, web specials and last-minute offers. Keep an eye out in the travel section of your local newspaper and revisit the airlines' websites regularly (or sign up for email alerts) to be sure of getting a good deal. One bonus of all the competition is that it is now possible to get one-way fares for half the price of a return.

Booking at least two weeks ahead is an immediate way to save money. If your travel dates include a weekend, you will also realize savings. Rates tend to vary widely – play around with dates and times to get the best fares. In general, for economy fares you should multiply the one-way price by three for a rough idea of the final cost of a return (including taxes and charges).

From the East Coast of the US, you should be able to get the five-hour flight to Vancouver for around US$280 in low season; booking early can sometimes get you a similar summer rate, but you should count on paying closer to US$580 in high season.

From Chicago, America West often offer the best fares, but you must change planes in Phoenix, upping the four and a half hour average flight time to seven hours. In low season, you can fly for around US$380; high season fares are more likely to average US$550.

Direct flights **from the West Coast of the US** will be cheaper, around US$235 in the low season and US$255 in the high. Flying to Vancouver **from other Canadian cities**, competition is fiercer than it is in the US. A low-season round-trip **from Toronto** will cost around $420 with a regular carrier or $225 with a no-frills airline (i.e. Westjet), while in high season, expect to pay $660 with Air Canada, around $495 with budget HMY, which flies exclusively from Vancouver to Toronto, and as little as $320 with the no-frills carriers, as long as you book well in advance. Low-season fares **from Montréal** are around $535 with the likes of Air Canada or $265 with the budget airlines; fares from Montréal may be as much as $760 with Air Canada, or as little as $305 with a no-frills carrier like Westjet. The no-frills carriers also offer excellent value from provincial Canada – a low-season round-trip from Edmonton or Calgary can cost as little as from $115 to $130 (as compared with the regular airlines' $250–300). Fares quoted include all taxes and fees.

Airlines and routeings

Air Canada ☎1-888/247-2262, ⊛www.aircanada.com. Also operates under regional Air Canada Jazz (⊛www.flyjazz.ca) and no-frills Tango (☎1-888/315-1390, ⊛www.flytango.com) brands.
Air Transat Canada ☎1-800/587-2672, ⊛www.airtransat.com. Charter airline.
Alaska Airlines ☎1-800/252-7522, ⊛www.alaskaair.com.
America West Airlines ☎1-800/235-9292, ⊛www.americawest.com.

American Airlines ☎1-800/433-7300, ⊛www.aa.com.
Canjet Airlines ☎1-800/809-7777, ⊛www.canjet.com.
Cathay Pacific ☎1-800/233-2742, ⊛www.cathaypacific.com.
Continental Airlines ☎1-800/231-0856, ⊛www.continental.com.
Delta Canada ☎1-800/221-1212, US ☎1-800/241-4141, ⊛www.delta.com.
HMY Airways ☎1-866/868-6789, ⊛www.hmyairways.com. Toronto–Vancouver; connections to LA and Las Vegas.
Jetsgo ☎1-866/440-0441, ⊛www.jetsgo.net. Low-cost Canadian carrier; connections with Newark, Florida and Las Vegas.
Lufthansa US ☎1-800/645-3880, Canada ☎1-800/563-5954, ⊛www.lufthansa.com.
Northwest/KLM Domestic ☎1-800/225-2525, International ☎1-800/447-4747, ⊛www.nwa.com, www.klm.com.
SAS Scandinavian Airlines ☎1-800/221-2350, ⊛www.scandinavian.net.
Skyservice ☎1-800/701-9448, ⊛www.skyservice.com.
United Airlines Canada ☎1-800/241-6522, ⊛www.united.ca, US ☎1-800/538-2929, ⊛www.united.com.
US Airways ☎1-800/428-4322, ⊛www.usair.com.
WestJet ☎1-888/WEST-JET or 403/250-5839, ⊛www.westjet.com. Low-cost Canadian airline.
Zip ☎1-866/4321-ZIP, ⊛www.4321zip.com. Owned by Air Canada but independently run.

Flight and travel agents

Airtech ☎212/219-7000, ⊛www.airtech.com. Standby seat broker; also deals in consolidator fares and courier flights.
Airtreks ☎1-877/AIRTREKS, ⊛www.airtreks.com. Round-the-world and Circle Pacific tickets. The website features an interactive database that lets you build and price your own round-the-world itinerary.
Educational Travel Center ☎1-800/747-5551 or 608/256-5551, ⊛www.edtrav.com. Low-cost fares worldwide, student/youth discount offers, and car rental and tours.
Flightcentre Canada ☎1-888/WORLD-55, ⊛www.flightcentre.ca, US ☎1-866/WORLD-51, ⊛www.flightcentre.us. Rock-bottom fares worldwide.
Long Haul Travel ☎1-866/548-4548, ⊛www.longhaultravel.com. Canadian partner of Airtreks (see above).

STA Travel Canada ☎1-888/427-5639, US ☎1-800/329-9537, ⊚www.statravel.com. Worldwide specialists in independent travel; also student IDs, travel insurance, car rental, rail passes, and more.
Student Flights ☎1-800/255-8000 or 480/951-1177, ⊚www.isecard.com. Student/youth fares, student IDs.
TFI Tours ☎1-800/745-8000 or 212/736-1140, ⊚www.lowestairprice.com. Consolidator with global fares.
Travel Avenue ☎1-800/333-3335, ⊚www.travelavenue.com. Full-service travel agent that offers discounts in the form of rebates.
Travel Cuts Canada ☎1-888/246-9762, US ☎1-800/592-CUTS, ⊚www.travelcuts.com. Popular, long-established Canadian student-travel organization, with worldwide offers and cheap domestic flights for students and non-students. Also student IDs. Also known as Voyages Campus in Québec.
Travelers Advantage ☎1-877/259-2691, ⊚www.travelersadvantage.com. Discount travel club, with cash-back deals and discounted car rental. Membership required ($1 for 3 months' trial).

Package tours

A day or so in Vancouver will often feature as the city break in longer adventure holidays to the Rocky Mountains or the Pacific North West of the USA. Even if the **package** aspect doesn't thrill you to pieces, these deals can still be more convenient and sometimes even work out to be more economical than arranging the same thing yourself, provided you don't mind losing a little flexibility. With such a vast range of packages available, it's impossible to give an overview – major travel agents will have brochures detailing what's available.

Tour operators

Adventure Center ☎1-800/228-8747 or 510/654-1879, ⊚www.adventurecenter.com. Hiking and "soft adventure" specialists worldwide. They offer a 15-day, land-only, no-camping trip encompassing the Rocky Mountains and the Pacific Coast, as well as Vancouver, from US$1540.
Adventures Abroad ☎1-800/665-3998, ⊚www.adventures-abroad.com. Adventure specialists with a 10- or 13-day Western Canada trip taking in Calgary, Banff, Jasper and Vancouver. The 13-day trip includes a whale-watching expedition. From US$1399, flights not included.
Contiki ☎1-888/CONTIKI, ⊚www.contiki.com. 18-

to 35-year-olds-only tour operator offering a 10-day land-only package from Seattle to Whistler, Vancouver, Jasper, and the Rockies. Tours start at US$1019.
Cosmos ☎1-800/276-1241, ⊚www.cosmosvacations.com. Planned vacation packages with an independent focus, often allowing afternoons free after active mornings. Offer 8- or 13-day Canadian Rockies packages, the latter with two days in Vancouver, from US $1309, a 13- or 15-day Totem Circle package, taking in Vancouver, the Rockies, and the Cascade Mountains from US $1349 and a 9-day Western Canada spectacular package from Calgary to Vancouver from US $899. All prices are land-only.
Globus ☎1-866/755-8581, ⊚www.globusjourneys.com. Planned land-only vacation packages such as a 12-day Best of Western Canada tour, covering the Rockies and a two-night stay in Vancouver from US $1749 and a 10- or 12-day Great Resorts of the Canadian Rockies tour, featuring rail travel and a sampling of top hotels in Vancouver and the Rockies, from US $2799.
Maupintour ☎1-800/255-4266, ⊚www.maupintour.com. Luxury independent and escorted land-only tours, including a ten-day independent tour of western Canada's national parks from US $1270, or a week-long Christmas stay in Vancouver, Victoria, and Whistler, for US$1645.
Moose Travel Network ☎905/853-4762 or 1-888/244-6673, ⊚www.moosenetwork.com. Company offering backpacker hop-on and hop-off coach tours in the summer (see opposite). Also organizes 2-4 day ski and snowboarding trips to the Sun Peaks, Big White or Silverstar resorts, from Vancouver. Prices from $199 to $249.
Suntrek Tours ☎1-800/SUNTREK, ⊚www.suntrek.com. Soft adventure specialists who offer a two-week Canadian Rockies trip ex-Seattle, with camping, from US$795.
Trek America ☎1-800/221-0596, ⊚www.trekamerica.com. Land-only walking and soft adventure tours all over Canada, year round. Among their "Trek America" offerings – camping adventure trips for 18–38-year-olds – is a 10-day Canadian Adventure trip US$649, a two-week Mountie trip exploring British Columbia and Alberta from US$909, and a three-week Canadian Parks West trip, from US$1129, all ex-Seattle, and all including a two-night stay in Vancouver. Open to all is a 12-day walking tour of the Canadian parks, also ex-Seattle, with one night in Vancouver. From US$905.
Trek Holidays ☎1-800/661-7265, ⊚www.trekholidays.com. Canadian agent that handles a vast array of deals from adventure companies worldwide. Included in their trips is a 15-day Rocky Mountains and Pacific Coast trip, with

accommodation in hotels, from $2554, land-only.
VIA Rail ⊛ www.viarail.ca. Although they don't organize tours, VIA's website does provide a lengthy list of US and Canadian operators who offer rail and sightseeing trips.
Viator ⊛ www.viator.com. Bookings for local tours and sightseeing trips in destinations around the world, including Vancouver and around.

By bus

Those travelling from anywhere other than Seattle in the US and nearby cities in Canada should think twice about enduring a long **bus journey** to get to Vancouver. It is, of course, one of the cheapest ways to travel (the daily **Greyhound** service from Seattle costs just $43 round-trip) and you arrive right in the city centre, but travelling by bus is pretty much the slowest way one can go. Canada's sheer landmass makes it a difficult country to travel by bus – the trip from Montréal to Vancouver takes at least three whole days – but if booked in advance, fares can be reasonable, if not much less than those offered by the no-frills air carriers. The **Moose Travel Network** (☎905/853-4762 or 1-888/388-4881, ⊛ www.moosenetwork. com) offers a completely different experience – a mini-coach service aimed at backpackers, it hits the major destinations on the travellers' circuit between May and mid-October (for winter packages, see opposite). The jump-on, jump-off service stops three days a week at youth hostels in the major cities and interesting smaller towns. Their West Pass covers Vancouver, the Rockies, Jasper and Banff and costs $419 ($399 with ISIC or hostelling membership).

Vancouver's main **bus terminal** lies alongside the VIA Rail Pacific Central Station (see

Bus passes

Bus pass	length of validity	cost (full/student rate)
Canada Pass	7 days	US$255/$228
	10 days	US$325/$291
	15 days	US$375/$334
	21 days	US$415/$370
	30 days	US$455/$404
	45 days	US$515/$458
	60 days	US$575/$510
CanAm Pass	15 days	US$379/$337
	21 days	US$419/$373
	30 days	US$469/$416
	45 days	US$539/$479
	60 days	US$609/$540
Ameripass	7 days	US$209/$186
	10 days	US$259/$231
	15 days	US$309/$274
	21 days	US$359/$319
	30 days	US$399/$353
	45 days	US$459/$407
	60 days	US$569/$504
West Coast CanAm Pass	10 days	US$265/$237
	21 days	US$345/$307

These Greyhound passes are available to North American and international travellers at major bus terminals or directly from Greyhound (see main text) or Greyhound Canada (☎1-800/661-8747 or 604/482-8747, ⊛ www.greyhound.ca).

below) and is used by Pacific Coach Lines (for services from Victoria and other parts of Vancouver Island), Maverick Coach Lines (from Whistler, Sunshine Coast and Nanaimo) and all Greyhound services.

By rail

Rail travel is the ultimate experience for those who enjoy sitting back, relaxing, and watching a beautiful landscape pass by. If you're on a tight budget or schedule, though, it often works out to be too ineffective for an enjoyable holiday. Canada's national **VIA Rail** services operate in and out of Pacific Central Station (☎604-3772 or 1-888/842-7245, ⊛www.viarail.ca), located in a dismal part of the city to the southeast of Downtown off Main Street at 1150 Station St. VIA Rail trains arrive here via Kamloops from Jasper, where there are connections from Prince George and Prince Rupert, and from Edmonton and points east. There are also four daily **Amtrak** (☎253/931-8917 or 1-800/872-7245, ⊛www.amtrakcascades.com) services from Seattle, ranging in price from US$22 to US35, plus a direct two-day route from San Diego with stops at all major West Coast US cities. Amtrak also links with VIA Rail at Winnipeg, Manitoba, if you want to make a much longer rail trip to Vancouver across western Canada.

Fares from the US are cheaper than air fares, provided you book ahead, Canadian rail fares tend to be as expensive as normal air fares, if not more so. The best economy fares – which can save you over thirty percent – are obtainable two to three weeks in advance. There are deals in place for students and seniors that offer between 50 and 100 percent off a second fare. US passengers booking VIA tickets should remember that these must be booked at least six days in advance, as paper tickets will be mailed. Year-round fares from Seattle are $46 round-trip, from San Diego around $180, but can reach Can$1050 from Montréal and Can$900 from Toronto.

VIA Rail passes and the North America Rail Pass can be purchased by anyone; the other Amtrak passes are only available to overseas visitors. Sales outlets include: **UK** 1st Rail ☎0845/644 3553, ⊛www.1strail. com; Trailfinders ☎020/7937 5400, ⊛www.trailfinders.com; **Ireland** USIT ☎0818/200 020, ⊛www.usit.ie (Amtrak only); **Australia** Asia Pacific Travel Marketing ☎02/9319 6624, ⊛www.aptms.com.au; **New Zealand** Holiday Shoppe (☎0800/808 480, ⊛www.holidayshoppe.co.nz) and United Travel (☎0800/730 830, ⊛www.unitedtravel.co.nz).

By car

Getting to Vancouver **by car** is easy enough if you're in the Pacific Northwest – coming from anywhere else, driving to Vancouver will take an inordinately long time. See p.19 for information on what's needed to cross the US/Canadian border.

From Seattle to Vancouver, you're looking at approximately 225 kilometres (140 miles),

Train passes

VIA Rail pass (validity)	off-peak rates	peak rates
Corridorpass (10 days)	$235	$235
Canrailpass (12 days in 30)	$448 ($403 students)	$719 ($647 students)
Amtrak pass (validity)	off-peak rates	peak rates
North East Rail Pass (5/15/30 days)	US$149/185/225	US$149/205/240
Coastal Rail Pass (30 days)	US$235	US$285
Far West Rail Pass (15/30 days)	US$190/250	US$245/320
East Rail Pass (15/30 days)	US$210/265	US$260/320
National Rail Pass (15/30 days)	US$295/385	US$440/550
North America Rail Pass (30 days)	$690, US$495 (students $621; US$445.50)	$975, US$699 (students $878; US$629.10)

which, not counting time waiting at the border, translates to about two and a half hours' driving time. **From San Francisco**, it's approximately 1520 kilometres (945 miles), or roughly fifteen and a half hours' drive. **From Montréal**, it's about 4900 kilometres (3045 miles), and driving, not counting stops, will take you about two days, and from **Toronto**, it's around 4375 km (2720 miles), a nonstop (and inadvisable) one day and 20 hours' drive.

You can of course **drive your own vehicle**, or you can **rent a car**. If you rent a car in the US, inform whomever helps you that you intend to take the car into Canada – just to be on the safe side, though this usually makes no difference. A few major North American **car rental agencies** are **Alamo** (☎ 1-800/522-9696, ⊛ www.alamo.com), **Avis** (US ☎ 1-800/331-1084, Canada ☎ 1-800/272-5871, ⊛ www.avis.com), and **Hertz** (US ☎ 1-800/654-3001, Canada ☎ 1-800/263-0600, ⊛ www.hertz.com). Keep in mind that prices for car rental are not cheap; unless you really want to drive, it will almost always be cheaper and more time-efficient to travel to Vancouver by plane.

Getting there by car

The approach to Vancouver by road is straightforward from the US and points to the east and north in Canada. From the western **United States**, follow Interstate 5 (I-5) from Seattle and Washington State to the border towns of Blaine (in the US) and White Rock (BC), about 210km or 140 miles from Seattle. You clear Canadian Customs at the Peace Arch crossing in Blaine (open 24 hours). If you return this way, you pass through US Customs.

Interstate 5 becomes the Canadian **Hwy 99** and leads west from White Rock and then north to Vancouver, where it becomes first Oak Street and then – six blocks after a left turn at Oak and 70th Avenue – Granville Street, a major artery that leads directly to the heart of Downtown. Note, however, that much of Granville is pedestrianized in the centre, and you'll have to be prepared to follow various one-way routes if your destination is in the Downtown core. Hwy 99 is also the route to follow if you're driving from the **ferry terminal** at Tsawwassen (for ferries

from Vancouver Island and the Gulf Islands): Hwy 17 runs from the terminal to connect with Hwy 99 just before the George Massey Tunnel.

If you're heading to the city from points in the **east** of Canada or central US, you should follow the main Trans-Canada Highway (Hwy 1), which crosses the Fraser River on the Port Mann Bridge and then cuts through the suburbs of southeast Vancouver before an exit at Cassiar Street to Hastings Street (Hwy 7A), which leads west about 7km to Downtown. Hwy 1 then continues over the Burrard Inlet on the Second Narrows Bridge before turning west to pass through North and West Vancouver.

If you're arriving from the **north** and Squamish, Whistler or the ferry terminal at Horseshoe Bay, then you'll follow the Trans-Canada south. If you're headed for Downtown on this route, take the Taylor Way Bridge to Vancouver-Hwy 99 exit (Exit 13) in West Vancouver and cross the Burrard Inlet on the Lions Gate Bridge to Downtown's West End district – note that you can expect delays on this route at busy times of the day.

Roadside assistance

Roadside assistance is available from the CAA – the Canadian Automobile Association (☎ 604/293-2222 or 1-800/CAA-HELP for emergency assistance, ⊛ www.bcaa.com) – who have reciprocal agreements with the AAA and motoring groups from other countries.

From the UK and Ireland

Finnair, Air Canada, British Airways, Lufthansa, Scandinavian Airlines and bmi british midland all fly direct daily **from the UK mainland** to Vancouver. All direct flights leave from London Heathrow with other airports offering add-ons and transfers; Manchester and Glasgow offer the most. It is sometimes cheaper to take flights from the UK to Seattle and then catch a bus, train or an internal flight, than it is to fly directly to Vancouver. Other non-direct routes include flying via the US to Vancouver, or via Amsterdam with KLM. If you want to take the charter route, there are once-weekly flights from Glasgow and Manchester and twice-weekly from London with Air Transat. A standard return **fare** from London Heathrow direct to Vancouver with Air Canada, the principal carrier, can cost as little as £395 from London in low season and between £485 and £740 in high season.

From Ireland you can fly direct via Vancouver from Belfast during the summer, and from Dublin via Amsterdam or Frankfurt year round; otherwise the main options are either charter flights or routeings via the UK mainland or a US hub airport, such as San Francisco or New York. Keep in mind that direct, nonstop flights can often – but certainly not always – be at a premium when compared with one-stop flights. From Ireland, low-season **fares** will be around €485 but high season fares can creep up to €1240 if booked late – if you book early enough, you might get a much more reasonable €500 or €600 fare.

Airlines and routeings

Air Canada UK ☎0870/5247 226, Republic of Ireland ☎01/679 3958, ⊛www.aircanada.com.
Air Transat ☎0845/712-5478, ⊛www.airtransat.com.
Aer Lingus UK ☎0845/084 4444, Republic of Ireland ☎0818/365 000, ⊛www.aerlingus.ie. Dublin to Boston; Boston to Vancouver.
American Airlines UK ☎0845/7789 789 or 020/8572 5555, Republic of Ireland ☎01/602 0550, ⊛www.aa.com.
British Airways UK ☎0845/77 333 77, Republic of Ireland ☎1-800/626 747, ⊛www.ba.com.
British Midland UK ☎0870/607 0555, Republic of Ireland ☎01/407 3036, ⊛www.flybmi.com.
Continental Airlines UK ☎0800/776 464 or 01293/776 464, ⊛www.continental.com/uk, Republic of Ireland ☎1890/925 252, ⊛www.continental.com/ie.
Delta UK ☎0800/414 767, Republic of Ireland ☎01/407 3165, ⊛www.delta.com.
KLM/Northwest Airlines UK ☎0870/507 4074, ⊛www.klmuk.com.
Lufthansa UK ☎0845/7737 747, Republic of Ireland ☎01/844 5544, ⊛www.lufthansa.co.uk.
United Airlines UK ☎0845/8444 777, ⊛www.unitedairlines.co.uk.

Flight and travel agents

Apex Travel Republic of Ireland ☎01/241 8000,

⊛www.apextravel.ie. Specialists in flights to Australia, Africa, the Far East, the USA and Canada.
Aran Travel International Republic of Ireland ☎091/562 595, ⊛homepages.iol.ie/~arantvl/aranmain. Good-value flights to all parts of the world.
Bridge the World UK ☎0870/444 7474, ⊛www.bridgetheworld.com. Specializing in round-the-world tickets, with good deals aimed at the backpacker market.
CIE Tours International Republic of Ireland ☎01/703 1888, ⊛www.cietours.ie. General flight and travel agent.
Co-op Travel Care UK ☎0870/112 0099, ⊛www.travelcareonline.com. Flights and holidays around the world.
Destination Group UK ☎020/7400 7045, ⊛www.destination-group.com. Good discount airfares.
Flightbookers UK ☎0870/010 7000, ⊛www.ebookers.com. Low fares on an extensive selection of scheduled flights.
Go Holidays Republic of Ireland ☎01/874 4126, ⊛www.goholidays.ie. Package tour specialists.
Joe Walsh Tours Republic of Ireland ☎01/676 0991, ⊛www.joewalshtours.ie. General budget fares agent.
Lee Travel Republic of Ireland ☎021/277 111, ⊛www.leetravel.ie. Flights and holidays worldwide.
McCarthy's Travel Republic of Ireland ☎021/427 0127, ⊛www.mccarthystravel.ie. General flight agent.
North South Travel UK ☎01245/608 291, ⊛www.northsouthtravel.co.uk. Friendly, competitive travel agency, offering discounted fares worldwide – profits are used to support projects in the developing world, especially the promotion of sustainable tourism.
Premier Travel Northern Ireland ☎028/7126 3333, ⊛www.premiertravel.uk.com. Discount flight specialists.
Quest Travel UK ☎0870/442 3542, ⊛www.questtravel.com. Specialists in round-the-world and Australasian discount fares.
Rosetta Travel Northern Ireland ☎028/9064 4996, ⊛www.rosettatravel.com. Flight and holiday agent.
STA Travel UK ☎0870/1600 599, ⊛www.statravel.co.uk. Worldwide specialists in low-cost flights and tours for students and under-26s, though other customers welcome.
Top Deck UK ☎020/7244 8000, ⊛www.topdecktravel.co.uk. Long-established agent dealing in discount flights.
Trailfinders UK ☎020/7628 7628, ⊛www.trailfinders.co.uk, Republic of Ireland

Airpasses

If you're planning to visit a number of destinations in North America, one of the various **airpasses** may save you a bundle on flights (but be sure to compare prices with what's available by booking direct). Typically these are unavailable to North Americans and must be booked overseas at the same time you book your flight to Canada or the US (some passes restrict your first flight to one country or the other). For most passes, like Continental's Visit USA (VUSA) pass, United's Skypass and Star Alliance's North America Airpass, you purchase a minimum of three and a maximum of eight to twelve coupons (depending on the airline), which are each valid for a single flight; costs average out around US$100–130 per flight segment, US$10–30 more in the June–August high season (if you can, ensure that your first flight is in May – fares are based on the first day of travel). Note that for any of these passes you may be required to fly to North America on whichever carrier (or partner of that carrier) is offering the programme; some airlines provide it to travellers on competitors' flights at extra cost.

There are also a number of train and bus passes, many of which are also available to Americans and Canadians (see boxes, pp.13 and 14).

℡01/677 7888, ⊛www.trailfinders.ie. One of the best-informed and most efficient agents for independent travellers; produces a very useful quarterly magazine worth scrutinizing for round-the-world routes.
Travel Cuts UK ℡020/7255 2082 or 7255 1944, ⊛www.travelcuts.co.uk. Canadian company specializing in budget, student and youth travel and round-the-world tickets.
usit NOW Republic of Ireland ℡01/602 1600, Northern Ireland ℡028/9032 7111, ⊛www.usitnow.ie. Student and youth specialists for flights and trains.

Tour operators

Airtours UK ℡0870/238 7788, ⊛www.uk.mytravel.com. Large tour company offering trips worldwide.
All Canada Travel & Holidays UK ⊛www.titanserver.co.uk/all-canada. Comprehensive Canada agent. Runs everything from escorted coach tours to adventure holidays and city breaks. Bookings through appointed travel agents.
AmeriCan Adventures UK ℡01295/756 200, ⊛www.americanadventures.com. Small-group camping adventure trips throughout the US and Canada.
American Holidays Belfast ℡028/9023 8762, Dublin ℡01/433 1009, ⊛www.american-holidays.com. Specialists in travel to the USA and Canada.
British Airways Holidays ℡0870/442 3820, ⊛www.baholidays.co.uk. Using British Airways and other international airlines, offers an exhaustive range of package and tailor-made holidays around the world.

Canada's Best UK ℡01502/565648, ⊛www.best-in-travel.com. Canada specialist offering a wide range of holiday options. Package and tailor-made holidays.
Thomas Cook UK ℡0870/5666 222, ⊛www.thomascook.co.uk. Long-established twenty-four-hour travel agency for package holidays or scheduled flights, with bureau de change issuing Thomas Cook travellers' cheques, travel insurance and car rental.

From Australia and New Zealand

Air Canada offers the only direct flight from **Australia and New Zealand** to Vancouver, from Sydney; travellers in other parts of the continent can either fly via Sydney or break their journey elsewhere. Options are flying with the likes of Air China or Singapore Airlines and connecting in an Asian city such as Hong Kong, Tokyo or Beijing, or going via the US, transferring at Los Angeles with Qantas, United or Air New Zealand; the same applies to charter flights.

Fares vary considerably, but not so much with the time of year, as fares remain fairly consistent whatever date you travel. Rather, price differences have more to do with the restrictions attached to your ticket. There are, for example, discounts for midweek travel and advance booking. Thus, a low-season round-trip fare **from Sydney** to Vancouver with Air Canada costs around Aus$1955, or Aus$2600 in high season; from Melbourne it's more likely to be

Aus$2050 in low-season, Aus$2990 in high; if you're travelling from New Zealand in low season, expect to pay around NZ$1945 **from Auckland** to Vancouver; NZ $2435 in high season.

Airlines and routeings

Air Canada Australia ☎1300/655 747 or 02/9286 8900, New Zealand ☎09/379 3371, ⊛www.aircanada.com.
Air China Australia ☎02/9232 7277, ⊛www.airchina.com.cn/english.
Air New Zealand Australia ☎13 24 76, ⊛www.airnz.com.au, New Zealand ☎0800/737 000, ⊛www.airnz.co.nz.
Cathay Pacific Australia ☎13 17 47, ⊛www.cathaypacific.com/au, New Zealand ☎09/379 0861 or 0508/800 454, ⊛www.cathaypacific.com/nz.
Japan Airlines Australia ☎02/9272 1111, New Zealand ☎09/379 9906, ⊛www.japanair.com.
Qantas Australia ☎13 13 13, New Zealand ☎0800/808 767 or 09/357 8900, ⊛www.qantas.com.
Singapore Airlines Australia ☎13 10 11, New Zealand ☎0800/808 909, ⊛www.singaporeair.com.
United Airlines Australia ☎13 17 77, ⊛www.unitedairlines.com.au, New Zealand ☎09/379 3800 or 0800/508 648, ⊛www.unitedairlines.co.nz.

Flight and travel agents

Flight Centre Australia ☎13 31 33 or 02/9235 3522, ⊛www.flightcentre.com.au, New Zealand ☎0800 243 544 or 09/358 4310, ⊛www.flightcentre.co.nz.
New Zealand Destinations Unlimited New Zealand ☎09/414 1685 ⊛www.holiday.co.nz.
Northern Gateway Australia ☎1-800/174 800, ⊛www.northerngateway.com.au.
STA Travel Australia ☎1300/733 035, ⊛www.statravel.com.au, New Zealand ☎0508/782 872, ⊛www.statravel.co.nz.
Student Uni Travel Australia ☎02/9232 8444, ⊛www.sut.com.au, New Zealand ☎09/379 4224, ⊛www.sut.co.nz.

Trailfinders Australia ☎02/9247 7666, ⊛www.trailfinders.com.au.

Tour operators

Adventure World Australia ☎02/8913 0755, ⊛www.adventureworld.com.au, New Zealand ☎09/524 5118, ⊛www.adventureworld.co.nz. Agents for a vast array of international adventure travel companies operating trips such as the six-day Whistler Winter Escapade from Aus$1137 (land only) or an eight day tour of the Rockies from Aus$1394.
Australian Pacific Touring Australia ☎1-800/675 222 or 03/9277 8555, New Zealand ☎09/279 6077, ⊛www.aptours.com. Highly regarded touring specialists offering longer than average tours such as the 29-day Rockies Explorer with Alaska Cruise, the 15-day Western Canadian Rail Adventure, or the 12-day Winter Wonderland of the Rockies tour.
Canada & America Travel Specialists Australia ☎02/9922 4600, ⊛www.canada-americatravel.com.au. North American specialists – accommodation, train travel, adventure sports, car rentals, Greyhound and other long-distance bus passes, cruises, escorted tours, independent travel, and more. Tours range from 2-day rail tours of the Rockies for Aus$519 to a 19-day independent Western Canada Adventure tour, from Aus$2449.
Contiki Australia ☎02/9511 2200, New Zealand ☎09/309 8824, ⊛www.contiki.com. Frenetic trips for 18- to-35-year-old party animals with a 10-day land-only package from Seattle to Whistler, Vancouver, Jasper and the Rockies. Tours start at US$1019.
Explore Holidays Australia ☎02/9423 8080, ⊛www.exploreholidays.com.au. A wide variety of Western Canadian tours, from a 2-day mini coach tour for Aus$435 to a 7-night self-drive tour, staying in B&Bs, for Aus$675.
Sydney Travel Australia ☎02/9220 9230, ⊛www.sydneytravel.com. US and Canadian flights, accommodation, city stays and car rental. They offer flights to Vancouver for Aus$2217 with an Aus$300 rebate to be used towards tours or accommodation.
Viator Australia ☎02/8219 5400, ⊛www.viator.com. Bookings for hundreds of travel suppliers worldwide, including those offering sightseeing tours of Vancouver from Aus$49.

Red tape and visas

Citizens of the EU, non-EU Scandinavia and most Commonwealth countries including Australia and New Zealand travelling to Canada do not need an entry visa but just a valid passport in order to stay up to six months, although the Canadian immigration officer who decides the length of your stay at the point of entry is more likely to allow you three. United States citizens simply need proof of US citizenship (a birth certificate or a valid passport, though not a US driver's licence) and some form of photo identification. If US citizens are entering Canada from another country, they must have a valid passport, naturalization certificate or green card. Permanent residents of the US should have their green card (US Resident Alien Card). There are joint US-Canada programmes available for regular low-risk travellers from the US to Canada, designed to speed up border-crossing.

All visitors to Canada have to complete a **customs declaration form**, which you'll be given on the plane or at the US/Canadian border. On the form you'll have to give details of where you intend to stay during your trip. If you don't know, write "touring", but be prepared to give an idea of your schedule and destinations to the immigration officer.

The Canadian immigration officers rarely refuse entry, but they may launch into an impromptu investigation, asking how much money you have and what job you do; they may also ask to see a return or onward ticket. Make sure you have proof of sufficient funds to support yourself. Travellers with criminal convictions (even those for drunk driving) should note that they may get refused entry to Canada. Ask the embassy before you go. Note also that although passing overland between the US and Canada used to be generally straightforward, there have been increasingly long delays since September, 2001, terrorist attacks on New York City and Washington, DC.

If you want **to stay for more than six months**, or if you plan to **study** or work – even temporarily – you will need a visa. Contact the Canadian embassy, consulate or high commission in your country for authorization prior to departure (see below for contact details). Once inside Canada, if an extension of stay is desired, written application must be made to the nearest Canada Immigration Centre well before the expiry of the authorized visit. The Government of Canada's "Canada International" website (🖳www.canadainternational.gc.ca) contains useful information and links for anyone planning to visit, study or work in Canada. If you plan to visit or transit through the **US**, check what the requirements are for nationals of your country as they may be different from those for Canada; more information can be found at 🖳travel.state.gov/visa_services.

Canadian high commissions, consulates and embassies

A full list of Canadian overseas representatives is available on 🖳www.dfait-maeci.gc.ca/world/embassies/menu-en.asp; offices that deal specifically with visas can also be found at 🖳www.cic.gc.ca/english/offices/index.

Canadian consulates abroad

Australia Canberra High Commission, Commonwealth Ave, Canberra, ACT 2600 ☏02/6273 3285, 🖳www.dfait-maeci.gc.ca/australia; Perth Consulate, 267 St George's Terrace, Third Floor, Perth, 6000 Australia ☏08/9322 7930 🖳www.dfait-maeci.gc.ca/australia.; Sydney Consulate General, Level 5, Quay West Building, 111 Harrington St, Sydney, NSW 2000 ☏02/9364 3000, 🖳www.dfait-maeci.gc.ca/australia.

Ireland Embassy, 65 St Stephen's Green, Dublin 2 ☏01/417 4100, 🖳www.dfait

-maeci.gc.ca/canadaeuropa/ireland. For visa services contact the Immigration Division in London. Belfast Consulate of Canada, Unit 3, Ormeau Business Park, 8 Cromac Avenue, Belfast BT7 2JA ☎ 02891/272060, ⊚ www.dfait-maeci.gc.ca/canadaeuropa/united_kingdom/embassy1-en.asp
New Zealand Wellington High Commission, PO Box 12049, 61 Molesworth Street, Thorndon, Wellington ☎ 04/473 9577, ⊚ www.dfait-maeci.gc.ca/newzealand
UK High Commission, Macdonald House, 1 Grosvenor Square, London W1K 4AB ☎ 020/7258 6600, ⊚ www.dfait-maeci.gc.ca/london. Also consular representation in Belfast, Birmingham, Cardiff and Edinburgh.

USA Embassy, 501 Pennsylvania Ave NW, Washington DC 20001 ☎ 202/682 7726, ⊚ www.dfait-maeci.gc.ca/can-am. ⊚ www.canadianembassy.org; 550 South Hope St, 9th Floor, Los Angeles, CA 90071 ☎ 213/346-2700, ⊚ www.dfait-maeci.gc.ca/los_angeles; 1251 Ave of the Americas, Concourse Level, New York, NY 10020 ☎ 212/596-1783, ⊚ www.dfait-maeci.gc.ca/new_york. Immigration services are also provided by Canadian consulates in Buffalo, Detroit and Seattle but not at the other Canadian consulates general in the US, namely Atlanta, Boston, Chicago, Dallas, Miami, Minneapolis, San Francisco, San Jose.

 # Insurance

The only thing worse than an accident or having something stolen on holiday is being out of pocket because of it. You'd do well to take out an **insurance policy** before travelling to Canada to cover against theft, loss and illness or injury, especially as Canada's generally excellent health service costs nonresidents anything from $50 to $1000–2000 a day for hospitalization. There is no free treatment to nonresidents but if you do have an accident, medical services will get to you quickly and charge you later.

Before paying for a new policy, however, it's worth checking whether you are already covered: some all-risks home insurance policies may cover your possessions when overseas, and many private medical schemes include cover when abroad. For residents from elsewhere in Canada, provincial health plans usually provide full cover for hospitalization but for a visit to a physician you may need to pay up front and seek reimbursement later. Holders of official student/teacher/youth cards in Canada and the US are entitled to meagre accident coverage and hospital inpatient benefits. Students will often find that their student health coverage extends during the vacations and for one term beyond the date of last enrolment. Some credit card companies also offer coverage if your holiday is purchased using your card, however this type of coverage tends to be quite minimal.

After exhausting the possibilities above, you might want to contact a specialist travel insurance company, or consider the **travel insurance offered by Rough Guides** (see box below). A typical travel insurance policy usually provides cover for the loss of baggage, tickets and – up to a certain limit – cash or cheques, as well as cancellation or curtailment of your journey. Most of them exclude so-called dangerous sports unless an extra premium is paid: in Canada this can mean scuba-diving, whitewater rafting, windsurfing, snowmobiling, skiing and trekking, though probably not canoeing or cycling. Many policies can be chopped and changed to exclude coverage you don't need – for example, sickness and accident benefits can often be excluded or included at will. If you do take medical coverage, ascertain whether benefits will be paid as treatment proceeds or only after return home, and whether there is a 24-hour medical emergency number. When securing baggage coverage, make sure that the per-article limit – typically under €500/US$750 – will

Rough Guide Travel Insurance

Rough Guides Ltd offers a low-cost **travel insurance policy**, especially customized for our statistically low-risk readers by a leading British broker, provided by the American International Group (AIG) and registered with the British regulatory body, GISC (the General Insurance Standards Council). There are five main Rough Guides insurance plans: **No Frills** for the bare minimum for secure travel; **Essential**, which provides decent all-round cover; **Premier** for comprehensive cover with a wide range of benefits; **Extended Stay** for cover lasting four months to a year; and **Annual** Multi-Trip, a cost-effective way of getting Premier cover if you travel more than once a year. Premier, Annual Multi-Trip and Extended Stay policies can be supplemented by a "**Hazardous Pursuits Extension**" if you plan to indulge in sports considered dangerous, such as scuba-diving or trekking. For a policy quote, call the Rough Guides Insurance Line: toll-free in the UK ☎0800/015 09 06 or ☎+44 1392 314 665 from elsewhere. Alternatively, get an online quote at ⊛www.roughguides.com/insurance

cover your most valuable possessions. If you need to make a claim, you should keep receipts for medicines and medical treat-ment, and in the event you have anything stolen, you must obtain an official statement from the police.

Health

It is vital to have travel insurance (see "Insurance" above) against potential med-ical expenses. Canada has an excellent health service, but nonresidents are not entitled to free health care, and medical costs can be astronomical, depending on the treatment. If you have an accident, medical services will get to you quick-ly and charge you later.

Doctors and pharmacies

Doctors and **dentists** can be found listed in the *Yellow Pages*, though for **medical emer-gencies** call ☎911. If you are bringing medi-cine prescribed by your doctor, bring a copy of the prescription; first, to avoid problems at customs and immigration, and second, for renewing medication with Canadian doctors, if needed.

As you would expect, Vancouver has scores of **pharmacies**, which can advise on minor ailments and distinguish between unfa-miliar brand names for the visitor. The 24-hr Shopper's Drug Mart has a central pharmacy location at 1125 Davie St (open 24hrs; ☎604/669-2424). For an alternative medicine pharmacy, try Semperviva, at 2608 West Broadway (☎604/739-1958, ⊛www

.semperviva.com), offering Vancouver's widest selection of herbal remedies, homeo-pathic medicine, and health products.

Specific health problems

Canada requires no specific vaccinations – but problems can arise when you're walking or camping in the Rockies and the surround-ing back country. Here, although tap water is generally safe to drink, it's always prudent to ask. You should also always **boil back-country water** for at least ten minutes to protect against the **Giardia** parasite (or "beaver fever"). The parasite thrives in warm water, so be careful about swimming in hot springs – if possible, keep nose, eyes and mouth above water. Symptoms are intestinal cramps, flat-ulence, fatigue, weight loss and vomiting, all of which can appear up to a week after infection. If left untreated, more unpleasant complications can arise, so see a doctor immediately if you think you've contracted it.

The most severe disease in the Vancouver area is **Rocky Mountain spotted fever**, a rickettsial illness spread to humans by hard ticks. Symptoms include the sudden onset of fever, headache, muscle pain and a subsequent rash. If you recognize any of these symptoms, seek medical help immediately. The disease can be tricky to diagnose in the early stages but without the right treatment, quickly, it can be fatal and between 3 and 5 percent of individuals who become ill with Rocky Mountain spotted fever die.

Lyme disease has been identified in Western Canada and is transmitted to humans through the bite of infected ticks. Manifestations of the disease include a rash where the tick is attached, fever, arthritis, facial palsy and other neuralgic symptoms. Try to avoid tick habitats, apply insect repellent frequently to your body and clothing, and check daily for ticks as prompt removal will help prevent infection. If you feel you have contracted the disease, seek medical help immediately; a course of antibiotics should cure you.

Blackfly and **mosquitoes** are notorious for the problems they cause walkers and campers, and are especially bad in areas near standing water. Horseflies are another pest. Late April to June is the blackfly season, and the mosquito season is from June until about October. If you're planning an expedition into the wilderness, you'd be well-advised to take three times the recommended daily dosage of vitamin B complex for two weeks before you go, and to take the recommended dosage while you're in Canada; this cuts down bites by up to seventy-five percent.

If you plan to do a lot of hiking or other outdoor activities, you might want to consider getting a rabies vaccination as well as booster shots for tetanus and diphtheria.

Once you're there, **repellent creams** and **sprays** may help: the best are those containing DEET. The ointment version of Deep-Woods Off is the best brand, with 95 percent DEET. If you're camping or picnicking you'll find that burning coils or candles containing allethrin or citronella can help. If you're walking in an area that's rife with pests, it's well worth taking a gauze mask to protect your head and neck; wearing white clothes and no perfumed products also makes you less attractive to the insects. Once bitten, an **antihistamine cream** like phenergan is the best antidote. On no account go anywhere near an area marked as a blackfly mating ground – people have died from bites sustained when the creatures are on heat. Also dangerous, and newly arrived in Vancouver (the first cases were confirmed in July 2003), is **West Nile virus**, a mosquito-born affliction with life-threatening properties. The risk of infection for humans is low but the disease could be contracted anywhere in the region. The most effective means of reducing the risk of infection with West Nile virus is, once again, to avoid mosquito bites (see p.48).

If you develop a large rash and flu-like symptoms, you may have been bitten by a tick carrying lyme borreliosis (or "**lyme tick disease**"). This is easily curable, but if left untreated can lead to nasty complications, so see a doctor as soon as possible. It's spreading in Canada, especially in the more southerly and wooded parts of the country; you should check on its prevalence with the local tourist authority. It also may be advisable to buy a strong **tick repellent** and to wear long socks, trousers and sleeved shirts when walking.

Travellers visiting the Vancouver region should also be aware of the disease **Hantavirus**, which is carried by the reddish-brown or grey deer mouse and passed to humans when they breathe in airborne particles released from the droppings and urine of infected rodents. Other animals do not pass the infection on to humans, even if they are exposed to the virus; nor does the virus cause any illness in them. Preventative measures include keeping away from rodent-infested areas, disposing of droppings of rodents quickly and carefully, and wearing dust-masks in areas with high levels of contamination or little ventilation. Symptoms generally appear within one to two weeks, but can take up to six. They initially resemble the flu, including a high fever, body aches, chills, but also trouble breathing. There is no specific cure for the disease; however, treatment in an Intensive Care Unit greatly reduces the risk of death.

Information, websites and maps

Information on Vancouver is fairly easy to track down, either over the Internet or, upon arrival, at the Tourist InfoCentre Downtown (see below); maps of the city and its surroundings are readily available from local bookstores.

Visitor information

The excellent **Tourist InfoCentre** (mid-May–Sept daily 8am–6pm; Sept–May Mon–Sat 8.30am–5pm; ☎604/683-2000, 682-2222 or 1-800/663-6000 or 1-800/435-5622, ☺www.tourismvancouver.com) can be found almost opposite Canada Place (see p.48) in the Waterfront Centre, 200 Burrard St at the corner of Canada Place Way. Besides information on the city and much of southeastern British Columbia, the office provides **foreign exchange** facilities, BC TransLink (transit or public transport) tickets and information, and tickets to sports and entertainment events through a separate Ticketmaster booth. Same-day tickets for events are also often available at a discount. It also has one of the most comprehensive **accommodation services**, backed up by bulging photo albums of hotel rooms and B&Bs: the booking service is free. Smaller kiosks open in the summer (July & Aug) in a variety of locations, usually including Stanley Park and close to the Vancouver Art Gallery on the corner of Georgia and Granville (daily 9.30am–5.30pm, Thurs & Fri till 9pm).

Websites

☺**www.city.vancouver.bc.ca** The city government's comprehensive site features links to almost everything you need, including an arts-events calendar, information on parks and gardens and maps of walking tours.

☺**www.canada.com/vancouver/vancouversun** The *Vancouver Sun*, the city's morning newspaper, provides news, sport and weather updates as well as film, art gallery and music listings.

☺**www.straight.com** The online version of *The Georgia Straight*, Vancouver's free news and entertainment weekly. This is your best bet for what's happening in the city.

☺**www.vancouver.visitorschoice.com** This comprehensive, professional website presents events, attractions, festivals, dining, shopping and accommodation information.

☺**www.canada.com/vancouver** This one-stop site features the best Vancouver newspapers, local news and listings.

☺**www.cbc.radio.ca** Vancouver's public radio station can be accessed live over the Internet for news and feature stories.

☺**www.gayvancouver.bc.ca** This source features gay and gay-friendly accommodations, businesses, restaurants, nightlife, events and services.

☺**www.hellobc.com** For trips around the province, visit this page for information on accommodation and travel ideas.

☺**www.coastandmountains.bc.ca** The Vancouver Coast and Mountains Tourism Board provides information and ideas for golfing expeditions, touring, outdoor activities, and general trips out of town.

Maps

The Tourist InfoCentre provide a comprehensive **map** of Vancouver, which, along with the maps in this guide, should be sufficient for your needs. If you're planning to use city transport, the excellent *Transit Route Map & Guide* is available from the there as well as from stores boasting "FareDealer" stickers.

Canada's leading map publishers, **MapArt**, the Vancouver-based **ITMB** and **Rand MacNally** all have maps of the whole of Greater Vancouver, with more detailed insets for the central area. MapArt also publish both a map and a street atlas of Vancouver and Fraser Valley, extending the coverage even further eastwards as far as Hope.

For more detailed mapping of the central area of the city, MapArt's *Vancouver FastTrack* is a handy concertina map with plans of Downtown, central area and the region. Insight Guides and National Geographic Society have laminated maps, combining detailed plans of the Downtown area with more general maps and tourist tips. MapEasy's plan, with its characteristic hand-drawn style, shows in addition to places of interest numerous hotels, restaurants and shops in Downtown, Granville Island and Stanley Park. Compass pocket-size map is a combination of two handy, if less detailed pop-out plans.

For those planning to venture further afield, ITMB have a contoured map of Vancouver's Northshore Hiking Trails at 1:50,000 and a road map *South West British Columbia* at 1:580,000. Mapping of Vancouver Island comes from ITMB at 1:400,000 with contours and hiking trials, or from Rand McNally and MapArt at 1:550,000 and 1:500,000 respectively, both with numerous street plans and the Gulf Islands. Both MapArt and Rand McNally also publish a street plan of the island's main town, Victoria, while ITMB have a special hiking map at 1:50,000 of the West Coast Trail in the Pacific Rim National Park.

Map outlets

Large general bookstores and online retailers usually have some maps of Vancouver but if you want to compare maps to find one that suits, you're better to try one of the following specialist map and/or travel bookshops or websites.

In Canada and the US

110 North Latitude US ☎336/369-4171, ⊛www.110nlatitude.com.
Book Passage 51 Tamal Vista Blvd, Corte Madera, CA 94925 ☎1-800/999-7909, ⊛www.bookpassage.com.
Distant Lands 56 S Raymond Ave, Pasadena, CA 91105 ☎1-800/310-3220, ⊛www.distantlands.com.

Globe Corner Bookstore 28 Church St, Cambridge, MA 02138 ☎1-800/358-6013, ⊛www.globecorner.com.
Longitude Books 115 W 30th St #1206, New York, NY 10001 ☎1-800/342-2164, ⊛www.longitudebooks.com.
Map Town 400 5 Ave SW #100, Calgary, AB, T2P 0L6 ☎1-877/921-6277, ⊛www.maptown.com.
Travel Bug Bookstore 3065 W Broadway, Vancouver, BC, V6K 2G9 ☎604/737-1122, ⊛www.travelbugbooks.ca.
World of Maps 1235 Wellington St, Ottawa, ON, K1Y 3A3 ☎1-800/214-8524, ⊛www.worldofmaps.com.

In the UK and Ireland

Stanfords 12–14 Long Acre, London WC2 ☎020/7836 1321, ⊛www.stanfords.co.uk. Also at 39 Spring Gardens, Manchester ☎0161/831 0250, and 29 Corn St, Bristol ☎0117/929 9966.
Blackwell's Map Centre 50 Broad St, Oxford ☎01865/793 550, ⊛maps.blackwell.co.uk. Branches in Bristol, Cambridge, Cardiff, Leeds, Liverpool, Newcastle, Reading and Sheffield.
The Map Shop 30a Belvoir St, Leicester ☎0116/247 1400, ⊛www.mapshopleicester .co.uk.
National Map Centre 22–24 Caxton St, London SW1 ☎020/7222 2466, ⊛www.mapsnmc.co.uk.
National Map Centre Ireland 34 Aungier St, Dublin ☎01/476 0471, ⊛www.mapcentre.ie.
The Travel Bookshop 13–15 Blenheim Crescent, London W11 ☎020/7229 5260, ⊛www.thetravelbookshop.co.uk.
Traveller 55 Grey St, Newcastle-upon-Tyne ☎0191/261 5622, ⊛www.newtraveller.com.

In Australia and New Zealand

Map Centre ⊛www.mapcentre.co.nz.
Mapland 372 Little Bourke St, Melbourne ☎03/9670 4383, ⊛www.mapland.com.au.
Map Shop 6–10 Peel St, Adelaide ☎08/8231 2033, ⊛www.mapshop.net.au.
Map World 371 Pitt St, Sydney ☎02/9261 3601, ⊛www.mapworld.net.au. Also at 900 Hay St, Perth ☎08/9322 5733.
Map World 173 Gloucester St, Christchurch ☎0800/627 967, ⊛www.mapworld.co.nz.

Arrival

Linked to almost every major city in the world and all of Canada, **Vancouver International Airport** receives 13 million visitors a year, making it the second busiest airport in Canada (after Toronto). Vancouver's **bus and train station**, Pacific Central, is located southeast of Downtown and links the city to many Canadian and a few American cities. Those coming in **by car** will find Vancouver's network of one-way streets to provide ample challenge, and the city rather congested, especially at rush hours.

By air

Vancouver International Airport (☎604/ 207-7077, ⊕www.yvr.ca) is situated on Sea Island, 13km south of Downtown. International flights arrive at the majestic new main terminal; domestic flights at the smaller and linked old main terminal. If you're an international passenger, you'll find a **tourist information** desk (daily 7am–midnight; ☎604/688-5515) as you exit customs and immigration and before entering the terminal's public spaces. On the left, before you exit to the public spaces, are desks for direct bus services from the airport to Victoria (Pacific Coach Lines) and Whistler (there are also services for Bellingham Airport (Seattle) and Sea-Tac Airport in the US available outside Arrivals: see below). There are also freephone lines to several upmarket hotels in the area. Domestic passengers also have a tourist information desk just before the terminal exit.

Departure tax

All passengers departing from Vancouver International Airport must pay an **Airport Improvement Fee** – $5 if travelling within BC, $10 within North America (including Mexico and Hawaii) and $15 outside North America. The tax is levied as you pass through to the gates and must be paid on the spot with cash or credit. Save time by pre-paying at the automatic machines dotted around the various check-in areas in national, international and US Departures.

The best way to get into Vancouver is on the private **Airporter bus** (6.45am–1.10am; $12, $18 round-trip; ☎604/946-8866 or 1-800/668-3141, ⊕www.yvrairporter.com)), which leaves every 15 minutes from a bay to the left immediately outside the main door of the international arrivals; domestic arrivals can walk here if you need visitor information or wait at the domestic arrivals pick-up outside the terminal. Helpful staff and a pamphlet with a useful map help you figure out which drop-offs on the shuttle's three routes are most useful. Note that if you're headed straight for the bus depot (see below) on route #3 you need to transfer to another Airporter service closer to Downtown: the driver will tell you all you need to know. Returning to the airport, buses run round the same pick-up points, including the bus depot.

Taxis into town cost about $25–30, limos $41.73. **Public transport** is cheaper, but slower and involves a change of bus – take the BC Metro Transit bus #100 to the corner of 70th Street and Granville (it leaves the domestic terminal roughly every 30min), then change to the #20 or #21 which drops you off Downtown on Granville Street. Tickets cost $3 during rush hour, $2 off-peak (weekdays after 6.30pm, Sat & Sun and all public holidays), and exact change is required to buy tickets on board. Make sure you get a transfer if the driver doesn't automatically give you one (see "City transport", p.28, for more on peak and off-peak times and transfers).

You can pick up direct **buses to Victoria** from the airport. Ask for details at the bus desk in international arrivals, or head straight

25

Vancouver is at the hub of transport links to many parts of western Canada. Deciding where to move **onward from the city** – and how to go – presents a wealth of possibilities. We've listed the basic alternatives, together with cross-references to more detailed accounts of the various options.

Alaska and the Yukon You can fly to Whitehorse in the Yukon directly from Vancouver, but there are no nonstop flights to Alaska from the city: all go via Seattle in the US. You can fly to Seattle or take a bus to Sea-Tac Airport in around three hours from Vancouver Airport or various Downtown hotels and other locations. You can **drive** to Alaska through southern British Columbia to Dawson Creek, where you can pick up the Alaska Highway, which runs through the Yukon to Fairbanks. Allow at least three days. Alternatively drive to Prince George, head west towards Prince Rupert and then strike north up the more adventurous Cassiar Highway to connect with the Alaska Highway in the Yukon. Using **public transport** you could take a Greyhound bus to Prince George (one day), connecting with another Greyhound to Dawson Creek and Whitehorse (two days). Buses link Whitehorse with other Yukon and Alaskan destinations. To reach Alaska by **boat** from Vancouver you need to go via Bellingham (in the US), Prince Rupert or Port Hardy on Vancouver Island.

British Columbia Two main **road** routes strike east from Vancouver towards Alberta and the Canadian Rockies – the Trans-Canada Highway and Hwy-3, both served by regular Greyhound **buses**. Both give access to the Okanagan, known for its warm-watered lakes and summer resorts, and to the beautiful mountain and lakes enclave of the Kootenays. VIA **trains** run through the region via Kamloops to Jasper (for the Rockies) and Edmonton three times weekly. Buses also serve the **Cariboo** region, the duller central part of the province. Several itineraries can be put together by combining car or public transport journeys in the BC interior with BC Ferries' connections from Port Hardy on Vancouver Island (see below) to either Bella Coola or Prince Rupert.

Calgary and the Canadian Rockies It takes between ten and twelve hours to drive to Calgary on the Trans-Canada Highway, and about ninety minutes less to reach the heart of the Canadian Rockies, Banff. Special express-service Greyhound buses operate over the same route. There is no longer a VIA Rail passenger service to Calgary. Very frequent one-hour flights connect Vancouver and Calgary, and charter operators and no-frills airlines offer highly competitive rates on this route (though cheap flights often leave very early or very late in the day).

Vancouver Island Numerous **ferries** ply between Vancouver and three points on its eponymous island – Swartz Bay (for Victoria), Nanaimo and Comox. Most leave from Tsawwassen and Horseshoe Bay, terminals about thirty minutes' drive south and west of Downtown respectively. As a foot passenger you can buy inclusive bus and ferry tickets from Vancouver to Victoria or Nanaimo. Car drivers should make reservations well in advance for all summer crossings (see p.220 for full details of getting to Vancouver Island). **Public transport** connects to the Pacific Rim National Park, the island's highlight, and to Port Hardy on the island's northern tip for ferry connections to Prince Rupert and Bella Coola.

to the hotel shuttle bus stop outside the international terminal. Pacific Coach Lines (⊕604/662-8074, 662-7575 or 1-800/661-1725, ⊛www.pacificcoach.com) runs between one and three daily direct services from the airport to Victoria depending on the time of year (1–3 daily year-round; 2–4 daily mid-May to late June and early Sept to Oct; 7 daily late June to early Sept; $36 single, $71 return).

By bus

Vancouver's main **bus terminal** at 1150 Station St is used by Pacific Coach Lines

(☎604/662-7575, ⊛www.pacificcoach.com) for Victoria; Maverick Coach Lines (☎604/ 940-2332, ⊛www.maverickcoachlines .bc.ca) for Whistler, Sunshine Coast and Nanaimo; and all Greyhound services (☎482-8747, ⊛www.greyhound.ca). It is in a slightly dismal area alongside the VIA Rail Pacific Central train station. It's too far to walk to Downtown from here, so bear left from the station through a small park, to the Science World–Main St SkyTrain station and it's a couple of stops to the city centre. Take the train marked "Waterfront"); tickets ($2) are available from platform machines. Alternatively, you can take a taxi Downtown from the station for about $6–8. There are **left-luggage** facilities here and a useful **hotel board**, whose freephone line connects to some of the city's genuine cheapies (but check locations) – some of whom will deduct the taxi fare from the terminal from your first night's bill.

By train

The skeletal **VIA Rail** services operate out of Pacific Central Station (☎604/640-3741 or 1-800/561-8630, ⊛www.viarail.ca); they run to and from Jasper (3 weekly), where there are connections for Prince George and Prince Rupert, and on to Edmonton and the east (3 weekly). VIA–Amtrak (☎253/931- 8917 or 1-800/872-7245, ⊛www.amtrak. com) operates one train a day between Vancouver and Seattle.

A second train station, belonging to the provincial **BC Rail**, at 1311 W 1st St, in North Vancouver (☎604/984-5246 or 1- 800/339-8752 in BC, 1-800/663-8238 from the rest of Canada and US, ⊛www.bcrail. com), once provided passenger services to and from Whistler, Lillooet and Prince George via 100 Mile House, Williams Lake and Quesnel. This service, however, has been suspended indefinitely, as have the popular **excursion trips** to Squamish aboard the *Royal Hudson* steam train.

By car

The approach to Vancouver by road is straightforward from the US and points to the east and north in Canada. From the western **United States**, follow Interstate 5 (I- 5) from Seattle and Washington State to the border towns of Blaine (in the US) and White Rock (BC), about 210km or 140 miles from Seattle. You clear Canadian Customs at the Peace Arch crossing in Blaine (open 24 hours). If you return this way, you pass through US Customs.

Interstate 5 becomes the Canadian **Hwy 99** and leads west from White Rock and then north to Vancouver, where it becomes first Oak Street and then – six blocks after a left turn at Oak and 70th Avenue – Granville Street, a major artery that leads directly to the heart of Downtown. Note, however, that much of Granville is pedestrianized in the centre, and you'll have to be prepared to fol- low various one-way routes if your destina- tion is in the Downtown core. Hwy 99 is also the route to follow if you're driving from the **ferry terminal** at Tsawwassen (for ferries from Vancouver Island and the Gulf Islands): Hwy 17 runs from the terminal to connect with Hwy 99 just before the George Massey Tunnel.

If you're heading to the city from points in the **east** of Canada or central US, you should follow the main Trans-Canada Highway (Hwy 1), which crosses the Fraser River on the Port Mann Bridge and then cuts through the suburbs of southeast Vancouver before an exit at Cassiar Street to Hastings Street (Hwy 7A), which leads west about 7km to Downtown. Hwy 1 then continues over the Burrard Inlet on the Second Narrows Bridge before turning west to pass through North and West Vancouver.

If you're arriving from the **north** and Squamish, Whistler or the ferry terminal at Horseshoe Bay, then you'll follow the Trans- Canada south. If you're headed for Downtown on this route, take the Taylor Way Bridge to Vancouver-Hwy 99 exit (Exit 13) in West Vancouver and cross the Burrard Inlet on the Lions Gate Bridge to Downtown's West End district – note that you can expect delays on this route at busy times of the day.

City transport and tours

Vancouver's public transport system is an efficient, integrated network of bus, light-rail (SkyTrain), SeaBus and ferry services, which are operated by TransLink (daily 6.30am–11.30pm; ☎604/953-3333 or customer relations ☎604/953-3040, ⓦwww.translink.bc.ca), formerly – and occasionally still – known as BC Transit.

Tickets are valid across the system for bus, SkyTrain and SeaBus. Generally they cost $2 for journeys in the large, central Zone 1 and $3 or $4 for longer two- and three-zone journeys – though you're unlikely to go out of Zone 1 unless you're travelling to the airport from Downtown which involves crossing from Zone 1 to 2. These regular fares apply Monday to Friday from start of service until 6.30pm. After 6.30pm and all day Saturday, Sunday and public holidays, a flat $2 fare applies across all three zones.

Tickets are valid for **transfers** throughout the system for ninety minutes from the time of issue; on buses you should ask for a transfer ticket if the driver doesn't automatically give you one. Otherwise, you can buy tickets individually (or in books of ten for $18

for Zone 1) at station offices or machines, 7-Eleven, Safeway and London Drugs stores, or any other shop or newsstand displaying a blue TransLink sticker (so-called "FareDealer" outlets). You must carry tickets with you as proof of payment. Probably the simplest and cheapest deal if you're going to be making three or more journeys in a day is to buy a **DayPass** ($8), valid all day across all three zones; Zone 1 monthly passes are $63. If you buy these over the counter at stores or elsewhere (not in machines) they're "Scratch & Ride" – you scratch out the day and month before travel. If you lose anything on the transport system go to the **lost property** office at the SkyTrain Stadium Station (Mon–Fri 8.30am–5pm; ☎604/682-7887 or 985-7777 for items left on West Van buses).

Useful and scenic bus routes

Some of the more important Vancouver **bus routes** are:

#1 Gastown–English Bay loop.

#3 and #8 Gastown–Downtown (Robson at Granville)–Marine Drive at Main.

#4 UBC and #10 UBC Granville Street–University of British Columbia–Museum of Anthropology.

#17 and #20 Downtown–Marine Drive; transfer to #100 for the airport at Granville and 70th Street.

#19 Pender Street (Downtown)–Stanley Park (Stanley Park Loop).

#23, #35, #123 and #135 – Downtown (Pender and Burrard)–Stanley Park.

#50 Gastown – False Creek–Broadway.

#51 SeaBus Terminal–Downtown–Granville Island.

#236 Lonsdale Quay terminal (North Vancouver)–Capilano Suspension Bridge–Grouse Mountain.

Some **scenic routes** are worth travelling for their own sakes:

#52 "Around the Park" service takes 30min through Stanley Park (April–Oct Sat, Sun & holidays only); board at Stanley Park Loop (connections from #23, #35 or #135) or Denman Street (connections from #1, #3 or #8).

#210 Pender Street–Phibbs Exchange; change there for the #211 (mountain

route) or #212 (ocean views) to Deep Cove.

#250 Georgia Street (Downtown)–North Vancouver–West Vancouver–Horseshoe Bay.

#351 Howe Street–White Rock–Crescent Beach (1hr each way).

If you don't want to use public transport, **car and bicycle rental** and **taxis** are easy to come by – see "Directory" on pp.211–213 for details.

Buses

The useful *Transit Route Map & Guide* ($1.95) is available from the infocentre and FareDealer shops, while free **bus** timetables can be found at the infocentre, 7-Eleven stores and the central library. You can buy tickets on the bus, but make sure you have the right change (they don't carry any); be sure to ask specially if you want a transfer ticket. Normal buses stop running around midnight, when a rather patchy "Night Owl" service comes into effect on major routes until about 4am. Note that blue **West Van** buses (☎604/985-7777) also operate (usually to North and West Vancouver destinations, including the BC Ferries terminal at Horseshoe Bay) in the city and BC Transit tickets are valid on these buses as well.

SeaBuses and ferries

SeaBuses ply between Downtown and Lonsdale Quay in North Vancouver, and they're a ride definitely worth taking for its own sake: the views of the mountains across Burrard Inlet, the port and the Downtown skyline are superb. The **Downtown terminal** is Waterfront Station in the old Canadian Pacific station buildings at the foot of Granville Street. There is no ticket office, only a ticket machine, but you can get a ticket from the small newsagent immediately on your left as you face the long gallery that takes you to the boats. Two 400-seat catamarans make the thirteen-minute crossing every fifteen to thirty minutes (6.30am–12.30am). Arrival in North Vancouver is at Lonsdale Quay, where a bus terminal offers connections to Grouse Mountain and other North Vancouver destinations. Bicycles can be carried on board.

The city also has a variety of small **ferries** – glorified bathtubs – run over similar routes by two rival companies: Aquabus (☎689-5858, ⊛www.aquabus.bc.ca) and False Creek Ferries (☎684-7781, ⊛www.granvilleislandferries.bc.ca). These provide a useful, very frequent and fun serv-

ice daily 7am–10.30pm (until 8.30pm in winter). Aquabus runs boats in a continuous circular shuttle from the foot of Hornby Street to the Fish Docks on the seawalk, to Vanier Park and the museums, to Granville Island (both $2), and to the Yaletown dock by the road loop at the east foot of Davie Street ($3). False Creek Ferries also runs to Granville Island ($2), and also to Vanier Park ($3 from Granville Island, $2 from the Aquatic Centre) just below the Maritime Museum – a good way of getting to the park and its museums (see p.92).

Both companies also offer what amount to **mini-cruises up False Creek**, with connections from Granville Island to Science World and the Plaza of Nations. You can pick up the Aquabus boat at the Arts Club Theatre on Granville Island, the foot of Hornby Street Downtown or – with False Creek Ferries – below the Aquatic Centre at the foot of Thurlow and northern end of Burrard Bridge, on Granville Island or below the spit and small harbour near the Maritime Museum in Vanier Park.

SkyTrain

Vancouver's single light-rail line – **SkyTrain** – is a model of its type: driverless, completely computerized and magnetically propelled, half underground and half on raised track. It covers 28km between the downtown Waterfront Station (housed in the CPR building with the SeaBus terminal) and the southeastern suburb of New Westminster. Only the first three or four stations – Waterfront, Burrard, Granville and Stadium – are of any practical use to the casual visitor, but the 39-minute trip along the twenty-station line is worth taking if only to see how the Canadians do these things – spotless interiors and Teutonic punctuality.

Trams

Owing to increasing pressure from preservation groups in the city, trams are slowly become a popular way to traverse Vancouver once again. Two electric trams have been restored and are in operation along the three-mile track between Science World and Granville Island, stopping at First Avenue and Ontario Street, and Leg-in-Boot Square. The Downtown Historic Railway

(☎665-3903) is in charge of the weekends- and holidays-only service run from late May to October.

Taxis

Taxis in Vancouver are efficient and reasonably priced and their drivers generally honest. Fares are generally $2.30 for the metre drop, and $1.25 for each 1km thereafter. Theoretically, taxis can be hailed on the streets when the sign on the roof is lit, or picked up at taxi ranks or stands around the city, but this can often be difficult in Vancouver. Taxi services can also be ordered by phone: try Black Top ☎604/681-2181, Maclure's Cabs ☎604/683-6666, Vancouver Taxi ☎604/871-1111, or Yellow ☎604/681-1111. Cabbies in Vancouver expect a ten to fifteen percent tip.

Driving

It's hard to see why anyone would want to **rent a car** while staying in Vancouver – the transport system is inexpensive and efficient and you can reach Victoria, Whistler and the Sunshine Coast using regular bus services. And if you're crossing to Victoria with a view to exploring Vancouver Island, you can hold off renting a car until you reach Victoria – this will save you the cost of taking the car across on the ferry, not to mention the extra hassle involved waiting in line to board at busy times.

If you do insist on **driving,** try and avoid bottlenecks outside the city centre (especially on the North Shore Bridges) between seven and nine in the morning and after 3pm on weekday afternoons. Unlike other parts of Canada, drivers in Vancouver are allowed to turn right at a red light; speed limits are usually no higher than 110km (65 miles) per hour outside the city, much less in urban and built-up areas.

Car rental

Car rental in Vancouver can be pricey when you take everything into account: it averages around $50/day or $300/week, excluding sales tax (14.5 percent), social services tax ($1.50/day) and a vehicle licensing fee (91¢/day). If you rent from an airport location, expect to pay a Concession Recovery Fee of 14 percent on top of everything else, although some companies will naturally factor this into their rates. You'll need to have a credit card to rent and, if you have an overseas driver's licence, an International Driver's Permit is recommended. Some car rental firms won't accept drivers under 25; others will charge a premium for younger drivers (minimum 21 years old).

Car rental agencies

Alamo ☎1-800/462-5266, ⓦwww.alamo.com.
Avis Canada ☎1-800/272-5871, ⓦwww.avis.ca, US ☎1-800/230-4898, ⓦwww.avis.com.
Budget Canada ☎800/268-8900, ⓦwww.budgetcanada.com, US ☎1-800/527-0700, ⓦwww.budgetrentacar.com.
Dollar US ☎1-800/800-4000, ⓦwww.dollar.com.
Enterprise Rent-a-Car ☎1-800/736-8222, ⓦwww.enterprise.com.
Hertz Canada ☎1-800/263-0600, ⓦwww.hertz.ca, US ☎1-800/654-3001, ⓦwww.hertz.com.
National ☎1-800/227-7368, ⓦwww.nationalcar.com.
Thrifty ☎1-800/847-4389, ⓦwww.thrifty.ca or ⓦwww.thrifty.com.
Via Route ☎514/871-1166, ⓦwww.viaroute.com.

City tours

First port of call for anyone considering an **organized tour** of any description should be the Tourist InfoCentre (see p.23), which carries rack upon rack of pamphlets and fliers advertising a wide range of walking, bus, plane, helicopter and other tours.

Bus, cab and car tours

City **bus tours** are offered by Gray Line (☎604/879-3363, ⓦwww.grayline.ca). Although the ticket price includes pick-up and drop-offs at your hotel, you will need to notify the company if you want to be picked up. The company's tours include the "Deluxe Grand City Tour" of the city's highlights (3hr 30min, $45) and a two-hour "Vancouver By Night" tour (2hr, $30). They also offer a "Double Decker Attractions Loop Tour", a hop-on, hop-off affair with stops at over twenty attractions in the city. Tickets are valid for two days and cost $27.10. Similar tours are also offered by Pacific Coach Lines (reservations required; ☎604/662-7575 or 1-800/667-1725, ✆www.pacificcoach.com), while Landsea Tours (☎604/662-7591 or 1-800/558-4955, ✆www.vancouvertours.com) have smaller "big-window" 24-seat buses. The Vancouver Trolley Company (☎604/801-5515 or 1-888/451-5581, ✆www.vancouvertrolley.com) has tours narrated by drivers in a red mock-San Francisco trolleybus that depart every 30 minutes from one of twenty-three stops around the city: the $26 all-day ticket (from 157 Water St in cruise season, or from your driver) allows you to get on and off at will at any of the stops. A full circuit of all 23 stops takes three hours.

Starline Tours (☎604/272-9187 or 1-888/755-2233, ✆www.vvv.com/home/starline) and Vancouver Special Tours (☎604/451-1600, ✆www.vancouverspecialtours.com) are just a few of the companies offering **nature** and **wildlife tours** of the Fraser River, Capilano Canyon, and other locations near the city. Taxi companies such as Black Top (☎604/731-1111) and Yellow Cab (☎604/681-1111) also often offer tours for up to five people: a 1hr 30min city tour costs around $70. Fridge's Early Motion Tours (☎604/687-5088) will take you round the city in a 1930 Model A Ford Phaeton for around $100 an hour.

Walking tours

Walkabout Historic Vancouver (☎604/720-0006 or 439-0448, ✆www.walkabouthistoricvancouver.com) offers two basic two-hour **walking tours** around Downtown–Gastown and Granville Island (2 daily at 10am and 2pm; $25; private tours and times can be arranged) with the tour guides dressed in nineteenth-century costume. Those interested in **architecture** might consider the architectural walking tours (Tues-–Sat, June–August, 1pm, $5) offered by the Architectural Institute of BC (☎683-8588 ex. 306, ✆www.aibc.bc.ca/pub_resources/aibc_outreach/architectural_walking_tour) For walking tours of Gastown, contact Gastown BIS (☎683-5650): tours last ninety minutes and currently depart daily at 2pm from Gassy Jack's statue in Maple Tree Square at the junction of Water and Carrall streets. Rockwood Adventures (☎980-7749 or ☎1-888/236-6606, ✆www.rockwood

adventures.com) offers guided **walking tours** of Stanley Park, Lynn Canyon, Capilano River Canyon, the rainforest at Lighthouse Park and of Bowen Island, the last with a return by floatplane. Hotel pick-ups are available. **Chinatown** can be explored with guides from the Chinese Cultural Centre ($5; ☎604/687-7793) – tours are scheduled for 11am and 1.30pm during the summer months, but have to be booked ahead during the rest of the year.

Horse and carriage tours

AA Horse & Carriage provide **horse-drawn tours** of Stanley Park in 20-person carriages between mid-March and mid-October: call (☎604/681-5115, ✆www.stanleyparktours.com) or visit the information booth on Park Drive east of the Rowing Club, the starting point for the leisurely one-hour trips around the park's best-known sights (departures every 20 to 30 minutes; from $20.55). A shuttle bus is available to the booth from ten Downtown locations.

The X-Tour

The popularity of *The X-Files* – the early seasons were filmed in and around Vancouver – has inevitably spawned a tour company offering visits to the locations associated with the TV series (☎609-2770 or ☎1-888/250-7211, ✆www.x-tour.com). The tours also include sites used in other films and shows. Pick-ups and drop-offs are available from Downtown hotels. Tours are by limousine with a guide, last around 3hr 30min and cost from $145.

Air and boat tours

Air tours are expensive, but they offer a superb way of seeing Vancouver and its magnificent natural setting. The easiest to access are offered by Harbour Air Seaplanes (☎604/274-1277 or 1-800/665-0212), which operates from the waterfront terminal at the bottom of the road one block west of Canada Place at the foot of Burrard Street. A wide variety of trips are available, from the 30-minute "Panorama Tour" of the city (from about $89) to half-day wilderness excursions, full-day trips to Victoria ($239) and the Sunshine Coast (from $229), and the "Fly 'n' Dine" package ($169). The last involves a flight to Snug Cove on Bowen Island for a romantic restaurant dinner at *Doc Morgan's Inn* and return to Vancouver by ferry and limousine. In a similar vein, Baxter Aviation (☎604/683-6525 or 1-800/661-5599, ⊛www.baxterair.com/tours.s) offer a 30-minute aerial *Vancouver Scenic* tour ($69–$129, depending on the number of passengers) and a 85-minute *Glacier and Alpine Lakes* tour ($179–$299) which includes a short photo stop. More expensive air options are offered by Helijet International (☎604/270-

1484 or 1-800/987-4354, ⊛www.helijet.com), whose range of helicopter tours depart from Vancouver Harbour and from the airport. Prices are from around $119 to $179.

For **boat tours**, contact Harbour Cruises (☎604/688-7246, ⊛www.boatcruises.com), which between May and October lays on 75-minute harbour tours (generally 3 daily; $19), the four-hour Indian Arm Luncheon Cruise (daily at 10.30am; from $50) and the three-hour Sunset and Dinner Cruise (daily at 6.30pm; from $65) aboard an authentic paddlewheeler, the MPV *Constitution*: it departs from the northern foot of Denman Street in Coal Harbour by Stanley Park.

Addresses

Most addresses in Downtown Vancouver are straightforward and easy to find. Most consist simply of a street or avenue and number (500 W Pender St), though on long streets and avenues the "cross" street or avenue has been added to help you find the relevant block (500 W Pender at/near/and Seymour). Where an address has several numbers, as in 150–1450 Robson, the first figure refers to the suite number, the second to the building number.

In **Downtown**, Carrall Street marks the axis from which streets and buildings are numbered and designated to east and west. To the west, numbers increase towards Stanley Park; to the east they increase towards Commercial Drive. Thus 500 W Pender would be five blocks west of Carrall. The axis for numbering to the south is the Canada Place Pier – there's no numbering to the north, as there's only the Burrard Inlet to the north of the pier. Thus numbers increase as you head south through Downtown towards False Creek and Granville Island.

The system works in the same way **off the Downtown peninsula**, although here Ontario Street marks the axis for numbering and designation to east and west, and all east–west roads are avenues and all north–south roads are streets.

Costs, money and banks

By Western European and major US city standards, Vancouver, which tends to be cheaper than the eastern Canadian cities, is very reasonably priced, with most basic items – from maps through to food, dining out and clothing – costing significantly less than back home. Rural US residents and Australians, on the other hand, will find prices about the same, if not less.

Daily costs

If you're prepared to buy your own picnic lunch, stay in hostels, and stick to the least expensive bars and restaurants, you should be able to get by on around **Can$55 /US$40/£25 per day**. Staying in a good B&B, eating out in medium-range restaurants most nights and drinking often in bars, you'll go through at least **Can$130/US$100/£60 per day**, with the main variable being the cost of your room. On **Can$200/$150/£90 per day** and upwards, you'll be able to live in relative luxury, enjoy a few city tours and eat well, though if you're planning to stay in the best hotels and to have a big night out pretty much every night, this still won't be anywhere near enough. As always, if you're travelling alone you'll spend much more on accommodation than you would in a group of two or more: most hotels do have single rooms, but they're fixed at about 65 percent (ie, not half) of the price of a double.

Restaurants don't come cheap, but costs remain manageable if you stick to the less pricey joints. A reasonable three-course meal with wine or beer can be got for around Can$25-30 per person, as long as you drink in moderation. **Tipping** at a restaurant is expected – usually fifteen percent – unless the service has been dire; taxi drivers expect a tip too, of the same amount. **Museum admission prices** are mostly in the Can$7/US$5/£3 range, but discounts of at least fifty percent are routinely available for children, seniors and students; indeed, **concessionary fares and rates** for teenagers, Canadian students and senior citizens are offered on all sorts of things, including public transport.

Finally, a word about **taxation**. Virtually all prices in Canada for everything from bubble-gum to hotel rooms are quoted without tax, which means that the price you see quoted is not the price you'll end up being required to pay. Across the province of British Columbia, which includes Vancouver, there's a **Provincial Sales Tax** (PST) of 7.5 percent on most goods and services, which rises to eight percent on hotel bills and ten percent in restaurants and bars; this is supplemented by the nationwide **Goods and Services Tax** (GST), a seven percent levy equivalent to VAT in Europe. As a small mercy, visitors can claim a **GST rebate** on certain goods and short-term accommodation of less than one month over the value of Can$50 and up to Can$200 per night. Claim forms are available at many hotels, shops and airports, or from any Canadian embassy. Return them, with **all original receipts**, to the address given on the form within sixty days of leaving Canada. Those returning overland to the US can claim up to a US$500 instant cash rebate at selected border duty-free shops. For more information, call either ☎902/432-5608 (outside Canada) or ☎1-800/668-4748 (within Canada), or consult ⊛www.ccra.gc.ca/visitors.

Currency

Canadian **currency** is the dollar ($), made up of 100 cents (¢) to the dollar. Coins are issued in 1¢ (penny), 5¢ (nickel), 10¢ (dime), 25¢ (quarter), $1 and $2 denominations: the $1 coin is known as a "loonie", after the bird on one face; the newer $2 coin is less inventively named a "twoonie". Paper currency comes in $5, $10, $50, $100, $500 and $1000 denominations. Although US dollars are widely accepted, it's often on a one-for-one basis, and as the US dollar is usually worth more than its

Canadian counterpart, it makes sense to exchange US currency.

At the time of writing, the **rate of exchange** is $2.20 to the pound sterling, $1.30 to the US dollar, $0.80 to the NZ Dollar, and $0.90 to the Australian dollar. For the most up-to-date rates, check the currency converter website ⓦ www.xe.com/ucc/.

Traveller's cheques

The main advantage of buying **traveller's cheques** is that they are a safe way of carrying funds. All well-known brands of traveller's cheque in all major currencies are widely accepted in Vancouver, with US dollar and Canadian dollar cheques being the most common. The usual fee for their purchase is one to two percent of face value, though this fee is often waived if you buy the cheques through a bank where you have an account. You'll find it useful to purchase a selection of denominations. When you **cash your cheques**, almost all banks make a percentage charge per transaction on top of a basic minimum charge.

In the event that your cheques are **lost or stolen**, the issuing company will expect you to report it immediately. Make sure you keep the purchase agreement, a record of cheque serial numbers, and details of the company's emergency contact numbers or the addresses of their local offices, **safe and separate from the cheques themselves**. Most companies claim to replace lost or stolen cheques within 24 hours.

ATMs, debit and credit cards

Vancouver is rife with **ATMs**, with a particular concentration in the city centre. Most ATMs accept a host of **debit cards**, including all those carrying the Cirrus coding. If in doubt, check with your bank to find out whether the card you wish to use will be accepted – and if you need a new (international) PIN. You'll rarely be charged a transaction fee, as the banks make their profits from applying different exchange rates. **Credit cards** can be used in ATMs too, but in this case transactions are treated as loans, with interest accruing daily from the date of withdrawal. All major credit cards, including American Express, Visa and MasterCard, are widely accepted in Vancouver.

Visa TravelMoney (ⓦ www.visa.com) combines the security of traveller's cheques with the convenience of plastic. It's a disposable debit card, charged up before you leave home with whatever amount you like, separate from your normal banking or credit accounts. You can then access these dedicated travel funds from any ATM that accepts Visa worldwide, with a PIN that you select yourself. When your money runs out, you just throw the card away. Since you can buy up to nine cards to access the same funds – useful for families travelling together – it's recommended that you buy at least one extra card as a back-up in case your first is lost or stolen. Travelex/Interpayment outlets sell the card worldwide (see ⓦ www.travelex.com for locations).

Lost or stolen card contact numbers

American Express ☏ 905/474-9280
Diners Club ☏ 1-800/554-7608
Mastercard ☏ 1-800/307-7309
Visa ☏ 1-800/847-2911

Banks and exchange

If you need to change money, Vancouver's **banks** usually offer the best deals. Banks are legion and although opening hours vary, all are open Mon–Fri 10am–3pm Monday–Thursday and Friday 10am–5 or 6pm. Outside these times, you might consider a **bureau de change** – try Thomas Cook, with several branches in the city. American Express cheques can be cashed at their Downtown office, 666 Burrard Street (Mon–Fri 8.30am–5.30pm, Sat 10am–4pm, closed Sun; ☏ 604/669-2813) at the corner of Hornby and Dunsmuir Streets.

Wiring money

Having **money wired** from home using one of the companies listed below is never convenient or cheap, and should only be considered as a last resort. It can actually be slightly cheaper to have your own bank send the money through. For that, you need to nominate a receiving bank in Vancouver and confirm the arrangement with them before you set the wheels in motion back home –

any large branch will do. The sending bank's fees are geared to the amount being transferred and the urgency of the service you require – the fastest transfers, taking two or three days, start at around £25/US$40 for the first £300–400/US$450–600.

Money-wiring companies

Thomas Cook Canada ☏1-888/823-4732;

Ireland ☏01/677 1721; UK ☏01733/318 922; US ☏1-800/287-7362, ☒www.us.thomascook.com. **Travelers Express Moneygram** Canada ☏1-800/933-3278; US ☏1-800/926-3947, ☒www.moneygram.com. **Western Union** Australia ☏1-800/501 500; Ireland ☏1-800/395 395; New Zealand ☏09/270 0050; UK ☏0800/833 833; US and Canada ☏1-800/325-6000, ☒www.westernunion.com.

Post, phones and email

Canada has an efficient postal system and a first-rate telephone network, and mobile network coverage has improved drastically over the last few years. Telephone booths and mail boxes are liberally distributed across the city and charges for both types of service are reasonable. Internet cafés are increasingly common, too.

Post

Canada Post operates branches in scores of locations, mostly as one part of a larger retail outlet, mainly pharmacies and stationery stores. The main **post office** is at 349 W. Georgia Street (☏1-800/267-1177) and is open 8am–5.30pm, Monday–Friday. There are also postal facilities in branches of stores such as Shopper's Drug Mart and Pharmasave. If you're posting letters to a Canadian address, always include the postcode or your mail may never get there. Apart from Canada Post branches or offices, **stamps** can be purchased from automatic vending machines, the lobbies of larger hotels, airports, train stations, bus terminals and many retail outlets and newsstands. Current **postal charges** are 48¢ for letters and postcards up to 30g within Canada, 65¢ for the same weight to the US, and Can$1.25 for international mail (also up to 30g).

Phones

Domestic and international **telephone calls** can be made with equal ease from public and private phones. **Public telephones** are commonplace, though the irresistible rise of the mobile means that their numbers will not

increase and may well diminish. All are equipped for the hearing-impaired and take coins. Most also accept pre-paid calling cards, as well as credit cards. Local calls cost 25¢ from a public phone, but are free on private phones (though not usually hotel phones).

When **dialling** any Canadian number, either local or long-distance, you must include the area code – ☏604 in Vancouver. Long-distance calls – to numbers beyond the area code of the telephone from which you are making the call – must be prefixed with "1". On public telephones, this "1" puts you through to the operator, who will tell you how much money you need to get connected. Thereafter, you'll be asked to shovel money in at regular intervals – so unless you're making a reverse-charge/collect call you'll need a stack of quarters (25¢ pieces) handy, if your call will be of any length.

To confuse matters, some connections within a single telephone code area are charged at the long-distance rate, and thus need the "1" prefix; a recorded message will tell you this is necessary as soon as you dial the number. To save the hassle of carrying all this change, you could consider either buying a telephone card back home (see below)

35

or here. As for **tariffs**, the cheap-rate period for calls is between 6pm and 8am during the week and all the weekend. Detailed rates are listed at the front of the telephone directory. Note also that many businesses, especially hotels, have **toll-free numbers** (prefixed by ☎1-800 or ☎1-888). Some of these can only be dialled from phones in the same province, others from anywhere within Canada, and a few from anywhere in North America; as a rough guideline, the larger the organization, the wider its toll-free net. Finally, remember that although most hotel rooms have phones, there is almost always an exorbitant surcharge for their use.

Useful phone numbers

Directory enquiries local (from private and public phones) ☎411; long-distance within North America from private phones ☎411, from public phones ☎1+ area code + 555-1212; international, call the operator ☎0.
Emergencies Police, fire and ambulance ☎911.
Operator (domestic and international) ☎0.
Phoning abroad from Vancouver To Australia: ☎011 + 61 + area code minus zero + number; to the Republic of Ireland: ☎011 + 353 + area code minus zero + number; to New Zealand: ☎011 + 64 + area code minus zero + number; to the UK: ☎011 + 44 + area code minus zero + number; to the US: ☎1 + area code + number.
Phoning Vancouver from abroad Dial your country's international access code, then the area code, followed by the number.

Calling home from abroad with a telephone charge card

One of the most convenient ways of phoning home from abroad is via a **telephone charge card** from your phone company back home. Using a PIN number, you can make calls from most hotels, public and private phones that will be charged to your home account – and not locally. Since most major charge cards are free to obtain, it's certainly worth getting one at least for emergencies; bear in mind, however, that rates aren't necessarily cheaper than calling from a Vancouver public phone – it's just more convenient not having to carry quarters around.

In the US, AT&T, MCI, Sprint, Canada Direct and other North American long-dis-

tance companies all enable their customers to make credit-card calls while overseas, billed to your home number. Call your company's customer service line for details of the toll-free access code in Vancouver. **In the UK and Ireland**, British Telecom (☎0800/345 144, ⊛www.chargecard .bt.com) will issue free to all BT customers the BT Charge Card, which can be used in Canada, along with a host of other countries. Alternatively, AT&T (☎0800/890 011, then 888/641-6123 when you hear the AT&T prompt) offers the Global Calling Card.

To call **Australia and New Zealand** from overseas, telephone charge cards such as Telstra Telecard or Optus Calling Card in Australia, and Telecom NZ's Calling Card can be used to make calls abroad, which are charged back to a domestic account or credit card. Apply to Telstra (☎1-800/038 000), Optus (☎1-300/300 937), or Telecom NZ (☎04/801 9000).

Mobile phones

If you want to use your **mobile phone** in Vancouver, you'll need to check cellular access and call charges with your phone provider before you set out. Note in particular that you are likely to be charged extra for incoming calls when abroad, as the people calling you will be paying the usual rate. The same sometimes applies to text messages, though in many cases these can now be received easily and at ordinary rates. The mobile network now covers almost all of the city and work on GSM 1900 – which means that mobiles bought in **Europe** need to be **triband** to gain cellular access.

Email

Vancouver is well geared up for Internet and email access with a healthy supply of **Internet cafés** – see below for a selection. In addition, note that many of the better hotels provide email and Internet access for their guests free or at a minimal charge.

One of the best ways to keep in touch while travelling is to sign up for a **free Internet email address** that can be accessed from anywhere in the world, for example Yahoo!Mail or Hotmail – accessible through ⊛www.yahoo.com and ⊛www

.hotmail.com, respectively. Once you've set up an account, you can use these sites to pick up and send mail from any computer with access to the Internet. In addition, ⓦwww.kropla.com is a useful website giving details of how to plug your laptop in when abroad; the site also lists international phone codes and provides information about electrical systems in different countries.

The media

Vancouver has a good selection of newspapers and magazines, featuring news and listings. The city's TV and radio offerings run the usual gamut found in major Canadian cities, ranging from the heavily commercial – and American-influenced – to more quality-oriented public broadcasting.

Newspapers

Vancouver has two local daily **newspapers**, the *Vancouver Sun* and the *Province*, the latter having a Sunday edition. Both provide an insight into every facet of the city, but the national *Globe and Mail* is better for international and Canada-wide coverage. The *Globe* is also Canada's main nationwide newspaper, its only rival being the troubled *National Post*. Initially a right-wing ranter, the *Post* was acquired by a media mogul with very strong Liberal connections, with an ensuing editorial bloodletting. Owing to the large Asian population in Vancouver, daily editions of the *Chinese Oriental Star* and the *Indo-Canadian Voice* are also widely available.

For great listings and entertainment news, try the free weekly *Georgia Straight*, which appears on Thursdays.

Magazines

The **magazine** to look out for if you want to know where the hip locals are shopping, eating and drinking is the originally titled *Vancouver Magazine* (ⓦwww.vanmag.com). Featuring a "cheap eats" section as well as extensive listings, this monthly is an excellent resource. A few **literary publications** deserve special note: *The Capilano Review*

has been going for over 20 years and is a leading voice in international arts. *Prism International*, published by the University of British Columbia, and *Room of One's Own* (ⓦwww.roommagazine.com) both publish new and established fiction writers, the latter exclusively by women. You will find the free shopping and tourist guide, *Where Vancouver*, in hotels and tourist offices.

TV and radio

Canadian TV is dominated by US sludge, though the publicly subsidized **Canadian Broadcasting Corporation** (CBC) does fight a rearguard action for quality programmes, from drama through to documentaries. The main local TV station is **BCTV**, a news and entertainment station, while **Vancouver Television** is a local entertainment station; **cable television** is commonplace, both in private homes and in the vast majority of hotel and motel rooms.

As regards **radio**, CBC Radio One (105.7FM) is Vancouver's frequency for the Canadian Broadcasting Corporation, an excellent source for public affairs, news and arts programming. For just news, try CFTR (680 AM) or CFRB (1010 AM). Vancouver's urban radio station, THE BEAT, can be found at 94.5 FM. For the latest pop sensations, tune in to Z95.3(95.3 FM) or FOX (99.3 FM). Classic rock is found on 101 ROCK 101 (101 FM), and alternative sounds are on CO-OP RADIO (102.7 FM) and Xfm (104.9 FM). JR-FM (93.7 FM) does country, and for clas- sical try CBC Radio Two (105.7 FM). The best site for sport is CKNW (98.0 FM). An excellent studio radio station featuring alter- native and world artists and listings is UBC's CiTR (101.9FM).

Opening hours and public holidays

Vancouver is a city for the traditional shopper, where artisan stores, cute bou- tiques, antiques vendors and ethnic markets still lord it over the urban mini-mall. Many places are closed on public holidays – though not the city's bars, restau- rants and hotels. Public transport keeps moving on holidays, too, operating a scaled-back restricted service. For a list of festivals and events, see p.206.

Opening hours

Shopping hours are fairly uniform, with most places open seven days a week, 9/9.30am–6pm Monday to Wednesday and Saturday, 9/9.30am–9pm Thursday and Friday, and 10am–5/6pm on Sunday. Malls have slightly longer hours and convenience stores, like 7-11, are routinely open much longer, often 24h. Liquor used to be on sale Monday–Saturday only, but the law has recently been changed and it can now be purchased from government liquor stores on Sundays, too. Hours at **museums** vary, but they are generally open daily (except Monday) from around 10/11am to 5pm or 5.30pm, with one late night a week, usually Thursday until 8pm. As for **restaurants**, these are usually open daily from 11/11.30 am to 11pm, with or without an afternoon break, from around 2.30/3pm to 5/6pm. **Bars** are open daily until 1am; **dance clubs** are often closed on Sunday and Monday nights – the rest of the week, they begin to get busy around 10pm and close at 2am.

Public holidays

New Year's Day Jan 1
Good Friday varies; March/April
Easter Sunday varies; March/April
Easter Monday varies; March/April
Victoria Day third Monday in May
Canada Day July 1
Simcoe Day first Monday in Aug
Labour Day first Monday in Sept
Thanksgiving second Monday in Oct
Remembrance Day Nov 11
Christmas Day Dec 25
Boxing Day Dec 26

Crime and personal safety

Canada has a very low crime rate in general, and while Vancouver is not the most crime-free of Canadian cities (that honour goes to Toronto), the city is very safe and largely free of violent crime. Some cases of smash-and-grab have been reported regarding cars with US licence plates and rental vehicles – travellers should avoid leaving their valuables in the car and park in a well-lit, central location.

Few citizens carry arms, muggings are uncommon, and street crime less commonplace than in many other major cities – though the usual cautions about poorly lit urban streets and so forth stand. Note also that the police are diligent in enforcing traffic laws.

Petty crime

Almost all the problems tourists encounter in Vancouver are to do with **petty crime** – pickpocketing and bag-snatching – rather than more serious physical confrontations. As such, it's good to be on your guard and know where your possessions are at all times. Thieves often work in pairs and, although **theft** is far from commonplace, you should be aware of certain ploys. Watch out, for instance, for the "helpful" person pointing out "birdshit" (actually shaving cream or similar) on your coat, while someone else relieves you of your money; being invited to read a card or paper on the street to distract your attention; or someone in a café moving for your drink with one hand while the other goes for your bag. If you're in a crowd of tourists, watch out for people moving in unusually close.

Sensible **precautions** against petty theft include: carrying bags slung across your neck and not over your shoulder; not carrying anything in pockets that are easy to dip into; and having photocopies of your passport, airline ticket and driving licence, while leaving the originals in your hotel. When you're looking for a hotel room, never leave your bags unattended and, similarly, if you have a car, don't leave anything in view when you park: vehicle theft is still fairly uncommon, but luggage and valuables do make a tempting target.

If you are robbed, you'll need to go to the **police** to report it, not least because your insurance company will require a police report. Remember to make a note of the report number – or, better still, ask for a copy of the statement itself. Don't expect a great deal of concern if your loss is relatively small, and don't be surprised if the process of completing forms and formalities takes ages.

Personal safety

Although generally you can walk around the city without fear of **harassment or assault**, and there are no clearly defined "no-go" areas as such, there are some rather shady locales at night – Pacific Central Station for one – and tourists and women travelling alone should always be on their guard. Consequently, and especially until you are familiar with the city's lay-out, it's always best to err on the side of caution, particularly at night. Using **public transport**, even late at night, isn't usually a problem – but if in doubt take a taxi.

In the unlikely event that you are **mugged**, or otherwise threatened, never resist, and try to reduce your contact with the robber to a minimum; either just hand over what's wanted, or throw money in one direction and take off in the other. Afterwards go straight to the **Vancouver City Police**, who can be contacted at ☎604/717-3535. For **emergencies** (police, fire, or ambulance), call ☎911.

Being arrested

If you're **detained** by the police, the arresting officer(s) must identify him/herself, giving his name and/or badge number, and tell you what you are charged with. At the police station, detainees have the right to free but reasonable use of a telephone and legal counsel. You must tell them your name, address and birth date, if they ask, but nothing more. For certain sorts of suspected offence – primarily gun- and drug-related – the police are likely to strip-search detainees, though these searches, and the frequency of them, remain controversial. They have a right to do this to detainees, but you have the right to insist on an officer of your own sex if you are to be searched.

Travellers with disabilities

Vancouver is renowned for being the "most accessible city in the world" for travellers with disabilities. All public buildings are required to be wheelchair-accessible and provide suitable toilet facilities, almost all street corners have dropped kerbs / sidewalk wheelchair ramps, as do the stairs at Robson Square, most major attractions and hotels are now required to have ramps and elevators. Public transportation is accessible, with most buses being equipped with wheelchair lifts and SkyTrain and SeaBus stations being equipped to handle wheelchair access.

Indeed, the city's public transport system (see p.28) is particularly disability-friendly, and publishes the *Rider's Guide to Accessible Transit*, available from Translink by calling ☎540-3400.

Contacts for travellers with disabilities

In the US and Canada

Access-Able ⊛www.access-able.com. Online resource for travellers with disabilities.
Directions Unlimited 123 Green Lane, Bedford Hills, NY 10507 ☎1-800/533-5343 or 914/241-1700. Travel agency specializing in bookings for people with disabilities.
Mobility International USA 451 Broadway, Eugene, OR 97401 ☎541/343-1284, ⊛www.miusa.org. Information and referral services, access guides, tours and exchange programmes.
Society for the Advancement of Travelers with Handicaps 347 5th Ave, New York, NY 10016 ☎212/447-7284, ⊛www.sath.org. Non-profit educational organization that has actively represented travellers with disabilities since 1976.
Wheels Up! ☎1-888/38-WHEELS, ⊛www.wheelsup.com. Provides discounted airfare, tour and cruise prices for disabled travellers, also publishes a free monthly newsletter and has a comprehensive website.

In the UK and Ireland

Access Travel 6 The Hillock, Astley, Lancashire M29 7GW ☎01942/888 844, ⊛www.access-travel.co.uk. Small, personal-service tour operator that can arrange flights, transfer and accommodation.
Holiday Care 2nd floor, Imperial Building, Victoria Rd, Horley, Surrey RH6 7PZ ☎0845/124 9971, minicom ☎0845/124 9976, ⊛www.holidaycare.org.uk. Provides free lists of accessible accommodation across North America.
Irish Wheelchair Association Blackheath Drive, Clontarf, Dublin 3 ☎01/818 6400, ⊛www.iwa.ie. Useful information provided about travelling abroad with a wheelchair.
Tripscope Alexandra House, Albany Rd, Brentford, Middlesex TW8 0NE ☎0845/7585 641, ⊛www.tripscope.org.uk. Registered charity providing free advice on international transport.

In Australia and New Zealand

Australian Council for Rehabilitation of the Disabled PO Box 60, Curtin ACT 2605; Suite 103, 1st floor, 1–5 Commercial Rd, Kings Grove 2208 ☎02/6282 4333, TTY ☎02/6282 4333, ⊛www.acrod.org.au. ACROD provides lists of travel agencies and tour operators for people with disabilities.
Disabled Persons Assembly 4/173–175 Victoria St, Wellington, New Zealand ☎04/801

9100 (also TTY), @ www.dpa.org.nz. Resource centre with lists of travel agencies and tour operators for people with disabilities.

For general assistance in Vancouver

In the city, there are various organizations that can provide help and assistance for those with disabilities. The **BC Paraplegic Association**, 780 South West Marine Drive (☎604/324-3611, @ www.canparaplegic. org), has lift-equipped vans for rent in and around the city; **BC Disability Sports** (☎604/737-3039, @ www.disabilitysport.org) can offer details of competitive and recreational sports and facilities in the city (including riding, sailing, climbing and track and field events); and the **BC Mobility Opportunities Society** (☎604/688-6464, @ www.disabilityfoundation.org) also provides sailing and other recreational activities.

Note, too, that if you are camping, the **BC Parks Disabled Access Pass** (call ☎250/356-8794 for details) offers free camping in all BC's provincial parks.

Disabled services in Vancouver

BC Coalition of People with Disabilities 204-456 West Broadway, Vancouver V5Y 1R3 ☎604/875-0188 or 604/875-8835 (TDD). Advocacy Access ☎604/872-1278.
Canadian National Institute for the Blind ☎604/431-2121, @ www.cnib.ca.
TransLink HandyDART. Specially adapted bus service ☎604/453-4634.
UBC Disability Resource Centre ☎604/822-5844 or 604/822-9049 (TDD), @ www.student -services.ubc.ca/drc/
Western Institute for the Deaf and Hard of Hearing 2125 West 7th Ave, Vancouver V6K 1X9, ☎604/736-7391 (voice) or 604/736-2527 (TDD), @ www.widhh.ca.

The City

The City

Downtown

Downtown is Vancouver's dazzling heart, home to its glittering high-rise skyscrapers and other modern architectural marvels. It is the area that contains many of the city's key shopping streets, a good deal of its prime office space, most of its big luxury hotels, one of its major galleries and its prime stretches of waterfront. The streets are also a pleasure to walk for their own sake, and some of your most enduring memories of Vancouver will probably involve turning a Downtown corner to be rewarded with a sudden and sensational view of the Pacific and the jagged peaks of the Coast Mountains.

Broadly speaking, the Downtown core is bounded by the waterfront to the north and south (Burrard Inlet and False Creek respectively), Stanley Park to the west and Gastown and Chinatown to the east. As the city has grown, however, so the Downtown area has spread. The area to the south is the one that has seen most recent change, in particular the revitalized and evermore funky warehouse neighbourhood of **Yaletown**, a small grid of streets that is attracting all sorts of new small businesses, specialist stores, bars, cafés and restaurants. Most of Downtown's other peripheral areas hold little interest; the **West End**, for example, is a pleasant but largely residential area bordering Stanley Park – with one or two interesting streets such as Denman – while much of the nameless southern area outside Yaletown is nondescript at best.

Where Downtown Vancouver differs from many North American cities is in the fact that people both live and work here, something planners from other North American cities are studying, and something that lends the area a vibrancy and dynamism often missing in other city centres. Neighbourhoods such as the West End and Yaletown, for example, feel like living communities, complete with markets and neighbourhood stores. In this they take their cue from Downtown's key street, **Robson Street**, a central axis that on hot summer evenings resembles a latter-day vision of *la dolce vita* – a dynamic meeting place crammed with restaurants, a mixture of designer stores and useful shops, late-night outlets, and bronzed youths preening in bars or cafés, or ostentatiously cruising in open-topped cars.

Downtown's other principal thoroughfares are **Burrard Street** – all smart shops, hotels and offices – and **Granville Street**, partly pedestrianized and also with plenty of shops and cinemas, but also, despite some efforts at rejuvenation, curiously seedy in places, especially at its southern end near the Granville Street Bridge – though even here, Yaletown and the False Creek waterfront's not-so-distant condominiums are beginning to push out the clubs, tat and nickel and dime stores as the ripple of gentrification spreads.

While you'll probably be tempted into exploring Robson if you step onto the street on your first day in Vancouver, the place you should actually aim to

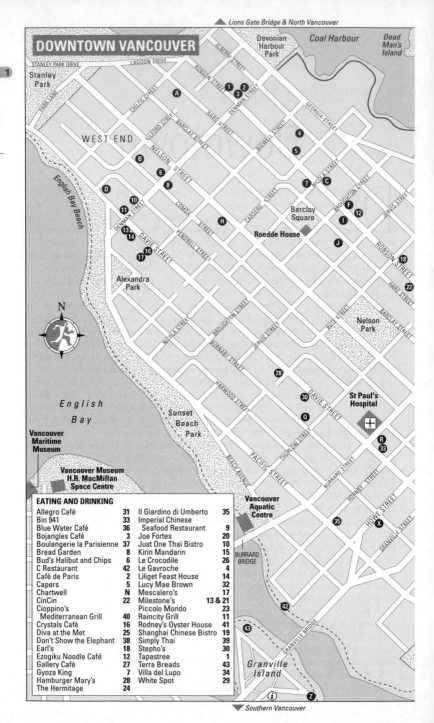

DOWNTOWN VANCOUVER

Lions Gate Bridge & North Vancouver

Coal Harbour

Dead Man's Island

Devonian Harbour Park

Stanley Park

STANLEY PARK DRIVE

LAGOON DRIVE

WEST END

English Bay Beach

Barclay Square

Roedde House

Alexandra Park

N

English Bay

Sunset Beach Park

St Paul's Hospital

Nelson Park

Vancouver Maritime Museum

Vancouver Museum H.R. MacMillan Space Centre

Vancouver Aquatic Centre

BURRARD BRIDGE

GRANVILLE BRIDGE

Granville Island

Southern Vancouver

EATING AND DRINKING

Allegro Café	31	Il Giardino di Umberto	35
Bin 941	33	Imperial Chinese	
Blue Water Café	36	Seafood Restaurant	9
Bojangles Café	3	Joe Fortes	20
Boulangerie la Parisienne	37	Just One Thai Bistro	10
Bread Garden	8	Kirin Mandarin	15
Bud's Halibut and Chips	6	Le Crocodile	26
C Restaurant	42	Le Gavroche	4
Café de Paris	2	Liliget Feast House	14
Capers	5	Lucy Mae Brown	32
Chartwell	N	Mescalero's	17
CinCin	22	Milestone's	13 & 21
Cioppino's		Piccolo Mondo	23
Mediterranean Grill	40	Raincity Grill	11
Crystals Café	16	Rodney's Oyster House	41
Diva at the Met	25	Shanghai Chinese Bistro	19
Don't Show the Elephant	38	Simply Thai	39
Earl's	18	Stepho's	30
Ezogiku Noodle Café	12	Tapastree	1
Gallery Café	27	Terra Breads	43
Gyoza King	7	Villa del Lupo	34
Hamburger Mary's	28	White Spot	29
The Hermitage	24		

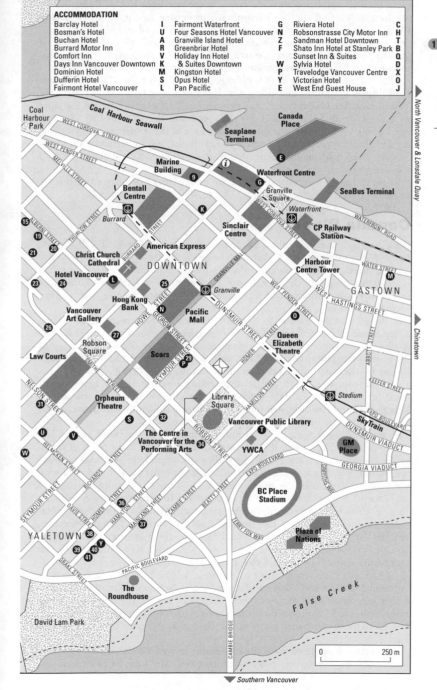

make your acquaintance with the city is at the northern end of Burrard. This is where you'll find the city's main **visitor centre** (see p.23) and **Canada Place**, a superb waterfront complex that provides a literal and visual introduction to Vancouver's past and present. Close by, you can enjoy an overview of the city from the **Harbour Centre**, a high-rise building with a panoramic viewing level. Then you might stroll up Burrard towards Robson to take in a medley of minor sights and buildings, of which the Art Deco **Marine Building** is the most compelling. On Robson, the main cultural lure is the **Vancouver Art Gallery**, the city's principal collection of art, where the chief attractions are first-rate travelling exhibitions and the paintings of Victoria-born Emily Carr. Finally you should take a look at the development that's taking Downtown's reach further south and southeast, and in particular the magnificent **public library**, a focus of this development and a striking piece of modern architecture to boot.

To get to Downtown, take the SkyTrain to Waterfront or Burrard, or bus #1 north on Burrard or #3, #4, #6, #7, #8, or #50 north on Granville.

Canada Place

Built as the Canadian pavilion for Expo '86, **Canada Place**, at 999 Canada Place Way (walkways open daily 24 hours; free; ☎604/775-7200, ⊛www .canada place.ca), which stands across from the main visitor centre (see p.23), is an architectural tour de force, housing the luxury *Pan Pacific* hotel, the city's principal cruise-ship terminal, restaurants, World Trade Centre and a glitzy convention centre.

Its design, and the manner in which it juts into the port, is meant to suggest a ship, a nod to the vital role of the city's port both past and present. This visual allusion is reinforced by the building's most distinctive feature, the five great 27-metre-high Teflon-coated fabric "sails" that make up its roof, a motif continued by the vast hotel and convention centre – the "mast" – which rises above the complex. Much of the surrounding area is currently being developed, primarily to expand the convention area to triple its current size, a half-billion-dollar scheme that will further transform a stretch of waterfront, which has been in a state of flux for more than 25 years.

It's unlikely you'll want to spend much time in either the hotel, convention centre or any other part of the interior, however, for the main point of interest for casual visitors is the "deck", or **walkways**, around the building's perimeter, a jutting pier the length of three and a half city blocks which is dotted with infoboards that describe the immediate cityscape and the appropriate pages of its history. These walkways start at an attractive **fountain** adorned with the flags of Canada's provinces and territories, and provide a superb viewpoint, with stunning vistas across the Burrard Inlet to North and West Vancouver, with the mountains and forest as a backdrop, and the huge green sanctuary of Stanley Park to the west on the Downtown waterfront. Key landmarks on the mountains across the water are **the Lions**, unmistakeable twin peaks reputedly named after their resemblance to the lions designed by Sir Edwin Landseer between 1857 and 1867 that stand at the foot of Nelson's Column in London. Other versions of how the peaks were christened suggest the innocuous name was adopted and vigorously promoted by city elders to help erase from the collective memory the name given to the landmarks by early settlers – Sheila's Paps.

Even better than the views of the mountains, however, is the window Canada Place offers on Vancouver's **port**, a constant buzz and hum of boats, helicopters and float planes; the activity is mesmerizing. Vancouver vies with Los Angeles and New York for the title of North America's busiest port. The harbour was first used, almost inevitably, for exporting timber in 1864 in the shape of fence pickets to Australia. Today, it handles around seventy million tonnes of cargo annually, turns over $40 billion in trade and processes 3000 ships a year from almost a hundred countries. The best way to see the port at closer quarters is to ride the SeaBus, the passenger ferry across Burrard Inlet that runs to Lonsdale Quay from a terminal in Waterfront SkyTrain station (see pp.111 and 29).

The alternative to enjoying the view is enjoying Canada Place's CN **IMAX cinema** ($9–16; screenings afternoon and evenings daily; ☎604/682-4629, 682-2384 or 1-800/582-4629, ⓦwww.imax.com/vancouver), a five-storey-high screen designed for spectacular special-format films (some 3-D) accompanied by high-powered IMAX Digital Sound. The number of films made for the format is limited, and they generally only last 45 minutes. They often involve boats, rock concerts, the natural world, space exploration and wildlife subjects – and are generally a waste of a good screen.

Burrard Street

After seeing Canada Place you could easily walk a few minutes to the east to explore Gastown (see p.64), or take in the handful of small sights that lie on or just off **Burrard Street**, a few minutes' walk to the south. Many of these are free and easily seen – in particular the Marine Building and Christ Church Cathedral. Others take a bit more time and require money up front, notably the Harbour Centre. When you've walked down Burrard you'll still be well placed for Gastown or – more pertinently if you wish to continue exploring Downtown – for Robson Street and the Vancouver Art Gallery.

Canadian Pacific Railway Station

Bear east on West Cordova and one block's walk away you pass the SeaBus Terminal and Waterfront SkyTrain station, both housed in the old **Canadian Pacific Railway Station** at 601 W Cordova St, a listed heritage building which comprises an imposing pillared exterior and airy atrium. It opened in 1915 as the western terminus of Canada's first transcontinental railway, a role it has long since surrendered to the drab CNR and VIA Rail terminal close to Science World in the southeast of the city (see p.88). The *Angel of Victory* (1922) bronze statue in front of the station was sculpted by Coeur de Lion MacCarthy and commissioned by the Canadian Pacific Railway (CPR) as a memorial to its employees who died in World War I. Copies of the statue – which portrays an angel bearing a dead soldier heavenward – are also found in front of the old CPR stations in Montréal and Winnipeg. More anodyne art is displayed inside the grandiose Neoclassical building, namely romantic scenes of the Canadian Rockies you might have seen as you travelled on the railway: they were painted by the wife of an early CPR executive. Otherwise the interior is given over to ticket machines, a coffee bar and a handful of very dull shops.

Harbour Centre Tower

Almost opposite the former Canadian Pacific terminus at 555 W Hastings at Seymour and Cordova stands the Cordova Street entrance to the very popular **Harbour Centre Tower** (daily: May–Sept 8.30am–10.30pm; Oct–April 9am–9pm; The Lookout! $10; ☎604/689-0421, ⓦwww.vancouverlookout

.com). Opened by the first man on the moon, Neil Armstrong in 1977, it was the city's tallest building for a long time and known by locals as the "hamburger", after its bulging upper storeys. On a fine day it's definitely worth paying to ride the stomach-churning, all-glass, SkyLift elevators that run up the side of the tower – 167m in a minute – to the fortieth-storey observation deck. This deck is known as "The Lookout!", and provides a glorious 360° view: free tours lasting between 25 and 45 minutes pointing out the city landmarks below are available every hour on the hour. The deck also offers a variety of mildly interesting video and other displays, plus an expensive revolving restaurant, the *Top of Vancouver Revolving Restaurant* (☎604/669-2220) – eat here and the ride up is free. The food's good as far as it goes, but the unique selling point here is the view. Note that while the ticket to The Lookout! is rather overpriced for what it delivers, it is valid all day (remember to keep your receipt) so you can return and watch the sunset or look out over the lights of Vancouver at night.

The Marine Building

Retrace your steps to Canada Place and turn left up Burrard Street. Almost immediately on your right, at no. 355 Burrard (near the intersection with West Hastings), stands the 25-storey **Marine Building** (lobby open office hours; entrance free), which English poet and architectural critic Sir John Betjeman called the "best Art Deco office building in the world".

Best Vancouver viewpoints

Vancouver is a city of ocean, mountains and high-rise buildings, so it comes as no surprise to find that there are several points in the city that command **magnificent views**. Here is a selection of the best:

Canada Place Great views of Vancouver's port, Stanley Park and the Coast Mountains above North Vancouver (see p.48).

Cypress Bowl Grouse Mountain may be a better-known mountain viewpoint, but the vistas from the service road (Cypress Bowl Road) in this provincial park are almost as spectacular (see p.123).

Empire Landmark Hotel Come in the evening to the revolving lounge and *Cloud 9* restaurant (☎604/687-0511) in this hotel at 1400 Robson St for a great view of the city at night (see p.159).

English Bay Admire the sunsets from the beaches on English Bay, or take up a position in the bar of the nearby *Sylvia Hotel* (see p.161).

Grouse Mountain Ride the cable car and chairlift to over 1200m for arguably the best of all views of Vancouver and its surroundings (see p.112).

Harbour Air Splash out a little for a tour or scheduled flight to Victoria or Nanaimo by float plane and wonderful aerial views of the city, ocean and Gulf Islands (see p.31). Baxter and West Coast Air offer similar flights from the same terminal just west of Canada Place (see p.32).

Harbour Centre Sweeping views over the city that on a good day extend as far as Mount Baker in Washington State (see p.49).

Lonsdale Quay You're almost at water level here, but the views across the Burrard Inlet to the Downtown skyline are none the worse for that (see p.111).

Mount Seymour The access road to Mount Seymour Provincial Park in North Van has two dedicated viewpoints for panoramas of the city (see p.121).

SeaBus The ferry between Downtown and Lonsdale Quay offers a first-hand view of the port and a fine panorama of the Downtown skyline (see p.29).

The enterprise was the brainchild of J W Hobbs, vice-president of G A Stimson, a Toronto-based finance company, and president of Hobbs Bros, a ship-owning concern. After the opening of the Panama Canal in 1914, Hobbs realized that Vancouver's already booming port would become still more prosperous. He also saw that its many maritime businesses would need premises near the waterfront with its customs house, immigration buildings and Canadian Pacific rail and Canadian National steamship terminals.

Completed in 1930, this was the tallest building in the British Commonwealth for ten years after it opened. It was intended as a paean in stone to Vancouver's maritime links – its basic appearance was designed to resemble a rocky headland, or, as its now-forgotten local architects McCarter and Nairne rather effusively claimed: "Some great marine rock rising from the sea clinging with sea flora and fauna, in sea green, flashed with gold".

Some seventy years on, the building's fascinating **facade** has featured in many a Vancouver-shot TV show or movie, its main sunburst door perfect for any film requiring a "period City Hall" shot. Across the facade are a series of stylized Art Deco **bas-reliefs** in brass, stone, terracotta and marble depicting old planes and various other forms of transport, complemented by a frieze of waves and other maritime motifs and settings. Such themes were radical at a time when architects were still largely preoccupied with Neoclassical and Neo-Gothic conceits.

Architects and designers came up with a host of ideas for sea creatures – snails, turtles, carp, scallops, seahorses, skate – to adorn every surface. Mingled with these are motifs further emphasizing Vancouver's transport links – boats and trains (to represent the city's status as a major port and rail terminus), stained glass which highlights the exploits of Captain George Vancouver (his ship, *Discovery*, is pictured on the horizon over the main entrance, with stylized Canada geese flying overhead), and a collection of aircraft, Zeppelins, cars and famous ships such as the *Golden Hind, Resolution, Beaver* and *Empress of India*.

The maritime theme continues inside the beautiful old **lobby** in which Hobbs envisaged a 27-metre "Grand Concourse" adorned in the manner of a Mayan temple laden with treasure. Blue and green tiles are offset by a vaulted ceiling lit by sconces designed to resemble ships' prows. Note the inlaid zodiac floor, relaid in marble in 1989 to replace the original "corkoid", or battleship linoleum, created by a Scottish firm that specialized in making similar floors for the big ocean-going liners of the day. Also outstanding are the fantastic Art Deco wood-and-brass elevator doors – among the most beautiful entrances in North America.

In its day, the building was guarded by liveried doormen, who would usher guests into the lobby where they would be met by five young women in sailor suits. These would then escort visitors the short distance to the lifts, which could climb 700 feet a minute, a staggering performance at a time when the average was 150. Take one to catch a glimpse of the equally beautiful wooden elevator interiors, inlaid with a variety of twelve different British Columbian hardwoods.

Much of the lobby, and building as a whole, might have been even more spectacular, but for the fact that work was interrupted by the Wall Street Crash. Some of the extravagances were reined in, but Hobbs withstood the effects of the Depression better than most, and pressed on with construction, lavishing a total of $2.3 million on his dream, $1.1 million over budget. The building's opening, was a failure, however, and almost everybody associated with the folly came to grief – including Hobbs. In 1933, after three years in which tenants could only be found for the first four floors, G A Stimson went bust, and the

Marine Building was offered to the city as a town hall for $1 million. The city declined. It was eventually sold to Guinness, the Irish brewing dynasty, for $900,000, considerably less than it had cost to build.

Local lore has it that it was from this building that a scion of the Guinness family looked over the Burrard Inlet and concluded that a fortune was to be made from property on the as yet largely undeveloped North Shore. By 1938, the family had built, at its own expense, the Lions Gate Bridge to encourage the growth and uptake of its holdings in North Vancouver (it was bought by the government as late as 1963). For decades, Guinness made more from its Canadian property portfolio than it did from brewing, its traditional activity. Today, the Marine Building has been returned to its former glory, some $20 million having been spent on restoration since the 1980s.

Christ Church Cathedral

Continue two blocks up Burrard Street and you'll come to the Anglican **Christ Church Cathedral** (daily 10am–4pm; services Sun 8am, 10.30am & 9.30pm, weekdays at 12.10pm; ☎604/682-3848), at no. 690 Burrard (near the corner of Georgia). A Neo-Gothic building begun in 1888 (making it the city's oldest church), it was completed in 1895 and is now all but hemmed in by modern skyscrapers.

The city's parish history began on December 30, 1888, when the first service was held – without a church – at 720 Granville St in what was then the town of Vancouver. In February 1889, a committee was formed to collect funds for the building of a church, eventually acquiring land from the Canadian Pacific Railway through the good offices of Henry John Cambie, chief engineer of the CPR's Pacific division and warden of the new church.

After the odd false start, the church was completed in 1895 and dedicated a year later. Don't be fooled by the sandstone cladding – inside, the building has a partly wooden frame of massive Douglas fir timbers culled from the forests of what is now south Vancouver. Initially, the building served simply as the parish church for the immediate area – then a predominantly residential neighbourhood – but as Vancouver grew it was made the city's cathedral in 1929. Inside, check out the mighty **organ**, built in 1949 after an earlier Wurlitzer gave up the ghost – it was rather cobbled together from war surplus parts and bits of the old Wurlitzer. Also look for the cathedral's emblem, a Celtic cross, which is dotted around the exterior and interior, and note the three-fish motif at its heart – it acknowledges the Coast Salish and other original West Coast inhabitants.

In 1971 the building and its stunning wooden ceiling narrowly escaped demolition when the local religious authorities wanted to cash in on its site, by now a prime piece of real estate. In the face of public opposition, the building was listed as a heritage site and thus protected in 1976. An outstanding Art Deco building nearby was not so lucky, and was demolished in 1991 to make way for the Cathedral Place mall and office development to the rear of the church. The cathedral authorities did, however, put together a canny real-estate deal with the developers of the nearby Park Place – though this involved not the land under the cathedral but the rights to the "airspace" above it, for which the church receives (and will receive) $300,000 a year for a hundred years.

Hotel Vancouver and the Hong Kong Bank

Cathedral Place stands close to the junction of Burrard Street and **Georgia Street**, which takes its name from the Strait of Georgia (or Georgia Strait) between Vancouver and Vancouver Island, which in turn takes its name from the British king, George III. The junction is dominated by the unmistakeable bulk of the **Hotel Vancouver** at 900 W Georgia St (see p.000), the city's leading traditional luxury hotel. This is the institution's third incarnation – the first, a four-storey wooden building, was built in 1886 by the Canadian Pacific Railway, which had been given 2400 hectares (6000) acres of prime Downtown land in return for making Vancouver the western terminus of the first trans-Canadian railway. The second hotel on the site was built in 1916 but quickly proved too modest; the third – the present pile – was begun in 1929 by architects John S. Archibald and John Schofield and completed ten years later. You'll soon learn to recognize the hotel's distinctive green-patina copper gables, built as part of the building's mock French-château design, which are visible from many points as you walk the city. The hotel also sports finely carved stone gargoyles (said to be copies of eleventh-century originals made for a variety of French cathedrals) and a large statue of the Roman god Hermes. Drop by the lobby if you want to see more – the concierge occasionally conducts tours, currently on Saturdays at 10.30am and 1pm.

Turn left east on Georgia at this point and, across the street at the first intersection with Hornby, take a quick look in the lobby of the **Hong Kong Bank** at 885 W Georgia St, notable for a gargantuan piece of kinetic art by Alan Storey known as *The Pendulum*. At 27 metres in length, the hollow "pendulum" is one of the world's largest, weighing in at 1600kg, though the term "pendulum" is slightly fraudulent, as it's helped in its six-metre swing by mechanical hydraulics at its fulcrum. The rest of the lobby is given over to temporary art exhibitions.

Vancouver Art Gallery

Downtown's main museum, the **Vancouver Art Gallery** (late April to mid-Oct Mon–Wed & Fri–Sun 10am–5.30pm, Thurs 10am–9pm; mid-Oct to mid-April Tues–Wed & Fri–Sun 10am–5.30pm, Thurs 10am–9pm; ☎604/662-4700, recorded information ☎662-4719, ⊛www.vanartgallery.bc.ca; $12.50) occupies a former courthouse at 750 Hornby St at Robson. The building was completed in 1911 and converted by leading North American architect Arthur Erickson during redevelopment in the 1970s of Robson Street and Robson Square (the latter is the sunken area of shops and cafés just east of the gallery).

When the gallery opened in 1983 it retained much of the courthouse's august grandeur, preserving its stolid stonework, Neoclassical pillars, ornate plasterwork and the glass-topped dome and rotunda that floods the building's four floors with natural light. Also preserved is the courtroom (now the gallery boardroom) of the former Chief Justice Allan McEachern, which was retained by Erickson in deference to its beautifully carved judge's bench: the room – every inch your idea of a typical North American "courtroom" – has been used in all manner of movies, most famously *The Accused* starring Jodie Foster. The courthouse's original architect, Francis Mawson Rattenbury, lived a life that might have provided material for any number of movies. Rattenbury, who was also responsible for the cream of Victoria's historic buildings (see p.227), retired to England, where he enjoyed only a short period of repose before being murdered in 1935 by his wife and her male teenage lover, the family chauffeur

In many ways this story is a lot better than the gallery's art – the permanent collection has over 80,000 works and is valued at over $100 million – but the only part of the collection you can be sure of seeing is the Emily Carr section on the top floor. The other three floors are given over to (admittedly excellent)

Emily Carr

Western Canada's most celebrated painter, **Emily Carr** was born in 1871 into a prosperous Victoria family. She led an artistic life that was almost clichéd – one that was eccentric, thwarted, ridiculed, bohemian and impoverished by turn, but also one that was ultimately successful and triumphant.

Things got off to a bad start. She was orphaned at an early age, and then her remaining family tried to persuade her against an artistic career, a way of life then deemed unsuitable for a woman. Ignoring their advice, she made her own way to San Francisco's California School of Art in 1890, aged just 19. Unable to make ends meet there, she was forced to teach for a living, an activity she continued on her return to Victoria in 1893.

In 1899, she travelled to Ucluelet on the west coast of Vancouver Island, where she came into contact with the art and culture of the indigenous **Nuu-chah-nulth**, an experience that would influence and feature in Carr's own work for the rest of her life. After a brief and unhappy sojourn in England, marked by illness as she trained at art schools, Carr returned to Victoria in 1904, where the provincial and largely hidebound world of early twentieth-century British Columbia viewed her lifestyle as wildly eccentric or worse. She often travelled with either a dog or parrot for company, and in time acquired a menagerie that included cats, cockatoos, a white rat named Susie and a Capuchin monkey known as Woo. Carr even made pinafores for her charges to wear on walks in the park with their owner.

In 1906, Carr moved to a studio in Vancouver at 570 Granville St. A year later she travelled with her sister to Alaska, and again encountered the aboriginal cultures and northern landscapes that would eventually colour her art. Four years later, still feeling her work lacked power and technique, she travelled to Paris, where she absorbed the lessons of the new art movements sweeping the city. Chief among these was the **Fauve** ("wild beast") school of painters, so called for the frenzied distortions, patterns and bright, almost violently coloured nature of its exponents' works. This was one of the most fertile artistic periods of the century, flourishing in one of Europe's most febrile cities, but Carr, unable to speak French and with a dislike of big cities, seems not to have met the likes of Picasso and the other groundbreaking artists of the time.

Returning to Vancouver in 1911, Carr exhibited work from her French sojourn. The show – and another in 1913 – was panned, her work rejected as impenetrable or offensive by British Columbia's staid critics. It wouldn't be until the late 1920s before Carr's work began to find fame. Her change of fortune followed her encounter with the **Group of Seven** painters, a celebrated assembly of eastern Canadian artists who, like Carr, looked to the Canadian landscape for much of their inspiration. Working with renewed confidence, and attaining a degree of international recognition in the process – but little financial gain – she made repeated visits to aboriginal villages and settings. Over the next ten years, she completed some of her most accomplished work, often working in the wilderness from a ramshackle caravan equipped with improvised shelters for her pets.

With her health failing – she would suffer four heart attacks – she began to write during a period of convalescence. Her first book, *Klee Wyck*, was published when she was 70, taking its name – "the laughing one" – from the name given to her by the Kwakiutl people of the Pacific coast. The book dealt with her travels and life among aboriginal people, and won the Canadian Governor General's medal for literature. Three other books followed – *The Book of Small* (a chronicle of her Victoria childhood), *The House of All Sorts* (about her career as a landlady), and *Growing Pains* (her autobiography). Carr died in 1945, secure in her status of Canada's first major female artist.

touring shows and rotating displays from the permanent collection. Thus you can never be sure quite what you will see of the latter, which does feature a rather sparse international collection with some of the lesser works of Warhol and Lichtenstein, as well as Italian, Flemish and British paintings spanning the sixteenth to twentieth centuries. In recent years, though, the gallery has made a determined effort to concentrate on contemporary works – videos, sculptures, installations and, in particular, photo-based and photo-conceptual art. In the last area the gallery boasts the largest such collection in North America, including wonderful pieces by Cindy Sherman (notably her "self" portraits), Jeff Wall, Rachel Whiteread, Jenny Holzer and the magnificent monumental photographs of Andreas Gursky.

But, of course, you can't be sure you'll see these, even if the fact that there are often three or four temporary shows means there's often something of interest – and the steep admission means casual visitors are taking a rather expensive chance unless you know you want to see a particular exhibition.

What redeems the space for a casual visitor is its excellent **Gallery Café** (Mon–Wed & Fri–Sat 9am–5.30pm, Thurs 9am–9pm, Sun 10am–5pm; see p.145) – which you can use whether you're visiting the gallery or not (there's a great outdoor terrace) – and the 200 powerful and almost surreal works and artefacts of Vancouver artist **Emily Carr** (see box, opposite). As with the permanent collection, however, not all these paintings are on show at any one time.

Southeast Downtown

Southeast Downtown is the area where the face of Vancouver is changing most dramatically. The district, bounded by Richards to the west, Robson to the north and False Creek to the south has seen considerable residential and other building since the early 1990s, the many high-rise developments a vivid expression – in contrast to many North American cities – of Downtown's vitality and the desire of people to live close to the heart of the city. The City of Vancouver, as opposed to Greater Vancouver, has shown a net increase in population, reversing a drift of people to the suburbs (which nevertheless continue to grow at a startling rate). It is a trend the city council has long made – and continues to make – a positive effort to encourage.

Much of Downtown's growth has traditionally tended towards the southeast, mainly because this was really the only way it could go – water lies to the north and south, while to the west much of the land is already taken up with the top-dollar properties of the West End. The down-at-heel area around Main and towards Chinatown and the east are still a gamble too far for most developers – though even here the first signs of gentrification are already visible.

For the time being, however, most of the action is on Homer and Hamilton, and on the False Creek waterfront, where numerous high-rise residential blocks have appeared. Things are also changing in the converted warehouse district of **Yaletown**, and around the eastern end of Robson Street, where a lacklustre area that once boasted only the 1983 **BC Place Stadium** – a large and otherwise unexceptional sporting and entertainment venue – has been joined by the sensational **Vancouver Public Library**, the Centre in Vancouver for the Performing Arts and the nearby General Motors Place – home to the Vancouver Canucks ice hockey team.

The Vancouver Public Library

Of southeast Downtown's new buildings, the most startling is the **Vancouver Public Library** (Mon–Wed 10am–9pm, Thurs–Sat 10am–6pm; also Sun

△ Jogging against the skyline

Oct–April 1–5pm; ☎604/331-3601) at 350 West Georgia St, built for over $100 million. When it opened in 1995, it was the most expensive public project ever sanctioned by the city, and, with over 1.2 million books and research items, one of North America's largest public libraries. To the casual observer the superb terracotta-coloured building resembles a Postmodern version of the Roman Colosseum, though architect Moshe Safdie apparently – and unconvincingly – claims the similarities between the two oval, arched and multitiered structures were unintentional. While many architects disdain it, regarding it as a vapid pastiche, it's almost universally admired by locals.

The library and its surrounding buildings – cafés, shops, library bookstore, day-care centre and seven-storey reading area occupy a city block – **Library Square** – bounded by Hamilton, West Georgia, Robson and Homer streets (the main entrance is at the corner of Homer and Robson). It's well worth walking into the library and taking the escalators to the upper floors, if only to admire the views. Otherwise take a break in one of the cafés or watch the world go by from the atrium and library steps, two favoured city places in which to hang out or catch some sun.

Yaletown

The knock-on effect created by the library and the area's new residential highrise is spreading quickly to surrounding streets. Interesting shops, cafés and restaurants are opening, and there's a smart "Y" just a couple of minutes' walk away (see p.14). It's worth noting, however, that, despite infocentre publicity brochures, large tracts around the southern end of Homer and other streets are still pretty dull. The most notable exception is the area known as **Yaletown**, a small, hip and genuinely captivating two- or three-street grid centred on Homer, Hamilton and Mainland streets between Drake Street to the south and Smithe to the north. It takes its name from the many Canadian Pacific railway workers who settled here in the 1880s, having followed the railway west from the town of Yale 180km away in interior British Columbia. At the time, it had more saloons per acre than anywhere in the world, and was considered one of North America's most lawless enclaves – the Mounties claimed it was too far a trek through the forest to make policing practicable.

Today, the area is still in a state of flux – much of it is still officially listed as a commercial zone, a legacy of the days when it was a warehouse and packing district. This said, you don't need to be a city planner to notice the changes that have – and are – transforming the area. Upper floors have become trendy lofts and offices for funky design, advertising, media and other companies. Below, the broad, raised walkways provide the perfect stage for café terraces, while the narrow, lofty or otherwise unusual spaces of the old warehouses have been taken over by often dramatically designed restaurants and bars. There are also plenty of small specialist shops, including a disproportionately large number of kitchen and interior-design stores. It's a great place to wander day or night, with an increasingly large choice of places to eat and drink.

At **Yaletown Landing** on the north shore of False Creek at the foot of Davie Street, you can catch the small **ferries** (see p.84) that ply from Science World, Granville Island and beyond. If you are headed to Granville Island (see p.82), this is a much better approach than walking across the Granville Street Bridge.

On and behind the False Creek waterfront, you'll come face to face with the most dramatic physical expression of Vancouver's dynamic development as a city. High-rise condominiums are mushrooming here, virtually all of them the work of Hong Kong property billionaire Li Ka Shing. The area was once a massive railway marshalling and switching yard that was partly transformed for the '86 Expo. After the world fair finished, the land was sold to the Hong Kong businessman for next to nothing on the understanding that he would build residential properties on the site. He did not disappoint, and the blocks have been going up at the rate of two or three a year for almost twenty years.

There are no specific sights in Yaletown or the False Creek waterfront developments to the south, but as you walk between the two or head for the former's shops, cafés and restaurants it's worth taking in **The Roundhouse** on Pacific Boulevard just off Davie, a legacy of the area's railway days, when the distinctively shaped building was used to repair and turn locomotives. Today, it's a community centre and showcase for local arts groups, but take a look inside to appreciate the interesting space and Engine 374, the locomotive that pulled the first passenger train into Vancouver in 1887.

The West End

The **West End** of the Downtown peninsula is bordered by Stanley Park and roughly delineated on its eastern flank by Burrard and Thurlow. There's not an awful lot to see here, for virtually the whole area is given over to affluent residential housing. Indeed, the large number of high-rise blocks and condominiums make this one of the most densely populated areas in Canada. At the same time, the area is tranquil and predominantly traffic free, which gives it the air of a cosmopolitan and close-knit small town – one reason, along with the proximity of the ocean and Stanley Park, that so many people want to live here.

The most visible part of the area for most visitors is the portion centred on **Robson Street**, which bisects the district. It contains the bulk of the city centre's shops, restaurants and – a distinctive feature – its high-rise apartment or suite hotels, many of which have been converted from former residential usage (see pp.132–134 for accommodation possibilities in these blocks). Most of the action on this street happens near its junction with Burrard, the interest and quality of shops and restaurants tailing off as you travel west.

Elsewhere, the inner grid of streets making up the West End's core contains one or two diversions you might make if you were walking west to Stanley Park, notably **Barclay Square**. None, though, is exactly compelling, and interest only really picks up on **Denmam Street**, focus for a buzzing café and restaurant scene. This has been prompted partly by its status in the late Seventies and Eighties as Vancouver's first "gay village" (the West End still has a sizeable gay community) and partly by its proximity to the park-fringed **English Bay Beach** and the overflow of strollers, joggers and visitors from nearby Stanley Park. It's a tremendous place to window-shop at the various speciality stores – small craft shops, galleries and delicatessens – or to wander at random, and a fine spot for lunch or a drink before or after a visit to the park.

Barclay Square and around

Barclay Square between Nicola and Broughton streets (and one block south of Robson) is a glimpse of an older West End, a one-block nineteenth-century fossil containing nine heritage homes built between about 1890 and 1910. Its centrepiece is **Roedde House** (guided tours only 2–4pm Wed–Fri; $4; ☎604/684-7040, ⓦ www.roeddehouse.org) at 1415 Barclay St in the square's southeast corner, a rare piece of domestic architecture by Francis Rattenbury, the architect responsible, among other things, for the *Empress Hotel* and

Parliament Buildings in Victoria (see p.227). Built in 1890 in the Queen Anne style, its interior and gardens have been beautifully restored to their period pomp.

Before the arrival of white settlers, the area had been the home of Musqueam and Squamish peoples for thousands of years. The first foreigners – three Englishmen – arrived in the 1860s, paying $550 for virtually the whole area, though the eventual owners, as in so much of western Canada, would be the Canadian Pacific Railway, which purchased the land in the late 1880s to build top-end residential properties. The biggest houses were built close to the ocean at English Bay, but plenty of other fine properties, such as those in Barclay Square, were constructed inland. Most were created before a boom in the first decade of the twentieth century which saw the building of the *Sylvia Hotel* (see p.132), for years Vancouver's highest structure, and many streets of less prestigious homes.

Less prestigious, that is, for the time, because today they are coveted for their rarity, the city elders having decided in the mid-1950s to try to attract more people to the Downtown area, both to shop and to live and work. One way to achieve this, they believed, was to provide more residential accommodation in the West End (much as has happened in Yaletown and around in the last decade), and over the next ten years many of the district's older buildings were torn down and replaced by over 200 high-rise developments.

Mole Hill to English Bay Beach

The eleven Edwardian homes at **Mole Hill**, near the corner of Comox and Bute, would have gone the same way as the West End's other buildings, but for a concerted campaign by local residents in the 1990s, two decades after the city had bought the properties with a view to renting them before tearing them down to make way for a park. While Barclay Square captures a slice of Vancouver in the 1890s, this enclave presents a picture of the area as it would have appeared in about 1925.

More fragments of the old city can be found on nearby **Pendrell Street** one block south. At the corner with Broughton Street, for example, at 1119 Broughton, is the grand former home of Thomas Fee, one of the leading architects and developers during the West End boom at the beginning of the twentieth century. On the southeast corner of Pendrell and Jervis stands **St Paul's Episcopal** church, built entirely in wood in 1905 in a Neo-Gothic style. In stark and hideous contrast, **Pendrellis**, a block away at 1254 Pendrell, is many people's candidate for the ugliest building in Vancouver. This multistorey paean to concrete was built in the 1970s as an old people's home and manages to contain not a single window.

Continue west on Pendrell and then turn left on Nicola and right on Davie and you come to **The Gabriola**, a far more enticing prospect at 1531 Davie on the right just beyond Broughton. This was one of the West End's first big mansions, built in 1900 for a sugar magnate, B T Rogers, who eventually sold up when lesser residential housing nearby caused the neighbourhood's stock to fall. The house was then divided into apartments but has been a restaurant under several names since 1975: its present incarnation is the *Macaroni Grill*, whose garden tables make a pretty spot to take stock on a sunny day.

Take Cadero or Bidwell southwest to the waterfront and you come to Beach Avenue and Alexander Park, the latter part of the stretch of parkland that fringes Sunset Beach to your left as you face the water and **English Bay Beach** to your right. Just beyond the park's northern tip stands a sculpture known as **Inukshuk** facing out over English Bay, a venerable Inuit symbol traditionally used as a symbol of hospitality and as an aid to navigation. It was moved here from the Northwest Territories' pavilion after the Expo '86 world trade fair. Continue along the bay northwards, past Denmam on your right, and you come eventually to the fringes of Stanley Park (see p.73).

Gastown and Chinatown

Vancouver's Downtown core is something of a historical accident, for the city's original Victorian heart – and its modern birthplace – actually lies to the east in an area known as **Gastown**, a designated historic district just a few minutes' walk from Canada Place and the rest of Downtown. The area takes its name from "Gassy Jack Leighton" (see box, p.63), an impossibly colourful publican whose bar – aimed at workers in a nearby lumber mill – provided the focus for a shanty village that by 1869 had been officially incorporated as the town of "Granville". Fire consumed much of this original settlement in 1886 (see p.264), but the arrival of the transcontinental Canadian Pacific Railway in 1887 brought renewed prosperity to the district and with it the birth of modern Vancouver. As a result, Vancouver is the only major Canadian metropolis that did not begin life as a fur-trading post.

Over the years, the city's Downtown focus moved west and the ghost of Gastown's boozy beginnings returned to haunt it, as its cheap hotels and warehouses became something of a skid row for junkies and alcoholics. Ironically, the area's dilapidation helped preserve the historic buildings, for no developer would touch the place. By the 1970s, however, the city was ready to bulldoze the entire area – together with much of **Chinatown** and Vancouver's other older eastern districts. A motley assortment of hippies, heritage buffs and Chinatown business people and inhabitants took to the barricades. The plans were shelved, but not before work began on one of the intended plazas and malls – Granville Square at 200 Granville St.

Gastown was then declared a historic site – the buildings are the city's oldest – one of two in the city (the other is Chinatown), and an enthusiastic $1.3 million beautification programme was set in motion. Many of the venerable two-storey stone and brick Victorian buildings were restored, old frontages were retained or reinstated, and the handful of streets and alleys were cleaned up and decked in hanging baskets of flowers. However, the end product never quite became the dynamic, city-integrated spot the planners had hoped, and was slated for years by locals as little more than a tourist trap.

Today, much of Gastown indeed has the look of a determined piece of city rejuvenation aimed at visitors – especially on **Water Street**, its main axis – and is distinguished by new cobbles, fake gas lamps, *Ye Olde English Tea Room*-type cafés, atrocious souvenir shops and a generally over-polished patina. At the same time, interesting cafés, clubs and restaurants are now slowly beginning to

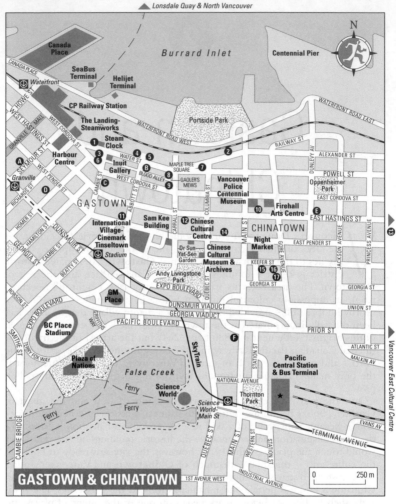

Lonsdale Quay & North Vancouver

GASTOWN & CHINATOWN

0   250 m

ACCOMMODATION		EATING AND DRINKING					
Budget Inn-Patricia Hotel	**E**	Alibi Room	**2**	Hon's Wun-Tun House	**16**	The Only Café	**12**
Cambie International Hostel Gastown	**C**	Bavaria	**8**	Incendio	**7**	Ovaltine Café	**10**
Cambie International Hostel Seymour	**A**	Blake's	**8**	The Irish Heather	**9**	Phnom-Penh	**17**
C&N Backpackers Hostel	**F**	Borgo Antico	**1**	Kent's Kitchen	**15**	Pink Pearl	**13**
Dominion Hotel	**B**	Buddhist Vegetarian		La Luna Café	**4**	Water Street Café	**3**
Victorian	**D**	Restaurant	**14**	The Old Spaghetti		Wild Rice	**11**
		Cordova Café	**6**	Factory	**5**		

make themselves felt, and though there's not an awful lot to see or do, the area's certainly worth a stroll for its better cafés, lively Sunday crowds and occasional points of interest such as a police museum and characterful old alleys.

Gastown's downbeat streets merge almost seamlessly into **Chinatown**, a no less shabby-looking area, but one that's redeemed by its obvious sense of

Gastown owes its existence to **Captain "Gassy" Jack Leighton**, a retired English sailor and riverboat pilot who arrived in Vancouver – then little more than a clearing in the woods – on September 29, 1867. He paddled ashore in a canoe accompanied by his aboriginal wife, his mother-in-law, his mother-in-law's cousin, Big William (brought along to do the paddling), a mangy yellow dog, two chairs, two chickens, $6 in cash and a barrel of whisky.

Born in Hull, England, in 1830, Leighton became a sailor on British and then American ships, apparently making the switch because the food was better on US vessels – and there was more of it. He worked aboard the clippers running across the Atlantic before jumping ship to join the Californian gold rushes of the early 1850s. Failing to find gold, he became a river pilot on the Fraser River, eventually opening a saloon in New Westminster – now a suburb of southern Vancouver – serving the prospectors travelling to the Cariboo region in the British Columbia interior during the Gold Rush of 1862.

His labours there, however, came to an abrupt end after a squabble with his American partner, after Leighton had left the friend in charge of the saloon while he visited mineral springs for the sake of his whisky-ravaged health. In his absence the friend laid on a spectacular Fourth of July celebration, sinking most of the saloon's profits into gunpowder, rockets, firecrackers and an extraordinary quantity of booze on the house. Leighton returned to find himself ruined.

Moving north, he quickly sniffed new entrepreneurial possibilities on the shores of Burrard Inlet after the opening there of the Hasting Mill, a lumber operation established in 1865. Workers at the mill could earn up to $1000 a month – an immense sum – and yet had virtually nothing to spend it on, certainly not liquor, mill bosses having forbidden the sale or consumption of alcohol on company property. The nearest drink was twenty miles away.

Leighton, so the story goes, promised the lumbermen drinks on the house if they helped him build a bar. Within 24 hours the new **Globe Saloon**, built on a spot named Luck-Lucky, or "grove of maple trees", by the local aboriginal inhabitants, was doing a roaring trade. Government officials from Victoria were quick to act and forced Leighton to add "bedrooms" to legitimize the bar. These proved so uncomfortable – the beds were little more than pillowless boards – that Jack felt obliged to offer a free early morning tipple to his bone-numbed guests. A second bar followed, accompanied by a shanty village of shacks that was soon christened **Gassy's Town**, partly after Leighton's tendency to "gas" – slang for being loquacious and given to long-winded monologues – and partly because of his repeated tendency to get heavily "gassed", or drunk.

In 1870, Royal Engineers surveyed the nine half-decent "buildings" making up the ramshackle "Town", a prelude to the incorporation of the six-acre site as the "town" of Granville, named after a British colonial secretary. The survey and its projected new roads left Leighton's bar stranded in the middle of a street, leading him to buy the town's first official lot for $65. Here, at the southwest corner of Water and Carrall, he built another saloon, a two-storey affair known as the **Deighton Hotel** with bar, billiard room, bedrooms and terrace. The point where the two streets met became known as Gastown, with Leighton its self-proclaimed "mayor". The name spread, despite Granville's official name – even British Admiralty charts of the time used the colloquial moniker.

Gassy Jack died in 1875, aged just 44 – his dying words were apparently a curse aimed at a barking dog – and was toasted at his funeral with drinks whose cost came to $165, a substantial sum at the time. His infant son died just six months later. The Deighton Hotel, for its part, would vanish in the great fire of 1886.

Today, Gassy Jack is remembered by a statue at Gastown's heart in **Maple Tree Square** (see p.65), supposedly on, or close to, the site of the original Globe Saloon. Vancouver's unlikely "founder", appropriately enough, is shown perched atop a whisky barrel.

community – this is very much a Chinese enclave – and the sights, smells and interest of its colourful streets, markets and cultural attractions. After Gastown, it's also the second of the city's two designated historic districts. The main sight here is the **Dr Sun Yat-Sen Garden**, a traditional Chinese Ming Dynasty garden, but you'll have as much fun simply wandering the streets, shopping for Chinese goods or eating in the many authentic restaurants.

Gastown

Gastown is a small and self-contained area that hinges on **Water Street**, so named because it stood on Vancouver's waterfront before land reclamation, the railway and new port facilities edged it further inland. Most of the area's shops, restaurants, cafés and points of interest lie on or just off the street, although as gentrification – people actually wanting to live here – and redevelopment take hold, so Gastown's prettier core is spreading east along Powell and Alexander streets.

At Water Street's eastern end lies **Maple Tree Square**, close to the site of Gassy Jack's original bars. Away from Water Street, Gastown's immediate vicinity contains one odd little attraction – a **police museum** – and a handful of appealing old streets and good bars, cafés and restaurants (see p.143 for details).

South and east of Gastown on and around **Hastings Street** beyond Homer Street lies a far, far seedier area altogether, a down-at-heel crisscross of streets that has yet to benefit from either gentrification or the improving effects of big city-funded renovation projects. Action is promised, but at present it's a grim sight – derelict buildings, boarded-up shops and battered streets; the domain of addicts, pimps, prostitutes, the derelict and the homeless. It is strongly recommended that you avoid this area after dark – and specifically the area near the junction of Main and Hastings – and preferably during the day as well, when you should consider a bus or taxi to take you to Chinatown. Most **crime** in these parts is drug-related, although it is certainly not as prevalent or violent as in some North American cities. During the day, however, the worst you can expect is the usual hassle from street people for spare change.

Start your tour of Gastown just east of the Waterfront SkyTrain and SeaBus terminal at the corner of Water, Cordova and Richards. This is an easy walk from Downtown, but **buses** #1, #3, #4, #7, #8 or #50 from Granville or Burrard will drop you on or close to the junction, which leaves you well placed to explore Water Street, Gastown's main artery.

Tours of Gastown

To explore Gastown and parts of Downtown with a guide, join one of the regular **guided walks** around the area with Walkabout Historic Vancouver (tours start daily at 10am and 2pm; $25 per person; for more information and details of departure points, call ☏604/720-0006 or 439-0448, ⊛www.walkabouthistoricvancouver). In addition to a Chinatown and Gastown tour, the company offers a Granville Island tour (see p.31) and a Downtown-Gastown tour. All routes are wheelchair-accessible.

Water Street

First stop along **Water Street** is **The Landing**, a period building at no. 375, constructed in two parts – western (1908) and eastern (1913). Originally known as the Kelly Douglas Building, it was built by Frank Douglas and Robert Kelly, who started a trading business in 1896. Two years later they grew rich supplying prospectors headed for the Yukon goldfields during the Klondike Gold Rush. The building was partly constructed using gold-rush receipts, serving as a warehouse and head office until 1946. Restored in 1988, it is now a small upscale mall with around 25 stores, and it's worth pausing here a moment or two to enjoy the harbour views from some of its stores and cafés. Among the more intriguing establishments here is the main office of the **BC Film Commission** (☎604/660-2732, ⓦwww.bcfilmcommission.com), where you can obtain details of films and TV programmes currently being shot in and around Vancouver. Note the steel rods running diagonally from the ground-floor windows to the top storey, part of the defence against earthquakes (it's a little-known fact that Vancouver sits on an area of seismic activity).

At the corner of Water and Cambie stands Gastown's main crowd-pleaser, the much-hyped, two-tonne **steam-powered clock**, the world's first. Built in 1977 to a design that had been sitting around for about a century, it's invariably surrounded by tourists armed with cocked cameras, all awaiting the miniature Big Ben's quarter-hourly toots and whistles or the bellowing performances on the hour that seem to presage imminent explosion. The steam comes from an underground system that was used to heat surrounding buildings; a plaque near the base of the clock explains how the whole thing works. The clock was designed by Ray Saunders, one of several figures immortalized in the **Magasin Building** at 322 Water St, where each of the column capitals of the facade features a bronze head of a figure connected in some way with the history of Gastown.

Along Water Street you'll find a considerable number of souvenir shops and other tourist tat, but also genuinely interesting diversions such as the **Inuit Gallery** (Mon–Sat 9.30am–5.30pm), at 345 Water St. This large commercial showcase features expensive Inuit sculpture, jewellery and other art and applied or decorative arts. At 165 Water St is a gift store that achieved fame of a different sort – it was here, apparently, that Bill Clinton bought a small statuette of a bear to take home as a gift for Monica Lewinsky.

Maple Tree Square and around

At its eastern end Water Street opens into **Maple Tree Square**, named – unsurprisingly – after a maple tree that grew here, and under which it's said Granville's worthies sat in 1885 to settle on the new name of "Vancouver" for their growing metropolis. In 1886, the year the name was adopted, a notice proclaiming the city's first civic election was posted to the tree. The present tree is not the original, but was planted on more or less the same spot. The **statue of Gassy Jack** was erected near the start of the area's rejuvenation. It lost its head in 1970, severed by unknown persons and eventually returned on payment of $50 ransom. Two or three little cafés on the square make a good place for a break before turning tail or taking a cab east – a block or so beyond here begin the Hastings' badlands (see opposite).

Close to Maple Tree Square is the **Byrnes Block** at 2 Water St, built after the great fire in 1886. This is Vancouver's oldest heritage building still on its original site; the older Hasting Mill store, which dates from 1865, was moved to 1575 Alma Rd in Kitsilano. One of the city's first brick buildings, it stands on the site of the two-storey Deighton House, the second of Jack Deighton's Gastown saloons (see p.63). Today it houses a café and residential premises.

Half a block south of the Byrnes Block and Water Street, two tiny, quaint alleys, Trounce Alley and **Gaoler's Mews**, run off Carrall Street into Blood Alley (no one seems to know how this last alley came by its evocative name). Gaoler's Mews was once home to Gastown's first police station, a log cabin and to its first chief of police, Jonathan Miller, who also doubled as postmaster and the port's main customs officer. Prisoners in Miller's care were rarely incarcerated, but usually lightly chained at the ankles and set to work on nearby road-building projects.

The Vancouver Police Centennial Museum

From Blood Alley, cross Carrall then follow East Cordova Street to the **Vancouver Police Centennial Museum** (May–Aug Mon–Sat 10am–3pm; Sept–April Mon–Fri 9am–3pm; $6; ☎604/665-3346, ⊛www.city.vancouver.bc.ca/ police/museum) at no. 240. A bizarre and fascinating little museum, it is inexpensive, easily seen and leaves you well placed for a short two-block walk south to the centre of Chinatown. The museum is housed in the city's old Coroner's Court Building and takes its name from the fact that it was established in 1986 to celebrate the centennial of the Vancouver police force.

The building has its own place in Vancouver folklore, not least for the fact that it was here that the actor **Errol Flynn** was brought after he died in Vancouver in 1959. Flynn arrived in the city in October 1959 with his best acting days well behind him. With him was his "personal assistant", a 17-year-old blonde girl not known for her secretarial skills. Within two days Flynn had dropped dead in his rented West End apartment. The body was brought to the Coroner's Court, where the pathologist conducting the autopsy is said to have removed a piece of Flynn's penis and placed it in formaldehyde to keep as a souvenir. The horrified chief coroner Glen McDonald, a rather more fastidious operator, is said to have pulled rank and reattached the missing piece of member to the corpse with sticky tape. The body was then dispatched to Los Angeles for burial. This was not the end of the story, for it emerged that somewhere between the West End and the morgue, a key to a Swiss safety-deposit box that Flynn wore round his neck had disappeared. When Flynn's lawyers opened the box three years later, the stock certificates and half a million dollars in cash they had expected to find were nowhere to be seen.

The **autopsy room** is still there, together with a suitably macabre selection of mangled and preserved body parts arranged around the walls. Check out the morgue's cooler, penultimate resting place of many over the years. Other rooms include a forensics lab, a simulated autopsy room, police cell and radio room, while a variety of thematic displays include sections on notorious local criminals, weapons seized from criminals (some pretty unusual), crime-scene reconstructions, gambling, uniforms, counterfeit money and a sizeable collection of firearms. Among the more light-hearted exhibits is a collection of model police cars from around the world. Finally, the museum's "Cop Shoppe" has an interesting line in police-related gifts and souvenirs.

To get to the museum by public transport, take buses #10, #16, #20, #23, #35 or #150 along Hastings St to Main then walk one block north to E Cordova.

Chinatown

A city apart, Vancouver's vibrant **Chinatown** is clustered mainly on Pender Street from Abbott to Gore and on Keefer Street from Main to Gore (buses #22 or #19 east from Pender, or #22 north from Burrard). Vancouver's 100,000-plus Chinese, the vast majority of whom live in the area, make up one of the largest Chinese communities outside the Far East – on a par with those of New York and San Francisco – and are the city's oldest and largest ethnic group after the British-descended majority. Many crossed the Pacific in 1858 to join the Fraser Valley Gold Rush; others followed under contract to help build the Canadian Pacific Railway. Most stayed, and found themselves treated appallingly (see box on pp.68–69), seeking safety and familiarity in a ghetto of their own, where clan associations and societies provided for new arrivals and the local poor and helped build the distinctive houses of recessed balconies and ornamental roofs that have made the area a protected historic site.

Unlike Gastown's gimmickry, Chinatown is all genuine – shops, hotels, markets, tiny restaurants and dim alleys vie for attention amidst an incessant hustle of jammed pavements and the buzz of Chinese conversation. Virtually every building replicates an Eastern model without a trace of self-consciousness, and written Chinese characters feature everywhere in preference to English. Striking and unexpected after Downtown's high-rise glitz, the district brings you face to face with Vancouver's multiculturalism, and helps explain why wealthy Hong Kong immigrants – who can afford to relocate – continue to be attracted to the city. There's an edge to Chinatown, however, especially at night and, though central districts are fine, lone tourists are better off avoiding Hastings and the backstreets.

Apart from the obvious culinary temptations – and it is the district's restaurants that bring most locals and visitors here – Chinatown's main points of reference are its **shops and markets**. One of the best markets is the open-air **night market** at Main and Keefer streets (May–Sept Fri–Sun 6pm–midnight), a cornucopia of sights, smells and sounds that seem all the more vivid as darkness falls. Interesting shops can be found across the district, with stores boasting fearsome butchery displays and such edibles as live eels, flattened ducks, "hundred-year-old" eggs and other stuff you'll be happy not to identify. Keefer Street stands out as **bakery** row, with lots of tempting stickies on offer like moon cakes and *bao*, steamed buns with a meat or sweet-bean filling.

More specific targets might include the Ten Ren Tea and Ginseng Company on the corner of Keefer and Main, which has a vast range of teas, many promising cures for a variety of ailments (free tastings). In a similar vein, it's worth dropping into one of the local **herbalists** such as Tung Fong Hung Medicine Company at 536 Main St to browse amongst their panaceas: snakeskins, reindeer antlers, buffalo tongues, dried seahorses and bears' testicles are all available if you're feeling under the weather. Ming Wo, 23 E Pender, is a fantastic cookware shop, with probably every utensil ever devised, while China West, 41 E Pender, is packed with slippers, jackets, pens, cheap toys and the like. A star among the **supermarkets** is the T & T at 179 Keefer St and Abbott, which has an extraordinary range of produce and is particularly distinguished, if that is the word, by its bizarre assortment of (live) seafood, among other things. For other shops in Chinatown, see pp.183–184.

Canada, and British Columbia in particular, owes a huge debt to the Asian labour and initiative that, almost literally in places, helped build the country. But for a province and city that now justly pride themselves on their multicultural elan, Vancouver and BC's past treatment of its Chinese immigrants makes for shabby reading.

The first large wave of such immigrants arrived on Canada's west coast in 1858, lured by the discovery of gold in the British Columbia interior. Another major migration to British Columbia followed in the early 1880s – some 11,000 arrived between 1881 and 1885 alone – when Chinese labourers were needed to help **build the Canadian Pacific Railway**. They were paid a dollar a day, half of what white workers were paid. Most headed for the BC and Albertan interior, where work on the railway was most intense. It's estimated that three Chinese died for every kilometre of track built in labour-intensive sections such as the Fraser Canyon in central British Columbia.

In Vancouver, a handful of Chinese arrivals formed a small settlement in **Saltwater City** – their name for Vancouver – along "Shanghai Alley", a small street close to what are now Carrall and Pender streets (today it's a sad and rather forlorn little alley). After the great **fire** that swept Vancouver in 1886, the Chinese were enlisted to help rebuild the young city and were leased sixty hectares of forest rent-free for ten years on the condition they clear and farm the land. Within a year, some ninety Chinese were living and working on and around Dupont (now Carrall) and Westminster (now Main) streets.

Elsewhere in British Columbia, the Chinese remained in the region once the railway – the main source of employment – had been completed. Thereafter they began to compete with local European-born and American workers for jobs in the burgeoning sawmills, lumber camps, mines and canneries. In the mid-1880s, for example, some 1500 of the estimated 2000 miners in British Columbia were Chinese. Crucially, they were prepared – or could be cajoled – to work for less than white workers.

The Sam Kee Building and around

Most visitors to Chinatown flock dutifully to the 1913 **Sam Kee Building**, two blocks west of Main and one north of Keefer at the corner of Carrall and Pender; at just 1.8m across, it's often claimed to be the world's narrowest building. The story goes that in 1912 the city authorities forcibly bought most of Sam Kee's land to widen Pender Street, but refused to compensate him for one tiny strip that wasn't required for the new street. Kee's neighbour had hopes of buying the strip for next to nothing, but didn't reckon on Kee, who decided to spite the neighbour and the authorities by constructing this slip of a building. Customers at his general store had to be served through the windows.

Behind it is the sombre **Shanghai Alley**, once a den of shops, restaurants, flophouses, public baths and worse – today it just looks rather forlorn. Opposite, at 1 West Pender, the **Chinese Freemasons' Building**, is a structure whose conservative Victorian appearance on Carrall says much about certain Chinese arrivals' determination to fit in with the prevailing Anglo-Saxon majority. Note, though, the building's Pender flank, which has fine examples of Cantonese recessed balconies. Dr Sun Yat-Sen (see p.71) sought shelter in the building for months, hiding from agents of the Qing (or Manchu) Dynasty he would eventually help overthrow.

Prejudice, violence and discrimination were the consequence. In Vancouver, this was made manifest when Chinese settlements on Dupont, along with shacks and tents on False Creek, were burned in **anti-Chinese riots in 1887**. A labour boycott was also effected, the railway being the only employer allowed to exempt itself from the ban on Chinese labour. This was accompanied by a general boycott of businesses that traded with the Chinese – such businesses were daubed with black crosses.

A more permanent expression of prejudice came soon after with the formation of the **Asiatic Exclusion League**, a racist organization that as late as 1907 was able to attract a crowd of 30,000 to an anti-Chinese parade on Cambie Street. Such leagues would survive almost to the middle of the twentieth century. Japanese and other Asian immigrants could expect the same welcome.

Given the pattern of prejudice, it was no wonder that the Chinese were forced to look to their own devices, or that Chinatown quickly developed as a self-contained enclave. Self-help became the order of the day. Chinese banks were formed, initially to facilitate the sending of money home. Benevolent societies helped new arrivals, the sick and elderly. Several generations would pass, however, before the barriers came down. The Chinese, for example, were denied citizenship and legal rights until as late as 1947. Fresh antipathy emerged among some Vancouver locals as recently as the mid-1990s when an influx of wealthy Hong Kong immigrants – who left Hong Kong because they feared the consequences of the British handover of the city to the Chinese in 1997 – sent property prices soaring (prices have since calmed down).

Today, while Vancouver's Chinatown still remains a distinctive Chinese enclave, there is no sense that it is also a ghetto. Most second-, third- and fourth-generation Canadians of Chinese ethnic origin are now fully integrated into the life and fabric of the city – and live in many different areas – something that seems only fitting given Vancouver's pivotal role in the increasingly important and interlinked markets of the Pacific Rim.

Dr Sun Yat-Sen Garden

Chinatown's chief cultural attraction is the small **Dr Sun Yat-Sen Garden** (May–mid-June daily 10am–6pm; mid-June to Aug daily 9.30am–7pm; Sept daily 10am–6pm; Oct daily 10am -4.30pm; Nov–April Tues–Sun 10am–4.30pm; $8.25; ☎604/662-3207, ⓦwww.vancouverchinesegarden.com) at 578 Carrall St near Pender St.

This was the first authentic, full-scale classical Chinese garden built outside China and it's still the only such garden in the Western Hemisphere. Named after the founder of the first Chinese Republic (see box p.71), who was a frequent visitor to Vancouver, the park was created for Expo '86 and cost $5.3 million, $500,000 of which came from the People's Republic – along with 52 artisans and 950 crates of materials. The latter included everything from limestone rocks from Taihu – whose jagged shapes are prized for this sort of garden – to the countless tiny pebbles that make up the intricately patterned courtyard pavements.

The whole thing is based on classical gardens developed in the city of Suzhou during the Ming Dynasty (1368–1644). China's horticultural emissaries, following traditional methods that didn't allow use of a single power tool, spent thirteen months in the city replicating a Suzhou Ming garden to achieve a subtle balance of Yin and Yang: small and large, soft and hard, flowing and

△ The Chinatown Night Market

immoveable, light and dark. These contrasts are achieved, among other things, by juxtaposing large and small stones, or rock with running water, numerous examples of which you will see in Sun Yat-Sen gardens. Every stone, pine and flower was carefully placed and has symbolic meaning. Unlike in Western gardens, where plants and shrubs tend to be grouped and planted in profusion, here they are used sparingly and with thought for their mystical and symbolic qualities. Any grouping is designed to give areas a special mood and unique character, and to reinforce the seasonal and cyclical nature of the garden.

Serenity, above all, was prized in Suzhou Ming gardens, which were designed to offer a retreat from humankind, allowing one to indulge a desire for mountains and water and turn one's back on the obligations of everyday life. Originally such gardens were designed by Taoist poets to encourage contemplation and inspiration – the calligraphic inscription above the entrance to the Sun Yat-Sen garden means "Garden of Ease". They always contained four principal elements in harmony – water, rocks, plants and architecture – and by combining elements of the natural landscape such as rivers, lakes and trees in small space, sought to concentrate the life force, or *qi*, which infuses them.

Free forty-five-minute **guided tours** are given on the half-hour and explain other elements of the Taoist philosophy behind the carefully placed elements. At first glance it all seems a touch small and austere, and isn't helped by a preponderance of sponsors' nameplates and the glimpses of the road, pub and high-rise building outside the walls. After a time, though, the chances are you'll find the garden working its calm and peaceful spell. Note that there are numerous exhibitions and events held in and around the garden throughout the year, including walking tours of Chinatown (currently Wed at 1.30pm; $10. Call ☎604/662-3207 to register and purchase advance tickets).

Dr Sun Yat-Sen in Vancouver

Dr Sun Yat-Sen was born in what is now Zhongshan in Guangdong province, China, in 1886. Despite being raised in a peasant family, he was sent at an early age to live with his elder brother in Hawaii, where he was exposed to a Western education. Eventually he became a doctor, but abandoned his career to further the cause of democracy in his native country, then under the autocratic control of the Qing (Manchu) Dynasty. The first Chinese leader of a political movement not to come from the gentry, he travelled around the world to raise money for political change, making three visits for this purpose to Vancouver in 1897, 1910 and 1911.

It was during the last of these that the city's Chinese community made their most telling contribution to revolutionary coffers. Sun Yat-Sen spoke daily during this visit at the Sing Kew Chinese Theatre (now vanished) in Shangahi Alley, and received the support of the Cheekungtong, a group of prominent Chinese freemasons. The group mortgaged their lodgings and other buildings to provide money for the cause, raising $35,000 in all, money that went to finance an abortive revolution in 1911 at Huang Hua Kang near Guangzhou, six months before the successful overthrow of the Qing (Manchu) Dynasty. To this day, a memorial at Huang Hua Kang lists the names of prominent Chinese-Canadian benefactors and communities from the period. Sun Yat-Sen became first president of the Republic of China a year later, but quickly relinquished the post to concentrate his efforts on the country's economic transformation. Following his early death in 1925 from liver cancer he was "canonized" and given the name Kuo Fu, or Father of the Country.

Chinese Cultural Centre Museum & Archives

Alongside the entrance to the gardens at 555 Columbia St, the1998 **Chinese Cultural Centre Museum & Archives** (Tues–Sun 11am–5pm; $3; ☎604/658-8880, ⓦwww.cccvan.com) is Chinatown's community focus. It is also a sponsor of New Year's festivities, fifteen days of processions, theatrical performances and other cultural events (call ☎604/687-6021 or visit ⓦwww.bcchinesenewyear.com for more information). It's an ugly building, the gate aside, but it hosts changing exhibitions and has a museum – the first of its kind – dedicated to Chinese-Canadian history and culture, including the Chinese Canadian Military Museum, designed to offer insights into the role of Chinese-Canadian soldiers who fought during the First and Second world wars. Guided tours of the museum are available ($4), together with tours of Chinatown (90min, $6: a combined museum and Chinatown tour costs $8). You can also attend 45-minutes workshops ($5 each) in *t'ai chi*, painting, knotting, calligraphy and Chinese music. Lunch is available for between about $5 and $10.

Next to the gardens and centre lies the small and slightly threadbare **Dr Sun Yat-Sen Park** (free), which, though less worked than the Dr Sun Yat-Sen Garden, is still a pleasant place to take time out from Chinatown. Hours are the same as for the garden, and there's an alternative entrance on Columbia Street and Keefer.

Stanley Park

One of the world's finest urban spaces, **Stanley Park** crowns the tip of the Downtown peninsula. It is a huge green heart of woodland, temperate rainforest, marshes, beaches and untamed landscapes that provides a link to the not-so-distant days when Vancouver was little more than a clearing in the west-coast wilderness. At nearly 405 hectares, it's one of the largest urban parks in North America – some twenty per cent larger than New York's Central Park. And, unlike many urban parks, it's very safe. It's also much frequented – an estimated eight million visitors a year – though it's worth stressing that only the outer edge is developed for recreational use – the rest is wild, with lots of wildlife as a result, including herons, coyotes, racoons, eagles, owls and more.

Ocean surrounds the park on three sides – ensuring some superb views – while its perimeter consists of a road (Stanley Park Drive) and the deservedly popular 10.5-kilometre cycleway and pedestrian Seawall Promenade. Much of the park's interior, by contrast, is nearly impenetrable scrub and forest, visited by relatively few people and criss-crossed by just a handful of trails (most of them well-maintained gravel paths). Around the fringes, on the other hand, and particularly along the park's southern edge – the area closest to Downtown – there are plenty of more conventional urban park trappings: lawns, flowerbeds, rose gardens, tennis courts, children's playgrounds, miniature railway, pitch and putt golf and lots of open, wooded or flower-decorated spaces where you can picnic, snooze or watch the world go by.

Best of all, the park has three good beaches: **English Bay Beach**, ranged along Beach Avenue; **Second Beach**, to the north, which also features a shallow onshore swimming pool; and **Third Beach**, further north still, least crowded of the three and the one with the best views of West Vancouver and the mountains. English Bay at the southern end of Denman Street is the most readily accessible from Downtown, and is particularly easy to visit after seeing the park. Away from the park's many natural delights, the main attraction is the highly popular **Vancouver Aquarium Marine Science Centre**, Canada's largest aquarium.

A neat **itinerary** for a half-day or so in the park and surrounding area – namely English Bay Beach and Denman Street a couple of blocks east of the park – would be to walk or take the bus to the park and stroll, cycle or skate all or part of the Seawall. It's between 8.8km and 10.5km if you do the whole thing, depending precisely where you start and finish, so factor this in if you want to tackle it in whole or in part. There's a slew of bike- and rollerblade-rental places nearby, and for more on what you can do in the park, see Chapter 16, "Sports and outdoor activities".

Some history

When George Vancouver sailed into the Burrard Inlet in 1792 he assumed the bulging knuckle of land that is now Stanley Park was an island. Later, in 1865, when settlers knew better, Edward Stamp earmarked its convenient position as a potential site for his first sawmill. When he made his plans clear to the indigenous Salish, however, they told him his log booms would never survive the powerful tides in the First Narrows waters near the proposed site. As a result, Stamp founded his mill elsewhere, and with it one of the nodal points that would eventually develop into Vancouver. The land that would become Stanley Park was thus largely ignored by loggers.

The rest of the peninsula now occupied by Vancouver, however, had already been partially logged in the 1860s, when Vancouver was still a twinkle in "Gassy" Jack Deighton's eye. However, in 1886 the newly formed city council – showing typical Canadian foresight and an admirable sense of priorities – moved to make what had by then become a military reserve into a permanent park. Impetus for the move came from Alexander Hamilton, land commissioner for the Canadian Pacific Railway, a company which was rarely far from the important decisions that shaped the nascent city. His motives were not entirely philanthropic, for the company hoped the proximity of the park would improve the value of its properties in the West End – and it was not disappointed.

Various Musqueam, Salish and other native villages were situated in the park – most of their inhabitants moved peacefully to North Vancouver – and several present-day hiking paths correspond to old aboriginal trails. Others follow the routes used by what loggers there were in the area to remove lumber. Otherwise, the city was preserving an almost virgin tract of wilderness.

The park's remaining first-growth forest of cedar, hemlock and Douglas fir, and the swamp now known as Lost Lagoon, was saved for posterity in the name of Lord Stanley, Canada's governor general from 1888 to 1893 (the same person who gave his name to ice hockey's Stanley Cup). He dedicated the park "to the use and enjoyment of people of all colours, creeds and customs for all time". The park was officially opened in 1888. At about the same time, and with equally admirable foresight, the Vancouver Board of Parks & Recreation was created, a body now responsible for almost 200 parks covering 1278 hectares of the city.

Getting to the park

Stanley Park is a simple though rather dull **walk** from most of Downtown – allow about fifteen minutes from the Vancouver Art Gallery – and a pretty lengthy one from the city's eastern districts such as Gastown and Chinatown. Beach Avenue to the south and West Georgia Street to the north are the best approaches if you're on foot, and lead to the southern and northern starts of the Seawall respectively. West Georgia Street becomes Stanley Park Causeway

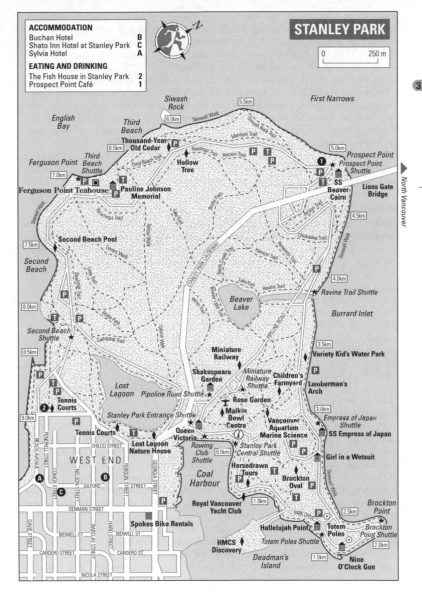

ACCOMMODATION
Buchan Hotel   B
Shato Inn Hotel at Stanley Park   C
Sylvia Hotel   A
EATING AND DRINKING
The Fish House in Stanley Park   2
Prospect Point Café   1

STANLEY PARK

0   250 m

in the park, cutting through the heart of the park en route for the Lions Gate Bridge and North Vancouver.

Perhaps a better approach than walking is to take a **taxi** or Stanley Park **bus** #23, #35 or #135 from the corner of Burrard and Pender streets Downtown, services which drop you near the so-called Stanley Park Loop just inside the park by Lost Lagoon and in summer continue deeper into the park to a point close to the Aquarium Marine Science Centre. If you're not coming from points on or near Burrard and Pender, other buses which will take you close to the park are the #1 which runs through the south side of Downtown along Davie and Beach Avenue (look for "Beach" on the front of the bus) – get off at the corner of Davie and Beach Avenue; and the #5 ("Robson") which runs along Robson to the corner of Robson and Denman Street.

Note that driving a **car** here can be foolish, especially at weekends, when parking is just about impossible. If you do drive, remember that traffic is one-way around the park, which means you have to use the park's West Georgia Street, or northern entrance. Parking meters are dotted around the park, both on the roads and in dedicated parking areas: most take credit cards if you don't have the right change. **Parking fees** are $1 for 45min (up to a maximum of $3 daily) between April and September (6am–9pm) and $1 for two hours the rest of the year (7am–6pm) up to a maximum of $4.

Getting around the park

Walking round the Seawall path – a distance of between 8.8 and 10.5km depending where you start – takes about two hours at a fairly brisk pace. If you want to rent a bike, go to the corner of Denman and West Georgia, where there's a cluster of **bike rental** outlets. Spokes, 1798 West Georgia St (☎604/688-5141, ⓦwww.vancouverbikerentals.com), is a big, busy place that's been in business since 1938 (from $3.75 an hour for a wide variety of bikes, including children's bikes and tandems with child trailers). You need to leave ID, and a cash, Visa or MasterCard deposit. Helmets, which are compulsory in BC, and locks are included in the rental. If this place looks too frenetic you might walk a few metres up the street to the smaller Bikes 'n' Blades (☎604/602-9899) which rents **in-line skates** as well. Directly opposite at 745 Denman St is another rental outlet, Bayshore Bicycle & Rollerblade Rentals (☎604/688-2453, ⓦwww.bayshorebike.ca). From Denman it's just a minute's pedalling to the park, but watch out for the traffic on the busy intersections off West Georgia and by the park entrance.

If you don't want to walk, cycle or skate, then there's a free TransLink "Stanley Park Shuttle" **bus service**, which runs on a 15-minute schedule in summer only (daily June–Aug/early Sept 9/10am–6.30pm; information ☎604/257-8400). It makes fourteen stops at the most popular sights around the park. You can transfer to the service from the #1 and #5 buses on Denman or the #23, #35 and #135 at Stanley Park Loop: both Denman and the Loop are a few moments' walk from the shuttle's stops at Stanley Park Entrance, Pipeline Road or the Vancouver Rowing Club. Another alternative is to take a **horse-drawn tour** of the park: see p.31 for details.

Note that drivers on Stanley Park Drive and cyclists on the Seawall Promenade must follow a **counter-clockwise route**. Walkers can obviously go in either direction, but if you insist on a clockwise approach you'll being going against the flow of both cyclists and of most other walkers. For this reason our account of the park follows a counter-clockwise route.

Around the Seawall

Stanley Park, especially on a busy Sunday, offers a good idea of what it means to live in Vancouver – the thrill of having great scenery on your doorstep and the passion of its inhabitants for the outdoors and for making the most of it by walking, biking, jogging or rollerblading around the **Seawall**. The wall was conceived in 1917 as a precaution against erosion but took almost sixty years to complete. Granite boulders had to be cut and trimmed on the beach to manageable 45kg blocks and then hauled to the wall. One man, James Cunningham, was the driving force behind the project, working on it until his death at the age 85 – 17 years before its completion. A plaque near the Siwash Rock (see p.79) honours his achievement.

If you're walking, biking or busing around the wall, there are any number of minor diversions en route, not to mention a couple of good places for snacks and a couple of exceptional **restaurants** for lunch or dinner. This tour assumes a counter-clockwise trip starting at the foot of West Georgia by the bus drop at Stanley Park Loop and Lost Lagoon. The Seawall is clearly divided, with lanes for cyclists and pedestrians, but keep an eye out anyway: if you're cycling, be sure to observe various speed restrictions and to follow the instructions to dismount for safety's sake at various blind corners and other indicated points.

From Lost Lagoon to Hallelujah Point

The first thing you see in the park is **Lost Lagoon**, a lake that started life as a tidal inlet and part of Coal Harbour. Its water all but disappeared at low tide, a process exacerbated when the bridge over the inlet was replaced by a causeway in 1916. By 1929, the area was cut off from the sea and had become a natural freshwater lake. In 1938, it was declared a wildlife sanctuary and the park board began to scatter seeds regularly to encourage birds. Walk its pretty waterfront path to admire the dozens of waterfowl species – including geese, several varieties of duck and a handful of rare trumpeter swans – that inhabit its shoreline.

The city side of the lagoon boasts the **Lost Lagoon Nature House** (July–Aug Tues–Sun 10am–7pm, rest of the year Sat & Sun 9.30am–4.30pm; free; ☎604/257-8544), which has displays on the park in general and the lagoon's flora and fauna. Its exhibits cover some of the animals that inhabit the area, notably racoons, beavers, coyotes, bald eagles, huge numbers of Canada geese and squirrels. Vancouver's Ecology Society (☎604/257-8544, ⊛www.stanleyparkecology.ca) runs **guided walks** from the centre on a Sunday ($5), and organizes a variety of other free or inexpensive activities, most aimed at children.

The lagoon's name was coined in a poem written on this part of the park by **Pauline Johnson** (1862–1913), a celebrated Indian princess born in Ontario of an English mother and Mohawk father. Her poetry on native life and lore achieved considerable fame in its day, and Johnson spent considerable time touring Britain and North America giving readings before settling in Vancouver. Here she learned of much of the city's particular aboriginal history and legend from Chief Capilano, a local elder, and then reworked them in a collection titled *Legends of Vancouver*. She spent much time canoeing in Lost Lagoon – her best-known poem is "The Song My Paddle Sings" – and is buried in the park at Ferguson Point (see p.80).

A few steps inland from the lagoon are the **Malkin Bowl**, an arena used for outdoor performances in summer (see p.208), and the **Rose Garden** and **Shakespeare Garden**, two of the park's horticultural highlights. The site was originally home to the park board's greenhouses, since moved, though the board still grows all the flowers – around 350,000 a year - used in the city's parks and gardens. Late spring and summer here sees hundreds of mostly old rose varieties and clematis in bloom (275 rose varieties in all, and 3000 individual bushes), while swathes of annuals bring colour to the beds later in the year. If you are keen on **gardens**, make a point of seeing the **Ted and Mary Grieg Rhododendron Garden** around the Pitch and Putt Course, at its best in mid- to late May, and the annual summer carpets of bedding plants at Prospect Point (see opposite).

Pass under the West Georgia Street underpass and you'll come to the private 1886 mock-Tudor **Vancouver Rowing Club**, fronted by a stature of Scottish poet Robert Burns. Close by stands a granite statue of Queen Victoria, designed in 1905 by James Blofield, who was also responsible for designing the city's coat of arms (motto: "By Sea, Land and Air We Prosper").

The Seawall path brings you to a parking area and **information booth**, a source of maps and the starting point for horse-drawn tours of the park (see p.31). Curving to the right you'll pass the private Royal Vancouver Yacht Club premises, while ahead, jutting into Coal Harbour and linked to the park by a narrow causeway, is **Deadman's Island**. This probably takes its name from an ancient Salish burial ground on the site, but it has also been an aboriginal battleground, a lumber camp, a squatters' village and a quarantine station during the smallpox epidemic in the city between 1888 and 1890. The military took it over in World War II for "temporary" use, but it remains an out-of-bounds military compound to this day known as the HMCS *Discovery*, the last remnant of the military reserve that once covered much of the park.

Continuing east, you come to **Hallelujah Point**, so called because the Salvation Army once held revival meetings here. On the seaward side of the path nearby is the **Nine O'Clock Gun**, which for many years since 1894 was fired nightly at 9pm, partly, it's said, to help ships' captains set their chronometers, and partly to indicate the curfew that once marked the end of the day's fishing. Its now performs at noon rather than 9pm, and is fired electronically rather than with a charge.

From Brockton Point to Prospect Point

The tip of **Brockton Point** represents the park's most easterly point, a belvedere for the port and the Lions Gate Bridge that appears to your left. The point was once the site of a pioneer graveyard, and it was here that one of the young city's first lumber magnates, Edward Stamp, cleared a site in 1865 for a sawmill. The proposed mill was moved further east (to the site of present-day Gastown), when Stamp discovered the currents of the Burrard Inlet here were too powerful to allow the creation of log booms.

Walk west around the point, past the unexceptional Brockton Point Lighthouse (closed to the public), and you'll pass the **Chehalis Monument**, a memorial to the nine people killed nearby when a tugboat was struck by the liner *Princess of Victoria* in 1906. Neither the tug nor any of the bodies were ever recovered. Moving on, you can't miss that most English of sights, a cricket pitch – a monument to Vancouver's powerful early links with Britain – nor a crop of **totem poles** created by the Haida, Kwakiutl and other native peoples. The totems form part of an aborted 1889 scheme to re-create an aboriginal village on the site. Look out for the carving of the woman with full lips and arms outstretched apparently in an embrace, a favourite backdrop for newlyweds having their photographs taken – they are presumably unaware that the totem represents the legendary "crazy bear woman who comes down from the mountains to steal children". As a quick guide to these totems' iconography, the whale represents the lordship of the sea, the eagle the kingdom of the air, the wolf the genius of the land, and the frog the transitional link between land and water. For further information on the totems, visit the **Brockton Visitor Centre** (see box p.74), which as well as further information on the totems has refreshments, toilets and the inevitable gift shop.

Almost a kilometre from Brockton Point you pass the bronze statue on a rock of the **Girl in a Wetsuit** (1972). It looks like a modern reinterpretation of Copenhagen's *Little Mermaid*, but the sculptor, Elek Imredy, maintains no connection at all was intended with the Danish statue. A short way beyond is a replica figurehead from the SS *Empress of Japan*, a memorial commemorating Vancouver's early trade with Asia. At the junction about 200m beyond, turn left on Avison Way and you'll come to the **aquarium** (see p.81) while a little beyond Avison Way, the Hummingbird Trail strikes south to a point just east of the information kiosk (see above) if you want to curtail your walk.

Stay with the Seawall, however, and beyond the Avison Way junction just inland you find **Lumberman's Arch**, once the site of a Salish village but now marked by a large arch of timber from vast Douglas firs erected in 1952 to honour logging workers – a strange memorial today given that most forestry companies would now give their eyeteeth for some of the trees protected in the park. Its meadow surroundings are a favourite for families and those seeking a siesta.

There's a refreshment stand here, and if you head a little further into the park from here you'll come to the Miniature Railway and **Children's Farmyard** (Easter to end of September daily 11am–6pm, Oct–Easter weekends only plus Christmas week and evenings in Oct, weather permitting, 11am–4pm; $4, under 12 $2; ☎604/257-8530), where children can admire farmyard and other domestic animals. This partly replaces the park's zoo, closed in 1993.

Also aimed at children, the **Miniature Railway** (same hours as Children's Farmyard; $3, under 12 $1.50; ☎604/257-8531) about 200m to the northwest appears equally popular with adults. It's estimated that the mini-locomotives, one of which is a copy of the first Canadian Pacific steam engine to pull a transcontinental train into Vancouver in 1887, carry as many passengers annually as all the Alaska-bound cruise ships combined. The train runs on a circuit through towering cedars and Douglas firs, a particularly good trip if you're in the city during October and the first week or so of November, when the railway turns into the **Hallowe'en Ghost Train**, a nocturnal ride through the woods, specially illuminated for the occasion. A similar lighted display takes place in winter, when the park board presents **Bright Nights** (daily 3pm–10pm early Dec to early Jan, except Christmas Day), when over 750,000 lights transform the park.

Back on the waterfront promenade, it's a little over a kilometre to the **Lions Gate Bridge**, roughly the halfway point on the Seawall. You could also walk here from the railway along Pipeline Road, enlivening this less attractive route by taking the short self-guided nature trail around Beaver Lake en route. Just beyond the bridge, a short detour from the main Seawall route cuts to **Prospect Point**, a sixty-metre-high basalt cliff and wonderful viewpoint that's home to the *Prospect Point Café* (☎604/669-2737) – good for coffee and a snack – public toilets, a colony of nesting cormorants and a cairn to the Hudson's Bay Company SS *Beaver*, the first ship to travel the entire west coast of North America.

From Siwash Rock to Ferguson Point

One kilometre west of Prospect Point lies **Siwash Rock**, an offshore outcrop, which has defied the weather for centuries. The rock has given rise to numerous native legends, the best known having a Squamish soon-to-be father named Skalish (or Skalsh) deciding to swim in **English Bay** until the waters made him free of physical and spiritual blemishes (the idea being that his newborn child should also thus start life free of stain). So impressed were the gods – Q' uas, the "transforming" god in particular – by this selflessness that they turned him into the rock as a reward: two smaller outcrops, purportedly Skalish's son and wife, stand in the woods overlooking the rock. Less romantically, the rock also served as a World War II battery site and searchlight position.

A popular summer barbecue spot among the locals, and a favourite place to settle down to watch the sunset, **Third Beach** lies 800m south along the Seawall, yet if you wish to cut back, about 100m before the beach Tatlow Walk cuts through the park to Lost Lagoon. Third Beach itself is relatively quieter than other English Bay beaches. It has lifeguards in summer from 11.30am to dusk. The celebrated Hollow Tree, the stump of colossal cedar, can be found just inland at the northern end of the beach, while on the path from the beach is a gargantuan cedar thought – at over 1000 years old – to be one of the world's oldest (and largest) trees.

Continuing along the Seawall from Third Beach brings you to **Ferguson Point**, home to a good though often busy *Teahouse in Stanley Park* restaurant, public toilets and to a memorial cairn and fountain that mark the grave of Pauline Johnson (see p.77).

Second Beach to English Bay

Another kilometre or so beyond the point brings you to the start of **Second Beach**. Although people do swim in the sea here and at Third Beach, most bathers prefer the large **swimming pool** (☎604/257-8370) next to Second Beach, generally open Victoria Day (third Mon in May) to Labour Day (early Sept). You pay a fee to swim here (25¢), though there is a small "spray" pool which is free. Offseason, or in windy weather, this can be an exposed and wind-chilled spot, so dress appropriately. Alongside the pool is the children's **Stanley Park Playground**, which has two play structures, one for older and one for younger children (busy at weekends and in summer).

While most people cut short their tour and head back to Lost Lagoon via Lagoon Drive or the parallel trails (see map p.75), the Seawall continues south for a little under a kilometre to Beach Avenue, passing another excellent restaurant, *The Fish House* (see p.155). Just south of Lagoon Drive is a corner of the park that contains, among other things, the pitch and putt golf course, putting greens, formal gardens and 17 free public tennis courts (first-come, first-served, but reservations possible on six pay courts May–Aug; call ☎604/605-8224). There is an additional bank of four free courts just below South Lagoon Drive near the Lost Lagoon Nature House.

From here you can continue back towards West Georgia Street and your starting point or continue along the waterfront and **English Bay Beach**, another great stretch of beach bordered with park and grass and Beach Avenue to the rear. This in turn gives way to Sunset Beach and its eponymous park, a slightly less appealing stretch of open waterfront. If you're following this route, it's best to peel off the beach early and wander down either Denman or Davie streets, both lined with interesting shops and cafés. Both are served by buses; Davie, if you follow it all the way, will take you to Yaletown (see p.57).

Vancouver Aquarium Marine Science Centre

The **Vancouver Aquarium Marine Science Centre** (daily: July to early Sept 9.30am–7pm; early Sept to June 10am–5.30pm; $15.95; ☎604/659-3474, ⓦwww.vanaqua.org) at 845 Avison Way is Stanley Park's most popular destination. The aquarium ranks among North America's best, and with over a million visitors a year is the most visited sight in Canada west of the Toronto CN Tower. It contains around sixty thousand living exhibits representing some six hundred different species, though in truth this is a relatively modest summation of the eighty percent of the world's creatures that live in water. Like the park zoo before it – now closed – the complex has been targeted by animal rights campaigners for its treatment of performing beluga and killer whales, not to mention cooped-up seals and otters. Given the aquarium's reputation as a tourist attraction, however, as well as its claims as a research centre, the campaigners have a long, uphill battle. The whales in particular are huge draws, but you can't help but feel they should really be in the sea, for all the hoopla surrounding their $14 million marine-mammal area.

At the aquarium's entrance stands a vast killer whale in bronze (1984), the work of celebrated Haida artist Bill Reid, whose famous *Raven and the Beast* sculpture forms the centrepiece of the Museum of Anthropology (see p.101). Beyond this there are several key areas to see. The **Arctic Canada** section in the Jean MacMillan Southern Arctic Gallery concerns itself with the fragile world of the Canadian north – everything from cod to beluga whales – with a chance to see whales face to face through glass and hear the sounds of whales, walruses, seals and other creatures in this icy domain. Special exhibits are devoted to Lancaster Sound off Baffin Island, an area whose position in the high Arctic is belied by the surprising richness of its marine life. The H. R. MacMillan Gallery here has an interesting **Whalelink** section, a more technically minded display devoted to current research into orca or killer whales. All round the aquarium, though, you have the chance to watch research sessions in progress, or watch feeding and "play" sessions with marine animals.

The **Pacific Canada habitats** of the Sandwell North Pacific Gallery perform a similar role for otters, beavers and other creatures of the waters of Vancouver, Georgia Strait, Vancouver Island and the rest of British Columbia. Other warm parts of the Pacific are examined in the MacMillan Tropical Gallery, with specimens such as sharks, sea turtles and coral-reef fish from Micronesia, Indonesia and the Philippines. From here you enter the domain of the **Amazon Rainforest**, a tremendous area which displays the bountiful vegetation, fishes, iguanas, three-toed sloths, poisonous tree frogs and other creatures of the rainforest in a climate-controlled environment: check out the hourly "rainstorms". Giant cockroaches and massive, hairy tarantulas are also often visible in the display. Closer to home, the **BC Waters Gallery** and **Ducks Unlimited Wetlands** displays are fairly self-explanatory – they're also fascinating, if less striking than the rainforest displays.

There's a café at the aquarium, the *Upstream Café*, if you need a reviving drink or snack, and **guided tours** behind the scenes: call, visit the website or enquire at the ticket office for details of tours, including 45-minute Trainer Tours ($20), where you learn what it takes to be an animal trainer; Animal Encounters ($175), face-to-face encounters with beluga whales (reservations ☎604/659-3552 or 1-800/931-1186); and sleepovers, where you get to see the attractions after everyone else has gone home.

Granville Island

One of Vancouver's most compelling sights, **Granville Island** is the city's most enticing "people's place" – one of the titles it likes for itself. It's a joy to visit for its own sake, and for the pleasure of milling around busy cafés, scouring market stalls piled with exotic goods, watching street performers, shopping in small specialist craft and other stores, eating a Sunday brunch looking out over the ocean or enjoying a late night-cap. As you would expect, the whole place is hugely popular – around 250,000 people come here each month.

More a peninsula than an island, Granville Island sits on False Creek – the arm of water that marks the southern edge of the Downtown peninsula – and lies half-hidden beneath the superstructure of the Granville Street Bridge which links Downtown to the city's southern suburbs. The word "island" in this context conjures up the wrong idea, for this is no green and bucolic retreat in a city setting, rather a deliberately jumbled collection of shops, restaurants and other businesses juxtaposed with a marina, open spaces, art school and light-industrial units, whose faint – and deliberately retained – whiff of warehouse squalor means the place never runs the risk of being quaint or pretentious.

The constant buzz of activity and variety of things – and people – to look at make it a tremendous and easy-going place to wander, and a superb place to shop, in particular for food – the endless ranks of stalls in the large, covered food hall here constitute one of North America's great markets. Most locals and tourists alike visit during the day, and especially at the weekend, but the restaurants, bars and the Arts Club Theatre, a performance space with bar and lounge (see p.170), are enough to keep the place alive at night.

East of the island at the other end of False Creek, and easily reached by ferry (see p.85), is **Science World**, distinguished by a striking geodesic dome which forms a prominent part of the city skyline, but whose science-related displays are somewhat disappointing. For details on getting to Science World, see p.89.

Some history

Granville Island began as little more than marsh and a couple of seaweed-laden sandbanks in False Creek, an area favoured by Vancouver's original Squamish inhabitants as winter fishing grounds. It came to the attention of white settlers in 1889, when a bridge was built linking the north and south shores of False Creek. First up were three contractors who circled the sandbars with stakes, intending to build a sawmill. They were soon seen off by the Canadian Pacific Railway, but only after the serving of a court injunction, an action which would result in years of squabbles over water and foreshore rights between the CPR, the provincial government, the city council, local businesspeople and the federal fishing and marine ministries.

All interested parties came up with their own plans, including a CPR for a

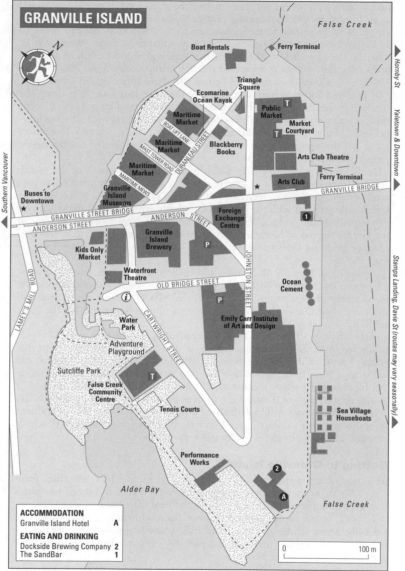

GRANVILLE ISLAND

False Creek

Boat Rentals

Ferry Terminal

Triangle Square

Ecomarine Ocean Kayak

Public Market

Market Courtyard

Maritime Market

BOAT LIFT LANE

Maritime Market

Blackberry Books

Arts Club Theatre

Maritime Market

MAST TOWER ROAD

Granville Island Museums

MARITIME MEWS

Arts Club

Ferry Terminal

Buses to Downtown

GRANVILLE STREET BRIDGE

GRANVILLE BRIDGE

ANDERSON STREET

ANDERSON STREET

Foreign Exchange Centre

Kids Only Market

Granville Island Brewery

P

JOHNSTON STREET

Waterfront Theatre

OLD BRIDGE STREET

Ocean Cement

Water Park

P

CARTWRIGHT STREET

Emily Carr Institute of Art and Design

Adventure Playground

Sutcliffe Park

False Creek Community Centre

Tennis Courts

Sea Village Houseboats

Performance Works

Alder Bay

False Creek

ACCOMMODATION

Granville Island Hotel **A**

EATING AND DRINKING

Dockside Brewing Company **2**

The SandBar **1**

0   100 m

LAMEY'S MILL ROAD

Southern Vancouver

Hornby St

Yaletown & Downtown

Stamps Landing, Davie St (routes may vary seasonally)

4

GRANVILLE ISLAND

colossal railway station and a \$10–million scheme for a port. In 1915 the new Harbour Commission pulled rank and paid the federal government \$1 for the land and then spent \$300,000 running railway tracks and a wooden road to the south shore of False Creek. The 760,000 cubic metres of slurry were dredged from the seabed and poured into a wooden stockade around the mudflats.

The reclaimed swampland opened in 1916 as "Industrial Island", a 14.5-

hectare area with 80 lots just three metres above sea level. It quickly prospered as an ironworks and shipbuilding centre, businesses having been attracted by virtue of its proximity to the ocean and to local sawmills and rail yards. In 1930, 1200 people worked on the site, a figure that grew during World War II, when, as the city's industrial fulcrum, it turned to the production of anti-torpedo nets, minesweeping ropes and other maritime-related war materials. In 1942, it was closed to outsiders to "guard island industries against saboteurs".

Its post-war fortunes were mixed to say the least, two huge fires being the worst of its various mishaps. The whole island was served by just one 20-centimetre water main, a conduit more often than not clogged with silt. One businessman, Major Chutter, unofficial "mayor of the island", observed that "there is not an area between Frisco and Prince Rupert which has so much valuable property and is so poorly served."

Dredging operations gradually filled in the area to the south of the island, effectively making it more of a peninsula than an island. The same operations were actually part of a never-realized five-stage plan to fill the whole of False Creek, a project that with the benefit of hindsight would, in robbing Vancouver of Granville Island and the False Creek waterfront, have changed the face of the city for the worse. Many industrial tenants then moved out, anxious to find cheaper land and keen to take advantage of the new possibilities offered by road haulage.

By the 1960s virtually all business and trade had moved on, further spurred on by the loss to fire of Wright's ropes and Pacific Bolts, hitherto among the island's industrial mainstays. Thereafter, the island's yards were abandoned, and the place then quickly became a rat-infested dumping ground for the city's rubbish.

Fortunately, in 1972, the federal government agreed to bankroll a $25-million programme of residential, commercial and industrial redevelopment that retained some of the old false-fronted buildings, tin-shack homes, seawall and rail sidings. Most of the renovation and new construction work (mainly modern business units, shops and the market building) had been finished by 1979 – and, despite years of doomsaying from politicians and city inhabitants alike, was immediately successful in attracting businesses and people. Work continues unobtrusively to this day, financed entirely by profits from the island, which employs 2500 people and is totally self-supporting.

Getting to Granville Island

The most direct approach to Granville Island is to take **bus** #50 (the "False Creek South" service) from Gastown or Granville Street: this drops you just a few steps from the entrance to the island and runs daily until around 12.30am. The walk south along Granville Street from Downtown and across the Granville Street Bridge might look like the obvious approach, but it's deceptively long, not terribly attractive, and probably only worthwhile on a fine day when you need the exercise.

Alternatively and more fun, tiny bathtub-sized private **ferries** are run over similar routes by two rival companies: Aquabus (☎604/689–5858, ⓦwww.aquabus. bc.ca) and False Creek Ferries (☎604/684–7781, ⓦwww.granvilleislandferries. bc.ca). Both provide useful and very frequent services between about 7am and 10.30pm (8.30pm in winter). Aquabus runs boats in a continuous circular shuttle from the foot of Hornby Street to the Fish Docks on Granville Island to Vanier Park and the museums (all $2), docking just below the Maritime Museum – a good way of getting to the park and its museums (see pp.92–94). It also runs to Granville Island ($2) and to the Yaletown dock by the road loop at the eastern foot of Davie Street ($3).

False Creek Ferries also runs to Granville Island ($2) and the Maritime Museum (Vanier Park) from the Aquatic Centre at the foot of Thurlow Street (Vanier Park is $3.50 from Granville Island, $2 from the Aquatic Centre), they also run from Granville Island to Yaletown ($3) and to Stamps Landing ($3) on the south side of False Creek en route to Science World ($5). You buy **tickets** on board with both companies. Note that many of the Vanier Park and Science World services only run daily in summer: in winter the services are restricted to weekends. Departures are between every five and 30 minutes, depending on the day (they are more frequent at weekends) and destination: Granville Island services to and from the Aquatic Centre are most frequent; those to Yaletown and Science World the least frequent.

Both companies also offer mini-cruises up False Creek, with connections from Granville Island to Science World and the Plaza of Nations. You can pick up the Aquabus boat at the Arts Club Theatre on Granville Island, the foot of Hornby Street Downtown or – with False Creek Ferries – below the Aquatic Centre at the foot of Thurlow and northern end of Burrard Bridge, on Granville Island or below the spit and small harbour near the Maritime Museum in Vanier Park.

Island practicalities

Granville Island is easy to negotiate, despite an ad hoc arrangement of "streets" – the jumble of industrial units, waterfront and other buildings hardly conform to the normal notion of a street – and public spaces designed to preserve a dynamic and open-plan feel. There's a good **infocentre** at 1592 Johnston St (daily 9pm–6pm; ☎604/666-5784, Ⓦ www.granvilleisland.bc.ca) for island-related information only, including maps. There's a **currency exchange** facility in the same building, displays on the island's history, a direct-call phone for taxis, change machine for parking (though you'd be well advised not to come by car) and ATMs on the wall outside. Public toilets stand adjacent.

Note that many of the island's shops and businesses close on Mondays, and that if you want a **bus back** to Downtown you should *not* take the #51 from the stop opposite the infocentre – it goes in the wrong direction: instead, walk out of the island complex's unmissable single road entrance underneath the bridge and at the junction the #50 stop is immediately on your right. The island has plenty of cafés and takeaway food stalls, as well as a couple of larger bar-restaurants. Details of where to eat and drink can be found on p.143 and p.161.

The island

Granville Island does not lend itself easily to any sort of set itinerary - the whole idea of the place is that it is unfocused and designed to encourage wandering. This said, there is one must-see target – the **market** in the Public Market Building (see p.87) – but the chances are you'll have most fun simply walking around the various galleries and specialist craft or book shops, grabbing a drink at one of the bars or cafés, and buying a picnic from the market to eat outdoors on the waterfront. Our reviews of the island's best shops and galleries are on p.179.

In addition to various commercial art galleries – several of which are collected in the **Net Loft Building** to the west of the market – you may also be able to catch an occasional temporary art exhibition at the **Emily Carr**

△ The Granville Bridge

Institute of Art and Design, 1299 Johnston St (☎604/844-3800), an art school based in two big buildings towards the south of the island: check directly with the infocentre or institute for details of the latest shows.

The Granville Island Brewery

One of the first buildings you'll see if you walk to the island from the bus stop under the girders of the Granville Street Bridge is the **Granville Island Brewery**, 1441 Cartwright St (tours June–Sept Mon–Fri on the hour noon–5pm, Sat & Sun on the half-hour 11.30am–5pm; $7; ☎604/687-2739), a small concern that, despite having no formal pub, offers guided tours that include tastings of its fine additive-free beers. Note that tour times change according to season, so call first to check the latest details. There's also a shop here where you can buy souvenirs, a selection of leading British Columbia wines, and the brewery's own beer – try the light, easy-to-drink Gastown Amber Ale, or the stronger Scottish Ale and Brockton Black, both dark beers with a rich, malty taste. If you want to drink these and other beers in a pub setting, then *The Keg* nearby sells most of the brewery's ales. The brewery is part of a long tradition of brewing and beer-drinking locally, it being claimed that Captain George Vancouver was the first white to brew beer here, when he used fresh spruce needles and molasses as the basis for a beer aimed to combat scurvy among his crew.

Tucked away before the brewery on the same side of the street is the excellent **Kids Only Market**, a collection of shops, cafés and activities aimed at children (see p.193). The children-only Water Park lies nearby (see p.195).

The Granville Island Museums

Across the street from the brewery and market stands a building containing a trio of small, linked, private museums at 1502 Duranleau St on the corner with Anderson (all daily 10am–5.30pm; $6.50 – ticket gives admission to all three museums; ☎604/683-1939). Unless you're a fishing or model boat enthusiast, the one with the most general appeal is the **Granville Island Model Trains Museum** (⊛www.modeltrainsmuseum.bc.ca), which has the world's largest collection of toy trains on public display. Most are displayed in cabinets, but there are also two working scale steam engines, photographs and related memorabilia, and a three-tiered O-scale working layout, with plans for other layouts in the future.

Also on the premises is the **Model Ships Museum**, whose collection of model sailing ships, submarines, warships and other maritime craft is more for the enthusiast. Much the same can be said for the **Sport Fishing Museum** (⊛www.sportfishingmuseum.ca), where devotees can linger over the 500-strong collection of reels (the world's largest), many stuffed fish, the world's finest fly plates, and numerous other salt- and freshwater fishing treasures.

The Granville Island Public Market

Far more general in its appeal than the Granville Island Museums, and a dominant feature amongst the maze of shops, galleries and businesses, the **Granville Island Public Market** (daily 9am–6pm) is the island's undisputed highlight. On summer weekends, it's packed with people and a phalanx of buskers. The quality and variety of **food** is staggering, and the endless groaning stalls of fruit, fish, vegetables, cakes, fruit, meat, cheese and other more exotic and gourmet foods are augmented by dozens of counters and cafés selling ready-made snacks and potential picnic ingredients.

If you can eat it or drink it, it's probably here; everything from fudge (visit *Old Worlde Fudge*), donuts (*Lee's*) and turkey (*Turkey Stop*) to tortillas (*La Tortilleria*), Belgian chocolate (*Brussels Chocolates*) and the inevitable muffins (*Muffin Granny*). Old favourites include the *Stock Market*, crammed with homemade stocks and meals, and the *Salmon Shop*, where you can buy some of the finest salmon in Canada, which is to say in the world. There is also a wide variety of takeaway outlets. Parks, patios and walkways nearby provide lively areas to eat and take everything in. The only drawbacks here are the sheer number of people on busy days and the foul flocks of pigeons, seagulls and other birds that assault you for food. Pick up a free **pamphlet**, *The Fresh Sheet*, for full of details about the market, recipes and forthcoming events.

Canoe rentals on False Creek

Granville Island has several marine-rental and charter outfits, including the opportunity to rent **canoes** for safe and straightforward paddling in False Creek and English Bay from Ecomarine Ocean Kayak, 1688 Duranleau St (☎604/689-7575, ⓦwww .ecomarine.com). The company also offers lessons. See p.199 and p.202 for further details and information on fishing and yacht charters.

Science World

Science World (Mon–Fri 10am–5pm, Sat & Sun 10am–6pm; Science World $12.75, OMNIMAX $11.25 for single feature, double features Sun & Wed evening $13.50; combination tickets $17.75 for Science World entry and one OMNIMAX film; ☎604/443-7440 or recorded 24-hour line 443-7443, ⓦwww.scienceworld.bc.ca) at 1455 Québec St and Terminal Avenue is one of Vancouver's most distinctive buildings, the Buckminster Fuller-designed geodesic dome it employs having been one of the main structural survivors of the city's Expo '86 world fair. The museum it now houses, however, is something of a disappointment, at least for adults. Probably only children, at whom the place is largely aimed, will be satisfied by the various sophisticated, hands-on displays, which include the opportunity to make thunderous amounts of noise on electronic instruments and drum machines.

Five major galleries on two levels deal with all manner of natural history and science-related themes – Eureka, the Sara Stern Search Gallery, KidSpace, Our World and Visual Illusions – and lots of demonstrations are held daily in each to help explain the science of water, fire and air. Activities include the chance to search for gold, crawl through a beaver lodge, wander a vast maze, explore a hollow tree, blow square bubbles, see the workings of a beehive, or play a tune by walking on a giant synthesiser. These displays are supplemented by regular touring exhibitions. Be warned that the place becomes very busy, especially on rainy days and before about 2pm during the school year, when vast parties of schoolchildren run riot. There's a gift shop and good-value *White Spot Triple O* restaurant-café if you need a retail or refreshment break.

The best things here if you're an adult are the building itself – at least its striking external appearance – and the chance to catch a special-format movie on the vast screen of the **OMNIMAX Cinema** on the third level near the top of the dome. As with all these giant screens, however, the number and variety of films adapted for the format is fairly limited – typically rock concerts and natural-history features. You can catch a glimpse of the building if you don't actually want to step inside by taking one of the ferry mini-cruises from Granville

Island or other points on False Creek served by Aquabus and False Creek Ferries.

Otherwise it's easiest to get here by taking the **SkyTrain** to Main St-Science World. Although relatively close to Chinatown, the museum is not easily reached from there – the roads are busy and the walk is grim – and the place is difficult to fit into a coherent itinerary. It's far more fun to see it as part of a **boat trip** from the island (see p.85), including it with Granville Island on a longer itinerary that also takes you to the nearby museums of Vanier Park (see pp.92–94) and perhaps Kitsilano and Kits Beach. Vanier Park can be reached either by ferry or by walking from Granville Island along the False Creek seawall.

Southern Vancouver

S outh of Granville Island and False Creek you enter a part of Vancouver that looks and feels very different from the city's core. Gone, for the most part, are the skyscrapers and glorious views of Downtown; in their place are streets, buildings and panoramas of far less architectural or visual impact – low-rise residential housing, malls and the other staples of suburbia. Save for one or two distinctive sights, this could be just about any suburb of any city in North America.

Much of this part of **southern Vancouver** you can ignore completely, notably the long run of undistinguished residential districts that stretch towards the airport, New Westminster and the Fraser River. The points that will concern you include **Vanier Park**, a big area of grass and trees that's noteworthy as the home to all but one of the city's main museums – the **Vancouver Museum**, the **Maritime Museum** and the H. R. MacMillan **Space Centre**: the last also combines the city's planetarium and observatory. To the west lies the **Kitsilano** district (better known simply as Kits), in its day something of a hippy enclave, but now a leafy and pleasantly gentrified residential area with a good beach and public swimming pool, funky cafés, restaurants, galleries and interesting stores. Further south lie **Queen Elizabeth Park** and **VanDusen Garden**, greenspaces that enliven the sprawl of the area's suburbs, and – to the west – the University of British Columbia (UBC) and its surroundings (see p.100). However, you're as likely to visit this area for its **beaches** (see box, p.92) as its sights, which stretch around much of the peninsula's northern shore from the busy but appealing Kits Beach in the east to the laid-back clothing-optional Wreck Beach on the western fringe of the UBC campus (covered on p.106 in Chapter Six).

You could easily incorporate a visit to the area's museums with a trip to Granville Island (see p.84), taking the **ferry** from False Creek and the island – it docks just below the Maritime Museum. Coming from Downtown, take the #22 Macdonald **bus** south from anywhere on Burrard or West Pender – get off at the first stop after the bridge and walk west a short distance on Cornwall Street and take the first right north on Chester Street to the park and museums.

Alternatively, walk or cycle the Seawall from Granville Island to Vanier Park and the rest of Kits. Don't tackle too much, however – certainly not the UBC and its Museum of Anthropology (see p.101), which you'll probably want to keep for another day.

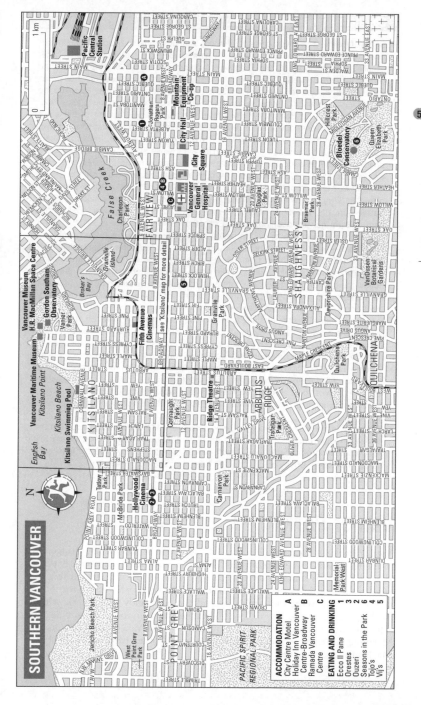

SOUTHERN VANCOUVER

N

1 km

0

ACCOMMODATION

City Centre Motel — A
Holiday Inn Vancouver
Centre-Broadway — B
Ramada Vancouver
Centre — C

EATING AND DRINKING

Ecco Il Pane — 1
Orestes — 3
Ouzeri — 2
Seasons in the Park — 6
Tojo's — 4
Vij's — 5

POINT GREY

PACIFIC SPIRIT REGIONAL PARK

West Point Grey Park

Jericho Beach Park

English Bay

Kitsilano Beach
Kitsilano Swimming Pool

Vancouver Maritime Museum
Kitsilano Point

Vancouver Museum
H.R. MacMillan Space Centre
Gordon Southam Observatory

Pacific Central Station

False Creek

Charleson Park

Granville Island

Broker's Bay

Vanier Park

Fifth Avenue Cinemas

KITSILANO

Hollywood Cinema

Ridge Theatre

ARBUTUS RIDGE

Tatlow Park

McBride Park

Connaught Park

Carnarvon Park

Trafalgar Park

Granville Park

Devonshire Park

VanDusen Botanical Gardens

SHAUGHNESSY

Braemar Park

Quilchena Park

WEST QUILCHENA

Memorial Park West

FAIRVIEW

City Hall

City Square

Mountain Equipment Co-op

Jonathan Rogers Park

Vancouver General Hospital

Douglas Park

Hillcrest Park

Bloedel Conservatory

Queen Elizabeth Park

91

Southern Vancouver's beaches

Some of the most tempting parts of southern Vancouver are its beaches, and in particular **Kitsilano Beach**, or "Kits Beach", named – like the district behind it – after Chief Khahtsahlanough (or Khahtsahlano), a Squamish chieftain of a band who once owned the area. It is edged by Cornwall Avenue west from Arbutus Street as far as Trafalgar Street, and you can take the 30-minute walk here from Vanier Park and the Vancouver and Maritime museums on the coast path or, from Downtown, take a #22 bus southbound on Burrard Street. Kits is the hippest and busiest of the city's beaches, especially popular with the university volleyball and rippling-torso crowd, as well as the more well-heeled locals. Families also come here, though, to take advantage of the warm and safe swimming area, while sunbathers can take up a position on the grass to the rear. There's a tremendous range of cafés and takeaway food outlets on Cornwall Avenue and, to a slightly lesser extent, on Yew Street.

At the western end of Kits Beach you'll find the world's largest outdoor **saltwater pool** (at 137m), at Yew and Cornwall (late-May to mid-June Mon–Fri noon–8.45pm, Sat & Sun 10am–8.45pm; mid-June–mid-Sept Mon–Fri 7–9am for adults only, 9am–8.45pm general opening, Sat & Sun 10am–8.45pm; $4.15; ☎604/731-0011) but easily reached if you're on the beach already by walking along the beachfront promenade: it is Vancouver's most popular outdoor heated pool. The shoreline path linking Kits Beach with other points east and west is a lovely place for an evening stroll, a bike ride or simply a place to take time out on a bench to watch the streetlife. Follow the path all the way east and it takes you to Granville Island by way of Vanier Park and the museums. The bars and restaurants of Kits fuel something of a party spirit on the beach, and there's always plenty going on.

Jericho Beach, west of Kits and handy for the youth hostel, is a touch quieter and serves as a hangout for the windsurfing crowd. Still further west, Jericho blurs into **Locarno Beach** and **Spanish Banks**, progressively less crowded, and the start of a fringe of sand and parkland that continues round to the University of British Columbia (UBC) campus. Locals rate Spanish Banks the most relaxed of the city's beaches, while Locarno is one of its most spectacular, especially at low tide, when the sand seems to stretch for ever. Bikers and walkers use the dirt track above Locarno, beyond which a broad sward of grass with picnic tables and benches runs to the road.

At low tide the more athletically inclined could walk all the way round to UBC (otherwise take the bus as for the Museum of Anthropology; see p.100), where the famous clothing-optional Wreck Beach (see p.106) lies just off the campus area below NW Marine Drive.

Vanier Park

Vanier Park sits on the waterfront at the west end of the Burrard Bridge, close to the residential and entertainment centres of West 4th Avenue and Kitsilano. The park itself is unremarkable, with large areas of open grass and few trees (and so offers little shade on a hot day), and is not worth visiting for its own sake unless you want some fresh air and the odd sandy little beach without trekking all the way to Kits or Jericho beaches. Its main role is to provide a setting for two of Vancouver's main museums – the Vancouver Museum and Maritime Museum – and the planetarium and other exhibits of the H. R. MacMillan Space Centre.

The Vancouver Museum

Founded in 1894, the **Vancouver Museum** (Mon–Wed & Fri–Sun 10am–5pm, Thurs 10am–9pm; $10; ☎604/736-4431, ⊛www.vanmuseum .bc.ca) in Vanier Park at 1100 Chestnut St is Canada's largest civic museum. The museum's purpose is to trace the history of the city and the lower British Columbian mainland. Its flying-saucer shaped building dates from 1968, when the museum moved to the park, and is a nod to the conical cedar-bark hats of the Haida and other aboriginal peoples, the area's earliest inhabitants. The strange fountain outside recalls the crab-like animal of native legend that guards the entrance to the city's harbour. By neat coincidence, it also evokes the astrological sign corresponding to July 1, Canada's birthday.

Though it's the main focus of interest at Vanier Park, the museum is not as captivating as you'd expect from a city of Vancouver's size and status. Though it claims to hold 300,000 exhibits, it's hard to know where they could all be, and a visit needn't take more than an hour or so. All this should change, as a multimillion-dollar refurbishment is on the cards that should give the museum more focus, a clearer chronological approach to the history of the city, and modern presentational devices that bring the museum into line with state-of-the-art museums such as Victoria's far superior Royal British Columbia Museum (see p.227).

As it is, the museum features a patchy collection of baskets, tools, clothes and miscellaneous artefacts of aboriginal peoples – including a huge whaling canoe, the only example of such a vessel in a museum – covering the 8000 years of native history before the arrival of white settlers. After this, the main collection weaves in and out of Vancouver's history up to World War I, full of offbeat and occasionally memorable insights if you have the patience to read the accompanying briefs. Some of the best of these are the accounts of early explorers' often extraordinary exploits – notably those of Simon Fraser (see p.262), the displays concerned with forestry and the lumber industry, and the immigration section, which re-creates what it felt like to travel in steerage, the cheapest class in the transatlantic boats that brought settlers to North America from Europe. The section of the chronological displays devoted to the twentieth-century is disappointing, at least for visitors coming from Europe where the artefacts on display are pretty commonplace – for the most part exhibits such as furniture and kitchen utensils would look more at home in an antique shop than a museum. Again, this may well change when the museum has undergone its refurbishment.

The H. R. MacMillan Space Centre

The **H. R. MacMillan Space Centre**, also known as the Pacific Space Centre (July–Aug daily 10am–5pm, Sept–June Tues–Sun 10am–5pm; evening laser shows at varying times Thurs–Sun; Space Centre $13.50, additional Virtual Voyage rides $6; evening laser shows $9.35; ☎604/738-7827, ⊛www .hrmacmillanspacecentre.com), incorporates the MacMillan Planetarium and a range of space-related displays and shows. Like the Vancouver Museum – to which it is close – it lies in Vanier Park and can be accessed at 1100 Crescent St or from the small ferry landing in the park. Its main draws are its star shows – the standard planetarium fare – and very loud, very brash evening laser and music extravaganzas. These are held in the H. R. MacMillan Star Theatre – there's an extra charge for the evening shows, but the 40-minute star shows (held several times daily, usually in the afternoon) are included in the general admission. The evening shows are very popular, so arrive in good time or make reservations.

Many of the centre's exhibits are high-tech and hands-on, especially in the Cosmic Courtyard, where interactive displays allow you to battle an alien, design a spaceship, guide a lunar robot or plan a voyage to Mars. Many displays also involve lots of impressive computer and other audiovisual effects, notably the Virtual Voyages Simulator, a flight simulator complete with the "motion" you might encounter during space travel and other journeys. The "rides" on the simulator last about five minutes (entrance is included with admission) and experiences range from collisions with a comet to trips on a rollercoaster and simulated space flights to the planets. The GroundStation Canada Theatre shows 20-minute films on various aspects of space roughly hourly from mid-morning.

The **Gordon Southam Observatory**, the small domed building close to the Space Centre, has a telescope that is usually available for public stargazing on clear weekend nights (call Space Centre or ☎604/736-2655 for current times); astronomers are on hand to show you the ropes and help you position your camera for a "Shoot the Moon" photography session of the heavens ($10).

The Maritime Museum

After the space-age look and high-tech displays of the Space Centre, the rather dated appearance of Vancouver's **Maritime Museum** (May–Sept daily 10am–5pm, Oct–April Tues–Sat 10am–5pm, Sun noon–5pm; $8; ☎604/257-8300, ⓦwww.vmm.bc.ca) is likely to come as a disappointing jolt. That said, the museum is a great place to bring children and will appeal if you have any feeling at all for ships and the sea. It is also close to the waterfront and a small jetty, or Heritage Harbour, used by ferries to and from Granville Island and the rest of False Creek (see p.85). It's also not too big, so there's no danger of museum-fatigue if you're finishing the day here after seeing Vanier Park's other two museums.

The collection itself features such treasures as original charts from George Vancouver's ships, lovely early photographs evoking late nineteenth-century Vancouver, and a vivid reconstruction of a tugboat bridge. Much of the rest of the presentation, however, doesn't quite do justice to the status of the city as one of the world's leading ports. The less-arresting displays, however, are redeemed by the wonderfully renovated 1928 *St Roch*, a Royal Canadian Mounted Police schooner that was the first vessel to navigate the famed Northwest Passage in a single season (see box, p.96) and to circumnavigate North America; a beautiful craft, it now sits in its own wing of the museum, where it can be viewed by guided tour only (tours run roughly every 30 minutes).

Special summer shows and exhibitions spice things up a little, especially for children, as do the Pirates' Cove and Children's Maritime Discovery Centre, full of computers for interactive games and education, model ships, telescopes trained on ships in the harbour and a store of seafaring costumes for dressing up. Outside, just north of the museum on **Heritage Harbour** (the quay for ferries to and from Granville Island), you can admire, free of charge, more restored old-fashioned vessels.

△ The Bloedel Conservatory in winter

The St Roch and the Northwest Passage

The Maritime Museum's star turn is the *St Roch*, celebrated as the first craft to make a single-season traverse of the fabled **Northwest Passage** around the American continent. This sea route continues to exert a romantic allure – and, in the wake of oil discoveries in the far north, an increasingly economic attraction as well. Crossed in its entirety fewer than fifty times, it is the world's severest maritime challenge, involving a 1500-kilometre voyage from north of Baffin Island west of Greenland to the Beaufort Sea above Alaska. Some 50,000 icebergs constantly line the eastern approaches and thick pack ice covers the route for nine months of the year, with temperatures rising above freezing only in July and August. Perpetual darkness reigns for four months of the year, and thick fog and blizzards can obscure visibility for the remaining eight months. Even with modern technology navigation is almost impossible: a magnetic compass is useless as the magnetic north lies in the passage, and a gyro compass is unreliable at high latitudes; little is known of Arctic tides and currents; sonar is confused by submerged ice; and the featureless tundra of the Arctic islands provides the only few points of visual or radar reference.

John Cabot can hardly have been happy with his order from Henry VII in **1497** to blaze the northwest trail, the first recorded instance of such an attempt. The elusive passage subsequently excited the imagination of the world's greatest adventurers, men such as **Sir Francis Drake**, **Jacques Cartier**, **Sir Martin Frobisher**, **James Cook** and **Henry Hudson** – cast adrift by his mutinous crew in 1611 when the Hudson Bay turned out to be an icebound trap rather than the passage.

Details of a possible route were pieced together over the centuries, though many paid with their lives in the process, most famously **Sir John Franklin**, who vanished into the ice with 129 men in 1845. Many rescue parties set out to find Franklin's vessels, HMS *Erebus* and HMS *Terror*, and it was one searcher, **Robert McClure**, who – in the broadest sense – made the first northwest passage in 1854. Entering the passage from the west, he was trapped for two winters, and then sledged to meet a rescue boat coming from the east. The **first sea crossing**, however, was achieved by the Norwegian **Roald Amundsen** in 1906, following a three-year voyage. Then came the successful *St Roch* voyage, led by a Canadian Mountie, **Henry Larsen**, in 1944. More recently, huge icebreakers have explored the potential of cracking a commercial route through the ice mainly for the export of oil from the Alaskan and new Beaufort fields and for the exploitation of minerals in Canada's Arctic north.

Kitsilano

The district of **Kitsilano** was named by the Canadian Pacific Railway, which – inevitably – had acquired most of the local land by the last decade of the nineteenth century. It half-heartedly acknowledged the area's previous aboriginal owners by adapting the name of Khahtsahlanough (or Khahtsahlano), a former chief of the aboriginal village, Sun'ahk, which stood on the site until its inhabitants were "dispersed" in 1901.

Kits has long been a desirable place to live, with its attractive 1920s houses and well-built apartment blocks. Attracting hippies and other counterculture types in the 1960s, it became Vancouver's equivalent of Notting Hill or Haight-Ashbury. Today's younger hipsters head for Yaletown, or the more gritty Commercial Drive to the east, but Kits is still hugely popular, thanks to the pleasant laid-back atmosphere that has survived from times past, and to an extremely healthy arts, culture and nightlife scene – the area has a plethora of good cafés, bars and restaurants, as well as interesting stores and galleries. These

KITSILANO

0   500 m

English Bay

ACCOMMODATION
Mickey's Kits
Beach Chalet   **A**

EATING AND DRINKING

Bin 941	**5**	Picasso Café	**10**
Bishop's	**4**	Planet Veg	**1**
Capers	**3**	Sophie's	
Flying Wedge	**2**	Cosmic Café	**6**
Lumière	**9**	Topanga Café	**7**
The Naam	**8**		

are dotted around the district, but for a good feel of the area, explore the streets on and around West Fourth Avenue.

Demand for property is outstripping supply, and the Kits effect is rippling outwards – real-estate brokers now talk of "Upper Kits" to describe more peripheral districts of what is anyway a loosely defined area – but the original area's borders are roughly Alma and Burrard streets to the west and east and the ocean and West 16th Avenue to the north and south. The district's young, reasonably moneyed and relaxed feel is epitomized by **Kits Beach**, the most popular of the city's beaches – there's a good hostel nearby (see p.140) if you want to hang out here and aren't too worried about the journey to Downtown.

Southern Vancouver's parks and gardens

Southern Vancouver's mostly residential suburban spaces south of Kits and Vanier Park have next to nothing to see, and, were it not for the presence of two of the city's major greenspaces, would be an area you would probably only visit in passing on your way to or from the airport. **Queen Elizabeth Park** is the larger of the two spaces, and while lacking the ocean-fringed setting of Stanley Park, or the wilderness of the North Shore's provincial parks, still attracts some six million visitors a year. The **VanDusen Botanical Garden** is smaller and, as its name suggests, has a more focused horticultural ambition than its near neighbour, but ranks as one of the continent's finest botanical gardens.

Queen Elizabeth Park

Queen Elizabeth Park (Bloedel Floral Conservatory open April to early Sept Mon–Fri 9am–8pm, Sat & Sun 10am–9pm; Oct & Feb–March daily 10am–5.30pm; Nov–Jan daily 10am–5pm; park free, conservatory $4; ☎604/257-8584 or 257-8570, ⓦwww.city.vancouver.bc.ca/parks) lies between Cambie St and Ontario St and W 29th Ave and W 37th Ave. It barely holds its own with Stanley Park – but then few parks do – yet still merits a visit if you're in this part of the city and relish the idea of a spacious, pretty and well-landscaped garden. It also lures visitors with its most distinctive attraction, the **Bloedel Floral Conservatory** (ⓦwww.bloedelconservatory.com), an indoor space at 33rd Ave at Cambie St that replicates the climate, flora and some of the fauna of desert, subtropical and rainforest habitats. The Floral Conservatory commands a 360-degree view of the city, and features 500 varieties of exotic plants and fifty species of birds. You'll also find many of the trappings of an urban park, including tennis courts, pitch-and-putt golf, lawn bowling, a roller-hockey court, Frisbee golf, a basketball area and the Nat Bailey Stadium, a fine place – evening or afternoon – to watch the city's Vancouver Canadians baseball team play (see p.204): the stadium's on the east side of the park at Ontario Street and 29th Avenue. **Bus #15** will get you here: it runs the length of Cambie from Pender in Downtown.

The 53-hectare **garden**, Vancouver's third largest, sits on the panoramic **Little Mountain**, the stump of an old volcano and the highest point on the south side of the city (153m). A winding road spirals gently up its slopes, passing through an arboretum en route to the summit. On the eastern slopes, in particular, you'll find examples of virtually every native British Columbian tree and shrub. The summit is partly taken up by two former quarries, originally used for building Vancouver's roads and by the Canadian Pacific Railway during the construction of the transcontinental railway at the end of the nineteenth century. The CPR offered the quarries to the city's parks department in 1919, but it was turned down, only passing to the city ten years later, by which time it was an eyesore, and derelict but for two holding reservoirs which provided some of the city's drinking water.

Both of these were reworked and landscaped after 1930 as the **Quarry Gardens**, vast rock gardens filled with flowers and shrubs, and dotted with ponds, fountains and tinkling waterfalls. Don't be surprised at weekends if you have to thread your way through wedding parties waiting to be photographed – it's not unknown for numerous pairs of newlyweds and friends to be here smiling for the camera in high season.

The quarries form part of the park's varied history, the area having started life in the 1870s as a timber camp. It then served as a dairy farm and Chinese vegetable garden before the quarries were worked in the first years of the twentieth century to provide stone for the large number of roads then being built in a nascent Vancouver. The area's transformation into a park was completed on the occasion of a visit by Britain's King George VI and Queen Elizabeth in 1939.

Bloedel Floral Conservatory

At the top of the Little Mountain, the **Bloedel Floral Conservatory**, a 43-metre-diameter dome made up of 1500 Plexiglas bubbles that presents a wonderful medley of sights, sounds and smells as you walk from the heat and humidity of a rainforest through subtropical habitats to end up in the dry heat of near desert. The bulk of the money ($1.25 million) required to build the dome came from the lumber industrialist Prentice Bloedel – ironically, given the timber industry's effect on the British Columbian landscape elsewhere. Around 500 species of plants from across the globe are collected within the dome, together with about 100 free-flying birds (around fifty species in all), among them numerous noisy and vividly coloured parrots. Close to the conservatory are various pieces of large-scale sculptural art, including Henry Moore's aptly titled *Knife Edge – Two Piece*, also donated by Prentice Bloedel. Close to the conservatory, and a pretty place to **eat** lunch or dinner, is the *Seasons* restaurant, West 33rd Ave and Cambie (☎604/874-8008 or 1-800/632-9422), where virtually every table has a view over the gardens to the city beyond. It's especially popular for brunch at weekends, and three fireplaces allow for outdoor eating on the terrace year round.

VanDusen Botanical Garden

Anyone with even remotely green fingers should visit the 22-hectare **VanDusen Botanical Garden** (daily: June–mid-Aug 10am to 9pm, May & mid-Aug–early Sept 10am–8pm, early Sept to end of Sept & April 10am–6pm, Jan–March & Oct–Dec 10am–4pm; April–Sept $7.50, Oct–March $5; ☎604/878-9274, ⓦwww.vandusengarden.org) at 5251 Oak St (at the corner of 37th Ave, between Oak and Granville) which is that rarest of things – a former golf course that became a piece of useful landscape. *Horticulture* magazine rates it – deservedly – as one of the world's top-ten botanical gardens, though the UBC Botanical Garden (see p.105) also has its fans among Vancouverites. It's easily seen, especially if you're also visiting Queen Elizabeth Park, as it lies on Oak Street just a few blocks west of its larger neighbour. If you're coming from Downtown, take **bus** #17, which runs the length of Oak.

The garden was a CPR-owned mess of bush and tree stumps in 1910, when it was leased to the Shaughnessy Golf Club, which remained in residence until 1960. It opened as a garden in 1975 and features many thousands of trees, shrubs and plants from around the world, all of which are well-labelled, making the tranquil walkways and shrubberies an education as well as a pleasure. Pick up a pamphlet which describes a self-guided tour of the garden at the entrance or join a guided tour: the latter generally run each afternoon in summer, weather allowing, but you should call for latest times and details. Various parts of the gardens are themed – there's a Rose Garden, Lake Garden and Rhododendron Walk, for example – but the trees and flowerbeds are designed so that there's something worthwhile to see every month of the year. One of the most popular areas, at least among children, is the **Elizabethan Hedge Maze**, made up of around a thousand pyramid cedars – each is only 1.5m high so that adults can keep track of their children's progress, or lack of it, from a grassy knoll nearby.

Events are held in the garden throughout the year, among them a major Flower and Garden Show, usually in the first week of June, and the Christmas Festival of Lights, when thousands of tiny lights illuminate the gardens. For more information, see Chapter 18, "Festivals and events".

The University of British Columbia

Though the **University of British Columbia** (UBC) might seem an unlikely point of interest, its world-class **Museum of Anthropology** is by far the best of the city's museums and galleries. The museum is devoted largely to the art and culture of the aboriginal peoples of the Pacific Northwest coast, highlighted by a sensational collection of totems and large-scale carved works.

Home to some 37,000 students, the vast 402-hectare campus is 13km from the city centre, and is located on the western edge of a large peninsula fringed by English Bay. Given the time you'll need to devote to reaching the site – allow at least thirty minutes by bus, car or taxi from Downtown (see below for transport details) – it's well worth taking in some of the other sights on and around the campus. If time is short, you should see two fine gardens – the beautiful **Botanical Garden** and smaller Japanese-style **Nitobe Memorial Garden**. On a longer trip, you might want to come prepared for a spell on the popular **Wreck Beach**, a stretch of sand infamous for its clothing-optional policy on sunbathing. If you want to swim in more decorous surroundings, the UBC Aquatic Centre is open to the public (see p.203).

If you have transport, or have cycled to the campus, then you might also want to explore the **University Endowment Lands**. This huge area includes the campus, but is also a domain of large tracts of forest and semi-wilderness. Much the same can be said of the countryside to the Lands' southeast, a protected 763-hectare area known as **Pacific Spirit Regional Park**, created in 1988 and almost twice the size of Stanley Park. Note that you *will* need transport to access these – you can't come to the UBC campus and easily walk to, or explore, the park or the Endowment Lands.

Getting to the UBC and the Museum of Anthropology

To get to the **UBC** and the **Museum of Anthropology** by **bus**, catch the #4 or #10 south from Granville Street and stay on until the end of the line, the "University Loop", near the centre of the campus. Other Downtown services include the #44 from Waterfront Station, or buses #9, #25, #41, #49, #99, #258 or #480 from various points in the city.

To reach the museum, turn right from the bus stop, walk along the tree-lined East Mall for about ten minutes, then turn left on NW Marine Drive and walk until you see the museum building signposted on the right (about another 5min).

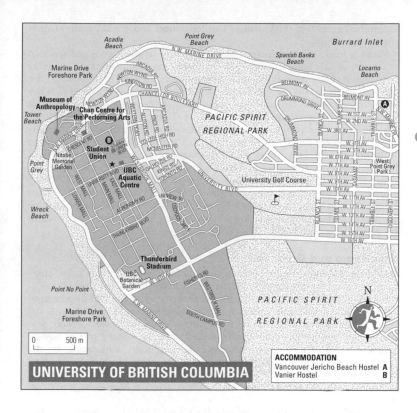

ACCOMMODATION
Vancouver Jericho Beach Hostel **A**
Vanier Hostel **B**

UNIVERSITY OF BRITISH COLUMBIA

0   500 m

To get here by **car**, the easiest route is to drive west along 4th Avenue – which becomes Chancellor Boulevard and then NW Marine Drive – until you reach the campus. Watch on the right for a sign indicating the museum car park.

The Museum of Anthropology

The superlative **Museum of Anthropology** (mid-May to early Sept Mon & Wed–Sun 10am–5pm, Tues 10am–9pm; early Sept to mid-May Tues 11am–9pm, Wed–Sun 11am–5pm; $9, free Tues 5–9pm; ☎604/822-5087, ⓦwww.moa.ubc.ca) at 6393 NW Marine Drive is devoted to the art and culture of the aboriginal peoples of the Pacific Northwest, and the Haida in particular. Its collection of carvings, totem poles and artefacts is unequalled in North America, and the superb modern galleries also feature artefacts from other aboriginal cultures. Not the least of the museum's attractions is its architectural élan, the building's modern and uncluttered appearance providing a perfect setting for its often ancient, strange and shamanistic works of art.

The university began its ethnographical collection – which now numbers 535,000 objects in its entirety – in 1927, but a museum to store them only started life in the late 1940s as an ad hoc arrangement in the basement of the university's main library. The present building was made possible by a grant from the federal government in 1971 to mark the centennial of British

Columbia's entry into the Canadian Confederation. Today, it is Canada's largest teaching museum.

Much is made of the museum's award-winning layout, a cool and spacious collection of halls completed in 1976 to a design by Arthur Erickson, the eminent architect also responsible, among many other projects, for converting the city's courthouse into the Vancouver Art Gallery. While the Great Hall is the most striking part of the building , one of its architectural highlights comes at the start, the vast entrance doors, carved in 1976 by four aboriginal sculptors. The doors' reliefs represent narrative episodes from the mythology of the aboriginal peoples of the Skeena Valley in central British Columbia. The entrance is flanked by cedar panels that mimic the shape of the traditional Salish "Bent boxes", simple rectangular cedar boxes with heavy lids. The two figures in red cedar at the top of the stairs outside represent the *Ancestor Figure* (1997) by Musqueam artist Susan Point – it holds a "fisher", a creature believed to have healing powers – and the *Welcome Figure* (1984) by Nuu-chah-nulth sculptor Joe David, carved in protest at logging on Meares Island off the west coast of his native Vancouver Island.

The Ramp and Great Hall

Inside, the **Ramp**, or walkway from the entrance, contains many large sculptures removed for safe-keeping in the 1950s from the cedar plank houses of British Columbia's aboriginal peoples. Some were decorative, and stood against interior and exterior walls; others served as massive posts to support roofs and other structural beams. Sculptures from houses of coastal peoples usually represent forebears, or powerful figures linked with the history of the houses' inhabitants. The sculptures are arranged geographically, with works by the Coast Salish (Musqueam, Saanich and Tsartlip) on both sides and, lower down on the left, works by northern peoples such as the Haida, Gitxsan (or Tsimshian) and Nisga'a. The gorgeous blanket here is a Musqueam work dating from 1997.

Still more outstanding is the remarkable **Great Hall**, the museum's centrepiece, a vast, airy space inspired by aboriginal "post and beam" cedar longhouses, which makes a perfect artificial setting – given that conservation concerns mean they can't be outdoors as they often should be – for the museum's thirty-odd **totem poles**. Though the exhibits themselves have very little by way of information, there is an information desk near the entrance, along with sourcebooks with photographic and written essays on aspects of Pacific Northwest aboriginal art and culture.

From the Great Hall, enormous 15-metre-high windows look out to the **museum grounds** where there are more poles and a re-created nineteenth-century Haida village (constructed in 1962), complete with family dwellings, mortuary house and longhouses built along the traditional north-south axis. Even the plants and grasses are those that would have been indigenous to a village of this type. The totems are memorial and mortuary poles, and date from 1951 to the present: the most recent was raised in 2000. You're free to wander around the grounds, something that's worth doing as much for the fabulous views of the ocean and distant mountains as for the exhibits.

Most of the poles and monolithic carvings, indoors and out, are taken from the coastal peoples of the Haida (see box p.104), Salish, Tsimshian and Kwakiutl (see p.267), all of whom have shared cultural elements. Scholars really don't know terribly much about the arcane mythology behind the carvings, but the best guess is that the many different animals correspond to different clans or the creatures after which the clans were named.

The rest of the collection

The museum's third main component is the **50th Anniversary Gallery** (gallery 3), created in 1999 to celebrate the museum's 50th anniversary. Its aim is to highlight the diversity and scope of Northwest Coast aboriginal art, past and present, which it does by combining beautiful examples of contemporary art in a variety of media – wood, textiles, semi-precious stones and so forth - with a range of high-tech interactive displays and computer links.

One of the museum's great virtues is that few of its major displays are hidden away in basements or back rooms; instead they're jammed into drawers and cases in the "Visible Storage Galleries" close to the Great Hall. In all, the collection boasts some 35,000 objects of cultural and archeological note – around half are open to scrutiny. More delicate items such as fabrics and works on paper are not displayed, though many are brought out of safekeeping for occasional exhibitions in the adjacent galleries 5, 8, 9 and 10.

Most of the permanent collection revolves around Canadian Pacific cultures, but the Inuit and Far North exhibits are also outstanding. So, too, are the jewellery, masks and baskets of Northwest aboriginal peoples in the **Masterpiece Gallery**, all strikingly delicate after the blunter and more monumental carvings of the Great Hall. Look out especially for the argillite sculptures of animals and other items, made from a jet-black slate found only on British Columbia's Haida Gwaii, or Queen Charlotte Islands. The **African** and **Asian** collections are also pretty comprehensive, if smaller and far less interesting, but appear as something of an afterthought alongside the indigenous artefacts. A small, more technically minded archeological section rounds off the smaller galleries, along with a three-gallery wing built to house the **Koerner Collection**, a rather incongruous assortment of six hundred European ceramics, dating from the fifteenth century onwards and left by a private collector.

The Raven and the First Men

The museum saves its best single sculpture for last. **The Raven and the First Men** is a modern sculpture designed by the celebrated Haida artist Bill Reid (1920–1998). Housed in a separate rotunda, it's the museum's pride and joy and has achieved almost cult status in the city, where you'll see it on any number of posters and postcards. Carved from a 4.5-tonne block of yellow cedar (made of 106 laminated timbers), the work took over three years to complete and required the almost continuous labours of five assistants.

As beautiful as the work is, however, its rotunda setting makes it seem oddly out of place – almost like a corporate display. The sculpture depicts the Haida legend of human evolution with stunning virtuosity, depicting figures squirming from a half-open clamshell, overseen by an enormous and stern-faced raven, the "trickster" of Haida myth who tempted humanity from its birthplace. Originally, so the legend goes, life began when the raven flew from the heavens to find the earth blanketed in snow. The bird stole the sun from the gods, and forged the rivers, oceans, forests and animals. It then found a clamshell on a beach, and coaxed five men from it with the promise of peace and prosperity. Eventually, it told them where they might find women.

Nitobe Memorial Garden

There are any number of very minor sights dotted around the museum, but they amount to nothing of genuine interest. For the exception, turn right out the front entrance and a five-minute walk brings you to the **Nitobe Memorial Garden** (daily: mid-March–mid-May & Sept–mid-Oct 10am–5pm;

The Haida

The **Haida** are widely considered to have the most highly developed culture and sophisticated art tradition of British Columbia's aboriginal peoples. Extending from the Haida Gwaii (Queen Charlotte Islands) to south Alaska, their lands included major stands of red cedar, the raw material for their huge dug-out **canoes**, intricate **carvings** and refined **architecture**. Haida trade links were built on the reputation of their skill – other British Columbian peoples considering the ownership of a Haida canoe, for example, as a major status symbol. Though renowned as traders and artists, the Haida were also feared **warriors**, paddling into rival villages and returning with canoes laden with goods, slaves and the severed heads of anyone who had tried to resist. Their skill on the open sea has seen them labelled the "Vikings" of the Pacific Northwest. This success at warfare was due, in part, to their use of wooden-slat armour, which included a protective face visor and helmets topped with terrifying images.

Socially the Haida divided themselves into two main groups, the **Eagles** and the **Ravens**, which were further divided into hereditary kin groups named after their original village location. Marriage within each major group, or *moiety*, was considered incestuous, so Eagles would always seek Raven mates and vice versa. Furthermore, descent was traced through the **female line**, which meant that a chief could not pass his property on to his sons because they would belong to a different *moiety* – instead his inheritance passed to his sister's sons. Young men might have to leave their childhood village to claim their inheritance from their maternal uncles.

Haida **villages** were an impressive sight, their vast cedar-plank houses dominated by fifteen-metre **totem poles** displaying the kin group's unique animal crest or other mythical creatures, all carved in elegantly fluid lines. Entrance to each house was through the gaping mouth of a massive carved figure; inside, supporting posts were carved into the forms of the crest animals and most household objects were similarly decorative. Equal elaboration attended the many Haida ceremonies, one of the most important of which was the **mortuary potlatch**, serving as a memorial service to a dead chief and as the validation of the heir's right to succession. The dead individual was laid out at the top of a carved pole near the village entrance, past which the visiting chiefs would walk wearing robes of finely woven and patterned mountain-goat wool and immense headdresses fringed with long sea-lion whiskers and ermine skins. A hollow at the top of each headdress was filled with eagle feathers, which floated down onto the witnesses as the chiefs sedately danced.

After **European contact** the Haida population was devastated by smallpox and other epidemics. In 1787, there were around 8000 Haida scattered across the archipelago. Their numbers were then reduced from around 6000 in 1835 to 588 by 1915. Consequently they were forced to abandon their traditional villages and today gather largely at two sites on the Haida Gwaii. At other locations the homes and totems fell into disrepair, and only at **Sgan Gwaii**, a remote village at the southern tip of the Haida Gwaii, has an attempt been made to preserve an original Haida settlement; the village is now a UNESCO World Heritage Site.

These days the Haida number around 2000, and are highly regarded in the North American art world; the late Bill Reid is among the tribe's best-known figures, and scores of other Haida craftspeople produce carvings and jewellery for the tourist market. They also play a powerful role in the Haida Gwaii's social, political and cultural life, having been vocal in the formation of protected sites such as the Gwaii Haanas National Park Reserve and other important aboriginal sites of historical and cultural significance.

mid-May–Aug 10am–6pm; mid-Oct–mid-March Mon–Fri 10am–2.30pm; $3 or $6 with the Botanical Garden, free mid-Oct–mid-March; ☎604/822-6038, ⓦwww.nitobe.org), a small Japanese garden near Gate 4, Memorial Rd, off West Mall that is good for a few minutes of peace and floral admiration.

Begun some forty years ago, it was created to honour Inazo Nitobe (1862–1933), who strove to improve trans-Pacific relations, and is considered the world's most authentic Japanese garden outside Japan – despite its use of many non-Japanese species. The garden is full of gently curving paths, trickling streams and waterfalls, as well as numerous rocks, trees and shrubs placed with precision and according to the balanced principles of Yin and Yang. It divides into the **Tea Garden**, whose arrangement is designed to inspire peaceful introspection, and the **Stroll Garden**, whose design follows the shape of the Milky Way and symbolizes a journey through life from youth to old age.

The UBC Botanical Garden

Almost directly opposite the Nitobe Garden, at 16th Ave and 6804 SW Marine Drive lies the larger **UBC Botanical Garden** (daily mid-March–mid-Oct 10am–6pm; rest of the year 10am–3pm; $4.50 or $6 with Nitobe Garden; ☎604/822-4208, ⓦwww.ubcbotanicalgarden.org), established in 1916 and Canada's oldest botanical garden. It claims some 10,000 different plants, shrubs and trees and consists of eight separate gardens – Alpine, Arbour, Asian, British Columbian Native, Contemporary, Food, Perennial Border and Physic. Horticultural experts rate this as better than the VanDusen Botanical Garden (see p.99), because its layout is more subtle and its displays better-organized: non-experts will find both gardens equally attractive. Also on site is the **Botanical Garden Centre**, with a shop that stocks one of the city's best selection of gardening books and gardening implements, as well as some of the rarer or more unusual plants and shrubs from the garden.

The Gardens

Non-gardeners will probably be most interested in the obviously impressive swaths of shrubs and stands of vast trees in the **David C Lam Asian Garden**. Surrounded by second-growth fir, cedar and hemlock, this, the largest of the gardens, is home to four hundred varieties of rhododendrons – more than any other Canadian garden and best seen in May. It also features roses, flowering vines, magnolias, hydrangeas and floral rarities such as blue Himalayan poppy and giant Himalayan lily.

The **Physic Garden** is a re-created sixteenth-century monastic herb garden, and though there are some macabre poisonous plants here, most of the flora are actually medicinal. Many of the plants were taken from the similar Chelsea Physick Garden in London, which in turn collected plants from Britain's Tudor and other medieval periods. Plants include foxgloves, which provide the heart remedies digitoxin and digoxin, and periwinkle, used in the treatment of leukaemia. Interpretative panels give you information about these and other plants, including those used to treat "violent blood" or "angry snake bite", and those used to make teas or grown to be strewn on the ground and in rooms to sweeten the often fetid air of medieval interiors.

The sloping four-hectare **British Columbia Native Garden** shelters some 3500 plants and flowers found across British Columbia in a variety of bog, marsh and other habitats – everything from coastal rainforest species to the flora of the arid semi-desert of the interior. The one-hectare **E H Lohbrunner Alpine Garden** manages to coax rare alpine varieties from five continents to grow at some 2000m lower than their preferred altitude, while the **Food Garden** produces a cornucopia of fruit and vegetables from a remarkably restricted area. It has some intriguing rarities – check out the strange apple-like espalier fruit, for example; the entire crop is donated to charity.

It's well worth taking one of the guided tours to spot things you might otherwise miss: the **tours** generally run once daily a couple of times a week; call the garden for latest details. Note that if you visit the Botanical Garden in winter you won't be disappointed, for there's even a special Winter Garden full of plants and shrubs adapted to seasonal cold.

Wreck Beach

Wreck Beach, about a kilometre south of the Nitobe garden, is well known in Vancouver mainly because it's a pristine patch of sand where, in Summer, you can strip off as many clothes as you like. In the past, the nakedness was a touch half-hearted and sporadic, and invited a fair amount of prudish tut-tutting. These days, the nudity is pretty much accepted and attitudes are more relaxed. The beach becomes fairly crowded and commercialized in summer, but there are plenty of driftwood logs and fallen tree trunks on the sand which allow you to lay claim to a private patch of sand.

The beach's reputation shouldn't hide the fact that it's also a very beautiful and broad strand, edged by the ocean on one side (with many shallow and often warm pools) and bordered by lofty trees on three other flanks. It's also well looked after, thanks to the Wreck Beach Preservation Society (Ⓦwww.wreckbeach.org), which, among other things, organizes beach events and prevents the commercial side of things getting out of hand. This means occasionally reining in the many food-sellers, body-painters, beach-casino operators and the like, though attitudes to all and sundry are pretty relaxed. For more on **nudism** in Vancouver, incidentally, visit Ⓦwww.vantan.ca.

Access is from SW Marine Drive near Gate 6 at the foot of University Boulevard. The beach can be a little tricky to find, but plenty of well-worn tracks, including numbered trails #3, #4 and #6, lead down the steep slopes above the beach, and just about any student on the campus will be able to point you in the right direction. On a busy summer day, you won't be able to miss the access, for parked cars are jammed bumper to bumper on SW Marine Drive above the trails to the beach.

Trail #4 leads down to Tower Beach to the north of Wreck Beach from Gate 4 a short distance south of the museum and before the Nitobe Garden. The best of the Wreck Beach sand is below trail #6, the trailhead for which you'll find just beyond the Nitobe Garden heading away from the Museum of Anthropology. To the south of this is the North Arm breakwater, separating the beach from log-booming grounds further to the south and east. The trailhead for #7, further round SW Marine Drive still, at the junction, leads to the Old Wreck Beach Trail, which runs south and west round the peninsula for a look at the uncommercialized section of the beach.

Pacific Spirit Regional Park

If you're out at the university and wish to hike or mountain bike in quiet but not terribly spectacular surroundings, take advantage of the **University Endowment Lands** and **Pacific Spirit Regional Park**, the latter on the east side of the campus. A huge tract of wild parkland – larger than Stanley Park, but visited by relatively few people – the non-campus part of the

Endowment Lands boasts 48km of trails and offers the chance to spot wildlife such as blacktail deer, otters, foxes and bald eagles. Best of all, there are few signs of human presence – no benches or snack bars, just the occasional signpost. The area was heavily logged at the start of the twentieth century, but much of the forest has regenerated

Much the same goes for 763-hectare Pacific Spirit Regional Park, the largest greenspace in the city, which until 1989 formed part of the Endowment Lands. It's an area that offers a combination of forest, foreshore and other natural habitats, and has 53km of walking, cycling, jogging and equestrian trails, most of them pretty flat. All the trails are well marked and signposted, so there's little chance of getting lost. If you do wander off-track, three major roads bisect the park to provide points of reference; park wardens also patrol the area. Note that after conflict between hikers and bikers (the park is especially popular with the latter), various trails have been set aside for hiking only, with 35km of mixed-use trails and 18km just for walkers.

If you have time to walk just one trail, plump for the **Swordfern Trail** (trail #24) in the park's southwest corner. It runs through typical British Columbia fir and cedar forest and starts from SW Marine Drive opposite the parking area and Simon Fraser Monument, the latter a memorial to the explorer who sailed down the river that bears his name in 1808. A trail from the road on the same side as the monument drops steeply through ancient forest towards the Fraser for views of the gargantuan log booms on the river – the largest such booms in Canada.

While you really need transport to access much of the park – or to give yourself a choice of trails – you can approach close to the park with public transport by taking the #4 or #10 **bus** towards the UBC (see p.100) and getting off at Blanca Street and W 16th Avenue, close to the park's main access points and 400m from the **Park Centre** (Mon–Fri 8am–4pm; ℗604/224-5739 or 432-6350) at 4915 W 16th Ave. The centre has trail maps and provides information on some of the park's key habitats, most notably the **Camosun Bog**, a rare wetland with its own distinctive flora and fauna: it's accessed by boardwalk from Camosun Street and West 19th Avenue.

North Vancouver

Norht Vancouver – or North Van as it's generally known – embraces most of the mountains, forests and residential districts that you see as you gaze across the Burrard Inlet from Vancouver's Downtown peninsula. The area contains some compelling sights, but the journey to North Van itself – preferably by SeaBus (see p.29) – is almost as alluring as anything you'll see when you get there, thanks to the mesmerizing views of the Downtown skyline and teeming port, a side of the city that's otherwise easily missed.

If you've no time or heart for longer trips to North Van, then you should at least make this crossing, spending an hour or so at Lonsdale Quay before catching the SeaBus back to Downtown. Lonsdale Quay is the SeaBus terminal on the north shore, home to a fine food and general market, somewhere that is well worth seeing but suffers by comparison with the even more impressive market on Granville Island.

Most of North Van is residential – the population of the incorporated City and District is about 48,000 – as is the neighbouring and rather confusingly named **West Vancouver** (West Van), which has a population of around 43,000. Both areas lie north of the Downtown peninsula and make up the so-called **North Shore**, but West Van is the name given to the district roughly west of the Capilano River, an area whose cosseted citizens boast the highest per capita income in Canada. North Van's eastern limit is the vast inlet of Indian Arm.

Few people cross the Burrard Inlet to view these leafy suburbs, however: the real reason to make the crossing is to sample North Vancouver's outstanding areas of natural beauty – Lynn Canyon Park, Grouse Mountain, the Capilano River and its environs, Mount Seymour Provincial Park, Cypress Provincial Park, Lighthouse Park and the Lower Seymour Conservation Reserve.

All the above parks offer fine **hiking** possibilities in summer, as well as **skiing** and winter activities on a range of good trails (see individual entries for some suggestions). However, for a straightforward and dramatic taste of the scenery – or if you only have time for one excursion – then you should make for **Grouse Mountain**, where a cable car whisks you to over 1200m for some superb views of the city and the surrounding area. Your best bet if you have more time and wish to hike is Mount Seymour, which is the closest park to Downtown if you want wild scenery. It is also easily accessible, thanks to the road that runs partway up the mountain. If you're really keen to make the most of the area's natural beauty, stay on the North Shore, where there are a handful of outstanding bed and breakfast options, some close to the major parks (see p.136).

North Vancouver's most advertised sight is the Capilano Suspension Bridge, a commercialized and overrated affair – it's a busy footbridge across a gorge – which you might catch on your return from Grouse Mountain. You might also ignore it completely in favour of the scenery – and an interesting salmon hatchery – elsewhere on the Capilano River. For the best seascapes close to Vancouver, make the longer trip to **Lighthouse Park** on the western tip of the North Shore, full of trails, sea views and magnificent virgin forest.

Vancouver's main visitor centre (see p.23) has plenty of information and accommodation listings for North Van, but you might also want to consult the area's own office, the North Vancouver Visitor Infocentre, 102–124 West 1st St, North Vancouver (☎604/987-4488 or 980-5332, ⓦwww.nvchamber.bc.ca), located just east of the Lonsdale Quay Market.

Some history

As with Downtown, North Vancouver's modern history has its roots in the lumber industry. While the Downtown area can be traced to the creation of Edward Stamp's Hasting Mill in 1865 (see p.264), the North Shore's Pioneer Mills – located around 6km east of the present Lions Gate Bridge – were already in operation three years earlier. The earliest transportation across the Burrard Inlet, aboriginal canoes aside, was provided in 1866 by a rowing boat operated by Jack Thomas, a gravel merchant, who, for a small toll, rowed mill workers to and from Gassy Jack's saloons (see p.63). In 1873 Jack settled in what today is West Vancouver, becoming the North Shore's first permanent white resident. With him was his aboriginal wife, Row'i'a, the granddaughter of Chief Ki'ep'i'lan'o, after whom the Capilano River and other city streets and landmarks are named.

Over the next 25 years, residents of what would become today's Downtown began to cross to the North Shore for picnics – in summer tents would stretch along much of Burrard Inlet shoreline – or to walk and ski on Grouse Mountain. In this they were helped by the inauguration of major ferry servic es to North Van in 1900 and to West Van in 1909. The construction of summer cottages and a few homes followed, but for the most part the area remained the domain of logging, fish canning and other industries. All this changed after about 1938, when the opening of the Lions Gate Bridge provided the spur for the development of the North Shore as a residential alternative to Downtown and the New Westminster suburbs.

If – and only if – the history of the area interests you, then it's worth visiting the small **North Vancouver Museum and Archives** at 209 West 4th St at Chesterfield Ave, four blocks north of Lonsdale Quay and one block west of Lonsdale Avenue (Tues–Sun noon–5pm; free; ☎604/987-5618). There's a range of period memorabilia and aboriginal displays, but the most fascinating exhibits are the many old photographs.

Getting to North Vancouver

The **SeaBus** from Downtown is the best and most practical approach to North Vancouver (see p.29) if you are using public transport (see below for car and bike options). Most of the places covered in this chapter are then accessible by bus or taxi from the bus terminal at Lonsdale Quay (see below), though in some cases you may need to change buses part way through your journey. Remember that if you come to North Van by SeaBus, you can take advantage of your ticket's 90-minute validity for onward bus journeys from Lonsdale Quay – long enough to get you to most of the destinations in this chapter. See p.29 ou don't cross the Burrard Inlet by boat, then there are two other

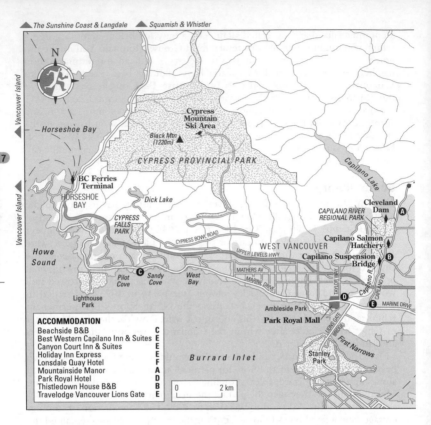

Vancouver Island ◄   *Vancouver Island* ◄   *Vancouver Island* ◄

ACCOMMODATION

Beachside B&B	C
Best Western Capilano Inn & Suites	E
Canyon Court Inn & Suites	E
Holiday Inn Express	E
Lonsdale Quay Hotel	F
Mountainside Manor	A
Park Royal Hotel	D
Thistledown House B&B	B
Travelodge Vancouver Lions Gate	E

approaches by **bus**, **bike** or **car** from Downtown and the south shore of the Burrard Inlet: one is via the Lions Gate Bridge to the west, the other via the Iron Workers Memorial Second Narrows Bridge well to the east. Note that both are busy during rush hours and at weekends. If you have a bike or car, then the Lions Gate crossing leaves you well placed for trips to Grouse Mountain, the Capilano River and Canyon, and Cypress Provincial Park and Lighthouse Park. The Second Narrows crossing is more convenient for Mount Seymour Provincial Park.

Buses across the Lions Gate Bridge are a mixture of TransLink and blue West Van buses. The latter are run by a different company, but accept TransLink tickets. TransLink buses that cross the bridge are the #240, #246, #250, #251, #252 and #257, of which the most convenient are the #240 and #246, both of which you can catch from stops Downtown on Georgia Street. West Van services from Downtown include the blue #241, #247, #253, #254 and #258. Almost immediately across the bridge is a major bus interchange, **Park Royal**, named after the adjoining shopping centre. Note that delays are common on the Lions Gate Bridge, especially during rush hour.

You have less choice of buses across the Second Narrows Bridge – the alternatives are the TransLink #28 and #210 or blue West Van #211, #214, #290 and #292. Almost immediately across this bridge is the third of North Van's

major bus interchanges, **Phibbs Exchange**, which you'll only need to use if you're heading for Mount Seymour.

Lonsdale Quay

Lonsdale Quay is the North Van terminus for the SeaBus catamarans that cross the Burrard Inlet from the Waterfront station terminal in Downtown (see p.29). As you alight from the boat, the bus terminal is immediately in front of you – buses (#226, #228, #229, #230, #236, #239, #242, #246) to all points leave from the two parallel bays here. The **Lonsdale Quay Market**, 123 Carrie Cates Court (April–Oct Sat–Thurs 9.30am–6.30pm, Fri 9am–9pm, Nov–March Sat–Thurs 9.30am–6.30pm Fri 9am–8pm; restaurants remain open later; ☎604/985-6261, ⓦwww.lonsdalequay.com) – which to all intents and purposes *is* Lonsdale Quay – lies a few seconds' walk to the right.

The quay, and the market in particular, were developed in the mid-1980s as part of an attempt to regenerate the area, prompted by the introduction of the SeaBus service and the success of the Granville Island market on the southern edge of Downtown. Development continues apace, the latest significant addition to the quay being the smart *Lonsdale Quay Hotel* (see p.137) directly above the market.

While not as vibrant as its Granville Island equivalent, the Lonsdale Quay Market is still an appealing place, with around eighty shops and stalls arranged over two levels – the first level is devoted mainly to fresh and cooked food, the second to small speciality shops. If you're travelling with children, you might want to make a beeline for the six stores that make up **Kids' Alley** on level 2, which features children's clothes stores, Games People (toys and games) and the unique Spark's Kutz for Children, a fun children's hairdressers.

The market also has great fresh fruit and vegetable stalls and numerous takeaway food counters selling a wide range of ethnic fast foods, mainly Far Eastern noodle and stir-fry stands, as well as other snack foods. The wooden promenades here make wonderful places to have a picnic or grab a coffee as you look out over the port, tugs and moored fishing boats towards the Downtown skyline. It's hard to see how these views can be improved, but if you want to escape the boardwalks for grass and trees, make for the small **Waterfront Park** just to the west of the bus terminal.

You'll find further shops and eating places on **Lonsdale Avenue**, North Van's key commercial thoroughfare, which strikes northeast from the quay, but there's little or nothing here to compare with what you'll find in the market.

Grouse Mountain

Named by hikers in 1894 who stumbled across a blue grouse (a bird), **Grouse Mountain**, 6400 Nancy Greene Way (daily 9am–10pm; cable-car tickets $24.95; ☎604/980-9311 or 984-0661, ⊛www.grousemountain.com), now lures about 1.1 million visitors a year. This deserved popularity owes itself to the views and the Swiss-built **cable-car ride** – on North America's largest cable cars (each carries 100 people) – which runs from the 290-metre base station to close to the mountain's 1250-metre summit. The eight-minute ride is exhilarating and the views of Vancouver and its surroundings at the top are sublime (be sure to visit on a clear day). You might also come here towards dusk to see the city's lights twinkle into life, or, better still, book a table in *The Observatory* restaurant at the summit, easily Vancouver's most panoramic restaurant. You'll be in good company – the restaurant, in a previous incarnation, was where one-time Canadian Prime Minister Pierre Trudeau brought the future Mrs Margaret Trudeau on their first date. Admission to the cable car is complimentary with advance dinner reservations.

The mountain rises above the Capilano River 12km from central Vancouver and some way to the north of the Capilano Suspension Bridge, Salmon Hatchery and Capilano River trails, so it's a good idea to combine some or all of these sights with a trip to the mountain. In summer it's also worth arriving early as queues build up fairly quickly. If you take one of the first cable cars you could be up and down the mountain in a couple of hours – there's not a huge amount to do at the summit – and then have time left to devote to the Capilano River, Lighthouse Park or Downtown. If you're in Vancouver in winter, then the mountain offers plenty in the way of skiing, boarding and other activities (see box p.114).

To get directly to the base station from Lonsdale Quay, take the special #236 Grouse Mountain–Pemberton Heights **bus** from the bus depot by the SeaBus terminal: the service usually departs from Bay 8. You can also take a #246 Highland bus from Bay 7 and change to the #232 Grouse Mountain at Edgemont Village or take the #232 from Phibbs Exchange. If you're coming by **car** from Downtown follow Georgia St through Stanley Park and cross the Lions Gate Bridge. Take the North Vancouver exit to Marine Drive, then turn left and follow Capilano Road for 5km. There's free parking in the gravel lot adjacent to the base station, but places go quickly.

The summit

Grouse Mountain's twin cable cars make up North America's longest aerial tramway and provide an exciting if expensive way of getting up and down the mountain. It's possible to walk up on the aptly named **Grouse Grind Trail** from the trailhead by the chalet at the base station, but it's not a great hike – a huge grind of a climb in a short distance (an ascent of 853m over 2.9km), with little by way of views. If you do fancy the challenge, be sure to use insect repellent. Allow one-and-half-hours if you're fit, two hours if you're not; the record for the ascent is 27 minutes and 18 seconds.

It's far easier, of course, to settle instead into the almost inevitable queue for the ticket office to the cable car; be sure to get here early. After eight minutes in the car (there are departures every 15 minutes) and two stomach-churning lurches over the tramway's twin towers, you reach the summit (or – at 1128m – as close to it as the tramway can manage), which, with its restaurants and tourist paraphernalia, is anything but wild. The **views**, though, are stunning, stretching across the city as far as the San Juan Islands 160km away in Washington State.

Have a quick look at the **interpretative centre** off to the right when you leave the cable car. A 25-minute film, *Born to Fly*, on the history of Grouse Mountain, an eagle's-eye view of southwestern British Columbia, is shown in the **Theatre in the Sky** downstairs (every half-hour in summer, hourly in winter; admission is included in your cable-car ticket). There are also a couple of cafés and a smarter restaurant if you need fortifying after your ascent. The first of the cafés, *Altitudes Bistro*, has panoramic views and serves contemporary West Coast food, but it fills up quickly; otherwise try *The Observatory* restaurant (see above). Ask at the interpretative centre, or the small information desk just beyond the centre, about easy **guided walks** (summer daily 11am–5pm): the Tribute to the Forest (30min) leaves on the hour, the similar Walk in the Woods every hour on the half-hour (35min).

Walk up the paved paths away from the centre for about five minutes – you can't get lost – and you pass a cabin office offering guided "gravity assisted" (read downhill) **bike tours** from the summit (May–Oct 3 daily; 20km trips cost from around $85, including the cable-car fee): behind the office you can sign up for expensive **helicopter tours** over the city (from $80). On the left up the path lies the site of the "Lumberjack Shows" (twice daily; free), involving various crowd-pleasing sawing and wood-chopping demonstrations. Just beyond this is the **Peak Chairlift** (also included in your ticket), which judders upwards for another eight minutes to the mountain's actual summit: views of the city and Fraser Delta are even better, only slightly spoilt by the worn paths and buildings immediately below you.

The latest attractions on the mountain are **four grizzly bears**, which were found as orphaned cubs (their mother had probably been shot by hunters). In an ideal world, the bears would not need to be taken in, and a certain amount of controversy raged for a while, but none would have survived long in the wild – and once used to humans, any return to the wild is in any case almost impossible. Today, most locals seem rather pleased to know the bears are there, and the animals have a generous amount of space in which to live. A big electric fence stops them from entertaining any thoughts of an escape that would be disastrous for them and, probably, anyone who bumped into them.

Grouse Mountain is a favourite for people wanting to **ski** or **snowboard** after work, and its brightly illuminated slopes and dozen or so runs are a North Vancouver landmark on winter evenings. The mountain has attracted locals since the early twentieth century, but in those days a skiing round-trip was a three-day affair. The first chalet appeared in 1926 soon after a toll road was cleared to the mountain: a double chairlift – North America's first – was built in 1949. Since then, the slopes have blossomed and their facilities continued to improve – 2000 saw the introduction of the $4.3 million Screaming Eagle, Vancouver's first high-speed quad chair.

The mountain is especially good for beginners or those learning to ski. Take two-hour drop-in **lessons** (Mon–Fri at 12.15pm, Sat–Sun & public holidays 10am & 2pm; single session $30, $62 with lift, $61 with rental and $93 with lift and rental; four sessions $99) or sign up for Snow School ski or boarding packages. Separate skill-improvement and women-only four-session courses are available. Register with Guest Services at the base station at least an hour before the start of a session. Cross-country skiing is also available on groomed and patrolled trails.

The resort's vertical drop is 384m and the base elevation 274m. Terrain is 30 percent novice, 50 percent intermediate and 20 percent expert. There are 25 runs (including three green, fourteen blue and six black diamond), the longest of which stretches for 2.4km: 13 runs are available at night and for snowboarding. Lifts include two aerial trams, one high-speed quad, three double chairs, two T-bars and two rope tows. There's also a 100-metre half-pipe for snowboarders.

A **day-pass** currently costs $39 ($29 at night) and allows you to ride the cable car and gives unlimited skiing or snowboarding. Five- and ten-day passes and season passes are available for $145, $290 and $625 respectively. Rental costs are $38 for skis or snowboards ($48 for high-performance equipment) and $24 for a suit. Skates, snowshoes, gloves and so forth are also available. Book online or call ☎980.9311 for rentals. If you're not skiing or boarding, then consider a sleigh ride (every 15 minutes from the base station), snowshoe tours (there are six snowshoe trails totalling 12.8km) or ice skating on a huge pond at the summit.

Call ☎980-9311 or 984-0661 or visit the website for more **information** on ski and snowboard rates, rental equipment, tours, lessons and regular snow, lift, run and weather reports.

Check with the office at the lower cable-car base station or the upper terminal chalet for details of long **hikes** – many are down below rather than up at the summit proper. The best stroll is to **Blue Grouse Lake**, a pretty lake north of the skyride (15min); the Goat Ridge Trail is for experienced hikers. More rugged paths lead into the mountains of the West Coast Range, but for these you'll need maps (see p.23).

The Capilano River

The lively little **Capilano River** rises in the mountains of the North Shore and empties into the Pacific 32km later just west of the Lions Gate Bridge. In the last 10km or so before it runs into the ocean, it boasts a range of natural sights and other attractions, most of which lie within a narrow strip of protected park on either side of the river and its gorge. To make best use of your time, the sights are probably best visited on the way back from Grouse Mountain, either by walking or by jumping off the #236 bus on its run back from the cable car's base station. From north to south the sights are the Cleveland Dam, Salmon Hatchery and Capilano Suspension Bridge. Further south lies Ambleside Park, a popular recreational spot alongside the point at which the river enters the sea. Although it's linked by trails to the sights further north, it's a place that is more easily seen from the shoreline road approaches to the east.

Much of the river is protected by the **Capilano River Regional Park** (daily May–Labour Day 8am–9pm, rest of the year 8am–5pm or dusk, whichever is later; ☎604/224-5739 or 432-6350, ⓦwww.gvrd.bc.ca), founded in 1926 after large-scale commercial logging ceased in North Van, making it one of the North Shore's first municipal parks. Most of the key sights are also linked by 26km of well-kept park **trails**, including the major **Capilano Pacific Trail**, on or near the river, and easily accessed from the road running parallel to the river on its eastern side. At its southern end, the road starts as Capilano Road and then becomes Nancy Greene Way towards Grouse Mountain. Be sure to walk some of the park's trails – the misty rainforest scenery, crashing river, cliffs and huge stands of timber are superb. Note that **no cycling is allowed on the park's trails**, only on the commuter cycling trail from West Van and North Van, which passes over the gravel road on top of the dam.

The Cleveland Dam

The barrier and attractive artificial lake of the **Cleveland Dam** divide the Capilano Lake from the river and sit at the northern edge of the river park about 1km south of the Grouse Mountain base station. From the parking area, toilets and picnic area off Nancy Greene Way you can walk across the top of the 195-metre-wide dam, built in 1954, and look down on the source of 40 percent of Vancouver and the Lower Mainland's (the city's hinterlands) drinking water – 17 billion gallons of water are stored and 100 million gallons released daily. The views also embrace forested slopes and surrounding peaks, including the two "Lion" mountains – named after their shapes – whose distinctive profiles you'll have seen from Downtown and elsewhere: they're the highest points on the North Shore range of the Coast Mountains, with **West Lion** reaching 1646m and **East Lion** topping 1599m.

A signboard map of local **trails** is located near the parking area: a good bet is the short **Giant Fir Trail**, which leads to what is probably the park's largest tree – a 500-year-old monster some 61m high and 2.4m in diameter. To access the trail, cross the dam and take the trail down the west side of the river. After about ten minutes' walk you come to a fork and a sign for the Great Fir Trail on your left. Continue past the eponymous fir and you reach another fork. Turn left and you come to the **Second Canyon Viewing Deck**, which offers a great view of the Cleveland Dam from below; take the right fork and you continue towards the salmon hatchery (see below). After a couple of minutes on the latter fork the Cable Pool Bridge will take you across the river for a quick route to the hatchery, but for a longer way round from this point (allow an extra 30 minutes) you could follow the Coho Loop Trail, crossing the river on the Pipeline Bridge before looping back up river to the hatchery. If you want to loop back to the dam's car park, a trail is signed back up the hill and along the east bank from the hatchery. Allow an hour for the full round hike from dam to hatchery and back.

Capilano Salmon Hatchery

The Capilano River's modern **salmon hatchery** (open daily June–Aug 8am–8pm, May & Sept 8am–7pm, April & Oct 8am–6pm, Nov–March 8am–6pm; free; ☎604/666-1790, ⓦwww.heb.pac.dfo-mpo.gc.ca), run by the province of British Columbia, is designed to help salmon spawn and thus replenish declining stocks. It's quickly reached by trail from the Cleveland Dam (see above) or a one-kilometre side road (or the Pipeline Trail) from the signed main entrance off Capilano Road. This access road comes about 200m after the busy roadside entrance to the Capilano Suspension Bridge. If you're coming on the bus up the hill from Vancouver, ring the bell for the stop after the Bridge.

Life started to become difficult for salmon on the Capilano River in 1889, when the river was partially dammed. It became critical in 1954, when the completion of the Cleveland Dam not only blocked the route of coho and steelhead salmon returning to spawn in the river's headwaters, but also destroyed 95 percent of the salmon's spawning territory and 75 percent of their rearing territory. To help the fish, the city authorities built a concrete weir and fish ladder that collected returning salmon on their way upstream. The fish were then transferred to tanks and carried above the dam to be released. This addressed the problems of the returning salmon, but not those of young salmon going the other way, which suffered predictably high losses as they plunged over the Cleveland Dam.

As stocks continued to decline, the city decided the only solution was to build a hatchery that would rear and release salmon *below* the dam. Work began in 1969 and was completed two years later at a cost of $3 million. Chinook salmon were also introduced, part of an attempt to create a self-sustaining run of this prized sport fish. The hatchery was the first of many similar schemes across the province.

It now nurtures a colossal number of fish a year, releasing 525,000 coho "smolts", or young fish, into the river, along with 600,000 Chinook and 15,000 steelhead. Some idea of the travails of the fish can be gained from the number of returning salmon – just 14,000 coho, 740 Chinook and thirty steelhead annually. The hatchery also conducts important scientific work, largely through the tagging of fish, thus allowing it to trace migration and ocean-survival patterns, and provides artificial "ladders" up the riverbed for those spawning salmon still doomed to head upstream.

You can view these ladders and, in season, catch a close-up glimpse of the struggling salmon through indoor glass panels. You can also see salmon at various stages of their development in eye-level tanks. There's always something to see, but different times of the year are more exciting than others: coho and steelhead adults start to return to the river in **June**, when you can see them "running" and watch the daily emptying of "traps" for the returning adults and the transport of coho adults above the dam. **Autumn** sees the continued return of coho and steelhead (until Dec) and the arrival of Chinook adults (Sept–Dec), along with tagging of smaller fish and the transfer of small "fry" to rearing troughs. **Winter** is quieter for large-fish activity, but the rearing activities of the centre means there's always something happening. The same goes for **spring**, when the "winter-run" steelhead adults ride the river until May and the smolts of all three salmon types are released.

The low, simple building is well designed and the information plaques on the work of the hatchery interesting, but it's a prime stop on city coach tours, so the place can often be packed. The scenic area below the hatchery – a lovely stretch of river and forest – is worth exploring, especially the pretty Dog's Leg Pool (1km), which is along a swirling reach of the Capilano River. A few minutes' walk along the river trails soon takes you into pretty scenery away from the hatchery crowds.

△ Skiing on Mount Seymour

Capilano Suspension Bridge

The Capilano River's most publicized attraction is the inexplicably popular 137-metre-long **suspension bridge** (daily: mid-May–Aug 8.30am–8pm, early May & Sept–mid-Oct 9am–7.30pm, late Oct & mid-March–mid-April 9am–6pm, late April 9am–6.30pm, Nov–mid-March 9am–5pm; $14.95 May–Oct, $10.25 Nov–April; prices exclude GST; ☎604/985-7474, ⓦwww.capbridge.com). Its main claim to fame, and one that attracts over 800,000 visitors a year, is that it is the world's longest pedestrian suspension bridge, dangling seventy metres above the vertiginous Capilano Gorge.

The first bridge here – a ramshackle affair of hemp rope and cedar planks – was built in 1889 by a local landowner, the Scottish civil engineer **George Grant Mackay**, to access his holdings across the gorge. Mackay was also a City Park Commissioner, and active in ensuring that Stanley Park, among other greenspaces, was preserved for posterity. He also bought and sold land on the British Columbia mainland, and founded the now large and prosperous fruit-growing town of Vernon in the Okanagan region in central southern British Columbia. His bridge's swaying and precarious construction attracted thrill-seekers (while its creaking caused local aboriginal peoples to nickname it the "laughing bridge"), making this Vancouver's oldest "attraction", though the present structure – which looks similar but is far more robust – dates from 1956. Famous names that have made the crossing include Marilyn Monroe, Katherine Hepburn, the Rolling Stones, Walter Cronkite and Margaret Thatcher – the last so enjoyed the experience that she did it twice.

Although part of the park, the footbridge is privately run as a money-making venture – something which rather counts against it, especially when you can have much the same sort of gorge, forest and river scenery for free up the road. Stick to the paths elsewhere in the park, therefore, and avoid the pedestrian toll, which buys you a walk across the bridge – scenic as far as it goes, but hardly hair-raising – miscellaneous tours, forestry exhibits and trails, the inevitable gift shop and café, a totem park, and a visit to an aboriginal carving centre; frankly none amounts to very much. Furthermore, if you want the suspension bridge experience – which, after all, amounts to little more than a view – there's one you can cross for free in Lynn Canyon to the east (see opposite).

Capilano Pacific Trail

The trail from the Cleveland Dam south past the hatchery and suspension bridge forms part of the scenic **Capilano Pacific Trail**, which you could, if you wanted a longer (and rewarding) walk, follow for virtually the whole length of the river south of the dam (about 7km) to its mouth near Ambleside Park in West Van (see below). Various loops and river crossings en route allow you to make circular routes – up one bank and down the other – if you don't want to walk the whole thing. Note that lower down the trail passes through less-arresting residential districts, but in its upper reaches you're walking through glorious forest habitats and along the river as it crashes over a tumble of rocks in a rush of white water.

Among the most interesting intersecting or branch trails is the Rabbit Lane Trail (4km return) close to the park's northern entrance near the dam, once used to haul lumber by the Capilano Timber Company – hence its gentle grades. Further south, the short secondary trail to **Ranger Pool**, though steep in places, is well worth a detour, thanks to the density of the evergreen cover, the profusion of ferns and the sheer peace and quiet of the forest.

Further south still, close to the coast and Hwy 1, you might access the park and its trails from Keith Road, east off Taylor Way. There's a trailhead here for the Capilano Pacific Trail signed by the Greater Vancouver Regional District (GVRD). The trail leaves the river for a while here and follows Keith Road for a distance, looking more like a country lane than a city road, despite its proximity to the Upper Levels Highway Bridge.

Ambleside Park

The Capilano Pacific Trail's conclusion (or start) is **Ambleside Park**, which runs west of the Capilano River's mouth as far as 13th Street. This is one of the North Shore's most popular parks, a magnet for strollers, joggers, dog-walkers or those who simply want to sit back and enjoy the buzz of marine activity offshore as well as the views of the Lions Gate Bridge and across the Burrard Inlet to Stanley Park. There's a long sandy beach (with calm water, despite the tidal currents further offshore), duck pond, playground, pitch and putt golf and one of the old ferry buildings from the early days of white involvement with the North Shore. People often come here at dusk in the summer, especially on Saturdays, when many of the cruise ships leave port – the ships and twinkling lights make a great spectacle. You're also likely to see plenty of fishermen from the Capilano Indian Reserve, on whose land the park stands.

Lynn Canyon Park

For a quick taste of backwoods Vancouver, the 250-hectare **Lynn Canyon Park** (7am–dusk; free) is a quiet, forested area between the Capilano River to the west and Mount Seymour to the east. It has a modest ravine and suspension bridge which, unlike the more popular Capilano Suspension Bridge (see opposite), you don't have to pay to cross. Several easy walks of up to ninety minutes take you through fine scenery – cliffs, rapids, waterfalls and the eighty-metre-high suspension bridge over Lynn Creek – all just twenty minutes' car or bus ride from Lonsdale Quay. Before entering the gorge, it's worth popping into the **Ecology Centre** in the park at 3663 Park Rd, off Peters Road (June–Aug daily 10am–5pm; Oct–Feb Mon–Fri 10am–5pm, Sat & Sun and holidays noon–4pm; donation suggested; ☎604/981-3103 or 987 5922, ⓦwww.dnv.org), a friendly and informative interpretative centre, where you can pick up maps and pamphlets on the park's trails and its many small mammals and other wildlife. You'll also learn about the area's ninety-year-old, second-growth forest – that is, forest that has grown after the virgin first-growth forest had been logged. Most of the original forest was gone by the early twentieth century, but in places around the park you can still see the stumps of gargantuan first-growth trees. The size of the second-growth trees and lush undergrowth provides a vivid illustration of the sheer fecundity of temperate rainforest and the benign effects of 150cm of rain a year for almost a century. Equally gripping are some of the forest's creatures, notably the aptly named banana slug, which can reach a length of 25cm from gorging on dead vegetation.

To reach the park take bus #228 from Lonsdale Quay to its penultimate stop at Peters Road, from where it's a signposted ten-minute walk to the gorge; alternatively, take the less frequent #229 Westlynn bus from Lonsdale Quay, which drops you about five minutes closer. If you're approaching by car from the south, take the Lynn Valley or Mountain Highway exits from Hwy 1 (both roads intersect near the park) and from Lynn Valley Road turn right onto Peters Road.

The Ecology Centre often offers guided walks in the summer (at 2pm daily in July and August), but you can just as easily follow the park's handful of **trails** yourself. The most popular walk is the easy **Thirty-Foot Pool Trail**, a 15-minute stroll from the parking lot up the east side of the canyon. It's a fairly level walk the short distance to and after the suspension bridge, with a set of steepish steps near the end. The 40-minute **Twin Falls Trail** is a longer loop that starts at the suspension bridge. Once across, take the boardwalk east, turning right at the fork and following signs to Twin Falls. Cross the wooden bridge, climb the steps out of the canyon and in the clearing at the top take the Centennial Trail north (following the fence) back to the car park. You can also hike part of the **Baden–Powell Trail**, a long-distance path from Horseshoe Bay to the west that runs through several North Shore parks (see box p.115). Its Lynn Canyon section takes about 75 minutes to trek and follows the Lynn Creek on its west bank.

Trails from the park also feed into trail systems in other parks, notably the **Lynn Headwaters Regional Park**, a large protected area with tougher trails into the Coast Mountains, and the Lower Seymour Conservation Reserve (see below), which borders the Lynn Canyon park on its northeast edge. The latter can be reached from a trail beyond the Thirty-Foot Pool by way of Lillooet Road, which marks the boundary between the two protected areas.

The Lower Seymour Conservation Reserve

Just northwest of the Lynn Canyon park lies the 5668-hectare **Lower Seymour Conservation Reserve**, formally known (and occasionally still referred to) as the Seymour Demonstration Forest (daily 8am–dusk or 9pm in summer; ☎604/987-1273, ⊛www.gvrd.bc.ca/lscr), bordered to the west by the Lynn Headwaters Regional Park and to the east by the Mount Seymour Provincial Park (see opposite). For years, this area was mostly off-limits, having first been ruthlessly logged and then restricted to the public until 1987 because its valuable watershed provided much of Vancouver's drinking water. Today, most of it is open, a large area of temperate second-growth rainforest, river flood plain and Alpine meadows in a spectacular glacier-carved valley containing the Seymour River, which bisects the reserve from north to south. At the river's and park's northern limit is the **Seymour Dam**, approached by the **Seymour Mainline Road**, a 12-kilometre paved road (bikers and walkers only at weekends), which shadows the river to its west and strikes off from the gatehouse near the reserve's southern limit.

The gatehouse is situated at the northern end of Lillooet Road and, if going by public transport, you need to take the #229 Lynn Valley bus to Dempsey Road and Lynn Valley Road. From here it's a ten-minute walk over Lynn Creek via the bridge on Rice Lake Road. By car, take exit 22 from Hwy 1 at the north end of the Ironworkers' Memorial Second Narrows Bridge. A large green GVRD sign at the intersection guides you towards the reserve past Capilano College and a cemetery.

The Mainline Road is a great favourite with bikers and in-line skaters (normally only the first 2km are open for recreational use on weekdays), but a myriad of biking and hiking trails (40km in all) strike off into the forest from the gatehouse and points along the road. From the car park it's 2.2km one-way to the Seymour River, where you could pick up the **Twin Bridges Trail** (7km round-trip) south or the more appealing, winding **Fisherman's Trail** north to Mid-Valley Bridge (5km one-way); return the same way on Mainline Road. For a short stroll, follow the 400-metre **Forest Ecology Loop Trail** from the car park, which emerges at Rice Lake before looping back. Generally, though, the trails here offer rather less variety than parks to the east and west; the river itself, though, and easier trails, will be a hit with children. Free organized tours with forestry officials run most summer weekends: call the above number for details.

Twin Bridges, Riverside, Fisherman's and other hiking trails are also open to **mountain bikers**, along with a range of other trails that run beyond the reserve's borders. The trails here are some of the best in the region for bikers, partly because they can be challenging, and partly because the forestry work here keeps much undergrowth in check and the trails clear: there is also little snow cover at lower elevations in winter.

Mount Seymour Provincial Park

Mount Seymour Provincial Park (always open; free) is the largest – at 3508 hectares – and most easterly of the North Shore's provincial parks close to Downtown. It is also the wildest, and the one – with Cypress Provincial Park (see p.123) – that most closely resembles the rugged, high mountain environments of the British Columbia interior. It protects the summit of the eponymous mountain, but also much of its lower slopes and hinterland. To get here by **bus**, take the #239 bus from Lonsdale Quay to Phibbs Exchange and then the #215 to the Mount Seymour Parkway-Indian River (1hr), from which point if you don't have a car you'll have to walk or cycle up the 13-kilometre **Mount Seymour Road** to the heart of the park.

The park dates from 1936 and is named after Frederick Seymour, governor of British Columbia from 1864 to 1869. Because of its height, the park straddles two bio- and geo-climatic zones – the coastal western hemlock and mountain hemlock zones. Below the 1000m mark you'll see old-growth Douglas firs and vast, beautiful western red cedars, mixed with lesser coniferous and deciduous trees. Above this height the forest comprises main mountain hemlock, yellow cedar and amabilis fir, with high alpine meadows swathed in wild flowers in spring. You may well see coyotes and deer close to the road, while in the back country cougars, black bears and bobcats are not unknown. Start eating a picnic and you're almost guaranteed a visit from the Canada jay, identified by its bright colouring and raucous call. Other indigenous birds include Stellar's jay (British Columbia's official bird), grouse, siskin, kinglet and – during autumn migrations – several types of hawk.

For further **information** on the park, call ☎604/924-2200, visit ⓦwww.gov.bc.ca/bcparks, or ask at the city visitor centre for the blue *BC Parks* pamphlet on the park. Among other things, the pamphlet has a good **map** which makes sense of the park's trails and their various links and permutations (see below).

Mount Seymour Road

Mount Seymour Road climbs from the park headquarters at the junction with Indian River Road to over 1000m, ending at a car park and the trailheads for several upper-mountain trails (see box p.123). En route it also passes four or five trailheads for lower and shorter (and generally less spectacular) trails, all explained and mapped on various infoboards at points up the road. The first of these is the **Old Buck Trail** (2.3km to junction with the Baden-Powell Trail;

2hr, 670m elevation gain), which leaves from near the park entrance across the road from the gatehouse. This shadows the approach road for just over a kilometre, picks up an old logging road before meeting and crossing the Baden-Powell Trail (see p.120), heads north to cross the approach road higher up and continues as the Upper Old Buck Trail-Perimeter, which rejoins the road higher up still.

Alternatively, keep following the road to the **Vancouver Picnic Area** (about midway up the road), a popular spot in summer. There are toilets here, picnic tables and a park information shelter plus the trailhead for the 750-metre **Mushroom Parking Lot Trail** (15 minutes), little more than a stroll into the woods, and the Old Buck Access Trail, an easy one-kilometre path (allow 30min), which runs east almost level to meet the Old Buck Trail coming up from the south.

Two kilometres beyond this picnic area you come to the popular viewpoint at **Deep Cove Lookout** – views are superb along much of the road, but they're especially good here – where signboards identify the city and other more distant landmarks below. Deep Cove Lookout offers trailhead access to some higher trails via the **Perimeter Trail** (1.5km, 45min, 240m elevation gain to Goldie Lake and connection to Goldie Lake Loop, see below) and Upper Old Buck Trail. Continue just under another 2km and on a sharp bend is the trailhead for the **Old Cabin Trail** (430m, 45min, 240m elevation gain), a connector trail which runs east to join the Perimeter Trail coming up from the south and the onward trail to Goldie Lake. Just a few hundred metres on is the end of the road and parking areas, toilets, picnic tables and park kiosk and information boards on the various trails that start here.

Trails in Mount Seymour Provincial Park

Several major trails from the parking area at the top of the road in the park proper are manageable in a day, but be aware that rain or fog can suddenly appear, while snow lingers as late as June. You must be properly equipped.

Among the easiest hikes is the **Goldie Lake Loop** (2km, 30min, minimal elevation gain), a half-hour stroll east from behind the First Aid station, passing through hemlock and cedar forest featuring the park's oldest trees, Douglas firs. About 500m down this trail, you can branch off (or add on) to the **Flower Lake Loop** (1.5km, 45min, elevation gain 150m) path that leads through sub-Alpine bog and pond habitats with a good chance of seeing several bird species.

Of similar length but with little climbing is the **First Lake Loop–Dog Mountain Trail**, which begins west of the chairlift and pushes though thick old-growth fir forest to First Lake (1km, 30min, minimal elevation gain). Here you meet the trail junctions for Dog Mountain or Mount Seymour – follow the trail west to the former (2km one-way, 40min, minimal elevation gain) for fine **views** of Vancouver and the Seymour River Valley.

The **Mount Seymour Trail** itself (4km, 2hr, 450m elevation gain) is the park's busiest, starting near the north end of the car park before traversing Brockton Point and First and Second Pump peaks. The reward for a fairly stiff climb is a panorama from Mount Seymour (1455m) that on clear days extends over the city to the Gulf Islands. Also popular is the **Mystery Lake Trail** (1.5km one-way, 45min, elevation gain 180m) which leads from the parking area straight into forest of fir, hemlock and cedar, reaching Mystery Lake (good for a cooling swim in summer) via an occasionally rocky route that shadows a ski lift with relatively few gaps in the trees for views. You can return the same

Winter on Mount Seymour

Mount Seymour (☎604/986-2261, ⊛www.mountseymour.com) has a developed skiing, snowboarding and **winter activities** programme. It has the city's highest base elevation in the car park at the top of Mount Seymour Road, and its 22 runs (the longest is 2.4km) are accessed by three chairlifts and a tow. The vertical rise is 330m and terrain divides into 40 percent novice, 40 percent intermediate and 20 percent advanced. Average snowfall is 300cm, or about half that of Cypress Mountain (see p.125) and a third that of Whistler (see p.256).

Shuttle services (☎604/718-7771 for information) run here daily in winter from various points on the North Shore, notably Lonsdale Quay and Phibbs Exchange. Skiing and other activities are available at night, and the mountain has excellent equipment rental and ski-school outlets. Lift passes cost $33 ($19 at night).

While the activities are franchised to a private operator, the provincial government's BC Parks put out two backcountry ski trails from the car park and park kiosk, where you'll also find the latest snow and avalanche reports (the latter are a real hazard). The **Mount Seymour Backcountry Access** runs 7km to the saddle between First and Second Pump peaks (allow 3hr return on skis, 4hr on snowshoes). The easier First Lake Trail loops out to the lake (with virtually no elevation gain) and picks up the Mount Seymour Trail for the return to the car park (1hr return on skis, 2hr on snowshoes).

way, or curve east around the lake and follow well-signed trails that either run up the mountain or drop more directly back to the parking area.

The wildest and most demanding hike for serious walkers is the **Elsay Lake** Trail (7km one-way, allow a full day, elevation gain 500m), which follows the Mount Seymour Trail until the divide just east of First Pump Peak, about 1km from Mount Seymour. From here it runs along an intermittently marked trail to the forest- and mountain-circled Elsay Lake, where there is a rough backcountry shelter. There is no loop return – the homeward leg retraces your outbound route. You are allowed to **camp** here and elsewhere north of Brockton Point within the normal park regulations – in essence, leave no trace and light no fires. Bring your own water as no potable water is provided anywhere.

Cypress Provincial Park

Cypress Provincial Park (always open; free) is the most westerly of the big parks that part-cover the dramatic mountains and forest visible from Vancouver's Downtown. It's also among British Columbia's most visited day-use parks and probably the most popular of the North Shore's protected areas. This is partly to do with its scenic diversity, but also its wilderness. The 3012-hectare park divides into northern and southern sections joined by a narrow corridor of land. The southern section (first designated in 1975) has road access in the shape of the **Cyprus Access Road** (or Cypress Parkway), some developed facilities, accessible trails and lots of rugged backcountry. The northern section (protected in 1982) is considerably wilder and can only be approached via the 29-kilometre Howe Sound Crest Trail (see p.125) from the southern section or by tracks from Hwy 99 and Howe Sound to the west.

To get here you really need a car or bike: the heart of the park, main car park, Alpine ski and principal trailheads in the southern section are at **Cypress Bowl** at the end of the access road, 15km north of exit #8 of Hwy 1-99 (the Upper Levels Hwy) at Cypress Bowl Road. Note that as you follow the road you'll pass a turn after 13km to the right for the **Hollyburn** Nordic skiing area, only really relevant if you are here in winter (see below) or wish to tackle one or both of the trails that start from this area (see below) To get within striking distance using public transport, take the #253 Caulfield/Park Royal or the #257 Horseshoe Bay Express **bus** from the Park Royal interchange. The Cypress Access Road, the main approach, has great **views** over the city and as far as Mount Baker in Washington State.

There's nowhere to **stay** in the park in summer, but backcountry **camping** is allowed, though only in the park's northern section, at some higher elevations above the Nordic and Alpine ski areas in the south, and along the Howe Sound Crest Trail, where there are four preferred sites: the plateau above Enchantment Lake (11km from Cypress Bowl), Magnesia Meadows (14.5km), Brunswick Lake (19km) and Deeks Lake (22km from Cypress Bowl). Campfires are not permitted and there are no facilities.

For more **information**, ask for the relevant *BC Parks* pamphlet at the city visitor centre (see p.23), call ☎604/926-6007 or 924-2200 or visit ⓦwww.gov.bc.ca/bcparks.

Trails in Cypress Provincial Park

Cypress Provincial Park's five major (and many minor) trails can be rugged and muddy, but they're always well marked, and even just a few minutes from the parking area you can feel in the depths of the great outdoors. Follow any of these walks and you'll soon see how the park came by its name, which is taken from the huge old red and yellow cedars that proliferate here. Trails depart either from the parking area at the top of the access road or from the Hollyburn Nordic ski area lower down the same road. In addition there are two much longer trails: the Howe Sound Crest and Baden-Powell Trail (see p.120), a 42-kilometre trail that runs across the North Shore from west to east and has two sections you can walk in the park.

The best short trails are those that kick off from the top of the access road in Cypress, starting with the easiest, the **Yew Lake Trail** (2km round-trip, 45min, minimal elevation gain), a self-guided interpretative trail that is wheelchair-accessible. It runs northwest from the car park through subalpine meadows, past the lake and has an additional short loop though a stand of old-growth forest. Almost equally easy, the **Black Mountain Loop** (2.5km round-trip, 45min, 100m elevation gain) also passes through subalpine meadows and skirts several small mountain lakes on the plateau southwest of Cypress Bowl, with short side trails to viewpoints over Yew Lake (see above) and the city. The more arduous **Cabin Lake Trail** (1km plus 7km round-trip, 3hr, elevation gain 275m) requires taking the Baden-Powell Trail for 2.7km from the Cypress Bowl car park, connecting with the Cabin Lake Trail itself on Black Mountain (1220m). This trail passes several small lakes and the Yew Lake Lookout before rejoining the Baden-Powell Trail for the return to Cypress Bowl.

One of the two main trails from the Nordic ski area, the **Four Lakes Loop**, also makes use of a segment of the Baden-Powell Trail. It starts at the BC Parks' information kiosk at the Hollyburn Mountain Nordic ski area car park – follow the Burfield Trail to the Baden-Powell Trail (100m past First Lake) and then follow this for 500m to pick up the West Lake and then Blue Gentian trails. At Blue Gentian Lake take the Lost Lake Trail past Lost Lake to Brother's Creek Trail for a return to Blue Gentian Lake. From here take the Blue Gentian Trail west for 300m back to the Baden-Powell Trail. The total loop is 7.2km via Brother's Creek (including 1km to First Lake, 1.7km to West Lake, 2.1km to Blue Lake and 3.2km to Lost Lake).

Winter in Cypress Provincial Park

Cypress Provincial Park has two closely linked ski and snowboard areas – the Alpine skiing area at Cypress Bowl (☎604/926-5612, ⍵www.cypressmountain.com) and the Nordic ski area (☎604/922-0825) at Hollyburn just to the southwest. There are a total of 23 runs, the longest being 3.2km, served by five chairlifts and a double rope-tow. The vertical rise is 512m, while cross-country ski trails total 16km, including 5km set aside for night skiing. The Nordic area also has dedicated snowshoe trails and there are special tobogganing areas. There is a licensed lounge and café on site. Full-day lift **passes** cost $42 ($15 for cross-country passes), with discounted half-day, night and season passes also available.

If you don't have **transport**, Cypress Mountain Sports, 510 and 518 Park Royal St, West Van, runs a shuttle (☎604/878-9229) several times daily in season from Lonsdale Quay, Horseshoe Bay, the Caulfield and Park Royal shopping centres. The same company also provides equipment, rental and repair services, and guided snowshoe treks for the area.

The ski operation is franchised by the provincial government to a private operator, but BC Parks marks three winter **backcountry trails**: obtain a free pass from the Cypress Mountain ticket office for access. The trails are; Hollyburn Hikers' Access (5km return to Hollyburn Mountain summit), from the BC Parks kiosk in the Nordic ski area; Black Mountain Plateau Winter Trail (7km round-trip, marked to summit of Black Mountain), which starts 50m from the BC Parks kiosk at Cypress Bowl; and – from the same starting point – the Bowen Lookout Winter Trail (3km round-trip) through the Yew Lake meadows.

The second trail from the Nordic ski area is the more ambitious **Hollyburn Peak Trail** (8km round-trip, 3-4hr, elevation gain 400m), which takes you to the top of Hollyburn Mountain (1325m) to the north for some sensational views – though the trail follows the rather dull powerline road before picking up the Baden-Powell Trail and last 1.3km of the Hollyburn Peak Trail.

Long-distance trails

The **Howe Sound Crest Trail** is a great choice for experienced hikers visiting Vancouver who want to do a little more than simple day hikes but aren't equipped or prepared for multi-day treks into the back country. That said, you will need decent equipment (tent, stove, sleeping bag, boots and so forth) to tackle the 29 kilometres of this trail (see p.188 for rental details). The trail starts at Cypress Bowl and follows the narrow corridor of protected land to Cypress Park's northern section, passing the Lions Peaks and wonderfully named Mount Unnecessary. It then descends to Hwy 99 just south of Porteau Cove Provincial Park and north of Horseshoe Bay. The trail is rugged and easily lost in parts, especially in bad weather, and is not recommended to inexperienced hikers beyond Bowen Lookout (and should not be attempted at all beyond this point in winter).

An even more challenging track, the **Baden-Powell Trail** is longer – at 42km – and, in running west to east across the length of the North Shore, it runs against the grain of the landscape, being forced to drop into and climb out of the many north-south valleys and creeks that run south to the coast. It is a trail that most casual visitors will tackle in the small sections that bisect some of the North Shore's protected areas, notably Cypress Park and Mount Seymour provincial parks. This said, given the proximity of North and West Van, you could easily arrange to walk the trail so as to leave it to overnight in hotels or bed and breakfast accommodation.

The trail was begun in 1967 as one of British Columbia's centennial projects and completed in 1971. Its western trailhead is just 2.5km southwest of Cypress Provincial Park in the car park at the north end of Eagle Ridge Drive, just off Hwy 1 (about 1km south of Horseshoe Bay). Buses will drop you nearby if you want to tackle this **first section of trail**: the distance from the trailhead to Cypress Bowl is 8.5km, with an elevation gain of 1014m (allow 5–6hr). The walk the other way – predominantly downhill – is clearly much easier. Alternatively, walk the section east from Cypress Bowl, a 9.5-kilometre trail with a 470m elevation change (more down than up). This will bring you out on Craigmohr Drive in residential West Van.

Lighthouse Park

The 75-hectare **Lighthouse Park** (always open; free) lies just west of Cypress Provincial Park (see above) on Beacon Lane, off Marine Drive, and offers a seascape and forest semi-wilderness at the extreme western tip of the North Shore, 8km from the Lions Gate Bridge. It was initially established in 1881 as a lighthouse reserve. Getting here by public transport is easy – the West Van #250 **bus** makes the journey all the way from Georgia Street in Downtown to a few moments' walk from the park entrance.

Smooth granite rocks and low cliffs line the park's shore, backed by huge Douglas firs up to 1500 years old, some of the best – and most accessible – virgin forest in southern British Columbia. It's the last vestige of first-growth forest in or near the city: it's a sobering thought to know that once the entire region would have looked something like this. You'll also see arbutus, identified by its smooth but often peeling orange bark – it's Canada's only native broadleaf evergreen. The rocks make fine sun beds, though the water out here is colder than around the city beaches. It's also a great place to bring a picnic.

If you want to walk, there are around 13km of trails. A signboard at the car park shows the paths, including the two easy trails to the 1912 Point Atkinson **lighthouse** itself – you can take one out and the other back, a return trip of about 5km which involves about two hours' walking, less for keen walkers. Although the park has its secluded corners (no camping allowed), it can be disconcertingly busy during summer weekends. For more **information** on the park, contact the infocentre or call ℡604/925-7200 or 925-7000.

Listings

Listings

8

Accommodation

Vancouver has plenty of central **accommodation** in all price brackets. At the top end are world-class Downtown hotels, such as the venerable *Hotel Vancouver* and *Four Seasons*, and glittering high-rise palaces that command magnificent views of the mountains and Downtown waterfront. Mid-range and inexpensive options rarely boast such panoramic positions, but it's still possible to find good central choices with plenty of character and quality for under $100.

The widest choice in all categories can be found in central Downtown, the most pleasant and practical base for exploring the city, so unless your budget is extremely tight there's really no reason to stay in any other location. As a result, our listings are arranged primarily **by price** rather than **location**, though we have also given the best choices in some of the city's more peripheral districts. That said, if you want to explore Downtown, there are few persuasive reasons for staying in North or West Vancouver, for example, where there are only a handful of hotels and bed and breakfast options, or in any location south of Granville Island or False Creek, unless you're headed for the youth hostel in Kitsilano.

Possible reasons for staying outside the Downtown core are if you wish to be close to the airport or a ferry terminal for an early getaway, want the peace and quiet offered by some of the excellent **bed and breakfast** options out of town, or are on a very tight budget, as there are plenty of **cheap motels** on the various strips in the city's northern, southern and eastern suburbs. The key locations are Capilano Road in North Vancouver and along Kingsway south of Downtown. Bear in mind, though, if you plan and book ahead, that Downtown **hostels** and the excellent YWCA offer rates to match all but the cheapest (and dowdiest) out-of-town motels.

And if you want peace and quiet but still wish to be central, you might plump for one of the smattering of hotels in the quieter and more residential West End, the area adjacent to Stanley Park – just to feel as if you're getting away from the bustle – as even here you're still effectively in Downtown. A central location doesn't necessarily mean high prices: there are excellent inexpensive or mid-range options – but you'll have to **book ahead** to secure a room in such places in midsummer. If you get stuck, there are two free **reservations services** to help out (see p.131).

In the budget bracket, you'd be well advised to steer clear of the area east of Downtown between Gastown and Chinatown. On the face of it this district has a large number of **inexpensive hotels**, but most are flophouses of a dinginess and unpleasantness that make them options of absolute last resort. These areas are also not particularly safe at night, and the back streets should be avoided at all times. There are a rash of especially dreadful places on Hastings

Street a few blocks either side of Main Street: don't be tempted into these on any account. Gastown itself has a couple of honourable exceptions, but these are often housed above a bar where live bands and late-night drinking may keep you awake till the small hours. Again, if you really need to stick to the rock-bottom price bracket, you're better off in the hostels, the YWCA or one of the marginally less-dodgy hotels north of the Granville Street Bridge, still in part a tame but tacky red-light area, but increasingly part of the gentrification process that is spreading from Yaletown.

Vancouver has two good Hostelling International **hostels**, plus a handful of other reasonable, privately run hostels. In addition to the hostels, relatively low-price accommodation is available in summer at the **University of British Columbia** at the University "Vanier Hostel", though the campus is a long way from Downtown, and many of the rooms go to convention visitors. If you're in the city for a longer period, check out the small ads in the *Vancouver Sun* newspaper for details of rooms and **apartments to rent**.

Surprisingly for a place so close to the great outdoors, Vancouver is not a camper's city – the majority of the in-city **campsites** are for RVs only and will turn you away if you've only got a tent. We've listed the few places that won't.

Out of season, hotels in all categories offer reductions, and you can reckon on thirty-percent discounts on the prices below. Many hotels will also offer discounted **weekly rates** in both high and low season. Remember, too, that the prices below are for doubles, though even the smartest hotels will introduce an extra bed into a double room at very little extra cost if there are three of you. As another way of saving money, or if you intend to be in the city for some time, it's also worth noting that many hotels have **kitchenettes** or fully fitted kitchens if you want to cook for yourselves.

Bed and breakfasts

Vancouver has a host of **bed and breakfast options**, but very few are cheap – reckon on $95 plus for a double – or central enough to make useful bases for sightseeing. However, if you choose well you can have access to beaches, gardens, barbecues and as little or as much privacy as you want. Watch out for places in Downtown that describe themselves as 'B&Bs'; in most cases these are just small hotels – often very nice but also as, or more, expensive than Downtown hotels in mid-range and expensive price brackets.

Bed and breakfast accommodations tend to close and open from year to year, so it's safest to book through agencies that keep their books up to date. However, most of these operate as a phone service only and require two days' notice – fine if you're planning ahead, but not much use if you need somewhere on arrival. In the latter case it's best to visit the city's main infocentre at the foot of Burrard Street (see opposite), where you can browse through folders containing details and pictures of dozens of bed and breakfast options and use the centre's accommodation service. In either case, make sure you know exactly where your B&B is located and how far you'll have to travel to see the sights.

If you need to use an **agency**, the following have accommodation throughout the city, in Victoria (see p.221), the Gulf Islands and beyond: Best Canadian Bed & Breakfast Network (☎604/738-7207, ⊛wwwbestcanadianbb.com); Emerald Park (☎604/878-1328, ⊛www.travelsuites.com); and Western Canada Bed and Breakfast Innkeepers' Association (☎604/952-0982, ⊛www.wcbbia.com).

Accommodation price codes

All the accommodation prices in this chapter have been coded using the symbols below, corresponding to Canadian dollar rates unless otherwise specified. Prices are for the least expensive double room in each establishment in high season, excluding special offers. Note, however, that many hotels in all categories have frequent off-season, weekly or weekend offers, and – if you're travelling in a group – that virtually all will introduce a third bed into a double room for only a few dollars. Many hotels will also allow children under a certain age – usually 12 years – to sleep free if they share their parents' room. Always enquire about deals.

Note, too, that room prices are quoted without BC's ten-percent **provincial hotel tax** levied on hotel rooms and added to your bill when you check out. The federal seven-percent **Goods and Services tax** (GST) is also levied, but visitors from outside Canada can claim a rebate on this, so keep all your receipts. Hotels and airports often provide rebate forms: for more information call ☎1-800/668-4748 in Canada or 902/432-5608 outside the country.

❶ up to $40	❹ $80–100	❼ $150–200
❷ $40–60	❺ $100–125	❽ $200–250
❸ $60–80	❻ $125–150	❾ $250+

Accommodation services

Vancouver is a busy city between June and September, and you should book rooms weeks, preferably months ahead, especially if you hope to stay at one of the better-known bargains. If you leave it until the last minute, have trouble tracking down a room, arrive in the city without a bed, or simply wish to browse accommodation in advance, the **tourist infocentre** (☎604/683-2000, ⓦwww.tourismvancouver.com) offers a free accommodation reservation service and extensive on-line listings.

Also invaluable is the official **Super Natural British Columbia** reservation service (☎1-800/435-5662 or 604/435-5622 within Greater Vancouver and 250/387-1642 outside North America; ⓦwww.hellobc.com). If you're prepared to leave things late, this service has access to a large database of rooms, and can sometimes offer better last-minute rates than those listed by the hotels themselves.

Downtown Hotels

Hotels are dotted across Vancouver's **Downtown** peninsula, so wherever you stay you won't be more than a few minutes' walk or a short bus or taxi ride from the main sights. The quietest and most peripheral places lie in the West End, which, despite their distance from the main core, have the advantage of being close to the beaches and green spaces of Stanley Park. East of here, the main Robson Street houses several hotels, many of them former high-rise apartment blocks that have been converted into big, bland but serviceable mid-price accommodation. These are reasonably convenient for both Stanley Park and the Downtown shops and galleries without being especially close – relatively speaking – to either. There are also hotels in all categories at the heart of the peninsula, with a great choice of upmarket options on or close to the waterfront.

On the area's southern and eastern fringes – Gastown and Granville Island – there are only a handful of hotels, but as gentrification takes hold, the old flophouses on the southern end of Granville and Howe streets are being converted by the mid-market hotel chains into functional mid-price places to stay.

Inexpensive

Budget Inn-Patricia Hotel 403 E Hastings St at Dunlevy Ave ☎604/255-4301 or 1-888/926-1017, ℗254-7154, ⓦwww.budgetpathotel. bc.ca. This 92-room hotel is well known among backpackers and budget travellers, and is widely advertised across Vancouver. However, the six-storey building is located a long way from Downtown in the heart of Chinatown (certainly too far to walk comfortably). This is an exciting or grim location, depending on your point of view, though some feel distinctly unsafe in the area and you wouldn't want to walk the surrounding streets in the small hours. The hotel itself is clean, well run, in relatively good condition, and the best of the many generally awful places in this district. Rooms are available in several price categories, and rates include a good breakfast at a nearby café. Free parking is available. ❸

Buchan Hotel 1906 Haro St at Robson and Denman ☎604/685-5354 or 1-800/668-6654, ℗685-5367, ⓦwww.buchanhotel.com. Some of the 61 rooms in this 1926 three-storey building are smallish and only half boast private bathrooms, but all are clean and priced accordingly (there's a $60 range from top to bottom for rooms of differing standards here). Try for rooms on the east side, which are brighter and overlook a small park, or the four "executive" front-corner rooms, which are well-furnished and the best in the house. On a quiet tree-lined West End, the hotel is not convenient for walking to Downtown; pick-up and drop-off for the airport shuttle (see p.25) is a five-minute walk away. Facilities include a laundry and in-house bike and ski storage, and rooms have TV but no phones. Children under 12 stay free in their parents' room. ❸

Burrard Motor Inn 1100 Burrard St near Helmcken ☎604/681-2331 or 1-800/663-0366, ℗681-9753. ⓦwww.vancouver-bc.com/ burrardmotorinn. A pleasantly dated motel with standard fittings: eighteen of the seventy rooms have kitchen facilities for self-catering (you'll pay an extra $5 for these), making this a good bet for families; some rooms look onto a charming garden courtyard. The general location isn't as convenient as some Downtown hotels, but you are still just four blocks from Robson

Street and from Yaletown to the east. Rooms have phone and TV; other facilities include a restaurant and free parking. ❹

Dominion Hotel 210 Abbott St ☎604/681-6666 or 1-877/681-1666, ⓦwww.dominionhotel. bc.ca. This is a nice, well-kept old hotel on the edge of Gastown, but it forms part of a popular pub and restaurant. Rooms come with phones (no TVs) and shared or private bathrooms, and if possible you should request one of the more recently renovated rooms with private bathroom well away from the live music. ❸

Dufferin Hotel 900 Seymour St ☎604/683-4251 or 1-877/683-5522, ℗683-0611, ⓦwww.dufferinhotel.com. Not far from the preferable *Kingston* (see below), the *Dufferin* tends to pick up its overflow. It's not as calm, cheap or pleasant as its rival, but does offer free parking, dining room and a choice of family rooms and rooms with and without private bathrooms. Noise and late-night bustle can be an issue here, as there is a (predominantly gay, but straight-friendly) pub on the premises. ❹

Kingston Hotel 757 Richards St at Robson ☎604/684-9024 or 1-888/713-3304, ℗684-9917, ⓦwww.kingstonhotelvancouver.com. One of Vancouver's best-known bargains, the Kingston is well run, clean, safe and handily situated on the eastern edge of Downtown. Its well-decorated interior successfully affects the warm and comfortable look and feel of a European-style hotel, though its 55 rooms are fairly small and standard in appearance. Nine have private bathrooms and TVs, while the rest have a phone (no TV), washbasin and share good bathrooms at the end of each corridor. There's also a coin laundry and a modest but free breakfast to start the day. Off-street parking is available half a block away from $10 a day. With the *Sylvia*, this is by far the best at its price in the city. Book well ahead. ❸

Sylvia Hotel 1154 Gilford St ☎604/681-9321, ℗682-3551, ⓦwww.sylviahotel.com. Located in a 1912 greystone, the *Sylvia* is an ivy-covered local landmark that was one of the city's first hotels and earliest high-rise buildings (some rooms are in a low-rise annexe added in the mid-1980s). It stands on English Bay virtually on the beach two blocks from Stanley Park, and its snug bar, quiet, friendly service, restaurant (with outdoor terrace for summer dining) old-world charm and sea views make it one of Vancouver's best in its price range. It's also a perennially popular place, making reservations for one of its 119 rooms essential. The lobby raises expectations – great stained-glass windows, plump chairs, red carpets and marble staircase – not fulfilled by the rooms, which are mostly relatively plain and come in seven different types (our price code covers only a handful of the very cheapest available: most are more expensive), all with private bathroom and, in the 23 suites (which are big enough for families), kitchen facilities. If you can, angle for one of the more expensive south- or southwest-facing rooms – they have the best views of English Bay and the sunset. Low-season rates are available between October and May. **❹**

Victorian Hotel 514 Homer St on the corner of Pender ☎604/681-6369 or 1-877/681-6369, ⓦ www.victorianhotel.com. The family-run *Victorian* is situated about as far east as you'd want, but remains within easy walking distance of Gastown and the rest of Downtown. It was built in 1898 as one of the city's first guesthouses, and has been carefully restored, and many of its rooms have high ceilings, hardwood floors, elegant bathrooms and period features such as original fireplaces and mouldings. Prices vary by up to $60 between double rooms, depending on whether they have private bathrooms and/or kitchenettes. All rooms have phones and small TVs; continental breakfast is included. **❸**

Moderate

Barclay Hotel 1348 Robson St at Jervis ☎604/688-8850, ⓕ688-2534, ⓦ www.barclayhotel.com. This is one of the nicer of several hotels at the north end of Robson (see also the *Greenbriar* and *Robsonstrasse* below), about half way between Stanley Park and the Vancouver Art Gallery. It features ninety rooms in several price categories (low-season rates are available) and a rather chintzy French rustic ambience in places. Given its rooms and facilities, which include air-conditioning, a restaurant and a licensed lounge, it's something of a bargain. **❹**

Bosman's Hotel 1060 Howe St between Nelson and Helmcken ☎604/682-3171 or 1-888/267-6267, ⓦ www.bosmanshotel.com. As long as

you don't want too many frills, this is a well-located hotel with free parking, restaurant and lounge just two blocks from Robson. It has 102 modern, air-conditioned rooms (all with TVs) at a range of prices, but some look on to Howe, one of the city's busier streets, so even with double-glazing, traffic may be an issue here. There is, however, an outdoor swimming pool for use in summer. **❺**

Comfort Inn Downtown 654 Nelson St ☎604/605-4333 or 1-888/605-5333, ⓕ605-4334, ⓦ www.comfortinnDowntown.com. There have been lodgings of sorts in this heritage building for years, but after a 1950s retro-inspired refit, complete with lots of black-and-white photographs and period neon, this boutique hotel now has a hip and stylish look. Rooms all come with high-speed Internet access, voicemail, dataports and air-conditioning. The room price includes a continental breakfast in *Doolin's Irish Pub*, and a pass to three clubs (*Roxy*, *BaBaLu* and *Fred's Uptown Tavern*) owned by the same management. The location is convenient for the restaurant and clubs of both Yaletown and the lower end of Granville St. **❺**

Days Inn Vancouver Downtown 921 W Pender St at Burrard ☎604/681-4335 or 1-877/681-4335, ⓦ www.daysinnvancouver.com. Something of a city institution, this old 85-room, seven-storey building in the financial district in the heart of Downtown has more character than most and lots of original Art Deco touches. Rooms are air-conditioned, but relatively plain for the price and ten have showers only, rather than showers and baths. Aim for a room away from the busy street, preferably one with harbour views. Facilities include restaurant, bar and valet parking ($10), and low-season deals are available from November to April. **❼**

Greenbriar Hotel 1393 Robson St at Broughton ☎604/683-4558 or 1-888/355-5888, ⓕ669-3109. ⓦ www.greenbriarhotel.com. The *Greenbriar* stands on a pleasant city block between Stanley Park and the heart of Downtown. Though nothing great to look at, the interior of this former apartment block has been nicely transformed into a variety of 32 one-bed and family suites with neat, modern decor and the option of fully equipped kitchens. Many rooms have sea and mountain views, and there's free parking, but Robson is busy day and night, so this isn't the most tranquil of locations.There's a $40 range from the cheapest to most expensive double. **⑥**

Holiday Inn Hotel & Suites Downtown 1110 Howe St between Davie and Helmcken ☎604/684-2151 or 1-800/663-9151 in the US and Canada, ⓕ684-4736, ⓦwww.atlific.com. The "Downtown" in the name of this is rather misleading, for while this large hotel is reasonably central, it actually stands at the Granville Island end of Howe Street. Unlike some of the dingier hotels nearby, this is a classy place, with lots of facilities, including sauna, pool and kids' activity centre, plus rooms with kitchenettes for self-catering. At this price – there is an extraordinary $220 range between top and bottom rates for doubles – there are also plenty of alternatives elsewhere. **⑦**

Riviera Hotel 431 Robson St at Nicola ☎604/685-1301 or 1-888/699-5222, ⓦwww.rivieraonrobson.com. More towards the Stanley Park than Vancouver Art Gallery end of Robson, the *Riviera* started life in the 1960s as an apartment building, but has been converted into a hotel with thirteen large studios and 27 twin-room/one-bedroom suites. All have well-equipped kitchens and balconies, with great harbour and mountain views from the rear (north-facing) side of the building. Free parking and weekly, monthly and low-season rates are available. **⑥**

Robsonstrasse City Motor Inn 1394 Robson St at Broughton ☎604/687-1674 or 1-888/667-8877, ⓕ685-7808, ⓦwww.robsonstrassehotel .com. Like the nearby *Greenbriar*, this hotel, midway between Stanley Park and the centre of Downtown, has a variety of double rooms and suites with kitchenettes at a wide range of prices. It's also air-conditioned, and offers free parking and a guest laundry. **⑤**

Sandman Hotel Downtown 180 W Georgia at Homer ☎604/681-2211 or 1-800/726-3626, ⓕ681-8009, ⓦwww.sandman.ca. This large hotel is the flagship of a reliable mid-price chain with hotels all over western Canada, and is well placed at the eastern edge of Downtown. The renovated rooms are bland but comfortable in the manner of chain hotels, and are well equipped and rather spacious: all have air-conditioning and some have kitchenettes. Underground parking is available and residents have access to an indoor swimming pool,

whirlpool and health club. The ground floor hosts the popular *Shark Club Bar & Grill* (see p.161). Low-season rates are available. **④**

Shato Inn Hotel at Stanley Park 1825 Comox St between Denman and Gilford ☎604/681-8920. If you can't get into the *Sylvia* (see p.132), then the *Shato* lies just a block to the northeast. It's a quiet, family-run place convenient to Stanley Park and the beach. All rooms have phones and TVs and some have balconies and/or kitchen units. Underground parking is available and rates are lower off season. **⑤**

Sunset Inn & Suites 1111 Burnaby St at Thurlow ☎604/688-2474 or 1-800/786-1997, ⓕ669-3340, ⓦwww.sunsetinn.com. This is one of the better modern high-rise apartment hotels on the fringes of the West End, offering studios or one-bed apartments that make it a good spot for a longer stay. The hotel has fifty spacious rooms in all, each with a balcony (though views are nothing special in this part of the city): most have recently been updated. Facilities include a laundry, free parking, exercise room and quiet location close to shops. Downtown is a ten-minute walk away. Low-season and weekly rates are available. **⑦**

Travelodge Vancouver Centre 1304 Howe St ☎604/682-2767 or 1-800/578-7878, ⓕ682-6225, ⓦwww.travelodge.com. This chain hotel has seen better days, and rates are rather high, but extensive restoration work is putting a new gloss on the place and making the prices rather better value. Ask for a refurbished room, and you'll get clean and comfortable interiors, air-conditioning, TV, free local phone calls, free parking and access to a restaurant and heated outdoor pool. Not terribly central, it is convenient for the Granville Island ferry jetty. **⑥**

West End Guest House 1362 Haro St near Jervis ☎604/681-2889, ⓕ688-8812, ⓦwww.westend guesthouse.com. This wonderful, small and carefully restored 1906 guesthouse lies in a quiet area despite being just a block from Robson. The Victorian feel is completely realized, right down to the gramophone in the old-time parlour, a lovely collection of old photographs of the city and the sherry and iced tea available in the afternoon. The seven bright, very attractive rooms (lots of antiques and your own stuffed animal) have private bathrooms and touches you'd expect in a luxury hotel – notably terry bathrobes, feather mattresses and your own slippers. Book well in advance. Full breakfast included and free loan of bikes. No smoking. ➐

Expensive

The Fairmont Hotel Vancouver 900 W Georgia St at Burrard ☏604/684-3131 or 1-800/441-1414, ⓕ662-1929, ⓦwww.fairmont.com. This venerable but thoroughly renovated 1939 hotel is the most famous and prestigious Vancouver hotel and the one to go for if money's no object and you want more traditional old-world style than some of Vancouver's world-class hotels, a Downtown location and all the refinements (spa, fitness centre, pool and so on) and attention to detail you'd expect in a hotel of this class. Doubles range from around $269 to $589, but low-season rates (down to about $190) are available. ➒

The Fairmont Waterfront 900 Canada Place Way ☏604/691-1991 or 1-800/441-1414, ⓦwww.fairmont.com. If the *Fairmont Hotel Vancouver* (see above) is too staid, then the company offers a more modern but equally illustrious alternative, this time a fabulous 489-room, multistorey affair on the dazzling Downtown waterfront. The location is unbeatable, especially if you have a room with a view, and everything about the place speaks of style and good taste. As in the Vancouver, the open-to-the-lobby restaurant and bar is a good place to eat or drink even if you're not staying here. Guests can use the health centre or third-floor heated outdoor pool, fringed by a herb garden whose produce is used in the hotel's restaurant, distinguished by huge floor-to-ceiling windows looking out over Coal Harbour. Doubles range from $295 to $625, with low-season rates available. ➒

Four Seasons Hotel Vancouver 791 Georgia St at Howe ☏604/689-9333 or 1-800/332-3442, ⓦwww.fourseasons.com. A Four Seasons hotel rarely disappoints, and Vancouver's is no exception. The location is perfectly central, located a block from Robson and the Vancouver Art Gallery, and the 385 rooms occupy a 28-storey high-rise building above the Pacific Centre mall. Rooms are enormous, the service immaculate, and the public spaces

stunning, none more so than the covered Garden Terrace, complete with lots of greenery, waterfalls and a superlative Inuit tapestry. If you're staying or not, you should definitely think about taking the buffet breakfast, served on this terrace – it's one of the best in the city (from $13). Similarly, the hotel's main restaurant, the *Chartwell* (see p.155), is widely considered among the city's elite, and is open to non-patrons. Doubles range from $400 to $570 for an executive suite. ➒

Granville Island Hotel 1253 Johnson St ☏604/683-7373 or 1-800/663-1840 in Canada and the US ⓕ683-3061, ⓦwww.granvilleislandhotel .com. If you stay at this modern and recently expanded hotel on the eastern edge of Granville Island, you'll be at the heart of one of the city's trendiest and most enjoyable little enclaves. This is not in the luxury bracket of places such as the *Pan Pacific* and the hotels above, but you still pay a premium for the location and spectacular waterfront setting, as well as for oversized bathtubs, health club, tennis courts and microwaves. A handful of rooms start at $159 but for some of the new and impossibly glamorous suites you're looking at up to $450. ➐

Opus Hotel 322 Davie St ☏604/642-6787 or 1-866/642-6787, ⓕ685-8690, ⓦwww.opushotel .com. Opened in August 2002, the *Opus* is a stylish, contemporary place to stay that lives up to Yaletown's hip reputation. Outside, it's just another seven-storey former warehouse, but inside the designers have got to work with the predictable bold palette of colours and materials (mosaic, marble, expensive fabrics) that are the minimum requirement of a modern city boutique hotel. The 97 rooms are equally fetching – expensive linens, firm beds, CD players, big windows and bathrooms you'd more than happily install at home. For the best views, ask for an upper south-facing room. Rooms start from $290, with suites coming in at $479, but off-season rates are far more manageable. ➒

Pan Pacific 300–999 Canada Place ☏604/662-8111 or 1-800/663-1515 in Canada, 1-800/937-1515 in the US, ⓦwww.panpacific.com. If you walk around Canada Place and wonder what happens in the magnificent white high-rise that rises above the complex's famous "sails" then wonder no more, for it's occupied by the *Pan Pacific*, the most expensive and spectacularly situated of Vancouver's modern luxury hotels. An eight-storey atrium and lobby set the tone, with vast 12m picture windows that look out over the harbour. All 504 rooms enjoy great views (the hotel rooms start on the building's eighth floor), and if you can get rooms 10 and 20 on each floor, then your bathroom will also have a sweeping panorama. Service and facilities are impeccable, while the heated outdoor pool and health centre are state-of-the art. **❾**

The North Shore

The North Shore embraces **North Vancouver** – the area across the Burrard Inlet opposite the Downtown peninsula – and **West Vancouver**, the mix of residential and open country along Marine Drive and the Trans-Canada Highway (Hwy 1) towards Lighthouse Park and Horseshoe Bay. Accommodation – and there isn't much – is concentrated mostly in the former, the moneyed enclaves of West Vancouver, which has some of the country's most expensive real estate, not being conducive to the notion of hotels and motels.

There is no point staying here if you want to get to grips with Downtown, even if you have a car, as traffic across the Lions Gate Bridge – the only vehicular access – is often bad. This said, there are several reasonably priced **motels** in the area, mostly just over the Lions Gate Bridge on or close to the junction of Capilano Road and Marine Drive. If you are using public transport, then you'll need to use either buses (which will also have to run the gauntlet of traffic on the bridge) or the SeaCat, a lovely crossing, but one whose novelty will wear off after several trips.

The main reasons you may want to be on the North Shore are to access the BC Ferries terminal at **Horseshoe Bay** easily or to be more handily placed for the hikes and other outdoor activities afforded by Grouse Mountain and the Capilano River, Mount Seymour and Lyonn Canyon parks. If this is your intention, there are some delightful **bed and breakfast** options close to the parks.

The city's reservation services (see p.131) can also help out here, but North Vancouver has its own **visitor centre** at 102-124 West 1st St (☎987-4488, ⓦ www.nvchamber.bc.ca) with information on the area's accommodation.

Inexpensive

Canyon Court Inn & Suites 1748 Capilano Rd ☎604/988-3181 or 1-888/988-3181, ⓦ www.canyoncourt.com. Take the North Vancouver exit or Exit 14 off Hwy 1 for this motel, which offers a variety of one- and two-bedroom suites, some with kitchens (for an extra $10). Facilities include an outdoor pool, Jacuzzi and laundry, and low-season rates are available: there is a $60 range from the cheapest to most expensive double room. **❹**

A Cottage Garden B&B 2810 Wembley Drive ☎604/980-9255 or 1-877/787-3813, ⓦ www.bedandbreakfasts.bc.ca. This two-room bed and breakfast is in Lyonn Canyon park and offers forest views that make you feel a long way from the city centre – which you are: to get here follow Hwy 1 and take exit 19 or 21. The rooms have a private entrance and shared bathroom and living room/kitchen. **❸**

Lynn Canyon B&B 3333 Robinson Rd ☎604/986-4741, ⓕ 986-4741, ⓦ www.vancouverinn.com. A Tudor-style home 13km from Downtown in lovely gardens and wooded setting close to the eponymous 250-hectare park and its hiking trails. There are two traditionally furnished rooms with private bathrooms, TVs, hot tub, open fires and a guest lounge. Rates include full breakfast and afternoon tea. **❹**

Travelodge Vancouver Lions Gate 2060 Marine Drive ☎604/985-5311 or 1-800-578-7878, ⊛www.lionsgatetravelodge.com. Noise can be a problem at this standard chain motel, given its busy (but convenient) position between the Lions Gate Bridge and Capilano Road. In its favour is the fact that it was refurbished in 2002, the rooms are air-conditioned, there's an outdoor pool, and rates are reasonable. ❸

Moderate

Best Western Capilano Inn & Suites 1634 Capilano Rd ☎604/987-8185 or 1-800/644-4227, ⊛www.bestwesterncapilano.com. Virtually on the junction of Marine Drive and Capilano Road, this is one of several chain motels just east of the Lions Gate Bridge. There are standard rooms or rooms with kitchenettes for an additional $20, as well as laundry, restaurant and outdoor summer pool. ❹

The Grouse Inn 1633 Capilano Drive ☎604/988-7101 or 1-800/779-7888, ⊛www.grouseinn.com. The Grouse Inn is located close to Downtown road links – one block east of the Lions Gate Bridge and one block south of Hwy 1 at Exit 14. Choose between eighty regular or superior rooms and one-or two-bedroom kitchen suites (the kitchens cost an extra $29). Rates include a continental breakfast and drop in low season. Among the facilities are air-conditioning, free parking, heated pool and a children's playground. ❺

Holiday Inn Express 1800 Capilano Rd ☎604/987-4461 or 1-800/663-4055 in Canada and the US or 1-800/HOLIDAY worldwide, ⊛www.hiexpressnv.com. One block north of the Capilano Road and Marine Drive intersection and just a few steps from the Canyon Court Inn & Suites and Best Western Capilano Inn & Suites (see above) – and with similar rates to the latter. Rates include continental breakfast and free local calls, and some rooms have kitchens and/or microwaves and fridges. In summer there's the option of a heated outdoor pool. ❺

Mountainside Manor 5909 Nancy Greene Way ☎604/990-9772 or 1-800/967-1319, ⊛www.mtnsideaccom.com. Situated off the road to Grouse Mountain (exit Hwy 1 at Capilano Road exit north and follow the Grouse Mountain signs for about 2.5km),

this ultramodern contemporary home offers four bright and airy bed and breakfast rooms with either en-suite facilities or private bathrooms, hot tub (with great view of the North Shore peaks), fireplaces, a guest sitting room with open fire, large deck and a pretty garden. Best rooms are the Panorama Room (with Jacuzzi and views of the city, mountains and the ocean as far as Vancouver Island) and the City Room (with four-poster and view of the city skyline). ❺

Thistledown House B&B 3910 Capilano Rd ☎604/986-7173 or 1-888/633-7173, ⊛www.thistle-down.com. This 1920 heritage building lies immediately east of the Capilano River park (just north of Edgemont Boulevard) and en route for Grouse Mountain, offering easy access to trails. En-suite rooms are tastefully restored and furnished with antiques, and there are lovely gardens; room rate includes a full breakfast and afternoon tea. Rooms are all non-smoking; low-season rates are available. ❻

Expensive

Beachside B&B 4208 Evergreen Ave ☎604/922-7773 or 1-800/563-3311, ⊛www.beach.bc.ca. You really are some way from Downtown here (12km plus, or 20 minutes by bus), but the location has other attractions, notably its position in a quiet cul-de-sac on a private beach between Sandy Cove and Pilot Cove (just east of Lighthouse Park), not to mention its panoramic views over the water to Point Grey and the city skyline. The upstairs guest area has floor to ceiling windows with binoculars to scout for seals, bald eagles and, occasionally, orcas and other whales. The two very stylish rooms have Jacuzzi (big enough for six) or hot tub, great oceanside patios, fridges, TV and video and en-suite bathrooms. ❼

Lonsdale Quay Hotel 123 Carrie Cates Court ☎604/986-6111 or 1-800/836-6111, ⊛www.lonsdalequayhotel. What you pay for the simple but tastefully appointed rooms here will get you smarter accommodation in Downtown, but you are paying for a location right on the Lonsdale Quay waterfront (which results in fabulous harbour views) and above the quay's superb market (see p.186): escalators from the market itself lead you to the hotel reception on the third floor. The hotel is bright and modern, and affects the usual design conceits and trimmings of the "boutique" property, including Internet access and spa, as well as offering bike hire and two restaurants. Posted room rates are as low as $80 off season, but generally this is an ❽

Park Royal Hotel 540 Clyde Avenue ☎604/926-5511 or 1-800/877-926-5511, ⓦwww.parkroyalhotel.com. Whereas most North Shore motels are a block or so east of the Lions Gate Bridge, this Tudor-style inn is one block west, over the Capilano River and close to the junction of Marine Drive and Taylor Way. This puts it virtually across the road from the vast Park Royal Shopping Centre, but the property itself sits on the river (you can fish for salmon from the grounds) and is shielded from the outside world by gardens. More intimate than the motels close by, it boasts an amiable English-style pub and Tudor Room restaurant for eating and drinking. Rooms are a touch small, but pay extra and you'll get more space and the chance of a garden view. ❼

South Vancouver

Whereas the North Shore has its obvious scenic attractions, it's hard to see any appeal in the accommodation found in the broad sweep of suburbs that make up south Vancouver. Prices are no keener than Downtown, though roads are less prone to congestion than the Lions Gate Bridge approach from the North Shore – and you also have the option of the SkyTrain, which bisects the area from Downtown to New Westminster.

With the honourable exception of the odd guesthouse near **Kits Beach** many of the lodgings here are motels, most notably the *Holiday Inn* and *Ramada* properties on West Broadway near Oak and the cluster on **Kingsway** southeast of the intersection with Victoria Drive. We've listed the cheapest options on Kingsway – price being the only real reason for being on this busy thoroughfare – but there's a substantial choice here of more expensive *Best Western*, *Days Inn* and other chain options. We have also given an option close to the **Tsawwassen ferry terminal** in case you need to catch an early ferry.

Inexpensive

2400 Motel 2400 Kingsway ☎604/434-2464 or 1-888/833-2400, ⓕ430-1045. These 65 basic motel bungalow units lie on Kingsway between 33rd Ave and Nanaimo/Slocan. Family suites and rooms with kitchenettes are available and there's free parking, with plenty of buses to Downtown from the doorstep. ❸

Biltmore Hotel 395 Kingsway ☎604/872-5252 or 1-800/663-5713, ⓦwww.biltmorehotel vancouver.com. If you are going to be on Kingsway, then this is the nearest of this busy road's hotels to Downtown. The 96 rooms are smallish, but they are air-conditioned, some have excellent city views, all have phones, there's free parking and a continental breakfast is included in the room rate. ❹

City Centre Motel 2111 Main St ☎604/876-7166 or 1-800/707-2489, ⓦwww .citycentermotelmotelhotel.com. Ignore the "City Centre" bit, because this standard motel is nowhere close: rather, it's on busy Main Street (between East 5th Ave and East 6th Ave), ten minutes' walk from the Science World-Main St SkyTrain station to the north. Rooms are air-conditioned, there's plenty of free parking, and rates are very competitive, but that's about it. ❸

Eldorado Hotel 2330 Kingsway ☎604/434-1341 or 1-800/667-2144, ⓕ434-5176. Just over 7km from Downtown a short distance north of the slightly more expensive *2400 Motel* (see below), this is a pretty rough and ready 46-room place with a pub lounge and little else. ❸

Mickey's Kits Beach Chalet 2142 1st Ave W at Yew St ☎604/739-3342 or 1-888/739-3342, ⓦwww.mickeysbandb.com. The youth hostel aside (see p.140), there's a surprising shortage of places to stay in the laid-back Kits district. This is the nicest of a limited choice: three quiet, private (non-smoking) rooms with the option of en-suite or shared bathrooms, plus TV, Web access and self-

Airport hotels

There are several choices close to the **airport**, though given the easy links to Downtown (see p.25), it's hard to see how you could get stuck either on arrival or be so pushed for time on departure that you have to check into what are invariably soulless retreats. However, if you are using an airport hotel, try to shop around, as there are invariably bargains and last-minute deals.

Fairmont Vancouver Airport
ⓣ604/207-5200 or 1-800/441-1414, ⓦwww.fairmont.com. There is no doubt where you want to be before or after flying if money is no object, and that's this luxurious and hugely convenient hotel, whose 392 extraordinary soundproof rooms are in the airport complex itself (access is via a walkway at the far end of the US departure hall). If you've ever thought that staying in an airport hotel was a waste of time, this place will make you think again. Everything hi-tech than can be crammed into a room has been crammed here, and everything has been designed to soothe the jet-lagged or harassed air traveller. Prices start at $189, but you'll almost certainly end up paying more

unless you check in during low season. The hotel is especially popular during the skiing season, when many people travelling long haul wisely spend a night here at the end of a trip before journeying to or from Whistler. ⓞ

Delta Vancouver Airport 3500 Cessna Drive, Richmond ⓣ604/278-1241 or 1-800/268-1133, ⓕ276-1975, ⓦwww.deltavancouverairport.com or www.deltahotels.com. Next choice, from the point of location, is this big 415-room hotel, 2km from the airport. The river setting is nicer than many an urban setting and the rooms were overhauled in 2002. There's a regular airport shuttle. Rates run from $119 to $259, but special deals can bring the price down to $99 or less. ⓞ

serve continental breakfast, and all just two blocks from the beach. Prices start at $75 but can go up to $140. ⓞ

Moderate

Best Western Tsawwassen Inn 1665-56 St, Delta ⓣ604/943-8221 or 1-800/943-8221, ⓦwww.tsawwasseninn.com. The main appeal of this *Best Western* is its location off Hwy 17 just 5km northeast of the BC Ferries' terminal at Tsawwassen. Rates include a continental breakfast and among the facilities are heated indoor pool, hot tub, sauna and dining room. ⓞ

Camelot Inn B&B 2212 Larch St ⓣ604/739-6941, ⓕ739-6937, ⓦwww.camelotvancouver .com. No complaints about the traditional look of this four-room Kits bed and breakfast, because it won the Vancouver's Heritage Honour Award in 2002 for the city's best-renovated home. The 1912 house and en-suite guest rooms have hardwood floors, lots of antiques and Persian rugs, and there's a good breakfast waiting in the morning. ⓞ

Holiday Inn Vancouver Centre-Broadway 711 Broadway West at Heather ⓣ604/879-0511 or 1-800/HOLIDAY, ⓦwww.hivancouver.com. It is hard to know why you would want to pay $160 and upwards for a double room in a big chain hotel outside Downtown, but if you want the security of knowing what to expect, this will do the job, with good chain-hotel rooms, lots of in-room and public facilities (indoor pool, sauna and a choice of restaurants). The best rooms have city, ocean and mountain views. ⓞ

Ramada Vancouver Centre 898 Broadway West ⓣ604/872-8661, ⓦwww.ramada.ca. The 118 rooms of this chain hotel are no more at the "centre" of anything than the *Holiday Inn* nearby (see above), which makes a similar locational claim, save for the busy stretch of Broadway north of Vancouver's city hospital. Rates are more competitive than its neighbour's, but otherwise facilities and rooms are what you would expect of a good mid-range chain. Watch out for the pub and its live entertainment (usually passable R&B) if you value peace and quiet. ⓞ

Hostels

Cambie International Hostel Gastown 300 Cambie St at Cordova ☏604/684-6466 or 1-888/395-5335, ⓦwww.cambiehostels.com. The 1897 *Cambie* is a private hostel located in Vancouver's oldest hotel and pub just off Gastown's main streets, and so has a much nicer and more central position than many of the city's hostels. Beds are arranged in two-, four- or six-bed bunkrooms and there are laundry, luggage-storage and bike-storage (but no cooking) facilities. There's a deservedly popular and inexpensive bar-grill with good patio (the *Cambie Saloon & Grill*) downstairs, so aim for beds away from this area if you want a relatively peaceful night's sleep. No curfew. $20 per person in a dorm room ($17.50 Oct–April); private double or quad rooms $22.50 perperson ($20 off season). Weekly rates available.

Cambie International Hostel Seymour 515 Seymour St at W Pender ☏604/684-7757 or 1-888/395-5335, ⓦwww.cambiehostels.com. This is the second, newer, calmer and more central of the *Cambie's* stable of hostels (there's a third on Vancouver Island). Like the Gastown hostel (see above), the management has made an effort to ensure that rooms in this heritage building are pleasant, secure and well kept, and provide laundry, storage, Internet and food and drink. No curfew. Pricing is slightly different to the Gastown hostel. Doubles in a bunk room cost $22.50 per person ($20 Oct–April) and $27.50 per person for a double bed ($22.50 offseason).

Central Station Hostel 1038 Main St ☏604/681-9118, 682-2441 or 1-800/434-6060, ⓦwww.centralstationhostel.com. This hostel opened near the main railway station in 2001 in the former *Ivanhoe Hotel*, a location that can be most kindly be described as "edgy". Each of the 104 rooms (renovated when the hostel opened) comes with sink, fridge and TV, and there's Internet access and an inexpensive restaurant and bar (with pool and darts) on site. Dorm beds $16 ($90 weekly), singles/doubles $40.

C&N Backpackers Hostel 927 Main St ☏604/682-2441 or 1-888/434-6060, ⓦwww.cnnbackpackers.com. This hostel is a well-known backpackers' retreat that, despite renovation and new management, is still not exactly dazzling and its location on the eastern edge of Downtown is hardly the best. Indeed, it is so far from anything but the Pacific Central Station and bus depot – which is 150m away – that it's hard to see why anyone should want to stay here unless you'd just got in on a late bus. No curfew. Beds at $14, $35 and $35 for a bunk (maximum of three- or four-bed dorms), single and double respectively. Weekly rates are available.

Global Village Backpackers 1018 Granville St at Nelson ☏604/682-8226 or 1-888/844-7875, Ⓕ682-8240, ⓦwww.globalbackpackers.com. *Global Village* has followed up the success of a popular hostel in Toronto with a zippy, bright hostel in Vancouver, although their chosen location on Granville Street – while central and away from the worst of this street's tawdriness – is not the quietest in the city. The hostel has 250 beds in two- and four-bed rooms, and offers a free shuttle from the bus–train station, secure lockers, modern kitchen and common area, games room and Internet access. No curfew. From $21 per person, doubles from $59.

Vancouver Central Hostel (HI) 1025 Granville St ☏604/685-5335 or 1-888/203-8333, ⓦwww.hihostels.ca. Vancouver's newest and smartest HI hostel on busy Granville Street is a far cry from the humble days of hostelling. It offers 226 beds in private double rooms with TV and en-suite bathrooms, four-bed dorms and air-conditioning in most rooms. Family rooms are also available. Facilities include a kitchen, pub, reading lounge and shuttle runs to the other city HI hostels and the Pacific Central Station. Check-in is at noon and check-out 11am. Dorm beds start at $20 for members and $24 for non-members. Private doubles start at $57.

Vancouver Downtown Hostel (HI) 1114 Burnaby St at the corner of Thurlow ☏604/684-4565 or 1-888/203-4302, Ⓕ684-4540, ⓦwww.hihostels.ca. The second of the city's two central official HI hostels is located in a former nunnery and health-care centre in the city's West End. There are 223 beds split up between shared and private rooms (maximum of four per room). Bike rental and storage as well as laundry, kitchen, Internet access and storage lockers are available. A free shuttle (look for the blue HI logo) operates between this hostel, the Jericho Beach hostel (see below) and the Pacific Central railway and bus terminal; if there's no bus, call the hostel to find when the next one is due. No curfew. Check-in 24 hours a day; check out by 11am. Reservations are essential. Beds cost $20 for members ($24 for nonmembers), private doubles $55 for members, $64 for nonmembers.

Vancouver Jericho Beach Hostel (HI) 1515 Discovery St off MW Marine Drive ☎604/224-3208 or 1-888/203-4852, ⨏224-4852, ⊛www.hihostels.ca. Canada's biggest Hostelling International youth hostel has a superb and safe position surrounded by lawns by Jericho Beach south of the city. The 286-bed hostel – a former barracks – fills up quickly, occasionally leading to a three-day limit in summer. There are dorm beds and ten private rooms (sleep up to six), which go quickly, with reductions for members and free bunks occasionally offered in return for a couple of hours' work. Family rooms are available. Facilities include kitchen, licensed café (April–Oct), bike rental and storage, storage lockers, Internet access and an excellent cafeteria. There is no curfew, but a "quiet time" is encouraged between 11pm and 7am. Check-in 24 hours a day. Dorm beds cost $18 for members, $22 for nonmembers. Doubles are $51 for members, $61 for nonmembers.

Vanier Hostel University of British Columbia (UBC), 5961 Student Union Blvd ☎604/822-1000, ⨏822-1001, ⊛www.conferences.ubc.ca. This hostel is on the UBC campus, which means it's a long way from Downtown (see p.100 for transport details), but close to the Museum of Anthropology and trails and

sights such as Wreck Beach (see p.106). As substantial bonuses, over and above your bed you get clean, safe accommodation (bed linen included), TV lounge, laundry, an Internet kiosk in the lobby, affordable campus food outlets and pubs and access to the University's fitness facilities, tennis courts and indoor and outdoor pools. Open early May to late Aug only. No curfew. Additional discounts are available for HI and ISIC cardholders on the room rates which start at around $25 single, $50 double.

YWCA Hotel-Residence 733 Beatty St between Georgia and Robson ☎604/895-5830 or 1-800/663-1424, ⨏681-2550, ⊛www.ywcahotel.com. Vancouver's excellent "Y" offers the best inexpensive accommodation in the city. It was purpose-built in 1995 in a handy east Downtown location close to the central library. The nearest SkyTrain station is Stadium, a five-minute walk. Top-value rooms (especially for small groups) are spread over eleven floors with a choice of private, shared or hall bathrooms. There are no dorm beds. TVs come with most rooms, plus there are sports and cooking facilities, Internet access, lounges, air-conditioning, laundry rooms as well as a cheap cafeteria and rooms with mini-kitchens. Open to men, women, couples and families. Check-in is 3pm, check-out by 11am. Singles cost $49 (mid-Oct–April), $51 (May) and $57 (June–mid-Oct); doubles ($56, $64 and $69 with shared bathroom, $75, $98 and $113 with private bathroom). If you are in a group, or family, four-person rooms (two double beds) are also available from $84, $113 and $132, plus $5 for each additional adult.

Campsites

In a city famed for its natural beauty and opportunities for outdoor activities it's something of a disappointment – and a municipal failing – that not only are there no public or private **campsites** in or near the city centre, but also that among the handful of sites that do exist none could be described as particularly memorable. To pitch a tent or hook up an RV you'll have to head to North Vancouver or the suburbs of Richmond and Burnaby, neither of which are places you'd choose to camp.

Burnaby Cariboo RV Park 8765 Cariboo Place, Burnaby ☎604/420-1722, ⨏420-4782, ⊛www.bcrvpark.com. This 237-pitch site

about 16km east of the city centre has luxurious facilities (indoor pool, Jacuzzi, laundry, free showers and convenience store) and a separate tenting area away from the RVs (for which there are full hook-up facilities). Take the Gaglardi Way exit (#37) from Hwy 1, turn right at the traffic light, then immediately left. The next right is Cariboo Place. Open year-round. $25–39.50 per site.

Capilano RV Park 295 Tomahawk Ave, North Vancouver ☎604/987-4722, ℉987-2015, ⊛www.capilanorvpark.com. This is a pretty unattractive place – think car park rather than verdant pastures – but it is the city's most central site for trailers and tents, located beneath the north foot of the Lions Gate Bridge and a short walk from the Park Royal Shopping Centre: exit Capilano Rd S or Hwy 99 exit off Lion's Gate Bridge. There are full RV facilities and hook-ups, plus swimming pool, free showers, washrooms and laundry, ice and water. Reservations (with deposit) essential June to August. $29.68–40.28 per site.

Park Canada Recreational Vehicles Inn 4799 Hwy 17, Delta ☎604/943-5811 or 1-877/943-0685, ⊛www.parkcanada.com. Convenient for the Tsawwassen ferry terminal to the southwest, this 145-pitch site has partial and three-way hook-ups for RVs and –

despite the name – some separate tent sites. There free showers, washrooms, laundry, heated pool, grocery store and, if this is your thing, the site's right next to a waterslide and golf course. Tent sites $18.50, RV sites $21–27.50.

Peace Arch RV Park 14601-40 Ave, Surrey ☎604/594-7009, ℉597-4220, ⊛www.peacearchrvpark.com. Calling this a city campsite is a bit of a stretch as it's in Surrey about 30km southeast of Downtown near the junctions of Hwy 99 and the King George Highway. However, it's a good place to pause before hitting Vancouver if you've driven up from the US. There are 250 tent and RV sites with full hook-ups, a games room and a swimming pool. $18.50–27.50 per site.

Richmond RV Park and Campground 6200 River Rd at Hollybridge and River Rd, Richmond ☎604/270-7878, ℉244-9713, ⊛www.richmondrvpark.com. Best of the RV outfits in terms of location, with the usual facilities (including free showers), but there are also tent sites; 14km from Downtown – take Hwy 99 N to the Westminster Hwy exit (#36) and follow the signs. April–Oct. $17–27 per site.

Eating

Vancouver locals eat out more than the residents of any other city in Canada: once you've been here for more than a few hours, it's easy to see why. The number and variety of restaurants is extraordinary, as is the range of European, Asian and Pacific Rim cooking (see box, p.144). Furthermore, the quality of the restaurants and the food they serve is generally exceptional, thanks to a demanding public and a plethora of superb natural ingredients, notably seafood. Most types of cuisine are available at prices that span the spectrum from budget to blowout but costs are generally lower than other major cities: if you want to eat well, you'll be spoilt for choice – and won't have to spend a fortune in the process.

The city's immigration history makes this a melting pot of different ethnic cuisines. **Chinese, Italian** and **Japanese** have high profiles, along with **French, Greek** and other European imports. **Vietnamese** and **Thai** are more recent arrivals, and these and other Far Eastern cuisines can often provide the best starting points – cafés and the ubiquitous fast-food chains aside – if you're on a tight budget.

For a city on the Pacific, specialist **seafood restaurants** are surprisingly thin on the ground, but those that exist are of high quality and often remarkably cheap. Seafood of some sort, however, crops up on most menus – salmon, a major fish in BC waters, is ubiquitous in all its forms, and an entirely different culinary experience to the mostly farmed salmon available in Europe. **Vegetarians** are well served by one or two specialist places, but will find an excellent choice of dishes in most "mainstream" restaurants.

Inexpensive options are provided by the countless **cafés** found around the beaches, in parks, along Downtown streets, and especially on Granville Island. Many sell light meals as well as coffee and snacks. **Little Italy**, the area around Commercial Drive (between Venables and Broadway), has always been good for cheap cafés and restaurants – though none for which you would make a special journey – but as new waves of immigrants fill the area Little Italy is increasingly dividing into "Little Vietnam", "Little Nicaragua" and so forth. Yaletown and the heavily residential **West End**, notably around Denman and Davie streets – Vancouver's "gay village" – are also booming, and boasts a selection of interesting shops and restaurants.

As far as **location** is concerned, restaurants are spread around the city, but are naturally more densely packed **Downtown** and sparser in North and West Vancouver. You'll eat well in several places in **South Vancouver**, but here the question is whether the blander, often suburban setting of restaurants and the distance from where you're likely to be staying make the journey worthwhile. Places in **Gastown** are generally tourist-oriented, with some notable exceptions, in marked contrast to **Chinatown**'s bewildering array of genuine and reasonably priced options. Downtown also offers plenty of chains and a huge selection, particularly where top-dollar places and fast-food outlets are concerned.

Further afield, the old warehouse district of **Yaletown**, part of Downtown's new southeasterly spread, is also a key – and still developing – eating and nightlife area. Good cafés and restaurants line 4th Avenue in **Kitsilano** and neighbouring West Broadway, though these require something of a special effort if you're based in or around Downtown. Perhaps try them for lunch if you're at the beach or visiting the nearby Vanier Park museum complex.

If you do go up market, don't feel inhibited by the need to dress up: Vancouver is a typically relaxed West Coast sort of city, and casual but neat will get you by in all but the stuffiest hotel or business-oriented restaurants.

If you're coming from Europe, note that "Entrées" in North America refer not to starters or appetizers, but to the main course. **Lunch** is generally served from about noon to 1 or 2pm, while **dinner** is served from 6.30pm, a little later in summer. **Smoking** in restaurants is prohibited – the bylaw is strictly enforced. Cafés and restaurants in our listings are **open** daily for lunch and dinner (and breakfast for cafés) unless specified.

Pacific Rim cuisine

Despite the range of options, many restaurants across the ethnic divides subscribe to the notion of **fusion cuisine** – often variously described as "West Coast", "Canadian" or "Pacific Rim". In practice, these descriptions are shorthand for (not always successful) cross-cultural approaches to cooking, something that's not confined to Vancouver by any means, but a trend that is particularly marked in a city able to exploit such a rich multi-ethnic mix. Italian is the most common staple – pastas, chicken dishes and so forth are common to a host of Vancouver restaurants – to which might be added ingredients, flavours or cooking techniques more commonly associated with Chinese and other Far Eastern cooking. Some of the wilder experiments of the late 1990s, however, have generally given way to cooking that is a little more restrained.

Canadian cuisine may also be shorthand for pasta (again), steaks, chicken, salmon, burgers and the other safe North American staples. In Vancouver, however, it can also be applied to restaurants that borrow from **aboriginal traditions,** which means food such as alder-smoked salmon, venison, grilled oysters, clam fritters and other more exotic dishes.

Cafés and light meals

Vancouver takes it coffee seriously, even by North American standards. Indeed, actress and comedian Bette Midler remarked in one performance in the city that she had "never seen so much coffee in all my life". The usual chains are ubiquitous, but there's no need to patronize the global conglomerates – there are plenty of small, individual places, and if you are tempted by a chain, then Vancouver's own *Bread Garden* cafés (see opposite) are good for coffee, bakery goods and breakfasts. For sinful treats, the name-says-it-all *Death By Chocolate* outlets are also excellent – be prepared for huge portions. Many cafés come and go quickly, but any stroll round **Granville Island** or **Yaletown** soon brings you to a place you'll be guaranteed good inexpensive food and snacks – and, invariably, the chance to sit outside in good weather.

Bavaria 203 Carrall St, Gastown (no phone). A simple, small and no-frills place with a couple of tables outside on Maple Tree Square almost in front of Gassy Jack's statue. Its inexpensive all-day breakfast is great value.

Blake's 221 Carrall St, Gastown ☎604/899-3354. One of several relaxed places on this short Gastown stretch of Carrall Street to drop by for a coffee, sandwich or snack and the chance to while away an hour writing a postcard or reading the newspaper.

Bojangles Café 785 Denman St, West End ☎604/ 687-3622, ⊛www.bojanglescafe.com. This West End institution is a little smarter than most cafés on a street full of small places to grab a coffee or snack. Lunches are well priced, with the "delux" sandwiches particularly good value. There's a small, sunny patio for outside eating and drinking.

Boulangerie la Parisienne 1076 Mainland St, Yaletown ☎604/ 684-2499. A café and bakery with a striking and very pretty all-blue interior that – true to its name – opens up French-style onto the pavement in summer.

Bread Garden 1040 Denman St at Comox St, West End ☎604/685-2996. Locals love to moan about the slow service, but food in these hyper-trendy deli-cafés is among the best – and best-looking – in the city. Great for people-watching. Also in Kitsilano at 1880 W 1st Ave at Cypress, and 812 Bute St, Downtown, off Robson.

Bud's Halibut and Chips 1007 Denman St, West End ☎604/683-0661. Generous and inexpensive portions of battered fish and fries (reckon on around $5 for the classic halibut and chip combo) from a West End institution that has been around for over twenty years.

Café S'Il Vous Plaît 500 Robson St and Richards St, Downtown ☎604/ 688-7216. Young, casual and vaguely alternative with good sandwiches, basic home-cooking and local art displays. It is close to the *Kingston Hotel* (see p.132) and central library. Open till 10pm.

Calabria Coffee Bar 1745 Commercial Drive ☎604/253-7017. Very popular café, known to locals as "Frank's", and tucked away from Downtown in the east of the city in Little Italy. Probably as close as you can get in Vancouver to the look and feel of a genuine Italian bar.

Capers 1675 Robson St, Downtown ☎604/687-5299. *Capers* is a three-branch chain of pristine supermarkets selling natural and organic foods, many of which can be bought as sandwiches and snacks in the on-site cafés. There is also a branch at 2285 West 4th Ave (☎739-6676).

Cordova Café 307 West Cordova St at Cambie, Gastown ☎604/688-3440. A café that showcases the work of local artists and serves good-value salads, light meals and daily soup-and-sandwich specials.

Crystals Café 1702 Davie at Bidwell, West End ☎604/682-5775. A good bet a block from Denman – and thus a block from the crowds – with a few outside tables.

Don't Show the Elephant 1207 Hamilton, Yaletown. Crazy modern teahouse-gallery on the edge of Yaletown where the funky Oriental-tinged design really counts for more than the teas. Be sure to visit the toilet.

Ecco Il Pane 238 West 5th Ave, South Vancouver ☎604/ 873-6888m ⊛www.eccoilpane.com. Superb Italian breads (try the delicious dolce mio fruit bread), which you can buy to take home or eat as accompaniments to, or mainstays of lunchtime soups and sandwiches, such as a cornmeal-crusted fried oyster panino. There is also an outlet in The Bay department store at 674 Granville St at Georgia.

Flying Wedge 3499 Cambie St, Downtown ☎604/874-8284, ⊛www.flyingwedge.com. If you want good, cheap pizza this is the place; thin-crust pizza by the slice (but no alcohol) and takeaway at various outlets, including the Waterfront Centre, 27-200 Burrard St ☎604/681-1122; Library Square, 207-345 Robson, Downtown ☎604/698-7078 (lunch only); the Royal Centre, 244-1055 West Georgia, Downtown ☎604/681-1233; 1059 Denman, West End ☎604/689-9700; and 1937 Cornwall Ave (for Kits beach) ☎604/732-8840).

Gallery Café Vancouver Art Gallery 750 Hornby St, Downtown ☎604/ 688-2233. Relaxed, stylish and pleasantly arty place at the heart of Downtown for coffee, good lunches and healthy, high-quality snack food and light meals (especially good desserts); also has a popular summer patio.

Hamburger Mary's 1202 Davie St and Bute, West End ☎604/687-1293. These may well be the best burgers in the city (though by no means the cheapest), but there are plenty of other things on the menu. Lots of people end the evening for a snack at this former West End diner. Outside tables when the weather is fine. Open very late (usually 3am). Recommended.

Kent's Kitchen 232 Keefer St between Main and Gore, Chinatown ☏604/669-2237. A café-restaurant that offers a mixture of Chinese staples and typical café snacks that is inexpensive even by Chinese standards.

La Luna Café 117 Water St, Gastown ☏604/687-5862. One of only a couple of places for coffee, muffins and snacks on Gastown's main street that has the char-acter – helped by a warm and welcoming, yellow-painted interior – to raise it above the usual tourist-oriented cafés in this part of the city.

The Only Café 20 E Hastings and Carrall St, Chinatown ☏604/681-6546. One of Vancouver's most famous institutions, founded in 1912, and worth the trip to a less than salubrious part of town to sample some of the best seafood in town and the old-world atmosphere. That said, this tiny greasy spoon (just 17 counter seats and two booths) has little more than seafood and potatoes on its menu; no toilets, no credit cards, no licence, and no messing with the service. Closed Sun.

Ovaltine Café 251 East Hastings St, Chinatown ☏604/685-7021. Beyond Main St and up the hill from *The Only Café* (see below), which it resembles, being a classic diner that's been around for over half a century. Easily

recognizable by the distinctive neon sign outside. Open 6am–midnight.

Picasso Café 1626 West Broadway, South Vancouver ☏604/732-3290. Staff here come from the Option Youth Society, which helps homeless young people. Service is enthusi-astic and the prices for the simple but well-prepared food are low – around $2 for soups, less than $5 for pancakes and the wonderful "Masterpiece" cheesecake.

Prospect Point Café Stanley Park. A position around midway round the Stanley Park Seawall and with great views of the ocean means this café has a large walk- or bike-by clientele, so it can become busy, espe-cially at weekends. But as a target for inex-pensive refreshment in Stanley Park it's perfect.

Sophie's Cosmic Café 2095 W 4th Ave, South Vancouver ☏604/732-6810. This 1950s-style diner is a Kits institution, packed for weekend breakfast and weekday lunch. It is renowned for its vast, spicy burgers, mussels, milkshakes, good vegetarian options and whopping breakfasts. Some may find its self-conscious kitsch a little too contrived.

Terra Breads Granville Island Public Market and branches ☏604/685-3102. Tremendous rustic, grainy and fresh-baked breads are the speciality here, with black olive, rose-mary, focaccia, cheese, onion, rye, raisin, grape, pine nut and other variations also available. You can also pick up the odd accompaniment and sandwich to combine with a drink from elsewhere.

Restaurants

In the listings that follow, restaurants are divided into **three price categories** according to the average cost of a three-course meal, including starter (appetiz-er), main course (often called "entrée" in Canada) and dessert. Bear in mind, however, that portions are often pretty generous, so by happily surviving on a main course, salad and wine by the glass, you can open up the possibility of eating in "expensive" places that might normally be beyond your budget. Bear in mind that you'll often enjoy the same dishes at lunch for considerably less than you would at the same establishment in the evening.

    Wine will push prices up a little, being generally rather overpriced, especially if you opt for French or New World wines. Reckon on at least $20 for a bottle of wine in a restaurant, much more if you want something reasonably good or interesting. Well worth a try are the emerging British Columbian wines, once something of a joke, but now winning prestigious international awards. Some are produced on Vancouver Island, but most come from in and around the Okanagan in the centre of the province, with Mission Hill one the top names.

Alcohol is expensive in Canada – don't be surprised if the drink portion of your bill comes to more than the cost of the food.

There is no provincial **tax** on restaurant meals, but seven-percent GST, a federal goods and services tax, is levied on the food portion of meals and added to bills. A ten-percent liquor tax is levied on alcohol, but many restaurants factor this into the listed price of a drink or bottle of wine. **Service** is rarely included, and you should definitely **tip** around 12 to 15 percent – unless the meal and service dictate otherwise.

Inexpensive: under $25

Moderate: $25–45

Expensive:over $45

Chinese

Boss Bakery and Restaurant 532 Main St, Chinatown ☎604/683-3860. There's many a spot in Chinatown where you'll feel you've crossed the Pacific to pitch up in Hong Kong or mainland China, but few like *Boss* which have a genuine Far Eastern atmosphere and yet also add an eccentric Western edge. Thus, while the clientele will almost certainly be mostly Chinese Canadians, the food might combine spaghetti with seafood or Chinese meatballs. Then, of course, there's Ovaltine, the milky bedtime drink, which you can have hot, cold or with raw egg. Inexpensive.

Floata Seafood Restaurant 400-180 Keefer St, Chinatown ☎604/602-0368, ⓦwww.floata.com. You can eat dim sum (see box, p.148) in many Vancouver Chinese restaurants but one of the most popular places to indulge is *Floata*, currently Canada's largest Chinese restaurant. Despite its size – the main dining area is nearly the length of a city block – it is not easy to find: it's on the third floor of a mall close to the Dr Sun Yat-Sen Garden. Dim sum is popular – and cheap, at lunch (choose from the carts being wheeled around by countless waitresses), but in the evening, menu items become more adventurous and more expensive: shark-fin and

Brunch

While brunch is not the institution in Vancouver it is in some North American cities, Sundays here are as potentially lazy as elsewhere, and the combination of fine settings – views of mountains, park and forest – and relaxed places to eat make the late-morning weekend meal an attractive proposition. Granville Island is an obvious location – but is busy at weekends, as are restaurants and cafés in Kits and Stanley Park. Turn up any time after 11am – and book to be sure of a table.

Recommended places which serve and specialize in brunch include the *Alibi Room* (see p.161), *Blue Water Café* (see p.154), *Bridges* (see p.155), *Café de Paris* (see p.149), *Cardero's* (see p.160), *Milestones* (see p.156), *Naam* (see p.154), *Seasons in the Park* (see p.156), *Sophie's Cosmic Café* (see p.146).

bird's-nest soups, Peking duck and so forth. Inexpensive–moderate.

Hon's Wun-Tun House 108-268 Keefer St at Gore St, Chinatown ☎ 604/688-0871. This canteen-like Cantonese spot started life more than twenty years ago as an inexpensive, basic and popular place known for the house specialities, "potstickers" – fried meat-filled dumplings – home-made noodles (go for those with shrimp, meat, dumplings or the spicy oyster, ginger and green onion) and ninety-odd soups (including fish ball and pig's feet). Success spawned other branches, and a slight smartening-up when the original place moved from Main Street, but the queues, good food, long menus (over 300 items) and low prices remain unchanged. It's invariably packed and hectic, but the service is efficient. Dim sum is available and there's a separate vegetarian menu. Also at 1339 Robson St. Inexpensive.

Imperial Chinese Seafood Restaurant 355 Burrard St, Downtown ☎ 604/688-8191, ⓦ www.imperialrest.com. A grand and opulent spot in the old Marine Building that serves fine, but pricey, Cantonese food (good dim sum, fresh egg noodles, delicious lobster in black bean sauce, pan-fried black cod and more) and looks nothing like the standard Chinese restaurant: the long dining room has white walls, smart royal-blue carpet and crisp, white table linen; windows run down one side, offering good city views. Expensive.

Kirin Mandarin 1166 Alberni St near Bute St, Downtown ☎ 604/682-8833, ⓦ www .kirinrestaurant.com. This was among the first of the city's smart Chinese restaurants when it opened in 1987, with a big business clientele and elegant, postmodern decor – green pastel walls, pink table linen and lots of black lacquer – that put it a world away from the more traditional and basic canteens of old-fashioned Chinatown. The superior food covers several Chinese regions: Cantonese (good scallops in black-bean sauce), Shanghai and the spicier dishes of Szechuan (try the hot chilli fish). Prices are high, but you're repaid with good food and great views of the mountains. Expensive.

Pink Pearl 1132 E Hastings St near Glen Drive, Chinatown ☎ 604/253-4316, ⓦ www.pinkpearl.com. This Vancouver institution is a big, fun, bustling and old-fashioned place with an unpretentious and highly authentic feel – but it's in a dingy part of town and ten blocks east of the main part of Chinatown. Expect to rub shoulders with Chinese families (and big wedding parties at weekends) and to eat your meal amidst considerable activity: service is brisk, unsmiling yet efficient. The food has a Cantonese slant, strong on seafood and great for dim sum (served daily): good bets are clams in black-bean sauce, spicy prawns or other fish and seafood options (crab, shrimp, scallops, oysters, rock cod and more) scooped from

Dim sum

Dim sum means "small heart" or "to touch the heart" and is a type of daytime Chinese snack, similar in many ways to brunch in the West. It originated in Canton, where most dishes are lightly cooked – steaming being the favoured method – and subtly flavoured. While there are over 2000 dim sum dishes, most Vancouver restaurants offer a selection of around 150, including popular dishes such as shrimp and pork dumplings, turnip cake, deep-fried sesame balls and steamed pork buns.

Jasmine tea or the strong black Chinese *bo lay* is usually brought to your table once you sit down. This is followed by a succession of carts piled with small plates and bamboo baskets of hot food, sometimes with savoury dishes on top, sweet below. Simply point to the dish you want; the waiter or waitress will mark your choices each time on a bill that stays at your table until the end of the meal.

Dim sum is served in most restaurants daily from about 10am to 2pm; lunch and Sundays are the busiest times. Be prepared for large crowds and big, gaudily decorated restaurants, featuring red and gold in most decorative schemes – colours chosen for their lucky associations. Best of all, dim sum is a cheap way of eating – you shouldn't spend more than about $10.

big glass tanks near the entrance.
Inexpensive.

Shanghai Chinese Bistro 1128 Alberni St,
Downtown ☎604/ 683-8222. A modern-
looking but less ostentatious and more reasonably priced alternative to the *Imperial* if
you want to eat Chinese Downtown. The
handmade noodles are a must – there's
also a daily noodle-making demonstration
for the curious. Dim sum is available, but
fresh seafood is the speciality. Open till
around 2 or 3am. Inexpensive.

Wild Rice 117 West Pender St, Downtown
☎604/642-2882, ⊛www.wildricevancouver.com.
A western take on Chinese food from a
former chef at *Bin 941* (see p.153), with
dishes and ingredients from across China
refined and reworked for Canadian consumption. Go for the bite-size tasters or
platters to share and don't worry too much
about cost – this is high quality food at
reasonable prices. Dishes might include
wild boar with jasmine rice and plantain,
rabbit wontons, winter melon salad, crispy
fried duck and warm rice pudding with
chocolate and ginger. There is a good,
short wine list and a choice of teas and
martinis. Moderate.

French

Café de Paris 751 Denman St, West End
☎604/687-1418. This bistro brings a little bit
of the Left Bank to Vancouver, with paper
tablecloths, lacy curtains, a mirrored bar
and popular French crooners such as Piaf
as background music. Good, solid French
staples like onion soup and *moules*, plus
more contemporary dishes like venison
with wild mushroom sauce and pot au feu
of duck. What you'll probably remember
most, however, are the amazing *frites*
served with all entrées – they're easily the
best and most authentic French fries in the
city. Good wine list with lots of French
choices, though the New World options
offer better value. Lunch Mon–Fri, dinner
Mon–Sat, brunch Sun. Moderate.

Cioppino's Mediterranean Grill 1133
Hamilton St, Yaletown ☎604/688-7466,
⊛www.cioppinosyaletown.com. It's hard to
categorize this inviting restaurant with
warm, cherrywood interior – the name
comes from San Francisco's cioppino fish
stew, but some food is French-influenced,
other Italian. Suffice to say, it's an attractive

and convenient place if you are in this part
of town. Perhaps the best thing to do is
sample a little of almost everything with the
tasting menu. If the food seems too expensive, make instead for the *Cioppino* wine
bar next door for a drink. Moderate–expensive.

Le Crocodile 100-909 Burrard St, entrance on
Smithe St, Downtown ☎604/669-4298,
⊛www.lecrocodilerestaurant.com. This plush,
French-Alsace up-market bistro pushes
Bishop's (see p.155) for the title of the
city's best restaurant and, unlike its rival,
it's located Downtown just a block south of
Robson Street. The punchy decor – bright
yellow walls – conjures up a suitable
Parisian feel, while the menu offers something for traditionalists and the more
adventurous alike – anything from classic
steak tartare, onion tarte, Dover sole and
calf's liver to more outré dishes involving
non-Gallic staples of the Pacific Rim. A
memorable meal is guaranteed – but check
your credit limit first. Lunch Mon–Fri, dinner
daily. Expensive.

Le Gavroche 1616 Alberni St, Downtown
☎604/685-3924. *Le Crocodile* may take the
culinary plaudits, but this top French
restaurant (with a West Coast twist) is not
far behind. It's a formal but amiable place
located in an old West End townhouse,
and while the food is excellent – with particularly fine sea bass with white beans or
veal tenderloin with lobster sauce – it's the
highly romantic setting that really sets this
place apart. The dining room is wonderfully
cozy thanks to dark-painted walls and a
big open fireplace, grand mirrors and old
paintings. Lunch Mon–Fri, dinner daily.
Expensive.

The Hermitage 115–1025 Robson St near
Thurlow St, Downtown ☎604/689-3237,
⊛www.thehermitagevancouver.com. Warm
brick walls, a big fireplace, crisp linen,
antique furnishing, French-speaking waiters
and a courtyard setting give this central
and very highly rated Downtown restaurant
a cozy almost European feel. The chef here
once cooked for King Leopold of Belgium
– the onion soup is unbeatable. If a simple
soup sounds too plain, you can also go for
classic calorie-laden French food, such as
duck Magret with an Armagnac sauce or
veal tenderloin with a wild mushroom
sauce. Lunch Mon–Fri, dinner daily.
Moderate.

△ Seafood, fresh from the Pacific

Lucy Mae Brown 862 Richards St, Downtown ☏604/899-9199. This intimate restaurant is one of the most popular in the city, and takes its name from the owner of a former brothel and boardinghouse on the site. The appealing decor is a rhapsody of blues, offset by stone and wood floors and high ceilings. Food changes regularly with the seasons, but is always lusty (lamb shanks or ahi tuna with capers) without forgetting its sophisticated French and West Coast inspirations. Downstairs is a secret, club-like little bar that opens late and has a sim-plified menu. Dinner only Mon–Sat. Moderate.

Lumière 2551 W Broadway near Trafalgar St, South Vancouver ☏604/739-8185, ⓦwww.lumiererestaurant.ca. This is in the first rank of Vancouver's restaurants. Cooking here is "contemporary French", a bit lighter than what you might expect to find at its rivals (see above), but no less pricey. A good option is to take one of the two set-price "tasting" menus offered each evening; one vegetarian, the other meat, fish and fowl. Visitors based in Downtown will need to take a cab here: you'll also need to book, for the simple, tasteful dining room accommodates just fifty diners. Closed Mon. Expensive.

Greek

Orestes 3116 W Broadway between Trutch and Balaclava sts, South Vancouver ☏604/738-1941. Good, basic food in one of the city's oldest Greek restaurants. Belly dancers shake their stuff Thursday to Saturday and there's live music on Sunday. Inexpensive.

Ouzeri 3189 W Broadway at Trutch St, south Vancouver ☏604/739-9995. A friendly and fairly priced restaurant on a part of the strip with several other good restaurants and cafés: not too far from the hostel or beach in Kitsilano. As with *Orestes* (see above) you'll find all the Greek standards, but the vegetable moussaka is a standout, as are the chicken livers and the prawns with ouzo and mushrooms. Inexpensive.

Stepho's 1124 Davie St between Thurlow and Bute sts, West End ☏604/683-2555. This cen-tral restaurant has simple interior, fine food, big portions, low prices, efficient service and is very popular (expect queues). The daily specials are always a good bet (go for the baby back ribs if they are available):

otherwise, avgolemono soup (a chicken broth with lemon and egg) is good, as are staples such as chicken, lamb or beef pita (with fries and tzatziki garlic sauce) or meat brochettes (souvlaki) accompanied by potatoes, rice pilaf or Greek salad. Recommended. Inexpensive.

Indian and Southeast Asian

Just One Thai Bistro 1103 Denman St, West End ☏604/685-8989, ⓦwww.thaihouse.com. A peaceful and authentic atmosphere prevails at this restaurant, thanks in large part to the exemplary and charming service, the palm trees, fresh flowers and numerous brass and porcelain Buddhas. The curries are delicious, as are the stir fries and tom yum goong (a spicy prawn and mushroom soup), but the house speciality is Thai bar-becue (meats, fish, seafood – all marinated and grilled and served with tangy peanut sauce). Inexpensive.

Phnom-Penh 244 E Georgia St near Gore St, Chinatown ☏604/ 682-5777; 955 W Broadway near Oak St, South Vancouver ☏604/734-8988. Excellent Vietnamese and Cambodian cui-sine (the menu is divided between the two), with some Chinese dishes, is served in this pair of friendly, family-oriented restaurants. Seafood is a strength, with a renowned spicy garlic crab, plus delicious garlic and pepper prawns (in season). Also try the bank xeo, a Vietnamese pancake filled with prawns and bean sprouts. Inexpensive.

Pho Hoang 3610 Main St at 20th Ave, Chinatown ☏604/874-0810; 238 E Georgia St, Chinatown ☏604/682-5666. The Main St Pho Hoang was the first and perhaps friendliest of the many Vietnamese pho (beef soup) restaurants now springing up all over the city. Choose from thirty soup varieties with herbs, chillis and lime at plate-side as added seasoning. Open for breakfast, lunch and dinner. The more recent Chinatown branch is right by the *Phnom-Penh* (see above). Inexpensive.

Simply Thai 1211 Hamilton St at Davie St, Yaletown ☏604/642-0123. This plain, modern but inviting Yaletown restaurant is packed at lunch (11.30am–3pm) and dinner, thanks to the keen prices as well as the good and very authentic food – the chefs are all from Bangkok.

Thai Urban Bistro 1119 Hamilton St, Yaletown ☏604/408-7788. A few steps from *Simply Thai*, and similar in most respects, *Thai*

EATING

Urban Bistro offers good, basic Thai food at low prices in a simple setting – except that it's likely to be less crowded. Inexpensive.

Vij's 1480 W 11th Ave at Granville St, South Vancouver ☎604/736-6664. *Vij's* East Indian cooking has deservedly won just about every award going in Vancouver for Best Ethnic Cuisine. At the time of writing you still couldn't make reservations – you simply line up with other hopefuls and enjoy the free tea and poppadoms while you wait. The menus change roughly monthly, but never let go of old faithfuls such as curried-vegetable rice pilaf with cilantro cream sauce or Indian lentils with naan and yoghurt-mint sauce. The vegetarian options are excellent. Dinner only. Moderate.

Italian

Allegro Café 1G-888 Nelson St, Downtown ☎604/683-8485. The location on the ground floor of an office building opposite the Law Courts may not be promising, but the recently revamped interior is surprisingly warm and romantic, while the Italian and Mediterranean food is excellent and good value for Downtown. Try the great soups (roast garlic a standout), exotic pastas (cappelli with scallops, leeks and Roma tomatoes) or ambitious mains (pan-seared halibut medallions in apple fennel butter sauce with celery-root chips). Puddings are also good: go for Cajun bread pudding or peanut butter pie, the latter courtesy of chef Barbara Reese, of the Reese Peanut Butter Cup dynasty. Inexpensive–moderate.

Borgo Antico 321 Water St, Gastown ☎604/683-8376, ⊛www.umberto.com. Gastown needs more restaurants like this, a restored warehouse under the same reliable ownership as *Il Giardino di Umberto*, though prices are lower here. A cobbled pavement leads to an old-fashioned iron-gate entrance, beyond which the arched dining room is decorated in warm, bold colours. Daily specials are always reliable choices, but carpaccio and rocket as a starter is recommended, as are the risottos and fresh grilled fish. Dinner daily, lunch Mon–Fri. Inexpensive to moderate.

CinCin 1154 Robson St, Downtown ☎604/688-7338, ⊛www.cincin.net. An excellent Downtown option with a stylish, buzzy setting of ochre-coloured walls, low lighting, long bar, open kitchen, lots of greenery and faux Renaissance statues. Plenty of fashion, politics, arts and media luminaries frequent the place, but it's never precious or showy. The refined Italian food merits the highish prices and includes top-grade home-made pastas, pizzas and desserts. Some of the best dishes, notably chicken and game, are cooked over the alderwood-fired open grill. Service is first rate and the restaurant also boasts one of the best wine lists in this or any other city, with plenty of wines by the glass. In summer, try to book an outside table on the terrace. Lunch Mon–Sat, dinner daily. Moderate–expensive.

Il Giardino di Umberto 1382 Hornby St, Downtown ☎604/669-2422, ⊛www.umberto.com. Sublime food with a pasta and game bias are served here to a trendy and casually smart thirty-something clientele. The atmosphere in the villa-like dining room is often animated, despite the muted Mediterranean-style surroundings (think burnt sienna-coloured walls, wooden beams). Some of the food is far more exotic than you'd ever find in Italy (reindeer loin, stuffed pheasant breast, ostrich in wild berry sauce). Weekend reservations are essential – this is something of a place to "be seen" – especially if you want to dine on the nice vine-trailed terrace. Lunch Mon–Fri, dinner daily. Expensive.

Incendio 103 Columbia St, Gastown ☎604/688-8694. This vividly painted pizzeria is just a block east of Maple Tree Square in Gastown, so its location is not as downbeat as some places closer to Chinatown. It features wood-fired pizzas, calzone, good salads and a range of other dishes. Inexpensive.

The Old Spaghetti Factory 55 Water St, Gastown ☎604/684-1288. Part of a chain and hardly alta cucina, but a standby if you're in Gastown and better than the tourist trap it appears from the outside, with its spacious 1920s Tiffany interior and a good range of pastas, chicken and other meat and fish dishes. A good place to go with children, as prices are low, there's plenty of room, the atmosphere is informal and the simple Italian food is likely to appeal. Inexpensive.

Piccolo Mondo 850 Thurlow St and Smithe St, Downtown ☎604/688-1633, ⓦwww .piccolomondoristorante.com. A nicely restrained dining room, just off Robson Street, that's not as formal as the austere red-brick facade, plain white walls and wooden floors first make it appear. The osso bucco is excellent, as are the veal loin and rather un-Italian starter of sweet-and-sour prawns; other good bets include zuppa di pesce or ravioli with salmon and ricotta. The wine list is also superb, drawing from a cellar of over 4000 bottles – it's won a fistful of *Wine Spectator* magazine awards. The clientele are expense-account types at lunch and smooching couples in the evenings. Lunch Mon–Fri, dinner daily. Moderate.

Villa del Lupo 869 Hamilton St, Downtwon/edge of Yaletown ☎604/688-7436, ⓦwww.villadellupo.com. Authentic, high-quality food in a renovated, unfussy and elegant Victorian-era "country" house on the eastern edge of Downtown. There's not a better osso bucco in Vancouver if you want to eat traditional Italian, though more sophisticated dishes include tuna loin with cracked black-pepper crust or sweetcorn broth with ricotta and spinach gnocchi. Expensive.

Japanese

Chiyoda 1050 Alberni St at Burrard St, Downtown ☎604/688-5050. Everything at this central robata (grilled food) bar, down to the beer glasses, was designed in Japan. Chic but convivial – the emphasis is on robata rather than sushi – and draws Japanese visitors and business people at lunch and the fashionable in the evenings. The day's produce is laid out on ice on the wooden counter in front of the grills – choose from around thirty different items (fish, prawns, oysters, aubergine and so forth) and then have your choice of food grilled, seasoned and returned to you on long paddles. Moderate.

Ezogiku Noodle Café 1329 Robson St at Jervis St, Downtown ☎604/685-8608. This tiny 70-seat Japanese ramen noodle house (with sister outlets in Tokyo and Honolulu) is a perfect place for quick, good food Downtown. The queues may look off-putting, but the turnover's speedy. Cash only and no alcohol. Inexpensive.

Gyoza King 1508 Robson St, Downtown ☎604/669-8278. Fight through groups of homesick Japanese students and tourists to enjoy the great comfort food (there is very little sushi here), casual atmosphere and funky, dark-walled interior of this excellent-value Downtown spot. Choose from more than 20 types of gyoza – succulent fried dumplings with a variety of fillings (the vegetable and spinach are great) with a soy dipping sauce. Or go for noodle and robust o-den soups, good-value specials, katsu-don (breaded pork chop with rice). Chase them down with one of many choices of beer and sit at the bar, the low front table or the higher Western tables. Inexpensive.

Koji 630 Hornby St, Downtown ☎604/685-7355. Gardens are rare enough Downtown, let alone in restaurants, so the very pretty Japanese patio with pines and river rocks here is a real treat. Sushi here isn't the city's best by any means, but Japanese visitors and locals come here for the garden, fair prices and other outstanding dishes, notably smoky black cod and grilled shiitake with bonito flakes, and for the generous boxed lunch at around $10. Breakfast and dinner daily, lunch Mon–Fri. Inexpensive.

Tojo's 777 W Broadway at Willow St, South Vancouver ☎604/872-8050, ⓦwww.tojos.com. Quite simply the best Japanese food in the city, which makes it a shame that the deceptively modest-looking sushi bar is some way from Downtown. Worth the journey, however – anything on the menu involving tuna is superb, but you should sample some of the many more unusual items (such as shrimp dumplings with hot mustard sauce) or standards such as lobster claws, crab and herring roe. This is sushi close to perfection – but at prices which make sure you savour every mouthful. Dinner only Mon–Sat. Expensive.

Spanish and Mexican

Bin 941 941 Davie Street, West End ☎604/683-1246, ⓦwww.bin941.com. It's not surprising that no one seems to have a bad word for *Bin 941*, or for its sister outlet at 1521 West Broadway in South Vancouver (☎734-9421). Both are tiny, on the slightly crazy side of funky, and packed long and late with people drawn by the up-tempo bars (the West Broadway location is marginally more subdued) and some of the city's best – and best-value – bite-size food. The menu's "tapatizers" include great fries ($3 for a mountain of hand-cut Yukon Gold potato fries), jumbo scallops, tiger-prawn tournedos, crabcakes, charred bok choy and many more. Open for dinner daily until 2am. Inexpensive.

Mescalero's 1215 Bidwell St, West End ☎604/669-2399. Very popular Mexican restaurant with fine, if predictable food: what draws people here are the fair prices, very lively atmosphere and the chance to eyeball the other fit young punters. Inexpensive.

Tapastree 1829 Robson St between Denman and Gilford, West End ☎604/606-4680, @www.tapastree.org. Vancouver's tapas craze of the 1990s has faded, but the best Spanish bars and restaurants (see also *La Bodega* on p.159) are still great places for inexpensive food and a relaxed early evening or wind-down late night. *Tapastree* has a vast choice of tapas whose inspiration goes way beyond Spain to include pork ribs with Chinese barbecue sauce, Asian seafood salad, lamb with sun-dried tomatoes and Gorgonzola, and Japanese aubergine with pesto. Late in the evening patrons are likely to include chefs from other restaurants who have just got off their shift – so you know the quality's got to be good. Dinner only. Inexpensive.

Topanga Café 2904 W 4th Ave near Macdonald St, South Vancouver ☎604/733-3713. A small but extremely popular Cal-Mex restaurant that's become a Vancouver institution. Prices are low and helpings large, a combination that has drawn hungry diners here for over twenty years and makes this a good place for people travelling with children. There are just forty places, so arrive before 6pm or after 8pm to avoid the worst of the waiting in line. Closed Sun. Inexpensive.

Vegetarian

Buddhist Vegetarian Restaurant 137 East Pender, Chinatown ☎604/683-8816. A Chinatown staple offering plenty of inexpensive items, set meals and a broad choice of dishes, including all-day dim sum. Inexpensive.

The Naam 2724 W 4th Ave near Stephens St, South Vancouver ☎604/738-7151,

@www.thenaam.com. The oldest and most popular health-food and vegetarian restaurant in the city. The ambience is comfortable and friendly – as you'd expect from a place with Kits's hippie-era origins – with live folk and other music as well as outside eating some evenings. Open 24hr. Inexpensive.

Planet Veg 1941 Cornwall Ave, South Vancouver ☎604/734-1001. There's limited inside seating at this mostly Indian fast-food and vegetarian option, but most Kitsilano patrons avail themselves of the take-out food (good for nearby Kits Beach and park for a picnic). Inexpensive.

Seafood

Blue Water Café 1095 Hamilton Street, Yaletown ☎604/688-8078, @www .bluewatercafe.net. This big restaurant has quickly become one of Yaletown's most popular fixtures, thanks to the sushi, fish and seafood, and to the attractive terrace and long interior, the last a dark, comfortable space of exposed beams and brick originally used as ballast in 1890s ships. There's an open kitchen for the fish and seafood staples (great halibut dishes, BC sablefish or salmon with pumpkin seed gnocchi), plus Eastern and Western bars (for sushi or ceviche, caviar and other treats respectively), and an Ice Bar, where you can indulge in chilled vodkas and freshly squeezed fruit juices. The service is amiable and unstuffy and quality is excellent, as you'd expect from a place run by James Walt, who has had stints at several other superb BC restaurants notably *Araxi* in Whistler (see p.257). Moderate to expensive.

C Restaurant 2-1600 Howe St near Pacific Blvd, Downtown ☎604/681-1164, @www.crestaurant.com. *The Fish House in Stanley Park* (see opposite) is *C*'s only serious rival for the title of Vancouver's best fish and seafood restaurant – and there are those that claim this is the best fish restaurant in Canada. The lengthy menu, which shows plenty of Southeast Asian influences, might include a choice from the "raw bar" – say a tartare trio of scallop, wasabi salmon and smoked chilli tuna – and fish such as Alaskan Arctic char. The taster of starters might include salmon gravlax cured in Saskatoon-berry tea, grilled garlic squid, abalone tempura and artichoke carpaccio – though the Skeena River sockeye terrine is unbeatable. Main courses might feature Maui hai tuna sashimi with 50-year-old balsamic vinegar or octopus bacon wrapping diver scallops with seared Québec fois gras. For a full insight into the chef's culinary powers, order the seven-course tasting menu. Views from the dining room are almost as good as the food. Expensive.

The Fish House in Stanley Park 2099 Beach Ave ☎604/681-7275, ◉www .fishhousestanleypark.com. The name more or less says it all. The leafy setting is pretty, the restaurant is housed in an attractive white-clapboard building, and the seafood is among the city's best. Inside, the three club-like dining rooms are painted in rich greens and whites offset by lots of dark wood. Indulge yourself at the Oyster Bar, order any available fish baked, broiled, steamed or grilled, or check out the daily specials. Obvious choices such as fish-cakes don't disappoint, but here it pays to be more adventurous: how about prawns flambéed with ouzo or ahi tuna with green-pepper sauce or – as one of several excellent vegetable accompaniments – red cabbage with fennel and buttermilk mash? Puddings are also superb: coconut cream pie is a particular winner. Excellent wine list. Expensive.

Joe Fortes 777 Thurlow St, Downtown ☎604/669-1940. This oyster bar-cum-chophouse and seafood restaurant is something of a city institution, noted as a hip place for high-spirited singles, among others, and the great bar (drinks and oysters) upstairs on the year-round roof garden and terrace. There are many varieties of oyster available, all as fresh as you like, plus ever-reliable fish dishes – the trio of grilled fish (choose from several types) at around $27 is always a winner. The atmosphere is lively and casual, the decor heavy on the mahogany and stained glass. There's also live music nightly. Moderate.

Rodney's Oyster House 1228 Hamilton St, Yaletown ☎604/609-0080. Not one of the most up-front Yaletown locations – it's tucked away in a relatively quiet dead-end street – but if you're after oysters, this fishing-shack lookalike is the place. "The lemon, the oyster and your lips are all that's required" is the pitch here. Expect anything

up to 18 varieties, from locally harvested bivalves to exotic Japanese kumamotos, all laid out on ice for you to choose from, and priced from about $1.50 to $3.50 each. There are also chowders and other dishes, plus other fresh seafood, notably Louisiana wild white shrimp and tremendous Fundy scallops. Or grab an appetizer and martini in the adjoining Mermaid Lounge. Inexpensive–moderate.

The SandBar 1535 Johnston St, Granville Island ☎604/669-9030. This is a great place to escape the bustle of Granville Island. The former restaurant on the site has been very tastefully renovated by the same group that owns the *Teahouse in Stanley Park*. You enter across stone bridges to find a foyer with a waterfall, an elevated rooftop waterfront bar, an open kitchen downstairs, and a main dining room reached by a wooden staircase. The food is mainly fish and seafood, but there are other West Coast dishes, as well as an enormous choice of wines. Moderate.

Contemporary and West Coast cuisine

Bishop's 2183 W 4th near Yew St ☎604/738-2025. Bishop's is consistently ranked as one of Vancouver's best restaurants. Although there's a frequent film-star and VIP presence, the welcome's as warm for everyone. The light and refined "contemporary home cooking" – Italy meets the Pacific Rim – commands high prices but is worth it. Menus change three or four times a year according to season: if in doubt, the daily special is invariably a winner. The dining room is all of an understated piece – candlelight, white linen and with a soundtrack of easy-on-the-ear jazz. Booking days (sometimes weeks) ahead is essential. Expensive.

Bridges 1696 Duranleau St, Granville Island ☎604/687-4400. This is an unmissable big, yellow restaurant upstairs; pub and informal bistro (the best option) downstairs, with a large outdoor deck. A reliable and very popular choice on Granville Island for a drink, snack (good nachos) or fuller meal of predictable pasta, fish and meat options. Inexpensive.

Chartwell Four Seasons Hotel, 791 W Georgia St, Downtown ☎604/844-6715. Don't let the fact that this is a hotel dining room put you off: the gracious, almost gentleman's club-like ambience is good if you want to dress up or have an indulgent lunch, and fine service, a great wine list and progressive Pacific Rim-influenced food make this one of the top restaurants in Vancouver. Ingredients are invariably organic and lavished on dishes that might include oxtail confit and sublime puddings such as white chocolate and lime mousse. Expensive.

Diva at the Met Metropolitan Hotel, 645 Howe St, Downtown ☏604/602-7788, ⓦwww .metropolitan.com. Like the *Chartwell* (see above), *Diva* has carved out a character completely separate from the hotel with which it's associated (a vast glass wall separates restaurant and hotel). The food is punchy and imaginative and the dining rooms are modern and clean-lined. The popular tasting menu is the best way to sample the food, albeit at some of Vancouver's highest prices. A great place for a treat or full-on brunch. Expensive.

Earl's 1185 Robson St, corner of Bute St, Downtown ☏604/669-0020. Come here first if you don't want to mess around scouring Downtown for somewhere to eat. The mid-priced, and often innovative, high-quality food is as eclectic as you please – everything from North American burgers to Far Eastern stir-fry and all points in between – and is served in a big, buzzy, open and casual-to-a-fault dining area. You can eat on the outside terrace in summer. Inexpensive.

Ferguson Point Teahouse Ferguson Point, Stanley Park ☏604/669-3281. A very pretty and romantic spot on the west side of Stanley Park with ocean view and outside dining that started in 1928 as a barracks but has evolved into a large English-style cottage. It makes the best place for a lunch or brunch during a walk or ride round the park. The food embraces most West Coast and French–Italian staples (fine carrot soup, good seafood and excellent steaks), though between 2.30 and 5pm daily the tearoom and patio serve simple light snacks and refreshments. Book a table on the terrace a day or so in advance. Moderate.

Isadora's 1540 Old Bridge St, Granville Island ☏604/681-8816. A popular Granville Island choice for a beer or a straightforward meal, Isadora's offers fine breakfasts, weekend brunches and light meals (with plenty of

good vegetarian and wholefood options) and a menu that covers most North American bases. There's lots of outdoor seating, but expect queues and slower service at weekends, particularly Sunday brunch. Closed for dinner Mon Sept–May. Inexpensive.

Liliget Feast House 1724 Davie St, West End ☏604/681-7044. This aboriginal restaurant – the only one of its kind in Vancouver – serves types of food you'll get nowhere else in the city: things like seaweed, steamed ferns, roast caribou and barbecued juniper duck. However, the cedar tables and benches inside, designed to resemble those of a Coast Salish longhouse, make the dining room a mite austere. Dinner only daily. Moderate.

Milestone's 1145 Robson St, Downtown ☏604/682-4477; 1210 Denman St ☏604/662-3431; Yaletown at 1109 Hamilton St at Helmcken ☏604/684-9112. Three popular mid-market chain restaurants with cheap drinks and standard but well-prepared and occasionally innovative North American food (especially good breakfasts) in very generous portions at the heart of Downtown (fast and noisy) and the English Bay Beach end of Denman Street (more laid-back).

Raincity Grill 1193 Denman St, West End ☏604/685-7337, ⓦwww.raincitygrill.com. The candles and a position near Davie St overlooking English Bay make for a romantic dining experience, but it is the food and wine, both of which make the most of British Columbian and Pacific Northwest ingredients (more than 100 varieties of Northwest and Californian wines by the glass are available) which are the main attraction – as you'd expect from a place which has connections with the outstanding *C Restaurant* (see p.154). The regional menu changes regularly, but you can always be sure to find salmon, seafood and other locally produced food (much of it organic) and at least four vegetarian options. Each dish comes with a suggestion for wine. Dinner daily, brunch Sat & Sun. Moderate.

Seasons in the Park Queen Elizabeth Park, Cambie at West 33rd Ave, South Vancouver ☏604/874-8008 or 1-800/632-9422. A pretty and panoramic position – at the heart of one of Vancouver's most popular parks – is almost enough to recommend this restaurant, but the food is as good as the romantic setting: certainly good enough for former presidents Yeltsin and Clinton, who both dined here. The menu always features fine fresh fish, seafood and local wines, but you'll also encounter dishes such as chicken breast stuffed with ricotta and pancetta in a port jus, a sun-dried tomato tart with Stilton and some cracking puddings. Moderate-expensive.

Tomato Fresh Food Café 3305 Cambie St, South Vancouver ☎604/874-6020. This busy place serves good simple food, with a fresh, health-conscious bias. It's way, way south of Downtown, so treat it as a good place to stop en route for the airport, Vancouver Island or the ferry terminal at Tsawwassen. Eat in or take away. Inexpensive.

Water Street Café 300 Water St, Gastown ☎604/689-2832. The café-restaurant of choice if you wind up in Gastown – it's located just across the street from the famous steam clock. The dining rooms (one downstairs, two upstairs) are pretty and relaxed, but in summer try to book an outside table. The menu at lunch and dinner is short and well planned, and mixes cuisines, but with a bias towards modern Italian-influenced cooking – salmon with soy sauce and balsamic vinegar, pasta with chicken, and dishes with Parmesan gratinée. Moderate.

Drinking

Vancouver has a reasonable assortment of **bars**, many a cut above the functional dives and sham pubs found outside the city in much of the rest of British Columbia. Most are in the same sort of locations as the major concentrations of restaurants (see p.143), but particularly in **Yaletown** and other **Downtown** locations. However, the distinctions between bars, cafés, restaurants and nightclubs can be considerably blurred, and the out and out pubs or bars that you might find in the US or European capitals are comparatively rare here: food in some form is usually available in drinking places, though the arcane licensing laws which made the provision of food a legal requirement were overhauled in April 2002. The same overhaul allowed 4am closing in certain cases. Note that the legal drinking age is 19.

However, while things are easing up bureaucratically, and bars stay open later than they did, there has been a long history of official disapproval of drinking in British Columbia, and a real renaissance in the city's drinking culture, and any proliferation of good places to drink, has still to happen. This said, many daytime cafés, bistros, tapas bars and restaurants – generated by the old "must-serve-food" legal clause – also operate happily as night-time bars, as do many of the clubs and live-music venues in our "Nightlife" chapter (see p.163). The city also has a good selection of **gay and lesbian bars** (see p.177).

Canadian beer

By and large, Canadian beers are unremarkable, designed to quench your thirst rather than satisfy your palate. Almost everywhere in Vancouver bars, ice-cold, light, fizzy beers rule the roost. Notable exceptions are provided by small microbreweries or brewpubs, but the market is still dominated by the two largest Canadian breweries, Molson and Labatts. Both offer remarkably similar beers – Molson Canadian, Molson Export, Labatts Ice, Labatts Blue – that inspire, for reasons that elude most foreigners, intense loyalty. There is also a niche market for foreign beers, although Heineken, the most popular, is made under licence in Canada; American beers such as Budweiser and Coors are common.

Drinking bottled beer will be more expensive than draught, which is usually served by the 170ml glass; even cheaper is to purchase it by the pitcher, which contains six or seven glasses.

Where Vancouver does score is in a handful of brewpubs and microbreweries, though these have a tendency to go out of business, change hands, merge or to lose impetus when a brewmaster moves on: the long reach of restrictive laws and provincial bureaucracy, as ever in anything to do with alcohol in British Columbia, doesn't help. Long-standing exceptions include the *Yaletown Brewing Company* (see p.160), *Steamworks Brewing Company* (see p.161) and the *Granville Island Brewery* (see p.87), through this last has no proper bar outlet. A new addition to the brewmaster community is *Dockside Brewing Company* (see p.162).

Vancouver also has several **brewpubs** and good **hotel bars** which are used by non-patrons of the hotel – one notable example is the *900 West* bar of the *Hotel Vancouver* (see below), which is a good place for an early or late-evening drink even if the hotel itself is beyond your budget.

Downtown

900 West 900 West Georgia St ☏604/684-3131. Hotel bars and lounges can be bland and anonymous affairs – not the bar of the *Hotel Vancouver*. Despite leading off the main lobby of one of the city's biggest and grandest hotels, is a cosy space of dark wood, comfortable chairs and low lighting. It's at its best immediately after businesses close, when it fills with an animated crowd catching a drink before heading home or moving on to a restaurant or club. Later in the evening it tends to be used more by hotel guests, and the atmosphere becomes more mellow.

Cloud Nine Empire Landmark Hotel, 1400 Robson St at Nicola St ☏604/687-0511. Vancouver has several bars with a view – notably the lounge in the *Sylvia* (see p.161) and *Bridges* on Granville Island (see p.162) – but none that can match the panorama from this super-sleek lounge bar on the 42nd floor of the *Empire Landmark Hotel*. The bar rotates, so your view changes by six degrees every sixty seconds. There's a modest cover charge for entry on Fri and Sat, but it's worth paying for the panorama.

DV8 515 Davie St between Richards and Seymour ☏604/682-4388. *DV8* is one of the city's trendier bars and lounges, but don't expect to get too much talking done stage-side, when the live bands and their vast sound systems kick in. The clientele is predominantly early 20s – skateboarders, snowboarders and the like.

Gerard Lounge 845 Burrard St between Robson and Smithe ☏604/682-5511. A smooth wood-panelled 25-seat lounge and piano bar in the smart *Sutton Place Hotel*, that aims – successfully – to re-create the look and atmosphere of an English gentleman's club, complete with leather chairs, tapestries, old oil paintings and wall-mounted stuffed animals. It all makes for elegant and rather distinctive Downtown drinking. This is also, at least until fashions change, one of the places to spot the stars currently filming in town – plus plenty of the wannabes.

Ginger 62 1219 Granville St ☏604/682-0409, ⊛www.ginger62.com. A dress code here requires that you are pretty well turned out, but it's worth making the effort (plenty of regulars do) to enjoy the louche and deliberately affected1960s style decor – red and gold room, couches, ottomans and big bar. Food consists of sophisticated tapas and Asian titbits.

La Bodega 1277 Howe St near Davie St ☏604/684-8815. This place towards the south of Downtown re-creates a Spanish bar that could almost be in Spain. As a result, it's one of the city's best and most popular places to drink, with fine tapas (great chorizo) and excellent main courses to mop up the alcohol (including sangria and other Spanish drinks). Food aside, though, it's chiefly dedicated to lively drinking. It's packed later on, especially on Friday and Saturday, so try to arrive before 8pm. Closed Sun.

Lennox 800 Granville St at Robson ☏604/408-0881. One of the city's busiest junctions is not perhaps the ideal place for a bar, but if you want a drink and time out from the Downtown bustle, this comfortable and straightforward pub is a good and convenient choice. The selection of beers and single malts is extremely good, but prices, given the site, are a touch over the odds. There's a small outside seating area for summer drinking and people-watching. Food is of the basic pub-grub variety, but the quality's reasonable.

Morrisey Pub 1227 Granville St between Davie and Drake ☏604/682-0909. Situated at the cheaper and less salubrious southern end of Granville, but this only halfway authentic "Irish" pub is better than the environs: spacious, lots of leather, dark wood and a fireplace. It's a cheerful and popular spot, with inexpensive beer and food. If you want something a little more out-there, try the affiliated *Ginger 62* (see above) a couple of doors down.

Shark Club Bar & Grill The Sandman Hotel, 180 W Georgia St ☏604/687-4275. This is currently the best and busiest of several sports bars in the city. This being Canada, ice hockey is popular, but you'll also catch basketball, baseball, soccer and American and Canadian football (especially the last, as it's close to BC Place, home to the local team). There are thirty screens, a 180-seat oak bar, more than twenty beers on tap, Italian food from the kitchen and lots of testosterone, though the place is by no means confined to rowdy jocks.

Sugar Refinery 1115 Granville St ☎604/683-2004. At the cheap end of Granville, but that's all grist to the hip and bohemian appeal of this second-floor mixture of bar, restaurant, art gallery and live-music venue. This, plus late opening (3–4am) and the eclectic range of its shows, attracts a cosmopolitan clientele of night owls, arty types, clubbers and movie-goers who don't want to go home (the Granville cinemas are close).

Urban Well 888 Nelson St at Hornby ☎604/638-6070, ☺www.urbanwell.com. The combination of club-like bar and restaurant, with nightly DJs and comedy and other event nights, has proved so successful that there are two *Urban Wells* in town – the one here in Downtown just two blocks from Robson and the other in Kitsilano at 1516 Yew St (☎737-7770). Chances are you'll have to queue for both at busy times.

Yaletown

Bar None 1222 Hamilton St ☎604/689-7000. A busy and reasonably smart under-forty-something Yaletown bar and club with brick and wooden beam interior where you can eat, drink, watch TV, smoke cigars (there's a walk-in humidor) play backgammon or shoot pool and listen to live music. A house band plays Mondays and Tuesdays, with a DJ the rest of the week, though patrons are generally a touch too cool to make fools of themselves on the small dancefloor. Closed Sun.

Section (3) 1039 Mainland St between Nelson and Helmcken ☎604/684-2777. With a name like this you know you're in for somewhere with certain pretensions, and the hyper-modern and self-consciously arty decor and knowing crowd don't disappoint. The bar is curved, the bar stools wrought-iron, the floor hardwood, the art bizarre and the booths silver. Music and food are similarly modern and eclectic.

Soho 1144 Homer St between Davie and Helmcken ☎604/688-1180. Less-in-your-face

trendy than some Yaletown bars, the *Soho* is a pub where you take tea, coffee and snacks, play billiards, eat a full meal, or drink in unfussy surroundings.

SuBeez Café 891 Homer at Smithe ☎604/687-6107. The sort of place you will love or hate, the *SuBeez* is a typical Yaletown warehouse-type place, with high ceilings supported by brutalist concrete columns. The lighting is low, the music alternative to a fault, and strange art on the walls competes with screens showing silent films. You can eat here (the menu is eclectic), but most of the regulars are here to drink. There's a sister establishment, the *WaaZuBee Café* on Commerical Drive.

Yaletown Brewing Company 1111 Mainland St at Helmcken ☎604/681-2739. There's no danger of missing this extremely large, modern bar and restaurant with its own six-beer on-site brewery. It's very popular, and one of the long-established leaders in the funky Yaletown revival. All the beers are excellent, as are the snacks and Italian and West Coast food in the restaurant, but this is a better place to drink than to eat seriously. The patio is good in summer, and if the weather's bad you can retreat to several cozy indoor rooms.

West End

Cardero's Marine Pub 1583 Coal Harbour Quay on Cardero St ☎604/669-7666. The location of this pub-restaurant is neither one thing nor the other, around midway between Stanley Park and Burrard, but the waterfront location and patio (heated on cooler evenings) at the northern end of Cardero St offer great views of the park, moored boats, Burrard Inlet and the North Shore. The clientele is mostly young and well-dressed, with many patrons en route to the adjoining restaurant, and the decor is low-key maritime.

Jupiter Café 1216 Bute St near Davie ☎604/609-6665, ☺www.jupitercafe.com. You need to be in the mood for the unsparing industrial look to this bar's design – all exposed air-conditioning pipes, black ceilings and superstructure – or concentrate on the softer edge provided by comfy chairs, rich fabrics and over-the-top chandeliers. There's a big outdoor drinking area, ideal for taking in the very mixed but never less than well-dressed punters. There is food – the usual pastas, burgers and a dozen ways with chicken – but it's something of an afterthought. Expect late opening (4am) most nights and comedy (Mon), live jazz (Tues–Thurs) and DJs (Fri–Sat).

Sylvia Hotel 1154 Gilford St and Beach Ave ⊕604/688-8865. There doesn't seem much to appeal at first glance in this nondescript and easy-going hotel bar, but it is popular for quiet drinks and superlative waterfront views, and makes a very pleasant retreat after a stroll in Stanley Park and/or English Bay Beach.

Gastown and around

Alibi Room 157 Alexander St between Columbia and Main ⊕604/623-3383, ⊛www.alibiroom.com. Various movie-makers and shakers put money into this unashamedly hip and happening bar-restaurant – and the result is a crowd that is trendy, but not to the extent that it spoils this as a good place for drinks and – perhaps – dinner. Excellent and eclectic food is served upstairs, with a short, modern menu and surprisingly reasonable prices; downstairs you can drink and venture onto the small dancefloor.

Blarney Stone 216 Carrall St ⊕604/687-4322. This lively pub and restaurant in Gastown features nightly live Irish music from house band and a dancefloor. If it looks a bit rough and ready, or just too plain rowdy, try *The Irish Heather* almost opposite across the street (see opposite). Closed Sun.

The Brickhouse Bar & Bistro 730 Main St ⊕604/689-8645. The edgy area around Main St and Terminal Ave is slowly yielding to the forces of gentrification, and this fine and welcoming bar is a sign of the changing times. It offers a relaxed and understated atmosphere, trendily kitschy fish tanks along the walls, plenty of comfortable couches, pool tables, good beer and an extensive selection of whiskies. Tapas and light bar food is brought down from the excellent bistro upstairs (open until 2am) and there are DJs and blues and other live-music sessions some evenings.

The Cambie 300 Cambie St ⊕604/684-6466. An obvious place to drink if you're staying at the linked hostel (see p.140), but the roomy (and invariably crowded) outdoor area and cheap pitchers of beer bring in a

fair number of locals and other passing trade. Inside, it's all smoke, pool tables and down-to-earth drinking.

The Irish Heather 217 Carrall St ⊕604/688-9779. This charming Gastown place is a definite cut above the usual mock-Irish pub, with an intimate bar, varied clientele – anything from students to local gallery owners – lots of nooks and crannies, live Irish music some nights and good Guinness (apparently it sells the second largest number of pints of the stuff in Canada). The Irish-influenced food – hearty stews and soups and so forth – is also excellent and there's an unexpectedly pretty outdoor eating and drinking area at the back.

Milk & Honey Lounge 455 Abbott St between Hastings and Pender ⊕604/685-7777. Don't expect to make much conversational headway against the occasionally booming music, but do come to the *Milk & Honey* if you're en route for the hip little gay- and lesbian-friendly *Lotus Sound Lounge* club downstairs. The bar area of the lounge is spacious and more laid back, with lots of comfortable chairs piled with velvet cushions. Closed Sun.

Steamworks Brewery Company 375 Water St ⊕604/689-2739. This Gastown microbrewery and pub sells about a dozen of its own rightly well-regarded brews and has plenty of different rooms. Upstairs, the drinkers are likely to include leery and besuited financial types; by the staircase, the old club-like setting – wood panelling, comfortable chairs and windows overlooking the harbour – appeals to a more congenial crowd; while the basement has the appearance and more beery atmosphere of a German beer hall. Friday night until about 9pm is when the place is liveliest.

Granville Island and Kitsilano

The Arts Club 1585 Johnston St, Granville Island ⊕604/687-1354. *The Arts Club's* popular *Backstage Bar and Grill*, part of its theatre complex, has seating with a waterfront view on Granville Island beneath the bridge, easy-going atmosphere, decent food and blues, jazz and other live music Friday and Saturday evenings. It's especially well known for its 50-plus selection of whiskies. Early in the week (notably Wed) it's a hang-out for art students from the nearby Emily Carr college.

Bimini's Tap House 2010 West 4th Ave between Arbutus and Maple ☎604/732-9232. Anglo-style pub at the heart of the West 4th Avenue "strip". Pool and cheap drinks attract a youngish crowd, but you can escape the hustle and the worst of the droning TV screens upstairs.

Bridges 1696 Duranleau St, Granville Island ☎604/687-4400. You can eat here (see p.155), but when the sun's shining it's hard to choose between the busy patio here and the *Dockside Brewing Company* (see below) as to which is the nicest place to have a waterside drink on Granville Island: *Bridges* is more central and thus more convenient.

Darby D. Dawes 2001 Macdonald St and West 4th Ave ☎604/731-0617. This pub – generally known simply as *Darby's* – is relatively handy for the youth hostel and Kits Beach. People often start the evening here with a beer or game of darts – meals are served 11.30am–7pm, snacks till 10pm – and then move on to the *Fairview* for live blues (see p.165). Live music (a mixture of jazz, blues and rock) in the pub is generally only played on Friday and Saturday evenings with jam sessions on Saturday afternoons.

Dockside Brewing Company 1253 Johnston St, Granville Island ☎604/685-7070. Beer buffs should try this sylish lounge in the *Granville Island Hotel* to sample some of the establishment's on-site microbrewery's ales. The atmosphere is relaxed and the generally well-heeled crowd thirty-something. Things tend to be more lively early in the evening, and in summer there's a fine outdoor patio.

King's Head 1618 Yew St between York and West 4th Ave ☎604/738-6966. Pleasant and very central Kits English-style pub just two blocks from Kits Beach. Upstairs there are plenty of hidden corners for a quiet drink.

The North Shore

Raven 1052 Deep Cove Rd ☎604/929-3834. Way out east on Deep Cove near the mouth of Indian Arm, so probably only appropriate if you've been in Mount Seymour Provincial Park just to the west (see p.121) or are a real beer fan, for there are half a dozen foreign imports and around twenty microbrewery beers. Whisky fans will also find a good selection of malts.

Rusty Gull 175 East 1st St between Lonsdale and St George ☎604/988-5585. Just a minute or so from Lonsdale Quay, this jovial neighbourhood pub is the most convenient place for a drink if you're on a flying visit to the North Shore or have time to kill before catching the SeaCat back to Downtown. Choice of beer and food is good, and you'll often be able to catch some live music, but the main draw here is the great view from the small patio over the warehouses and docks towards the Downtown skyline.

Sailor Hägar's 86 Semisch Ave at West 1st St ☎604/984-7669. A brewpub with six good local-brewed beers on tap (plus a wide selection of other microbrewery and imported beers), uphill and about 200m west of Lonsdale Quay. The interior is unexceptional, save for a big oak fireplace, but this is part of the appeal of what is a non-nonsense neighbourhood pub. The outdoor patio has fine views of Vancouver, and there's good pub and Scandinavian-influenced food.

Nightlife

Vancouver offers plenty to do come sundown, laying on a varied and cosmopolitan blend of **live music**, clubs and discos. Clubs here are just as adventurous as in other Canadian cities such as Toronto, particularly the fly-by-night alternative dives in the backstreets of Gastown and Chinatown. There's also a choice of smarter places (where you need to dress up) and more conventional clubs, a handful of discos and a smattering of good **gay** and **lesbian** clubs and bars. The city's northerly latitude occasionally makes for unreliable weather, but summer nightlife often takes to the streets in West Coast fashion, with outdoor bar terraces and – to a certain extent – beaches becoming venues in their own right. And when the fine weather does arrive, it allows the city to host a range of **festivals**, from jazz to theatre (see Chapter 17 for details of the main events).

The most comprehensive **listings** guide for nightlife is *The Georgia Straight* (ⓦ www.straight.com), a free weekly published on Thursdays and available in dump bins at stores and other points around the city. Many other free magazines devoted to different musical genres and activities are available at the same points, but they come and go quickly. Selected club listings can also be found by visiting ⓦ www.clubvibes.com, ⓦ www.wildvancouver.com or ⓦ www. Vancouver-nightlife-info.com, while ⓦ www.vancouverjazz.com/directory offers a list of jazz venues, but without critical commentary. The **Jazz Hotline** (ⓣ 604/872-5200) offers details of current and forthcoming jazz events. For detailed information on **gay and lesbian** events see p.175.

Tickets for many major events are sold through Ticketmaster, with forty outlets around the city (ⓣ 604/280-3311 for general tickets or 604/280-4444 for rock concerts, ⓦ www.ticketmaster.ca); they'll sometimes unload discounted tickets for midweek and matinee performances. Half-price and last-minute same-day tickets are available via "Tickets Tonight" (ⓦ www.ticketstonight.ca) at participating venues, or through the outlet at the main TouristInfo visitor centre at 200 Burrard St (see p.23).

Live music

Vancouver's night-time **venues** are generally ill-defined places, and few restrict themselves solely to live music. Many clubs offer live music all or some nights of the week, often with DJs and dancing on the same evenings or on non-live music nights. Clubs may also offer many types of music, from rock one night to jazz or 1970s revival bands the next. You'll also find live music and/or dancing in some of the places we've listed in Chapter 10 "Drinking".

Here we've concentrated on places where music is predominant. They are dotted across the city and showcase a variety of largely local bands, none of which is likely to make the big time – Ontario-born but Vancouver-raised Bryan Adams having proved a notable exception. Mainstream **rock** groups are the most common bill of fare, though **jazz** is generally hot news in Vancouver, with many spots specializing in the genre. And, while Vancouver isn't as cowpoke as, say, Calgary, it does have several clubs dedicated to **country music**, though many are in the outer suburbs. At the other end of the spectrum to these small clubs, the 60,000-seat Pacific Coliseum and other bigger venues such as the Orpheum Theatre are on the touring itinerary of most international acts.

Cover charges in most smaller clubs and venues are typically a few dollars (anything from $5 to $20), but creep up when bigger acts perform. Prices are also higher on Friday and Saturday: the most you would expect to pay would be in the region of $40 to get into somewhere like *Richard's on Richards* (see p.166), one of the city's smartest clubs.

Rock

The Cave Plaza of Nations, 750 Pacific Blvd and Cambie St ℡604/603-8597, ℮cavenightclub@shaw.ca. A loud and young, progressive dance and live-music club with a big1000-plus capacity. It's blessed with five bars, a staggeringly loud sound system and a huge and invariably packed dancefloor – think warehouse or aircraft hangar.

Commodore Ballroom 868 Granville St and Smithe St ℡604/280-4444 or 739-7469, ℗www.commodoreballroom.com. The city's best mid-sized venue (there's room for 990 people) benefited from a $1 million face-lift after being empty for three years, a makeover that to general rejoicing retained its renowned 1929 dancefloor and Art Deco patina. There is an adventurous music policy that embraces many different types of band (rock, pop, jazz and blues), and they feature a new DJ every two to three weeks.

Piccadilly Pub 620 West Pender near Granville ℡604/682-3221. The "Pic" is a long-established pub with a guarantee of raucous music of some description (garage, rock, punk, rockabilly) most nights, usually Thursday to Saturday. It's a laid-back, non-poseur sort of place aimed at those who simply want beer, music and a good time.

Railway Club 579 Dunsmuir St and Seymour St ℡604/681-1625. This is one of the city's best small – the place is tiny – venues, a long-established favourite with excellent bookings, casual atmosphere and a wide range of live music (folk, blues, jazz and

rock). It's also a good place just for a drink and a game of darts – the upstairs pub is quieter and more relaxed than the stage bar downstairs. There's a separate "conversation" lounge where it's more peaceful, so it's ideal if you don't want to come here just for the music. If you arrive before 10pm at weekends be prepared to pay a nominal "private-club" membership fee.

Roxy 932 Granville and Nelson St ℡604/331-7999, ℗www.roxyvan.com. The *Roxy* – "where life is like a beer commercial" – has been around for a while, providing a successful, casual and fun place for the city's UBC college crowd and people in from the 'burbs. Four bars feature slick bartenders showing off their moves and there are live bands most nights – often the two very competent "house" bands – with an emphasis on 1950s to 1970s music. Also has theme dance nights and karaoke sessions.

Sonar 66 Water St and Abbott St ℡604/683-6695, ℗www.sonar.bc.ca. This is one of central Vancouver's best and most heavily patronized music venues, largely by virtue of its cool, funky vibe and convenient mid-Gastown location. In the past, Britain's clubbing magazine *Ministry* has voted it one of the world's top twenty nightclubs, and though fashion can be fickle, the ranking looks likely to remain justified for some time. The live music nightly often seems something of a distraction – the place is also a good dance club and known as something of a pick-up spot. The clientele is mainly a casual bunch of 19- to 24-year-olds, and the music anything from jazz, reggae, trance and soul to rock, hip-hop, techno and progressive house. Bar food and piano lounge until 9pm, when the band strikes up and the more serious dancing and partying begin.

Jazz, blues and country

Arts Club Theatre Backstage Lounge 1585 Johnston St, Granville Island ☏604/687-1354. Given Granville Island's popularity, at least by day, it has surprisingly few places to sip a late-night beer or catch some live music. This good lounge, tucked away behind one of the city's best-known small theatres (see p.170), makes up for the shortage elsewhere. It's a nice spot to hear R&B, jazz and blues, or watch the boats and the sun set on False Creek. It's also pretty lively most nights, which may have something to do with the fact that it has one of the best selections of whiskies in Vancouver. There's a cover charge at weekends and occasional weekdays, depending on the band.

Boone County Cabaret 801 Brunette Ave, Coquitlam ☏604/523-3144. Suburbia's favourite country-music club is some 20km east out of town just off the Trans-Canada (take bus #151) in residential Coquitlam. The cramped 300-capacity place is invariably raucous and crowded. Closed Sunday and Monday.

Capone's 1141 Hamilton St ☏604/684-7900. Capone's is one of the better fixtures that has opened up in burgeoning Yaletown. On the face of it, the place is primarily a restaurant – mostly pizza and pasta – but it also takes its jazz seriously, and there's a stage for nightly live performances. The restaurant's layout is oddly long and narrow, however, so arrive early or book a table near the stage if you want a decent view of what's going on.

Cellar Restaurant & Jazz Club 3611 West Broadway ☏604/738-1959, ☏www.cellarjazz.com. Kitsilano has only recently acquired clubs, and this tiny 70-seat red-walled basement with black booths and low tables is one of the most popular, frequently offering the best live jazz in the city four or more nights a week (generally Wed–Sat). Join the enthusiastic crowd for top local outfits or big international names.

Fairview 898 W Broadway at the Ramada Inn ☏604/872-1262. Good local blues and 1950s rock'n'roll in something resembling a pub atmosphere – fans seem unperturbed by the hotel setting – which means there's generally a lively buzz but precious little room to move on the small dancefloor. Snacks are served during the day and good-value meals in the evening. Live music nightly from Monday to Saturday, with a cover charge at weekends depending on the band.

Hot Jazz 2120 Main St and 5th Ave ☏604/873-4131, ☏www.hotjazzvancouver.com. Hot Jazz is the oldest and most firmly established jazz club in the city. Music is mainly traditional – swing, Dixieland and New Orleans – performed by both local and imported bands. On Saturday nights you'll occasionally be treated to a big band. A jumping (and invariably full) dancefloor and large bar ensures the place swings past midnight. This is a club, so you'll have to pay a nominal annual membership fee unless you manage to be signed in as a guest by a member. Wednesday is jam night; closed Monday and Sunday.

Purple Onion 15 Water St ☏604/602-9442, ☏www.purpleonion.com. This is a casual dance club and music lounge combined, and one that is well situated right in the heart of Gastown. You can expect top-notch live jazz, funk and Latin music in one area (usually a house band); DJs, dancefloor, cigars, oysters and cabaret in the other. It's a very popular place of long standing, so expect to queue Friday and Saturday. The cover charge (from $5) includes entry to both club and lounge.

Yale 1300 Granville St and Drake St ☏604/681-9253. An outstanding venue and the place in the city to hear hardcore blues and R&B – check out the hall-of-fame photographs in the entryway of the blues maestros who've played here. It has a relaxed air, big dancefloor and occasionally presents outstanding international names alongside lesser home-grown talent. You can often attend jam sessions of up to 50 players at once, currently on Saturday (3–8pm) and Sunday (3pm–midnight). The venue sometimes closes on Monday and Tuesday, so call for details.

Clubs and discos

Many of the live-music venues above double as **clubs** and **discos** – the boundaries between the three are generally pretty blurred – and as in any city with a healthy alternative, student and music scene there are also plenty of fun, one-off clubs that have an irritating habit of cropping up and disappearing at speed. Most clubs of note or long standing are dotted around Downtown, Gastown and – increasingly – at the southern end of Richards and Granville – while the fly-by-night places are more likely to spring up on and around Main Street and Commercial Drive. See *The Georgia Straight* listings weekly for the latest. Cover charges are usually nominal, and tickets are often available (sometimes free) at record shops.

Au Bar 674 Seymour St ☎604/648-2227. Downtown club for suits and miniskirts, with martinis the (expensive) drink of choice. Strict dress code and vetting on the door (you'll spot the Seymour Street queues from afar), but the exclusive air is what attracts punters. If you get in, people-watching may prove the most entertaining part of your evening. Three bars and small dancefloor with safe Top 40, hip-hop and R & B.

Atlantis 1320 Richards St ☎604/662-7707, ⊛www.atlantisclub.net. This newly renovated club has cutting-edge music, lights and dancefloor, and a sharp clientele to match. There's plenty of room at the rear bar for a drink and a break from the music, with hip-hop currently on Saturdays and a wide range of sounds on theme nights the rest of the week.

Caprice 967 Granville St. Club ☎604/685-3288, lounge 685-3189, ⊛www.capricenightclub.com. This recent club is the relocated and reincarnated *Luv-a-Fair*, which for years was one of the city's best. Its airy, modern successor, a converted cinema, looks like living up to its high standards, with an excellent dancefloor and state-of-the-art sound, light and video systems. If you don't want to dance, then the *Caprice Lounge* alongside offers a quieter retreat where you can eat and chill out in front of a fire and large-screen TVs.

Plaza Club 881 Granville St ☎604/646-0064, ⊛www.plazaclub.net. A popular, no-nonsense dance club with great sound and lighting in a former cinema in central Granville St location. Music has a strong British bias, but there are also theme nights. Saturday is very popular, so expect to queue.

Richard's on Richards 1036 Richards St and Nelson St ☎604/687-6794, ⊛www.richardsonrichards.com. This well-known club and disco – probably the best-known in the city – has been around for years and invariably invites sneers from young and hip clubbers. This is because it's a smart, trendy and somewhat pretentious place – check out the valet parking – aimed at the older, richer and better-heeled set. It's also hugely popular, so be prepared for long waits. And put on something other than T-shirt and sneakers – there's a dress code. Music is generally safe covers from the occasional live bands and recorded Top 40 and other mainstream dance fodder. Open Thurs/Fri–Sat.

Shine 363 Water Street ☎604/408-4321. Conveniently located and happening Gastown club which attracts some of the city's top DJs, notably Dicky Doo. Understated decor, with comfortable retro 1960s couches and all-white colour scheme provide a sophisticated setting for house, reggae, soul, R & B, hip-hop and other sounds. Dress up a touch, or you'll feel out of place.

Voda Westin Grand Hotel, 783 Homer St ☎604/684-3003, ⊛www.voda.com. Arrive early in this very roomy hotel lounge near the central library and chances are it'll be empty. Come later and you'll find it heaving, for this is one of the newer and most popular of the city's clubs. The sleek look and fittings – wood panelling, back-lit bar, lots of candles, waterfalls, rocks, angled beams – are offset by the generally very elegant and fashion-conscious clientele. Don't wear your jeans. Music for the smallish dancefloor covers most bases, from R & B and funk to electro and old-school house. Closed Sunday and Monday.

Comedy

It's not that the inhabitants of Vancouver have no sense of humour, just that it's proved difficult here over the years to make money out of clubs that offer comedy and nothing else. As a result there's currently only one dedicated comedy club of long standing, though the success of the occasional comedy nights at *Urban Well* may well encourage other clubs and bars to follow suit – see *The Georgia Straight* (see p.163) for the latest details.

Urban Well 888 Nelson St at Hornby ☎604/638-6070, ⊛www.urbanwell.com. There's generally only comedy one or two nights a week (currently improvisations on Monday plus Tuesday or Wednesday depending on venue), but a good bar and good value have proved so successful that there are now two *Urban Wells* in town – the one here in Downtown just two blocks from Robson and the other in Kitsilano at 1516 Yew St (☎737-7770). Chances are you'll have to queue for both at busy times.

Yuk Yuk's Plaza of Nations, 750 Pacific Blvd and Cambie St ☎604/687-LAFF. Vancouver's longer-established central comedy club presents top US and Canadian stand-up acts. Shows generally kick off at 9pm, with extra performances on Saturday and Sunday at around 11.30pm. It's worth booking at weekends. Closed Monday and Tuesday.

The performing arts

Vancouver serves up enough top-quality highbrow culture to suit the whole spectrum of its cosmopolitan population and its visitors, with plenty of unusual and avant-garde **performances** to spice up the mainstream entertainment you'd expect of a major North American city. It also boasts a wide range of festivals devoted to the performing arts, the best of which are included in the calendar of events in Chapter 17 (see p.206). This being a well-integrated multicultural city, Vancouver also offers a range of performances that fully acknowledges and involves all parts of its diverse population.

As the western capital of Canada's **film industry**, Vancouver is favoured by Hollywood studios in their pursuit of cheaper locations and production deals. It's therefore no surprise that the spread of **cinemas** is good – though the films shot in the city, with the odd exception, are rarely more than B-movie action flicks or "straight-to-video" offerings. Home-produced and Hollywood first-run films play in the Downtown movie houses on the central "Theatre Row" – the two blocks of Granville between Robson and Nelson streets – and at other big complexes, and there's no shortage of cinemas for more esoteric productions.

Major performance spaces

Centre in Vancouver for the Performing Arts 777 Homer St ☎604/602-0616, ⓦwww.centreinvancouver.com. In 1996 the Queen Elizabeth Theatre (see below) was joined by this world-class 1824-seat complex, an impressive three-level modern space opposite the central library – it was designed by the library's architect, Moshe Safdie: check out the amazing mirrored staircase and dramatic glass cone in the lobby. It has had a chequered career, the original owners having gone bust, and until 2002 the building sat empty. Now owned by Hong Kong property developers, it is once again hosting large-scale productions of popular theatre, musicals and other spectaculars, but check with the tourist office or website for latest details.
Chan Centre for the Performing Arts 6265 Crescent Rd, University of British Columbia ☎604/822-2697, ⓦwww.chancentre.com. The1400-seat Chan Shun Concert Hall, the main space of the three-hall UBC performance complex, has the best acoustics in the city, and hosts shows by outside and university music, drama and other groups, as well as fashion shows, world music and other events. The UBC has a smaller Recital Hall at Gate 4, 6361 Memorial Rd.
Orpheum Theatre 884 Granville St at Smithe ☎604/665-3050 or 876-3434, ⓦwww.city.vancouver.bc.ca/theatres. The refurbished and beautifully ornate 3000-seat Orpheum is Vancouver's oldest theatre. Built in 1927 as a cinema – the original Wurlitzer organ survives – it is all Rococo gilt, deep red carpets, ornamental plaster and chandeliers topped off by a painted, dome ceiling, and serves as the headquarters of the well-respected Vancouver Symphony Orchestra and several small choirs.

Information and tickets

For information on the Vancouver arts scene, call the **Arts Hotline** (☎604/684-ARTS or 684-2787, ⊚www.allianceforarts.com) or visit their office (Mon–Fri 9am–5pm) at 100-938 Howe St. The **Jazz Hotline** (☎604/872-5200) offers details of current and forthcoming jazz events. The **Dance Centre** (☎604/606-6400, ⊚www.thedancecentre.ca) fulfils the same function for dance.

Also useful are the listings pages of *The Georgia Straight* weekly (widely available in dump bins around the city and online at ⊚www.straight.com), the monthly *Vancouver Magazine* (⊚www.vanmag.com) or the *Vancouver Sun* (the Thursday edition contains a weekly listings magazine, *Queue*) and *Province* newspapers.

For gay and lesbian listings, pick up the free *Xtra! West* magazine from dump bins around town, but especially the West End. For classical-music recitals, check the above sources or fliers posted at the city's main classical-music stores, notably Sikora's Classical Records, two blocks from the SeaBus terminal at 432 W Hastings St (☎604/685-0625).

Tickets for most musical, theatrical and other events can be obtained from individual box offices or through Ticketmaster (☎604/280-4444, ⊚www.ticketmaster.ca), which has around forty outlets around the city. Cut-price **same-day tickets** for events can often be obtained from the "Tickets Tonight" desk (⊚www.ticketstonight.ca) at the main Burrard Street infocentre (see p.23).

Queen Elizabeth Theatre 600 Hamilton St at Dunsmuir-Georgia. Information ☎604/299-9000, tickets ☎604/665-3050, ⊚www.cityvancouver.bc.ca/theatres. This modern 2929-seat theatre is the chief focus of the city's performing arts, playing host to a steady procession of visiting theatre, opera and dance troupes, and even the occasional big rock band. It also houses the smaller 668-seat **Vancouver Playhouse**, used for smaller recitals, dance, chamber pieces and by the resident Vancouver Playhouse Theatre Company, responsible for around six productions annually between May and September.

Classical music

Vancouver has many of the ingredients required for a thriving classical music scene, not least an excellent symphony orchestra and several outstanding performance spaces. It also has a wide range of societies and ensembles which cater to more specialized areas of the classical canon, such as baroque, choral and chamber music.

Early Music Vancouver 1254 West 7th Ave ☎604/732-1610, ⊚www.earlymusic.bc.ca. This society, one of several musical associations in the city, promotes medieval, Baroque and other early music, preferably played with the original instruments of the time. Concerts are held at venues across the city, including St Andrew's Wesley Church at 1012 Nelson St, the Chan Centre and UBC Recital Hall, 6361 Memorial Rd, during the Early Music Festival in July and August (see p.208).

Festival Concert Society ☎604/736-3737 the **Vancouver Academy of Music, 1270 Chestnut St at Kits Point in Vanier Park.** The society organizes inexpensive Sunday morning concerts including jazz, folk or classical recitals – at the Queen Elizabeth Theatre (see opposite).

Music-in-the-Morning Concert Society ☎604/873-4612, ⊚www.musicinthemorning .org. This society began modestly in June Goldsmith's front room but now organizes innovative and respected morning concerts of old and new music with local and visiting musicians. Concerts are held at 10.30am (Sept–May Tues–Fri);"Rush hour" concerts take place five times a year in the Vancouver Art Gallery, 750 Hornby St (see p.53).

University of British Columbia School of Music Recital Hall, Gate 4, 6361 Memorial Rd ☎604/822-5574, ⊚www.music.ubc.ca. The UBC presents around eight major and many smaller performances during January and February and between September and November. Many of the concerts are free.

Vancouver Bach Choir 805-235 Keith Rd, West Vancouver ☎604/921-8012, ⊕www.vancouver bachchoir.com. The city's top non-professional 150-strong choir performs between three and five major concerts yearly of Bach and other choral works at the Orpheum Theatre (see p.168). Its Christmas sing-along performance of Handel's *Messiah* is something of a city institution.

Vancouver Cantata Singers 5115 Keith Rd ☎604/921-8588, ⊕www.cantata.org. Various locations are used by this 40-strong, semi-professional choir for performances of traditional and contemporary choral music.

Vancouver Chamber Choir 1254 W 7th Ave ☎604/738-6822, ⊕www.vancouverchamber choir.com. This is Vancouver's best and most internationally renowned professional choir. Founded in 1971, the choir performs at a dozen locations, including the Orpheum, the Chan Centre and even the *Fairmont Waterfront Hotel* and *Hotel Vancouver* (see p.52).

Vancouver New Music Society 837 Davie St ☎604/663-0861, ⊕www.newmusic.org. This association is responsible for promoting cutting-edge twentieth-century and contemporary classical music, including opera, mixed-media dance and film performances. It presents around seven major concerts annually between September and June, usually at the Vancouver East Cultural Centre (see opposite page), and occasionally links with other orchestras and musical organizations to present festivals of new music.

Vancouver Opera 500-845 Cambie St ☎604/638-0222, ⊕www.vanopera.bc.ca. The Vancouver Opera produces four operas during its season (Oct–May) at the Queen Elizabeth Theatre: productions enjoy an excellent local and national reputation. Productions consist of operas from the mainstream repertoire, often performed by stars of international opera, and works by more obscure Canadian composers. The box office is open Mon–Fri 9am–4pm.

Vancouver Recital Society 304-873 Beatty St ☎604/736-0363, ⊕www.vanrecital.com. Hosts two of the best and most popular cycles in the city – the summer Chamber Music Festival (usually at St George's School) and the main Vancouver Playhouse recitals (Sept–April). Catches up-and-coming

performers plus a few major international names each year.

Vancouver Symphony Orchestra 601 Smithe St ☎604/876-3434, ⊕www.vancouver symphony.ca. The highly regarded VSO presents most concerts at the Orpheum or the Chan Centre (see p.170) but also sometimes gives free recitals in the summer at beaches and parks, usually culminating in a concert on Whistler Mountain. Its repertoire includes so-called "Masterworks" (great classical works), "Casual Classics" (lighter works from the classical canon), "Kid's Koncerts" (aimed at school children) and "VSO Pops", a mixture of pop, Broadway and other show tunes. The box office (Mon–Fri 1–5pm) is at the Orpheum Theatre at Smithe and Granville (see p.168).

Theatre

Theatre in Vancouver is what you would expect from a vibrant, urbane and multicultural city. It has a healthy mainstream, but also a number of smaller and long-established perform-ance spaces that feed productions – and actors and actresses – onto larger stages, both literally and metaphori-cally. Film and TV star Michael J. Fox, for example, graduated from the Arts Club Theatre (see below) on Granville Island. There is also a thriv-ing community theatre scene, and plenty of opportunities to catch a performance outdoors during some of the city's summer festivals.

Arts Club Theatre 1585 Johnston St, Granville Island ☎604/687-1644, ⊕www.artsclub.com. Established in 1964, this is one of the leading lights in the city's drama scene, and one of the most active. Performances are staged at several venues: the 425-seat main stage offers mainstream drama, comedies and musicals; the bar next door presents small-scale revues and cabarets; while the most recent stage, the 650-seat refurbished Art Deco Stanley Theatre at 2750 Granville St south of Broadway – a former vaudeville theatre and movie house – offers a mixture of musicals, long-run shows and mainstream and avant-garde plays by Canadian and other dramatists.

The Arts Club's Granville Island Revue Stage also hosts the popular "Vancouver Theatresports League" (☎604/687-1644), improvisational comedy based on audience contributions. Shows are currently held nightly at 7.30pm on Wednesday and Thursday and three times nightly at 8pm, 10pm and 11.45pm on Friday and Saturday.

Firehall Arts Centre 280 E Cordova St and Gore St ☎604/689-0926, ⊛www.firehall.org. The leader of Vancouver's community and avant-garde pack, presenting mime, music and visual arts. The 150-seat theatre is housed in a historic fire station and generally hosts three major (often ground-breaking) productions each season from the resident Firehall Theatre Company, as well as cutting-edge contemporary dance. There's also a nice lounge and gallery, plus an outdoor stage for summer shows.

Performance Works 1218 Cartwright St, Granville Island ☎604/606-6425 or 604/689-0926. A converted warehouse is the setting for this intimate performance space given over to a wide range of small-scale and usually contemporary productions.

Presentation House Theatre 333 Chesterfield Ave, North Vancouver ☎604/990-3474. The North Shore is short of venues, largely having to make do with this former 1902 schoolhouse, the setting for contemporary theatre productions and performance art.

Theatre Under the Stars Malkin Bowl, Stanley Park ☎604/687-0174 or 257-0366, ⊛www.tuts.bc.ca. July and August productions by "TUTS" at the Malkin Bowl – built in 1934 as a bandstand – are fun, popular and lightweight (and, note, not free), but can suffer from being staged in one of Canada's rainiest cities. Try for a dry night – productions will be cancelled on very bad days – and bring something to sit on and something warm to wear. For other outdoor theatrical productions, see "Bard on the Beach" on p.207.

Vancouver East Cultural Centre1895 Venables St and Victoria Drive ☎604/251-1363, ⊛www.vecc.bc.ca. This highly renowned 350-space in East Vancouver – known colloquially as the "Cultch" – is housed in a late nineteenth-century former church adapted for performance, and is used by a highly eclectic mix of drama, dance, mime and musical groups. Performances are usually modern, sometimes controversial and almost always far better than the "neighbourhood" tag – suggesting small-scale local productions – that the place modestly attaches to itself. To get here take bus #20 from Downtown to Commercial Drive at Venables and walk east two blocks uphill.

Vancouver Playhouse Theatre Company Hamilton St at Dunsmuir St ☎604/665-3050. One of western Canada's biggest theatre companies. It usually presents six top-quality shows, from the mainstream theatrical canon, employing some of the region's premier performers, directors and set designers during its October to May season.

Waterfront Theatre 1411 Cartwright St, Granville Island ☎604/685-6217. This popular and intimate 240-seat theatre is used by three resident and several occasional local companies. You can therefore expect a wide range of shows – anything from musicals to improvisation – plus drama workshops and readings.

Dance

Vancouver serves dance enthusiasts well, especially those whose bent is for contemporary dance, an area where the work over many years of talented individuals such as Karen Jamieson has provided the impetus for a flourishing and nurturing environment for modern choreography. Many leading lights of the city's dance world, as well as those from further afield, come together for the annual Dancing on the Edge See below and p.208).

Anna Wyman Dance Theatre 707-207 West Hastings St ☎604/685-5699, ⊛www.anna wyman.com. Although its repertoire is wide, this troupe specializes in contemporary dance. As well as shows in a variety of conventional spaces, it occasionally puts on free outdoor performances at Granville Island and at Robson Square near the Art Gallery.

Ballet British Columbia 1101 West Broadway ☎604/732-5003, ⊛www.balletbc.com. The province's top company performs – along with major visiting dance companies – at the Queen Elizabeth Theatre (see p.169). The corps is highly respected, and known for its bold and powerful performances and its sophisticated approach and interpretations. It presents both modern and more traditional dance.

Films and filming in Vancouver

Vancouver's burgeoning film and TV industry – as a production centre it now rates third in terms of size behind Los Angeles and New York – has seen it rather hyperbolically dubbed "Hollywood North". Others, more unkindly, have christened it "Brolleywood" – Hollywood with rain – not least *The X-Files* lead David Duchovny, who lamented that it rained "400 inches a day". The star's unhappiness with the climate was apparently one of the reasons the show fled Vancouver after five seasons had been shot in the city.

That said, *The X-Files* was a major catalyst for a business that sprang from a venture worth just US$12 million in 1978 to an industry that now generates at least $650 million plus $1 billion in indirect revenues.

The reason is simple – money. It simply costs less to produce films and TV in Vancouver, though there are those who claim, Duchovny's complaints aside, that it was the weather that first lured *The X Files'* makers to the city – the rainy, overcast days were perfect for the sombre pall that infused many of the show's early episodes.

True or not, the US producers of this and other shows loved the favourable exchange rates, the cheap (and union-lite) labour, the easy flight from LA and, above all, the wide range of locations that easily double for US locations. Tenements, skyscrapers, alleys – especially the alleys – docks, waterfront and more need little or no disguise to double for New York, Philadelphia, Chicago or other Stateside cities.

Thus remakes of *Perry Mason* and *Ironside*, for example, feature the Vancouver Art Gallery, while chunks of the city also appeared in Schwarzenegger's *The Sixth Day*. Vancouver can also do London, Hong Kong and Russia, appearing as the last in *The Russia House* with Sean Connery. Inland, British Columbia offers forests, lakes, mountains and, around Kamloops, areas of near desert – much of *First Blood*, for example, Sylvester Stallone's first Rambo movie, was shot in and around Hope in the Fraser Valley east of Vancouver, the town being wasted by Stallone in spectacular fashion near the film's end.

The merits, or otherwise, of *First Blood* aside, the majority of films and TV shows made in Vancouver are usually forgettable at best, and B-movie straight-to-video or unmitigated rubbish at worst. Better or better-known outings include *The Accused*, with Jodie Foster, *Little Women*, *We're No Angels* (with Sean Penn), *This Boy's Life* (Robert de Niro) and *Bird on a Wire* (Mel Gibson and Goldie Hawn).

In the same way that Vancouver- and Canadian-produced films may be little known, so there is a long roster of "American" stars who actually hail from the land of the maple leaf : Dan Ackroyd, Jim Carrey, Christopher Plummer, Keanu Reeves, Donald Sutherland and William Shatner, with Pamela Anderson, Raymond Burr (of *Ironside* and *Perry Mason* fame), Michael J. Fox and James Doohan (the immortal Scotty in *Star Trek*) hailing from Vancouver itself. One Bill Pratt also worked in the city as a 22-year-old, and might have remained a longshoreman-cum-stage hand had he not moved to Hollywood and changed his name – to Boris Karloff.

Among local film-makers, the best-known name is Atom Egoyan, who grew up in Victoria, and has been responsible, among others, for *Speaking Parts* (1989), *The Adjuster* (1991) and *Exotica* (1994).

To find out more about the city's film and TV business, pick up *Reel West* magazine from newsstands (www.reelwest.com), or contact the BC Film Commission (hotline 604/660-35690, www.bcfilmcommission.com), which provides updates on movies and TV series currently being filmed in the city.

THE PERFORMING ARTS

EDAM Western Front Lodge, 303 East 8th Ave ☏604/876-9559, ⓦwww.edamdance.org. Experimental Dance and Music was founded in 1982 by six dancers and a musician and has long favoured developing dance through improvisation. It often presents multimedia productions mixing dance, film, music and art at a variety of venues. It also offers courses and summer schools.

Karen Jamieson Dance Company 4036 W 19th Ave ☏604/893-8807. Jamieson is an award-winning choreographer whose company, founded in 1983, often uses solely Canadian composers and artists, and incorporates aboriginal themes into its work.

Kokoro Dance Company 1201-207 W Hastings St ☏604/662-7441, ⓦwww.kokoro.ca. An innovative company whose name means "heart" in Japanese and whose works combine elements of modern dance and traditional Japanese dance. Most performances are held at the Vancouver East Cultural Centre.

Scotiabank Dance Centre 677 Davie St ☏604/689-0926. This new dance centre in a former bank building was converted by Arthur Erickson, architect of the Museum of Anthropology and other Vancouver buildings. It provides studio and rehearsal space for around 30 companies, and is open to the public for workshops, classes, exhibitions and other events. It also houses the Vancouver Dance Centre (☏604/606-6400, ⓦwww.thedancecentre.ca), a major source of information on dance in Vancouver and beyond. Contact it for details of the major Dancing on the Edge Festival in July (for more on the festival, see p.208).

Film

Vancouver may feature prominently in the world of film production, but this is a city that still appears to be no more or less obsessed with watching films than any other place its size. This said, it has plenty of multiplex screens for first–runs, with a cluster on Granville, and several repertory movie houses dotted around the city's fringes that cater to more dedicated film buffs. Cinema enthusiasts should time a visit to the city to coincide

with the Vancouver International Film Festival (North America's third largest) in late September and October (see p.209).

Capitol 6 820 Granville Mall ☏604/669-6000. This complex is one of the biggest first-run venues in the centre of the city, and – as it's bang in the middle of Downtown and shows all the new releases – the main 1000-seat screen makes a good first choice if you want to see the movies of the moment. Screens in the upstairs theatres are much smaller.

Cinemark Tinseltown 88 Pender St at Abbott ☏604/806-0799. Just two blocks south of Water St and the heart of Gastown, this multi-screen in the International Village complex has the most modern and high-tech of the city centre's first-run cinemas, with big screens, underground parking and good seating.

Denman Cinema 1737 Comox St at Denman ☏604/683-2201. A good choice in the West End if you need a break after Stanley Park or want to catch a movie before or after hitting the cafés and bars on Denman Street. Expect second-run or near first-run films at good prices.

Fifth Avenue Cinemas 2110 Burrard St at W 5th Ave ☏604/734-7469. Fiveplex cinema in south Vancouver run by the founder of the Vancouver Film Festival. It is one of the better in the city for art-house or more arty first-run films.

Hollywood 3123 West Broadway between Tutch and Barclay sts ☏604/738-3211, ⓦwww .hollywoodtheatre.ca. A Kitsilano repertory cinema which can also always be relied on for good (and good-value) double bills and second-run (or just over first-run) movies.

Pacific Cinémathèque 1131 Howe St near Helmcken St ☏604/688-3456, ⓦwww.cinematheque.bc.ca. The nonprofit film society that runs this screen is devoted to furthering the understanding of cinema and contemporary visual arts. As part of its brief, it shows a good range of arthouse, overseas and experimental films. All of which makes it the best non-mainstream cinema in the city. The programmes can be hit or miss, but any film buff will find something to tempt them.

Raja Cinema 639 Commercial Drive at Georgia ☏604/253-0402. The place to come when only Bollywood will do.

Ridge Theatre 3131 Arbutus St at West 15th Ave ☎604/738-6311, ⊛www.ridgetheatre.com. A little too far south to catch its target Kits audience, but still a great neighbourhood place for second-run, classic and other films. Look out for its provocatively paired double bills and late-lunch (1.30pm) "Movies for Mommies" screenings. Built in 1950, it's virtually unchanged – there's even an enclosed "crying room" for parents with boisterous children or howling infants.

The Blinding Light! 36 Powell St ☎604/684-8288, ⊛www.blindinglight.com. A great 100-seat Gastown venue for diehard film buffs who can expect to see all manner of offbeat, experimental and plain crazy films (sample title: *Jesus Christ Vampire Hunter*), as well as home movies, crazed animation, and lunacies such as industrial and training films from the 1950s and 1960s. It helps host the Vancouver Underground Film Festival and presents theme nights such as "bring-your-own-movie" sessions.

Gay Vancouver

W hile it may lack the profile or élan of San Francisco, Vancouver enjoys the same laid-back West Coast attitudes and joie de vivre. The city boasts a large, vibrant and unabashed gay and lesbian community, much of which is culturally and politically active. There's also a lively and diverse scene when it comes to entertainment and nightlife, with plenty of clubs – theme nights are a popular phenomenon – drag shows and up-to-the-minute bars and discos.

It hasn't always been this way, homosexuality having only been decriminalized in Canada in 1969. This followed a slow process of protest and liberalization which started five years earlier with the creation in Vancouver of the Association for Social Knowledge, Canada's first openly gay and lesbian discussion forum. Today, the easygoing self-confidence of the city's gays and lesbians is traced by many to 1990, when Vancouver hosted "Celebration 90: Gay Games III and Cultural Festival", a week-long event that attracted 8500 participants to around thirty sports and associated cultural events.

Change has continued apace, and today the city's now-progressive attitude is making it a prime destination for gay couples wanting to wed, same-sex marriages having been made legal in 2003. At the same time, a slightly ageing population and a general shift in lifestyles have led the city's gay and lesbian culture to diversify beyond clubs and pubs in recent years. Now there's a plethora of courses and group activities available in the city – anything from gay quilting to gay ping-pong and gay square-dancing.

Gay and lesbian events

The main draw in Vancouver's gay calendar is **Pride**, which celebrated its twenty-fifth anniversary in 2003. It usually takes place over three days during the first long weekend in August. Special events are held in clubs across the city, while the traditional parade along Denman and Beach has, by general consent, become bigger and better each year, with ever-more exuberant floats. Over the years, the parade has spawned stalls and stages at Sunset Beach up to Davie Street, with lots of beer gardens and live performances. For further information contact Vancouver Pride Society (☎604/687-0955 or 604/737-7433, ⊚www.vanpride.bc.ca); special club events can be found in listings in editions of *The Georgia Straight* or *Xtra! West* (see p.176) free magazines in the week or so preceding the event.

The Queer Film and Video Festival (⊚www.outonscreen.com) takes over the city's movie theatres shortly after Pride in August. It marked its 15th anniversary in 2003. Other noteworthy events include the Gay Ski Week (☎604/899-6209, ⊚www.outontheslopes.com), which has attracted thousands every year since its inception in 1991. Event organizers also now have a summer event, with riding, biking and rafting among warmer-weather activities.

That's not to say the city's gay nightlife is second-rate. Davie Village, which runs from Burrard along Davie to Denman, is where you will find the highest concentration of long-established gay clubs, pubs and stores, though there are plenty of other venues throughout the city; lesbians, for their part, have traditionally gathered on or around Commercial Drive (The Drive). Most clubs are late-night opening, usually until 4am, a relatively new freedom following the relaxation of licensing laws.

While there are no vast **events or festivals** in the manner of Sydney's Mardi Gras or San Francisco's Pride, there are plenty of one-off and occasional events that have become, or are becoming permanent fixtures. These include the city's "Pride" event (see box p.175) and the Stonewall Festival in June, a mixed bag of cultural and other events, usually held in Grandview Park on Commercial Drive between Charles and Williams streets.

Contacts, media and information

The best source of information pertaining to gays and lesbians is **Xtra! West** (ⓦwww.xtra.ca), a free fortnightly newspaper produced by the not-for-profit Pink Triangle Press. It's available from kerbside boxes, and music, video and other stores around the city, and has articles on news, events and people, as well as a classified section and full gay and lesbian nightlife and entertainment listings.

The paper also provides an exhaustive directory for its invaluable touch-tone phone service, which embraces a very wide range of information and contacts in the gay and lesbian community. All you do is call ☎604/684-XTRA, press 1 at the main menu, then dial the four-figure extension from a directory of some 120 different contacts and organizations. These range from the AIDS Vancouver Help Line (ext 2016) through to the Vancouver Gay and Lesbian Choir (ext 2298) and Vancouver Leather Alliance (ext 2035). Also useful for listings and contacts is the monthly *Outlooks* (ⓦwww.outlooks.ca) magazine.

In other **media**, *Out On TV* is a weekly news programme, which airs on Saturdays at 10pm: it's informative, if a little parochial. Visit ⓦwww.OutOnTV.com for further details. You might also want to check out cable stations 20/51, Tuesdays and Fridays, on PrideVision. Various **radio shows** also cater to a gay and lesbian audience: currently broadcasting are Queer FM every Sunday between 6 and 8pm on CITR 101.9 FM with a lesbian show on Thursdays at 8pm on Co-op Radio 102.7 FM; further information ☎604/822-1242. There are also gay and lesbian shows on CFUV in Victoria (101.9 FM).

Other general contacts include the **Gay & Lesbian Centre Help Line** (☎604/684-6869) and the **Gay & Lesbian Business Association** (☎604/253-4307 or 604/739-4522), the latter being a source for gay- and lesbian-friendly businesses in the city. The **Gay Lesbian Transgendered Bisexual Community Centre** – The Centre for short – has a good library at 1170 Bute (☎604/684-5307). Little Sister's Book and Art Emporium at 1238 Davie St (☎604/669-1753) sells everything from dildos to greetings cards, and also has a comprehensive noticeboard. It also sells tickets for various events, as does GayMart at 1148 Davie (☎604/681-3262). Mainstream bookstores such as Chapters (see p.181) also have good gay and lesbian sections. For more specific contacts, Vancouver Women in Leather is for women into **leather, fetish and or bondage and S & M** (☎604/779-6434, ⓦwww.vwleather.com). Fetish fans should also look at the Sin City night at

Club 23 (see p.178), currently held on the second Saturday of every month: there is a strict fetish dress code. Visit ⓦwww.gothic.bc.ca/sincity for more information and latest venues.

BiVancouver (☎604/787-4330, Ⓔbivancouver@hotmail.com) is for **bi-sexual** and bi-friendly people of all ages; VASM is for bondage and/or S & M fans (☎604/684-XTRA, extn 2123, ⓦwww.vasm.bc.ca), who should also visit ⓦwww.bodyperve.com or ⓦwww.vancouverdungeon.com for details of monthly pan-sexual nights, play parties and special nights at The PumpJack pub (see p.178) and other venues.

Event organizers

The Hershe bars (ⓦwww.flygirlproductions.com) are popular lesbian nights held in different venues mainly on the Sunday of any holiday/long weekend. Other useful websites to visit if you are looking for one-off events and information include ⓦwww.lesbigay.com, ⓦwww.twpe.ca , ⓦwww.lesbiannation.com, ⓦwww.flygirlproductions.com and ⓦwww.tbbproductions.net.

Nightlife

Gay and lesbian **clubs** tend to open and close with alarming speed, so it is always worth checking listings magazines (see p.163) and flyers and posters for latest details. Gay and lesbian pubs tend to rather better established, and to help you find a place operating, or still with a gay and/or lesbian emphasis, we have indicated which bars and clubs below have been open for some time. A word of warning: while Vancouver is a welcoming city for the gay traveller, it is still important to keep your wits about you. There has been the odd case of queer-bashing, as in most cities, and a man was murdered in the cruising area of Stanley Park in 2001.

Pubs and restaurants

Big C Grill 3941-3943 Main St ☎604/871-9096. Drop by this gay-owned and operated diner if you are browsing the shops and galleries of Antique Row at 23rd and Main. Good for breakfast, lunch and dinner, and there is a licensed rear patio. Often shows paintings and other art by local artists.

Café Luxy 1235 Davie St ☎604/669-5899. Davie Village and the West End have no shortage of gay-friendly places to eat and drink, but this stands out by virtue of its fresh, home-made pastas and jazz-groove DJ nights, currently every Tuesday.

Dufferin 900 Seymour St and Smithe St ☎604/683-4251, ⓦwww.dufferinhotel.com. This is one of the city's key places for gay men to shake their stuff on the dancefloor, but it also hosts a lot of drag-nights – the Buff at the Duff drag shows (Mon–Thurs) are an institution – as well as featuring strippers, go-go boys (Fri and Sun) and karaoke.

Fountainhead Pub 1025 Davie ☎604/687-2222, ⓦwww.thefountainheadpub.com. A popular and pleasantly buzzing place at the heart of Davie Village for good food, drink (including microbrewed beers) and a large, heated patio from which to spy on all the street action. Also has a pool table, darts and multiple TV screens. Tends to attract a slightly older, more mellow crowd.

Global Beat 1249 Howe St ☎604/689-2444. A gay-owned restaurant and lounge with billiard tables that makes a good place for an inexpensive meal (fine Italian-influenced food) or a drink – there's no heavy cruising – to start the evening, especially if you're heading to *Odyssey*, a club which stands right next door (see p.178).

Oasis 1240 Thurlow ☎604/685-1724, ⓦwww.theoasispub.com. Vancouver's only gay piano bar. Comfortable upstairs place for people who want to be heard above the music. Long list of martinis and a tapas menu, with daily specials and a rooftop patio. Open 9pm until late daily.

PumpJack Pub 1167 Davie St ☎604/685-3417, ⊛www.pumpjackpub.com. A spacious spot and Vancouver's leather bar of choice: it's favoured by Western Canada Leather Pride and the so-called BC Bears, a gay affiliation for those with a penchant for the hairy and/or bearded (visit ⊛www.bcbears.com for more information). Arrive early to guarantee a window-side barstool to watch the men go by. There are pool tables and uniform nights. Expect queues at the weekends.

Sugar Daddy's 1262 Davie St ☎604/632-1646. Another West End gay rendezvous of some standing, thanks to video sports, big-screen TVs, and good burgers, beer and margaritas. Open for lunch and dinner daily.

Clubs

Club 23 23 West Cordova ☎604/662-3277. A cool, dark split-level club, perfect for the various theme nights held here, such as the naked parties held by the Pacific Canadian Association of Nudists (☎604/684-9872 ext 2026, ⊛www.p-can.org), "Lesbians on the loose" and "Sin City" fetish nights.

Fluid 1066 West Hastings ⊛www.twpe.ca. A gay tea dance is currently held here on the second Sunday of the month, along with other more risqué theme nights.

Heritage House Hotel 455 Abbott St ☎604/685-7777. The three bars here host a number of gay and lesbian nights: *Charlie's Bar and Grill* on the main floor fills up with women only on Saturdays and *Chuck's Pub* has "Guys in Disguise" on Fridays and men-only on Saturdays; call for latest details. The *Lotus Sound Lounge* downstairs has a women-only dance club (Fri) and a lesbian hang-out every Wednesday to Saturday at the Lick Bar. There are some mixed nights and occasional fetish and other theme nights. Call before you go for latest permutations and times.

Lava Lounge 1180 Granville St ☎604/605-6136. This is a gay and lesbian club with different theme nights several times a week: "Sexy Friday" has go-go boys, while "Soirée la Femme" is a girls-only night every third Sunday of the month.

Numbers 1042 Davie St and Burrard St ☎604/685-4077. This is a cruisy multilevel venue that has been in business for over twenty years, with a gay disco, kitschy mirrored dancefloor, movies and pool tables upstairs, men and women downstairs – but with very few women. Tends to attract a slightly more mature crowd. As with virtually all other clubs listed here, there is a wide variety of theme nights.

Octane 1188 Davie St ☎604/688-0677. A hip club and bar with DJs and a happening, youngish crowd. Best of the spinning is at the late-night event on Sundays. There's currently live jazz on Saturdays.

Odyssey 1251 Howe St near Davie St ☎604/689-5256, ⊛www.theodyssey nightclub.com. A young gay and bisexual club with house and techno disco and theme shows on most nights. Expect to queue on Fridays and Saturdays as it currently has the reputation as the hippest and wildest place in town.

Sublime 816 Granville St Ⓔsublimenightclub@hotmail.com A good place to wind up in the small hours if you're still raring to go at the weekend: the after-hours dance club runs from 1 to 6am on Fridays and Saturdays.

Twilight 686 West Hastings St ☎604/633-3988. The club has the occasional gay theme nights and guest DJs. Currently the Luce night on Sundays invites you to "dress fabulous and be glamorous".

Bathhouses

F212 Steam 1048 Davie St ☎604/689-9719, ⊛www.f212.com. This bathhouse is found at the heart Davie's gay "Village" in the West End. There is a second, co-owned F212 Steam in the suburbs at 430 Columbia St (☎604/540-2117) near the SkyTrain station.

Hastings Steam & Sauna 766 East Hastings ☎604/251-5455. This ambient bathhouse has been open since 1926, and caters to a varied straight and gay clientele – the more cruisey area is downstairs. It's open seven days a week from 11am to 11pm.

M2M 1210 Granville St (downstairs) ☎604/684-6011. A Downtown spot that caters to the leather, steam, jocks and Levi fraternity.

Shopping

Vancouver affords excellent **shopping** possibilities. Unlike many colder Canadian cities, it has largely eschewed the larger indoor mall, and offers a wide variety of smaller speciality stores and a good selection of markets. It also has the range of designer and other upmarket outlets you would expect in a city of this size and wealth, as well as the predictable rash of souvenir and other tourist shops.

In **Downtown,** the key shopping thoroughfare is **Robson Street**, and in particular the stretch near the corner of Burrard Street, an intersection which supposedly has the highest pedestrian count of any city block in Canada. Robson's character has changed in the last few years, its former array of small European restaurants and speciality stores having given way to smart designer-clothing stores – with the emphasis on youth fashion – slick cafés and upmarket restaurants. Here you'll also find flagship stores for national and international chains, such as Banana Republic, Gap, Nike, Roots, French Connection, Zara and Chapters.

These days, the funkier (and more expensive) speciality stores are to be found in **Yaletown,** which has plenty of fashion, furniture and home-design stores. For food and fun browsing in small offbeat shops, **Granville Island** and its superb market have no rivals – though it can be very busy, especially at weekends. In **Gastown,** the weight of souvenir shops is leavened by speciality stores – the cigar stores on Water Street in particular. It also has some of the finest galleries of Inuit and other aboriginal art in the city.

Away from Downtown, **Chinatown** boasts a good night market and plenty of food shops and stores selling Chinese kitchenware and goods. To the south of Downtown, **Kitsilano**'s best speciality, secondhand and bookshops cluster on **West 4th Avenue** between Burrard and Alma streets. There are also retail hotspots on Broadway, and though this is an emerging shopping street it doesn't yet have West 4th's eclectic mix of stores – anything from clothing, home furnishings and candles to books, sportswear and crystals.

Further south still, the **South Granville** enclave – the ten-block stretch of Granville Street from about West 7th to 17th Avenue – is a key shopping area. Once a place where older, wealthy denizens of old-money Shaughnessy came to shop, the area now has a trendier edge, with clothing stores and delicatessens complementing upscale galleries and stores selling antiques, Oriental carpets, furniture and men's and women's designer clothes.

You'll also find lots of interesting small stores – especially antique shops – plus cafés, bookshops and clothing stores to the west, between 19th and 27th avenues on **Main Street**. Another small corner of Main Street at 4th Avenue is rapidly being colonized by artists' and designers' studios, small cafés and specialty stores and galleries.

Much further afield, there are a handful of ethnic enclaves with food markets and stores aimed at the local community – though in all cases the areas' original ethnic identities are quickly being blurred by the arrival of Downtown hipsters and other new inhabitants. This is especially true of **Commercial Drive** east of Chinatown and the railway and bus station – more commonly known as the "Drive" – and in particular the stretch from 1st Avenue to Venables Street in East Vancouver, which for years was the city's **Little Italy**. The delis, coffee bars and the Italian mammas are still in evidence, but the ethnic mix (Vietnamese, Korean, Chinese and others) is now far more varied, as is the range of trendy clothing stores, bookshops and interesting speciality outlets.

Much the same can be said of **Little Greece**, to the west in Kitsilano, where the traditional Greek-dominated area of Broadway from Trafalgar to Waterloo streets now has a far more diverse ethnic mix – though several good Greek restaurants and cafés survive. Further south, a district where the ethnic flavour is still marked is the **Punjabi Market** – on Main Street between 49th and 51st avenues – where in the Guru Bazaar and other stores you'll find a wide range of Indo-Pakistani goods such as saris, fabrics and Indian spices and food. The area is also crammed with lots of tiny jewellery stores – bartering is acceptable in most.

The **opening hours** of most Vancouver stores are Monday to Saturday 9/10am to 5.30/6pm (7pm for malls), with late openings on Thursdays and Fridays until 9pm. Many stores on Robson Street stay open until 9pm every night, at least in summer. Most malls and stores on Robson and other Downtown malls also open on Sunday, though hours are generally a little shorter – typically 10am or noon to 5pm. Opening times that are markedly different are given in individual entries below.

Aboriginal arts and crafts

Coastal Peoples Fine Arts Gallery 1024 Mainland St ☎604/685-9298, ⊛www.coastalpeoples .com. This airy modern gallery was one of the first in Yaletown to deal in aboriginal art and artefacts. It sells small totems, paintings, prints and Inuit sculpture at top-dollar prices, but specializes in fine gold and silver jewellery. This is the place where you're likely to find the work of both established and up-and-coming artists.

Hill's Native Art 165 Water St ☎604/685-4249, ⊛www.hillsnativeart.com. If the art of Water Street's museum-like galleries is too precious or expensive then Hill's, established in 1946, has a selection of items and artefacts aimed more squarely at ordinary visitors – T-shirts, prints, books, CDs of aboriginal music and so forth – as well as paintings, sculptures, masks and – if you have $35,000 to drop – full-sized totems.

Images for a Canadian Heritage 164 Water St ☎604/685-7046, ⊛www.imagesforcanada .com. This government-licensed gallery sells some of Canada's finest (and most expensive) pieces of Inuit and other Pacific Northwest aboriginal art. The quality of its pieces makes it more of a museum than a store or gallery, a feeling reinforced by its tasteful brick and wood-beamed setting. Check out the fine soapstone sculptures and reindeer-antler carvings by Kevin Peters.

Inuit Gallery of Vancouver 206–220 Water St ☎604/688-7323, ⊛www.inuit.com. Like the similar and nearby Images for a Canadian Heritage, this gallery showcases some of the finest and most expensive Inuit art available on the open market – masks, works on paper, ceremonial bowls, stone and bone sculptures, painted chests, wood and argillite carvings and much more. Prices are high, but it's worth admiring the exquisite pieces even if you have no intention to buy. Often there's work here by some of the top names in aboriginal art, notably Bill Reid, Richard Davidson and David Neel.

Khot-La-Cha Salish Handicrafts 270 Whonoak St, North Vancouver ☎604/987-3339. Crafts, sweaters, jewellery and inexpensive accessories are part of the large selection of goods at this Salish-run store a block off Capilano Rd.

Leona Lattimer Gallery 1590 West 2nd Ave at Fir St ☎604/732-4556, ⓦwww.leonalattimer.com. A great-looking gallery just west of Granville Island with a wide range of Pacific Northwest peoples' prints, paintings, sculpture, masks, jewellery, totems: not everything is expensive – prices for most pieces range from a few to a few hundred dollars.

Marion Scott Gallery 481 Howe St ☎604/685-1934, ⓦwww.marionscottgallery.com. This gallery is now in its third decade, and remains noted for its contemporary aboriginal art, and in particular Inuit prints, drawings and sculpture.

Spirit Wrestler Gallery 8 Water St ☎604/669-8813, ⓦwww.spiritwrestler.com. The Gastown location precludes low prices, but then the work here was never going to be inexpensive, for the gallery, as its name suggests, specializes in high-quality sculpture and graphics by leading aboriginal artists inspired by shamanism.

Antique shops

Salmagundi 321 West Cordova St ☎604/681-4648. A Gastown hoard of covetable items, some hidden in the 100-odd drawers of an old Japanese medicine chest.

Uno Langmann 2117 Granville St near West 6th Ave ☎604/736-8825, ⓦwww.langmann.com. It's unlikely you'll be buying anything here unless you've recently come into an inheritance, but if you're nearby it's worth looking in on a treasure trove that is more museum than shop. Particularly good for eighteenth- and nineteenth-century Canadian paintings.

Vancouver Antique Centre 422 Richards St ☎604/669-7444. A heritage building with around 15 antique stores on two floors.

New stores are opening in neighbouring buildings.

Books and magazines

Antiquarius 609-207 W Hasting St at Cambie St ☎604/669-7288. A treasury of secondhand books across a wide range of subjects, plus old magazines, posters, photographs, sheet music and a small assortment of bric-a-brac and antiques.

Banyan Books and Sound 3608 West 4th Ave between Stevens and Trafalgar ☎604/732-7912, ⓦwww.banyen.com. Tremendous bookshop devoted to all things New Age, organic gardening, alternative medicine and healing, yoga, Buddhism and other mind, body and spirit titles. Also sells CDs, incenses, yoga mats and other associated articles.

Barbara-Jo's Books to Cooks 1128 Mainland St near Davie St ☎604/688-6755, ⓦwww.bookstocooks.com. A specialist store that was inspired by a similar shop in London's Notting Hill and is typical of the imaginative shops opening in Yaletown. It stocks over 2500 cookery, food and wine books, plus literary works and fiction titles with a food theme. It also hosts occasional talks and lectures and has a demonstration kitchen where you can watch dishes from various books being prepared.

Blackberry Books 1663 Duranleau St, Granville Island ☎604/685-4113, ⓦwww.bbooks.ca. This Granville Island store isn't large, but makes up for in eclectic good taste what it lacks in size and range of titles. It is also the sort of small, specialist bookstore with a knowledgeable staff that appeals to the variety of bookish babyboomers that frequent Granville Island on Saturday and Sunday mornings.

Chapters 788 Robson St at Howe St ☎604/682-4066 or 1-888/648-0889,

---

Antique hunting

Though a long way to come from Downtown, **Antique Alley** at New Westminster, near Westminister Quay, contains a dozen or more antique shops and hosts a flea market on Saturdays in summer.

A better-known and more accessible alternative to Antique Alley, **Antique Row,** on Main St south of King Edward Ave features a run of antique shops between 16th and 25th avenues on Main Street. Sunday afternoon is the busiest time for browsers. Stand-out stores include Legends, 4366 Main St (☎604/875-0621), which is great for retro and vintage clothes and jewellery, and Deeler's Antiques, 4391 Main St (☎604/879-3394), a labyrinth of antique-crammed corridors.

@www.chapters.ca. Many of Vancouver's more highbrow inhabitants were less than pleased when Chapters, a vast bookshop chain, opened this megastore in the city. Smaller and much-loved stores such as the more traditional Duthie's felt the heat and closed. However, the sheer range of titles – it has over 110,000 in stock – comfortable chairs and pleasant, airy feel of the store have won people round, and it's hard to fault either the service or the presentation. The travel section on the street-level floor is particularly good for outdoor activity or natural history guides to British Columbia and the Canadian Rockies. There are also vast sections devoted to international newspapers and magazines and a music store with the chance to listen to a wide range of CDs before you buy. There is another reasonably central outlet at 2505 Granville St (☎731-7822).

Duthie Books 2239 West 4th Ave between Vine and Yew ☎604/732-5344, @www.duthie.com. Duthie had been Vancouver's main bookstore chain since 1957 until financial Armageddon forced the closure of all but this large and browser-friendly Kits store.

Granville Book Company 850 Granville St ☎604/687-2213 or 877/838-BOOK, @www.granvillebooks.com. A welcome if incongruous addition to the heart of the Granville St entertainment strip; good staff, lots of newspapers and magazines and long hours (daily 9am–midnight).

Kidsbooks 3083 West Broadway at Barclay St ☎604/738-5335. The city's biggest children's bookshop, though it doesn't confine itself to books: there are also puppets, games, toys and occasional readings. There is another branch in North Vancouver at 3040 Edgemount Boulevard (☎986-6190).

Little Sister's Book & Art Emporium 1238 Davie St between Jervis and Bute ☎604/669-1753, @www.lsisters.com. It took a Supreme Court ruling to halt the periodic raids by Customs officers looking for "pornography" at this gay, lesbian and transgender bookstore in the West End. It has a wide range of books, videos and magazines, plus a section devoted to adult "novelties". Open daily 9am–11pm.

MacLeod's Books 455 W Pender St at Richards St ☎604/681-7654. A great place to browse for well-priced secondhand books, with a particularly good stock of fiction and non-fiction titles relating to western Canada. It

also has a smaller selection of antiquarian titles.

Magpie Magazine Gallery 1319 Commerical Drive between Charles and Kitchener ☎604/253-6666. If you don't find the magazine you want among the 5000 or more titles on sale here (the city's biggest selection), then you probably won't find it anywhere.

Wanderlust 1929 W 4th Ave between Cypress and Maple sts ☎604/739-2182. A Kitsilano store (five blocks back from the beach) with everything you could want from a travel bookshop, including many hundreds of books, maps, guides and travel accessories.

Crafts and jewellery

Circle Craft The Net Loft, Granville Island ☎604/699-8021. Main draws in this shop, one of several in the Net Loft ensemble opposite the Public Market, are ceramics, jewellery and sculpture made from "retrieved" items.

Forge & Form 1334 Cartwright St ☎604/684-6298. The studio just beyond the False Creek Community Centre doesn't look much, but it's the working base of two master gold- and silversmiths, Dietje Hagedoorn and Jürgen Schönheit. Their work has been bought by the likes of X-Files star Gillian Anderson, among others, in particular their "tension-set" stones – stone held in place without a setting.

Gallery of BC Ceramics 1359 Cartwright St, Granville Island ☎604/669-5645, @www.bcpotters.com. This gallery opposite the False Creek Community Centre is owned and run by the Potters Guild of British Columbia. At any one time you can buy or admire the work of around 100 guild members. Pieces range from the functional – domestic tableware and the like – to sculpture and other display pieces. Prices cover a correspondingly wide range. A wide range of books on ceramics and pottery is also available.

Henry Birks & Sons 698 West Hastings St ☎604/669-3333. An institution since 1879, which makes this traditional jeweller almost as old as the city itself.

Martha Sturdy Originals 3039 Granville St ☎604/737-0037, @www.marthasturdy.com. Sturdy is celebrated across North America for her jewellery and designs in glass,

Galleries

Vancouver has a plethora of small private art galleries, with a particular preponderance of established and somewhat staid outlets on a southern stretch of Granville Street between West 3rd Avenue and West 7th Avenue and beyond. For listings, check *The Georgia Straight* (see p.37), the *Vancouver Magazine* or visit ⓦwww.art-bc.com and ⓦwww.preview-art.com, site for the free quarterly gallery magazine *Preview*. Many galleries have free openings on the first Thursday of every month from 5 to 8pm. If you want to browse among the best, Buschlen Mowatt, 111-1445 West Georgia St (☎604/682-1234, ⓦwww.buschlenmowatt.com), is generally considered the city's foremost mainstream gallery.

furniture and cast-resin homeware. Her pieces are expensive, as you'd expect of work that has been exhibited in museums and galleries across the country.

The Crafthouse 1386 Cartwright St, Granville Island ☎604/687-7270. A glorious showcase for the work of decorative and functional pottery, textiles and other crafts by Canadian (and mostly BC) artists. The gallery is run by the non-profit-making Crafts Association of British Columbia.

Chinese goods

Buddha Supplies Centre 4158 Main St at 26th Ave ☎604/873-8169. This extraordinary store sells over five hundred deliberately combustible items, all designed as *joss* – paper replicas of earthly belongings that are burned at Chinese funerals to help make the deceased's life in the underworld more pleasant. Buy $1-million denomination notes from the Bank of Hell or more ambitious and equally materialistic items such as a paper cellular phone, CD player, fax machine or a paper penthouse complete with carport and Mercedes.

Keefer Chinese Bakery 251 E Georgia St near Main St ☎604/685-2117. You have plenty of bakeries to choose from in and around Chinatown, but a wide range of high-quality cakes, buns and tarts make this one of the best. Coconut buns and barbecued pork buns are tasty buys. As with most food stores in Chinatown, the customers are mostly local Chinese-Canadians.

Ming Wo 23 E Pender at Carrall St ☎604/683-7268. Ming Wo has some ten outlets around the city selling an amazing selection of Chinese and other kitchenware. If you ever wanted a gigantic cleaver, this is the place to come, but you'll also find more innocuous items such as woks, pasta machines, plates, knives and serving bowls.

South China Seas Trading Company Granville Island Public Market ☎604/681-5402. An outlet that sells fresh Chinese and Asian produce, noodles, Asian cookbooks and a wide variety of specialist spices, sauces, and hard-to-find ingredients such as Thai basil, fresh kaffir lime leaves, rambutans and mangosteens.

Superior Tofu 163 Keefer St ☎604/682-8897. The name doesn't quite say it all, for this store sells soy drinks, soy puddings and take-away lunch specials as well as fresh, smooth, pressed, firm or fried tofu.

T & T Supermarket 179–181 Keefer St near Abbott St ☎604/899-8836. The shelves here and at other T & T supermarkets around the city are a cornucopia of Chinese food and other Asian products, many of them likely to be of mind-boggling obscurity and unknown culinary purpose unless you have profound knowledge of Chinese cooking. If you're just browsing, be sure to look in the seafood bins – full of extraordinary-looking creatures of the deep – and to take in the many exotic fresh fruits and vegetables.

Ten Ren Tea & Ginseng Company 550 Main St ☎604/684-1566. Canada's best-stocked tea shop is filled with jars of medicinal and drinking teas of all descriptions from China and around the world. A Chinatown institution, the store sells strong black China teas and others more familiar to Western palates, but you might also try delicately scented teas such as jasmine, ginger flower and chrysanthemum. American, Korean and Siberian ginseng are also available.

Tung Fong Hung Medicine Company 536 Main St ☎604/688-0883. Chinatown is full of herbalists, but if you only have the time for one, then Tung Fong Hung is the first choice for product. A lot of what is on sale is frankly of dubious efficacy – dried seahorse and sliced deer antler, for example – though you can't help but be fascinated by the various potions, powders, lotions and other concoctions on display. Some of these "cures" can have side effects, so don't embark on a course of treatments without advice – there is an on-site herbalist for consultations.

Cigars

La Casa del Habano 980 Robson St ☎604/609-0511, ⓦwww .lacasadelhabanocanada.com. Havana House is one of Cuba's largest suppliers of cigars and this central store with a walk-in humidor avails itself of many hundreds of examples of its stock. Smokes here cost from a few dollars to more than a hundred.
Vancouver Cigar Company 1093 Hamilton St ☎604/685-0445 or 1-888/94-CIGAR, ⓦwww.vancouvercigar.com. It's said that the infamous cigar in the Bill Clinton and Monica Lewinsky affair was acquired during Clinton's visit to Vancouver for a world summit. This Yaletown store was perhaps too far from the *Waterfront Hotel* where he was staying to be the source, but it does have one of the city's better selections of Cuban and other cigars, with all leading brands such as Bolivar, Cohiba and Romeo y Julieta. There's also a full range of accessories. The store stays open until midnight from Thursday to Saturday.

Condoms

Rubber Rainbow Condom Company 953 Denman St ☎604/683-3423 or 1-888/423-7193. A visit to this fun store lays to rest forever the notion that Canadians are strait-laced or in any way uptight. It stocks thousands of condoms from around the world in an eye-opening range of colours and designs. The good-natured staff will answer just about any question you care to pose on the subject.

Department stores

The Bay 674 Granville St at Georgia St ☎604/681-6211, ⓦwww.hbc.com. There's no missing The Bay, a big old-fashioned department store outlet for the famous Hudson's Bay Company. The company began trading fur in the seventeenth century, its trading posts being the seeds from which many Canadian towns and cities eventually grew. Today, it has stores such as The Bay from coast to coast, as well as other lucrative business interests. While you can no longer buy furs here, you can still buy the Hudson's Bay Company's celebrated original "point" blanket, whose colourful stripes once referred to the number of beaver pelts each blanket was worth as a trade. Otherwise this has the reasonable prices and all the predictable clothes, shoes and household goods you would expect of a department store, including designer concessions such as Polo, Tommy Hilfiger and DKNY.
Sears 701 Granville St and Robson ☎604/685-3121. Famous US mid-market name in the huge retail space vacated by a noted Canadian department-store name, Eatons, after the latter company's financial meltdown.
Urban Fare 177 Davie St ☎604/975-7550, ⓦwww.urbanfare.com. Yaletown and the smart denizens of False Creek's condominiums got the impossibly hip supermarket they deserved in this supremely slick store. Supermarket basics are complemented by lots of organic and ethnic foods, an olive bar, a pasta bar and lots of high-quality prepared foods. Some idea of the shop's ambition can be gained from the fact that while it bakes much of its own bread, many of the basic ingredients are flown in from Poilâne, one of France's best bakeries.

Household and design

Birks 698 West Hastings St ☎604/669-3333. When many Canadian couples get married they send their wedding list to Birks , a chain with a reliable stock of fine china, glassware, silver and the like.
Casa 420 Howe St ☎604/681-5884. Offers the best in contemporary tableware, expensive gifts and stationery.
Chintz & Company 950 Homer St ☎604/689-2022. Large landmark store on the northern edge of Yaletown, an area that is home to more than its share of design and homeware stores. This one covers all bases from fabrics to furniture.
Drinkwater and Company 4465 West 10th Avenue ☎604/224-2665. It may not look much from the outside, but professionals

and public alike storm this family-run kitchenware store for all manner of cooking and other hardware.

Inform 97 Water St ☎604/682-3868. Large Gastown showroom for the best in modern furniture from B&B Italia, Philippe Starck, Mies van der Rohe and other leading names.

Liberty Design 1295 Seymour St ☎604/682-7499, ⊛www.libertyinside.com. A vast two-storey Yaletown store that has become a favourite among Vancouver's design-conscious shoppers looking for furniture, designer items and other beautiful things for the home from around the world.

Living Space Interiors 1110 Mainland St ☎604/683-1116. Cutting-edge Italian and French designs in furniture and other household must-have items at a central Yaletown location.

Glasses

Eyes on Burrard 775 Burrard St ☎604/688-9521. Large and central eyewear store known for its witty window displays and the latest frame styles from Persol, Boucheron, Paul Smith, Oliver Peoples and others.

Granville Eyeland 1666 Johnston St, Netloft Building ☎604/488-0909. If you want a new pair of spectacles, join the long line of locals and celebrities (including Elton John, Ed Asner and Robin Williams) who have patronized designer Klaus Sebök's Granville Island studio. The attention to detail is minute – Sebök, who has been in the trade for over 35 years, takes a cast of the bridge of your nose to ensure a perfect fit – while the variety of materials used can border on the ludicrous: buffalo horn, leather and salmon-skin frames are all available. One client wanted – and was made – glasses in 18-carat gold. Cost? $17,000 the pair.

Malls

The Landing 375 Water St ☎604/687-1144, ⊛www.mcleangroup.com. The Landing occupies a superbly restored 1905 warehouse in Gastown and includes a mostly upmarket selection of souvenir stores, restaurants and elegant designer outlets such as Polo-Ralph Lauren.

Pacific Centre ☎604/688-7236, ⊛www.pacificcentreshops.ca. Vancouver's major central Downtown mall stretches

north from Robson St for almost three blocks between Dunsmuir and Pender streets: to the east and west it is bordered by Howe and W Georgia streets. The emphasis among its more than two hundred stores is on clothes and shoe stores, but there are plenty of speciality shops such as Crabtree & Evelyn (toiletries and cosmetics), the Nike Shop and major general-clothing stores such as Holt Renfrew, a sort of Canadian version of Saks Fifth Avenue. A three-storey waterfall is the main non-retail highlight. Another 115 top-end and mid-priced speciality stores are enclosed in the adjoining Vancouver Centre, which has its main entrance at 650 W Georgia St (☎688-5658).

Park Royal Shopping Centre 2002 Park Royal South, West Vancouver ☎604/925-9576, ⊛www.shopparkroyal.com. This is one of those mega malls (actually two facing malls) in which you could, if forced, probably spend your entire life without having to leave – 250 stores, cinemas, golf range, bowling, a food court and various special events are all on hand. The malls are astride Marine Drive just west of the Lions Gate Bridge.

Royal Court 1055 W Georgia St at Burrard St ☎604/689-6711. This underground mall is something of a poor relation among the Downtown malls, but only because it's smaller than its rivals – it has around sixty stores and a food hall. The variety of shops and services is good, however, with everything from high-fashion boutiques to emergency dental clinics. One of the more fascinating stores is Geomania (☎683-2818), which sells crystals, minerals and fossils, plus works in stone.

Sinclair Centre 757 W Hastings St ☎604/666-4484, ⊛www.sinclaircentre.com. The Sinclair Centre is a classy mall that occupies four historic converted buildings – the old Vancouver Post Office (1910), Winch Building (1911), Customs Examining Warehouse (1913) and Federal Building (1937). Most of the stores are upmarket outlets such as Armani or the ultra high-fashion Leone store. Also here – in the Upper East Galleria – is Dorothy Grant (☎681-0201), a celebrated Canadian designer whose clothes, accessories and jewellery are inspired by traditional Haida and other aboriginal art and culture. The mall also has a food court.

Maps and guides

International Travel Maps 552 Seymour St near Dunsmuir St ☎604/687-3320, ⓦwww.itmb.com. This Downtown store – sometimes known by its former name of World Wide Books and Maps – offers an extensive selection of world travel books, guides and maps, as well as an excellent selection of specialist guides to Vancouver and a bewildering range of outdoor and other activities in British Columbia. You can also buy detailed hiking maps of the province. There's another outlet at 530 West Broadway (☎879-3621).

The Travel Bug 2667 West Broadway at Trafalgar ☎604/737-1122. A tiny store crammed with maps, guides and accessories on the funky strip of small shops, cafés and restaurants on the stretch of Broadway from Larch to Bayswater.

Wanderlust 1929 West 4th Ave at Cypress ☎604/739-2182. Kitsilano point of pilgrimage for maps, guidebooks, luggage and other travel accessories.

Markets

Chinatown Night Market 200 Keefer St and 200 Pender St ☎604/682-6786. May–Sept Fri–Sat 6.30pm–1.30am. Two separate blocks in Chinatown are closed to traffic for three nights a week in the warmer months of the year to make way for booths, tables and stalls selling a wide variety of fruit and vegetables, imported clothes, cooked food and miscellaneous junk, fake luxury goods, art and trinkets. The area is crowded and the atmosphere buzzing.

Granville Island Public Market 1669 Johnston St ☎604/666-5784, ⓦwww.granvilleisland.bc.ca. Daily 9am–6pm. Closed Mon in winter unless a public holiday. This covered food market is by far the best in the city, and contains a staggering array of fresh fruit and vegetables, fish, meat, pastas, chocolates, hams, cheese and a variety of gourmet foods and wines. Stalls that are particularly worth hunting out include Dussa's (☎688-8881) for ham and cheese, and the Stock Market (☎687-2433). The latter has a wonderful concept, selling home-made soup stocks and sauces by the litre, plus three daily soups to take home or eat there. It also sells a wonderful seven-grain hot

cereal for breakfast topped with apple sauce, maple syrup and cream. Currently there's also a Farmer's Truck Market on the island every Thursday from 9am to 6pm. See also p.87.

Lonsdale Quay Market 123 Carrie Cates Court, North Vancouver ☎604/985-6261, ⓦwww.lonsdalequay.com. Sat–Thurs 9.30am–6.30pm, Fri 9.30am–9pm. A smaller and only slightly less exhilarating version of the Granville Island Public Market (see above), this market just seconds away from the North Vancouver SeaBus terminal (see p.29) has one floor devoted primarily to fruit and vegetable stalls and food counters, and an upper floor given over to fashion stores, bookshops and gift stores. Perhaps the best thing here, however, is the view across the water to Downtown.

New Westminster Quay Public Market 810 Quayside, New Westminster ☎604/520-3881, ⓦwww.westminsterquay.com. Mon–Thur 10am–7pm, Fri 10am–8pm, Sat 9am-6pm, Sun 10am-6pm. It's hard to see why you would want to pay a special visit to this market 25 minutes by SkyTrain from Downtown, for it's a pale imitation of Granville Island and Lonsdale Quay markets, with a similar mixture of food stalls, speciality stores and food court. But it's worth a look if you happen to be down here, especially if you combine a visit with a walk along the river.

Robson Public Market 1610 Robson St at Cardero St ☎604/682-2733. Daily 9am–9pm. This long-established neighbourhood food market is something of an aberration on a street that has an increasing number of high-rent designer shops and smart restaurants. It has plenty of fruit and vegetable stalls, a couple of good bakeries, a salmon stall and an outstanding butcher, R B Meats. The upper level has a food court with ethnic restaurants (French, Italian, Japanese, Greek and such) and takeaway concessions.

Vancouver Flea Market 703 Terminal Ave; admission 60¢; ☎604/685-0666. Sat & Sun 9am-5pm. Vancouver's largest flea market lies close to the bus and rail terminal about five-minutes' walk from Main St SkyTrain station. There are more than 350 stalls, and while many sell little more than T-shirts, cheap trinkets or sheer tat, you'll also find plenty of junk, old books, used tools, secondhand clothes and other flea-market staples. As ever with this sort of place, you'll have to arrive early if you want to find the real bargains or treasures.

Music and video

A & B Sound 556 Seymour St at Dunsmuir ☎604/687-5837, ⊛www.absound.ca. One of several outlets in this chain whose sales often produce the best deals on new CDs (they also produce queues which can stretch a city block or more). There's a big selection and the chance to listen before you buy.

Black Swan 3209 West Broadway between Blenheim and Trutch ☎604/734-2828. First-rate independent store with informed staff and a discerning selection of new and used CDs and vinyl (including some rarities) in most genres, but particularly rock, jazz, blues, folk and world music.

D & G Collectors Records 3580 East Hastings ☎604/294-5737, ⊛www.bid-wiser.com. Lots of vintage gems from the 1950s and 1960s, rarities, and CD reissues of ancient recordings from the 1920s and other eras.

Highlife Records and Music 1317 Commercial Drive between Charles and Kitchener ☎604/251-6964,

⊛www.highlifeworldmusic.com. Excellent world-music specialist which has been in business over 20 years. Also has a selection vintage instruments.

The Magic Flute 2203 West 4th Ave ☎604/736-2727, ⊛www.magicflute.com. Classical music specialist at the heart of the Kitsilano shopping district. Carries a big selection, including works by local orchestras and other city ensembles, plus some jazz, world music and soundtracks.

Zulu 1972 West 4th Ave at Burrard St ☎604/738-3232, ⊛www.zulurecords.com. Not only is this the most amiable record store in the city, it's also the best for secondhand records, tapes and CDs, as well as a big selection of imports, rare vinyl and non-mainstream music. A newer store, without the secondhand stock, can be found nearby at 1869 West 4th Ave (☎738-0856).

Sam the Record Man 568 Seymour St and branches ☎604/684-3722. Music retailing the way it used to be: a family-run business with low-key stores, good stock and knowledgeable staff.

Virgin Megastore 788 Burrard St at Robson St ☎604/669-2289, ⊛www.virginmega.com. This is the only place in Vancouver you'll need to visit for CDs, videos, laser discs and music

and other entertainment books. Housed in Vancouver's former public library, this is the largest music store in Canada, a vast retail area over three floors with over 150,000 titles. The store is extremely central and prices, at least if you're coming from Europe, are far better than anything you'll find at home. There are some 140 listening stations where you can listen to a choice of four hundred CDs – these always include the current top 20 titles – as well as a good selection of computer multimedia software for Mac and PC.

New and vintage clothing

Aritizia 1110 Robson St ☎604/684-3251. Main outlet for a chain that carries clothes for young women by Canadian and Vancouver-based designers that you probably won't find elsewhere.

Atomic Model 1036 Mainland St ☎604/688-9989. Yaletown store that imports leading women's high-fashion lines and diffusion lines such as Is (Voyage) and Urchin (Mark Eisen) and much-frequented by models, stylists and other industry people.

The Block 350 West Cordova ☎604/685-8885. Carries a good assortment of women's clothes by a variety of mostly Canadian designers and is the main Vancouver outlet for clothes by UK company Ghost.

Deluxe Junk Co 310 West Cordova St at Cambie ☎604/685-4871,

⊛www.deluxejunk.com. The "junk" in the name is no accident – this Gastown store is full of the stuff – but among the mountains of unwearable polyester there's always the possibility of uncovering a real find. The store is just moments from *Tapestry Vintage Clothing* and *Virgin Mary's* (see below).

Dream 311 West Cordova St between Homer and Cambie ☎604/683-7326. Overflows with distinctive clothes and jewellery by local designers. It's one of several small shops on Cambie (including some vintage stores – see below) where you can find good small clothes outlets and interesting local designers.

Gregori 1010 West Georgia ☎604/681-5288. A good first stop for all the top Italian menswear labels, from Armani to Umberto Bilancione.

Holt Renfrew Pacific Centre Mall, 633 Granville St ☎604/681-3121. A definite first choice for one-stop designer shopping. All the leading labels on three floors plus cosmetics and an excellent selection of shoes.

Legends Retro-Fashion 4366 Main St at East 29th Ave ☏604/875-0621. It's a long way to come from Downtown, but this treasure trove is much loved by vintage connoisseurs both for the often immaculate condition of the old clothes, hats and accessories and the fact that most are unique and often out-of-the ordinary gems.

Leone Sinclair Centre, 757 West Hastings St ☏604/683-1133, ✆www.leone.ca. Look out for the stars shopping at this elegant and top-end store which is filled with Sui, Mui Mui by Prada, Dolce & Gabbana, Versace, Armani and other leading labels.

Mark James 2941 West Broadway ☏604/734-2381. Menswear central, with all the major Italian and other labels (Byblos, Boss, DKNY…) plus a jeans/sportswear section in a different part of the store.

Roots Canada 1001 Robson St at Burrard ☏604/683-4305, ✆www.roots.ca. Think The Gap with a Canadian twist and a slightly more varied range. This chain stocks lots of sports and casual wear, leather jackets and footwear.

Tapestry Vintage Clothing 321 Cambie St ☏604/687-1719. A convenient Gastown store where you'll always turn up something interesting among the vintage women's clothing.

True Value Vintage Basement Level, 710 Robson St at Granville ☏604/685-5403. One of the city's best-known and most central vintage stores, with clothing from the 1920s through to the 1990s, including a big selection of used Levis, lots of fake fur, leather jackets, evening wear, period

swimwear and accessories.

Virgin Mary's 430 Homer St between West Hastings and West Pender ☏604/844-7848. Another good little shop in the Gastown cluster of secondhand and vintage stores near Cambie.

Wear Else? 1766 West Fourth Ave ☏604/221-7755. A chain with several city locations. A good bet for reasonable work and leisure basics from reliable labels; also has a good selection of accessories.

Sporting goods stores

Comor 1090 West Georgia St at Thurlow ☏604/899-2111, ✆www.comorsports.com. Comor is one of the city's major ski and winter-sports retailers, and it stocks a full range of skis, snowboards, clothing, skates, sunglasses and other items from leading manufacturers such as Oakley, North Face, Salomon, Patagonia, K2 and Rollerblade. The stores also do repairs, feature a wide range of rental equipment and will deliver free to major Downtown hotels. There's another outlet in Kitsilano near Granville Island at 1918 Fir St (☏731-2163).

Europe Bound Outfitters 195 West Broadway and Columbia ☏604/874-7456. This store is part of a chain with outlets across Canada, and carries a full range of top-name outdoor brands.

Lululemon Athletica 2113 West 4th Ave ☏604/732-6111, ✆www.lululemon.com. The man behind this store, Chip Wilson, was also the brains behind the celebrated Westbeach shop (see below). Pick up the absolute latest (and hottest) in sports gear and yoga wear (yoga is *huge* is Vancouver), with

Outdoors and sports equipment

Given its setting and the spectacular scenery on its doorstep, it's no surprise that Vancouver is one of the best cities in North America if you're looking for equipment for hiking, camping and numerous other outdoor activities. *Mountain Equipment Co-op* (see below) was one of the first major outdoor stores, and its existence has led to several other similar stores opening nearby on the three blocks of West Broadway around Cambie and Columbia streets.

Stores in this axis include Altus, 137 West Broadway (☏604/876-2525); Great Outdoors Equipment, 222 West Broadway (☏604/872-8872); and A J Brooks, 147 West Broadway (☏604/874-1117).

Farther west, a similar thing has happened at the junction of West 4th and Burrard, but this time you'll find a concentration of skate, surf, diving, ski and snowboard stores for sales and rentals. Key players here are Pacific Boarder, 1793 West 4th Ave (☏604/734-7245); The Boardroom, 1717 West 4th Ave (☏604/734-7669); Thriller, 1710 West 4th Ave (☏604/736-5651); and Westbeach (see below).

own-label goods and leading brands such as Gaia.

Mountain Equipment Co-op 130 W Broadway at Columbia St ☎604/872-7858, ⓦwww.mec.ca. This is Canada's largest outdoor-equipment and supplies store and something of a Vancouver institution. Because this block-long, city institution really is a co-operative, you need to pay $5 membership to make a purchase, but you'll soon recoup this if you buy something from the store's staggering range of tents, boots, winter sports gear, climbing gear and other outdoor activity equipment and clothing. For skiing and other winter-sports gear, see below.

Ruddick's Fly Shop 1654 Duranleau, Granville Island ☎604/681-3747, ⓦwww.rudfly.com. The oldest and best fly-fishing shop in western Canada, and the first stop for all things fishing, including rods (notably Orvis), clothing, accessories and custom-tied flies.

Westbeach 1766 West 4th Ave ☎604/731-6449, ⓦwww.westbeach.com. An internationally renowned sports board and skateboarding store which is something of an institution, almost as well known in Germany and Japan as it is in Vancouver. It has its own line of street and technical gear, and often hosts skateboarding shows.

Shoes and leatherware

Boys' Co 1044 Robson St ☎684-5656.
Browns Pacific Centre and other locations ☎604/683-4740. Browns has been in the shoe-selling business for half a century and has some thirty stores across the city. It sells its own-brand Browns and Bravo labels, as well as an extensive range of designer labels such as Ferragamo, Timberland, Bruno Magli, Donna Karen and Manolo Blahnik. The most central stores are in The Bay and Holt Renfrew in the Pacific Centre (see p.185).

David Gordon 822 Granville St ☎604/685-3784. A long-established store specializing in all sorts of boots, from Western to Doc Martens, as well as accessories and other fashionable and alternative street footwear.

Ingledew's 535 Granville St near the Pacific Centre ☎604/687-8606, ⓦwww.ingledews.com. Ingledew's has been a byword for good shoes, bags, accessories and other leatherware since 1915. It also trades on its excellent service. For more shoe shops, head to Robson St.

John Fluevog 837 Granville between Robson and Smithe ☎604/688-2828, ⓦwww.fluevog.com. Cult name Fluevog has made a splash in the international fashion world, noted for his inspired takes on traditional shoes and his funky urban footwear – and for some pretty outrageous platforms, fetish and other items that are more high art than high fashion.

Stéphane de Raucourt 1067 Robson St ☎604/681-8814. If you're looking to drop a large sum on an exquisite pair of Italian women's shoes, then this smart store is for you.

Specialty food and drink

A Bosa & Company 562 Victoria Drive near Turner St ☎604/253-5578. This sensational Italian delicatessen two blocks east of Commercial Drive has been run by the same family for three generations. It stocks more than 2500 items of food – the cheeses, olive oils and hams are exceptional – as well as a wide range of Italian kitchenware and gadgets.

All India Food 6157 Main St near 49th Ave ☎604/324-1686. All the Indian spices and produce you can imagine under one (very large) roof in the Punjabi Market area. Many people come here just for the amazing sweet outlet – All India Surat Sweets – where you can sample a buffet of brightly coloured sweets and sugar-saturated Indian puddings. The store is also known for its fine samosas.

First Ravioli Store 1900 Commercial Drive ☎604/255-8844. Almost anything and everything Italian can be purchased at the most venerable and celebrated of Vancouver's Italian supermarkets.

Fujiya Japanese Food 912 Clark Drive at Venables St and branches ☎604/251-3711. This store east of Chinatown (five blocks west of Commercial Drive) stocks a big range of Japanese food and kitchenware. It also prepares fresh fish for sushi and sells sushi to take away.

Kaplan's Delicatessen & Restaurant 5775 Oak St at 41st Ave ☎604/263-2625. Just southwest of Queen Elizabeth Park, Kaplan's is as authentic a 1940s Jewish delicatessen as you could wish for, selling a wide range of kosher food, a big spread of sandwiches and 265 other menu items.

Les Amis du Fromage 3655 West 10th Ave ☎604/732-4218. This store's 400-plus cheeses would put many a French cheese shop to shame.

Longliner Sea Foods 1689 Johnston St ☎604/681-9016. Granville Island market has several fresh salmon and seafood stalls: this is generally considered the best, and is favoured by many of the city's chefs.

Murchie's Tea & Coffee 970 Robson St near Burrard St ☎604/669-0783, ⓦwww.murchies.com. A western Canadian institution (there's another branch in Victoria (see p.233) and several other outlets dotted around Vancouver), Murchie's is sells more than forty different blends of coffee and around fifty types of tea.

Parthenon Wholesale and Retail Food 3080 W Broadway near Bayswater St ☎604/733-4191. This Greek grocery and deli south of Jericho Beach (four blocks west of Alma St) sells, among other things, everything you need to make the consummate Greek meal. It also has a big selection of prepared foods to take away.

Kids' Vancouver

H ave no fears if you're travelling to Vancouver with children – the city is a child-friendly place, with plenty of sights that appeal to youngsters and adults alike. It also has attractions designed specifically with children in mind, numerous parks and gardens, boat and plane tours, and a wide miscellany of good cafés and restaurants – many with outdoor seating – where children won't be out of place. You'll also have few problems finding places to change or feed younger children in hotels or major malls. The city is also physically safe, save in parts of Chinatown and its environs (see p.39), though you should exercise caution in places and situations with obvious potential for problems – on or near water, on busy streets and junctions, and on upland trails in the parks of the North Shore and elsewhere.

The city has plenty of sources of information and ideas for travel with children (see box p.192), especially when it comes to **organized tours** (see p.30) – seaplane tours, if you can afford them, with the great views and thrill of taking off in a small plane, should be sure-fire winners (see p.31). Less expensive but equally appealing tours include whale-watching – there is more of a choice of tours from Victoria (see p.232), but trips also run from Vancouver – and the many boat, horse-drawn and wildlife ventures possible in and around the city.

One of the best ways to indulge your children is to time your visit to Vancouver to coincide with the city's **International Children's Festival**, an annual event held for a week each May in colourful tents set up in Vanier Park. It draws over two hundred children's entertainers – jugglers, magicians and the like – and storytellers from around the world. Tickets for events go on sale through Ticketmaster (see p.163) in March, but are also available at the festival. Many events sell out quickly, but even if you miss your show of choice, the small daily admittance fee to the festival allows you to enjoy the myriad free events and performances laid on outside the show tents. There are also lots of activity tents for children such as dance or kite-making. For information, call ☏604/708-5655 or visit ⓦwww.youngarts.ca. Many of the city's other festivals will also appeal to children – see p.206 for further details.

Note that most sights that charge an **entrance fee** usually allow some children to enter free, typically those under five or six. Some sights are more generous than others, however – the Vancouver Art Gallery, for example, allows children under 12 in without charge, whereas at Science World and the Vancouver Aquarium the cut-off is a more miserly four years old. Some, but by no means all sights offer better-value **family tickets**, allowing entrance to two adults and two (occasionally three) children.

Our account below briefly highlights the various child-friendly sights, activities and attractions around the city. For fuller details see the relevant sections of the guide.

The main Vancouver visitor centre (see p.23) is a good place to start for **information and ideas** on activities for children, especially for organized tours. It is also the place to pick up the free annually updated *Kids' Guide Vancouver*, which you'll also find at the visitor centres at the Peace Arch Border Crossing on Hwy 99 in Surrey and on the domestic and international arrivals levels at Vancouver International Airport. It carries a map and suggests around 100 places and ideas for activities with children.

The **Granville Island Kids Only Market** (see opposite) also usually has free information, news sheets and factsheets such as *BC Parent* and *West Coast Families*, whose pages contain listings and calendars of events. There are also several dedicated **websites**, the best being ⊛www.kidsvancouver.com, which has extensive listings and ideas under 14 headings such as Rainy Days, Playgrounds, Animals and Parks & Gardens. It also includes good practical information on parking, safety, access to public transport and a tip-filled "Good to Know" section. Also good for listings – but with less in the way of practical help – is ⊛www.travelforkids.com and the more informal ⊛www.findfamilyfun.com, a jolly, colloquial site compiled by local parents and their children.

Major sights

Downtown attractions that should keep children happy include **Canada Place** (see p.48), which has fun views of the port, an IMAX cinema, and boats, seaplanes and helicopters taking off; if you're lucky, you'll be able to admire the vast cruise ships that often dock here and, if you're luckier still, watch one of the ships as it leaves or comes into port. Cinema aside, this is best kept for a sunny day, as the walkways are largely exposed to the elements. Be sure to have a few quarters (25¢) to feed into the telescopes around the walkways.

You'll also want clear weather to make the most of the views, as you will nearby at the **Harbour Centre** (see p.49), where the lifts and viewing deck offer captivating city panoramas. Better still, children can safely run round the enclosed viewing area while you relax with coffee. On **Robson Street**, children should like the waterfalls, pools and fountains of Robson Square, while the adjacent Vancouver Art Gallery (see p.53) holds regular monthly events aimed at children (usually on the third Sunday of the month), with lots of hands-on activities, shows and drop-in art-making sessions.

To the east, the buskers and steam-powered clock in **Gastown** (see p.64) and its toots and whistles provide a few moments of light relief (every quarter-hour in the case of the clock); close by there's also the **Dr Sun Yat-Sen Garden** (see p.69), where at noon daily children can feed the fish and turtles (older children will enjoy Chinatown's night market – see p.67).

Across in North Vancouver, the **SeaBus** is a fun ride in its own right, with the lure of the Lonsdale Quay Market (see p.186) and its sights, sounds and dedicated kids' stalls as an additional treat for children. Another fun ride is the cable-car trip up **Grouse Mountain** (see p.112). Older children with a scientific bent also enjoy learning about the life cycle of salmon at the **salmon hatchery** in Capilano River (see p.115); younger children here should be captivated by the sight of leaping salmon and the many fish in the various tanks and viewing areas.

South of the Downtown core, **Science World** (see p.88), has countless hands-on displays and an Alcan OMNIMAX screen which are very much aimed at children; it's also one of the places on False Creek accessed by small ferries (see p.84) – of obvious appeal to children – that ply back and forth between Downtown, Granville Island and Vanier Park.

Granville Island

Granville Island (see p.82) is a major attraction, great in the sun or rain, and one whose general buzz, street performers and market sights, smells and sounds should captivate children of all ages. It also boasts a Duck Pond (great for toddlers), several small museums (the model ship and model train museums have obvious appeal for children), plenty of child-friendly cafes and restaurants, Sutcliff Park (lots of grassy areas, picnic tables and a long promenade) and a dedicated Kids' Playground and Water Park (see p.195). Many of the shops and workshops should also be fun – among other things, children can watch glass being blown and boats being made and repaired.

Best of all is the Kids Only Market, one of the city's key children's attractions. It is housed in a four-storey building near the entrance to the island at 1496 Cartwright St (daily 10am–6pm) and boasts around thirty children's toy shops – selling kites, books, puppets, crafts, clothing and much more – plus a play area, food outlet, and an indoor playground known as the Adventure Zone and Circuit Circus. It's a busy, not to say chaotic place at weekends. On Saturdays in summer free events happen around the island, including clowns, magicians, musicians and face-painters.

Museums

Vancouver's finest museum, the Museum of Anthropology (see p.101), should interest children by virtue of the scale and spectacle of the totems and other carvings in its main hall. Granville Island's Model Trains Museum and Model Ships Museum (see p.87) are other attractions with built-in child-appeal. In nearby Vanier Park, the Vancouver Museum is of more limited allure, unlike the more compelling Maritime Museum (see p.94) and its historic boats and displays – notably the St Roch and tugboat wheelhouse – and the Pirates! display and Children's Maritime Discovery Centre, where, among other things, children can play on the computers, use the telescopes trained on boats in English Bay, go through the wall full of drawers filled with model boats and maritime artefacts, and dress up in pirate clothes and other naval uniforms. Close by are the more modern planetarium and multimedia displays of the H.R. MacMillan Space Centre (see p.93). Children whose eyes don't glaze over in museums may also want to visit the well-stocked children's library in the Vancouver Public Library (see p.55).

Further afield, the BC Museum of Mining, off Hwy 99 about 45 minutes' drive from Downtown en route for Squamish (see p.251), has an underground train, guided tour of the mine, gold-panning area and live demonstrations of mining equipment.

Parks, gardens and animals

Most first-time visitors, or those with limited time, should make for Stanley Park (see overleaf), the city's obvious open-space destination for those with children.

In southern Vancouver, the flowers of the **VanDusen Garden** at Oak Street and 37th Avenue probably won't appeal, but the Elizabethan Hedge Maze just might – adults can keep an eye on their charges from a grassy mound alongside. In **Queen Elizabeth Park** (see p.98), children should respond enthusiastically to the fifty-odd varieties of exotic bird in the Bloedel Conservatory.

Across on the **North Shore**, Cypress Provincial Park, Lynn Canyon, Lighthouse and Mount Seymour parks are full of easy, fun trails and boulders and fallen trees to scramble over – Lynn Canyon also has a suspension bridge over rapids (see p.119), Lighthouse Park has tidal pools and Cypress Falls boasts two cracking waterfalls. Be careful, however, as many of these parks have areas of wilderness. Much gentler is **Ambleside Park** (see p.119), with a flat sand beach, playground and small summer water park. Further afield, the spectacular **Shannon Falls** (see p.251) on the way to Squamish should capture children's imagination.

Stanley Park

Stanley Park vies with Granville Island as Vancouver's most compelling destination for those travelling with children. There is a huge variety of things to do here, from the obvious lure of the big attractions such as the **Vancouver Aquarium** (see p.81), with its whale and dolphin shows and many exhibits specifically aimed at children, to the more low-profile sights such as the Miniature Train and Children's Farmyard, where children can look at peacocks, Shetland ponies, pigs, cows, chickens and other barnyard animals. There are also several **beaches** and swimming areas such as the heated pool at Second Beach (see p.80) and plenty of open spaces – notably the Stanley Park Playground – for youngsters to run off excess energy. You can also rent children's bikes, rollerskates and in-line skates, as well as "jogging" buggies and hitch-on bike buggies for small children. Then there are the many peripheral or incidental temptations: Stanley Park horse-drawn Tours (see p.31); the Nine O'Clock Gun (fired at noon daily); the totem poles at Brockton Point; and the host of ducks, geese and swans (don't feed them) on Lost Lagoon and Beaver Lake.

Zoos and animals

You might – if you are lucky – see birds, small creatures and big mammals in the wild in the parks of the North Shore: black bears and cougar, among others, roam the Coast Mountains, for example, and there are plenty of opportunities for birdwatching on and around the Fraser Delta. In the city itself, however, Stanley Park's Vancouver Aquarium and Children's Farmyard (see above) are about the only places to take children to see animals.

A little further afield is **Maplewood Farm** (Tues–Sun 10am–4pm; $3.25, special events $5; ☎604/929-5610, ⊛www.maplewoodfarm.bc.ca), located in the heart of North Vancouver at 405 Seymour River Place. The two-hectare site was one of many farms that once operated in the area, but which were put out of business by the big agricultural holdings in the Fraser Valley. The BC parks department saved this one from oblivion, and it now has around 200 barnyard animals, including pigs, sheep, donkeys, ducks and chickens. Various special events take place throughout the year, among them pony rides, a summer Sheep Fair, Country Christmas Weekend, 101 Pumpkins Day (late October) and Farm Fair (mid-September). Right next to the farm is the **Maplewood Mudflats Bird Sanctuary,** great if your children are birders.

About 45 minutes' drive and 48km east of the city is the **Greater Vancouver Zoo** (daily April–Sept 9.30am–7pm, Oct–March 9.30am–

4pm; $9; ☎604/856-6825, ⓦwww.
greatervancouverzoo.com), a 48-
hectare site at 5048-264th St,
Aldergrove, with around 125 species
of animals either roaming relatively
freely or in spacious enclosures.
Creatures here include lions, ele-
phants, tigers, buffalo, elk, zebras,
giraffes, hippos, a rhino and camels.

Games and amusement parks

Playdium (Sun–Thurs 11am–11pm,
Fri & Sat 11am–2am; price varies;
☎604/433-7529, ⓦwww.playdium.
com) is a multi-level complex at
Metrotown in Burnaby in South
Vancouver at 4700 Kingsway, which
contains a vast array of electronic and
other games for children and adults.
For a more old-fashioned experience,
visit the **Playland Family Fun
Park** (daily mid-June–early Sept
11am–9pm; Sat, Sun and public holidays May–mid-June & early Sept to
end of Sept 11am–7pm; $20.95, chil-
dren $9.95 for unlimited rides). This
amusement park is in Exhibition Park
(or Hastings Park) at East Hastings St
and Cassiar St and can be reached on
buses #14 or #16. There are around
35 rides, including an old-fashioned
roundabout and wooden rollercoaster, plus an arcade of electronic games
and a Nintendo Pavilion.

Beaches, water and swimming

Vancouver has plenty of places to
swim, including several good beaches, though as the best temperature
you can hope for in the ocean is
about 18–21°C (65–70°F) you may
want to take younger children to
some of the indoor pools: diehards
can compromise by swimming in the
fresh- and saltwater outdoor pools.
The city also has a small dedicated
water park on Granville Island for
younger children and a monster park
out of the city with a range of watery
and other attractions that should
appeal to children of all ages.

Swimming pools and water parks

Granville Island Water Park Granville Island
☎604/257-8195. Open and supervised daily
10am–6pm in summer, weather allowing.
This water park and adjoining adventure
playground are near the False Creek
Community Centre (which has changing
facilities) off Cartwright St to the right as
you enter the island (behind the island's
infocentre). The park has a central wading
pool with fire hose for the children; the
playground has a waterslide and lots of
rope- and log-built facilities.
Kitsilano Beach and Pool The seawater at
Kits Beach (see p.97) may be a touch cool
for adults, but it doesn't seem to worry
children. Lifeguards are on duty all summer.
Nearby, the area's grassy spaces have
swings and monkey bars. Kits' heated
outdoor pool lies right by the water and has
a gently sloped section for youngsters: it's
busy on summer weekend afternoons, so
time a visit for the morning.
**Splashdown Park 4799 Nu Lelum Way,
Tsawwassen** ☎604/943-2251. If you have
time to kill before catching a ferry, or your
children clamour for the joys of a water
park, this big complex three minutes' drive
from the Tsawwassen ferry terminal south
of Vancouver offers 13 vast slides,
swimming pool, giant hot tub, picnic areas,
inner tubes and basketball and volleyball
courts. Open summer 10am–8pm, weather
allowing; $20; family tickets $70 for entry to
park excluding water attractions.
Stanley Park Children can swim in the
supervised pool at Second Beach (it also
has waterslides) or splash around at the
water adventure playground across from
Lumberman's Arch. See p.79 for details.
UBC Aquatic Centre ☎604/822-4522,
ⓦwww.aquatics.ubc.ca. The university's
Aquatic Centre next door to the Student
Union Building and bus loop boasts two
fifty-metre pools (one indoor, one outdoor),
with lots of large inflatable toys, inner tubes,
basketball nets and floating mats in
summer for children. Drop by the pools on
a visit to the Museum of Anthropology (see
p.101), but call for pool hours first, as only
certain times are designated for the general
public.

16

Sports and outdoor activities

C ome up with an outdoor activity and chances are you'll be able to indulge in it somewhere in or around Vancouver. The city's close prox-imity to scenic mountains, forests and ocean make it a superb play-ground for outdoor enthusiasts of every stripe: snow-covered slopes for skiing and snowboarding; woodland and wilderness for hiking, climbing and mountain biking; and open water for sailing, kayaking, diving and other aquatic sports – with ample opportunities for running and in-line skating, golf, tennis and more. Beyond Vancouver lies the vast interior of British Columbia, where immense areas of wilderness constitute an almost limitless natural playground. Whistler is the most obvious out-of-city destination (see p.254), thanks to its well-deserved reputation as one of North America's finest winter-sports resorts, but other centres, such as Squamish (for climbing and windsurfing) and Powell River (for diving), are also outstanding.

Vancouver's options for watching sports rather than doing them are more restricted, for this is not a city with any great teams in the top **spectator sports**, the one notable exception being ice hockey, where the Vancouver Canucks play in the National Hockey League. If you're not too worried about the quality of your sport, you can watch baseball and Canadian football, among others, at a variety of first-class venues. If you wish to see top-flight basketball, however, note that the NBA's Vancouver Grizzlies are no more – the team has relocated to Memphis.

The city is packed with companies aimed at helping you find and enjoy your chosen activity, and the initial **contact details** on the following pages are meant simply to set you on the right track. The tourist infocentre (see p.23) has the lowdown on numerous activities and will book tickets for some of the bigger sporting events. You'll also find plenty of contacts and background at the city's larger outdoor shops. For more information, order or pick up a copy of *The Vancouver Book*, the infocentre's official visitor's guide, or visit Ⓦ www.tourismvancouver.com.

Outdoor activities

Certain activities in Vancouver have their obvious seasons – skiing and winter sports being the most obvious – though even here you should note that there can be surprising exceptions. In Whistler, for example (see p.254) you can ski year-round, not just in winter, thanks to summer glacier skiing. You'll also find that the winter season in Whistler may be longer than the slopes close to Vancouver itself. Hiking, too, can be a year-round activity, though you should be aware of the very real risks involved in cold-weather hiking at higher altitudes even in parks close to the city. Fair-weather activities such as golf are self-evident, but don't overlook things like birdwatching, which can be most rewarding during spring and autumn migrations, or fishing, which also has seasonal variations.

Bicycling

Bicycling is popular in Vancouver, whether it's mountain biking or cycling on city trails or in Stanley Park – see p.76 for details on where to rent bikes. Most rental outfits provide maps with recommended routes, as do most bicycle shops around the city. Expect to pay from about $3.75 an hour, $15 a half-day and $25 to $30 for a full day. You may also find that some hotels and hostels, particularly in the West End, hire or loan bikes to guests. For **further information**, contact Cycling BC (☏604/737-3034, ⓦwww.cycling.bc. ca). Bear in mind that the law in BC requires you to wear a helmet when cycling.

There are any number of routes to choose from, with a total of 16 designated cycleways totalling 129km in the city. The most obvious and popular is the flat 8.8-kilometre run around the **Stanley Park Seawall** (allow an hour; see p.76), a combination of paved surface, trail and road. The Seawall circuit forms part of one of the city's most scenic and popular routes, which runs westward from Canada Place Pier and finishes up in Pacific Spirit Regional Park via the Seawall, English Bay and Sunset beaches, Granville Island, Vanier Park and Kitsilano and Jericho beaches. Other designated routes are the ten-kilometre run around **False Creek** and the **BC Parkway** (19km) which shadows the SkyTrain route from Science World–Main Street to New Westminster.

More ambitious rides take you to Spanish Banks from Granville Island (17km round-trip) and to **Horseshoe Bay** in North Vancouver by way of Stanley Park, the Lions Gate Bridge and Marine Drive (40km round-trip).

The best of the mountain-biking trails are found in North Van's **parks and mountains** (see Chapter 7). Winter cross-country ski trails are used by bikers, notably on Hollyburn Mountain in Cypress Provincial Park – Hollyburn Ridge alone has some 16km of trails. The steep Good Samaritan Trail on Mount Seymour is a notorious route – recommended for very fit bikers only.

You can take bikes on the SeaBus to get to North Van (see p.109) and on some of the small Aquabus ferries from Downtown to Granville Island (see p.84).

Birdwatching

The wide variety of habitats in and around Vancouver provides shelter for over 360 species of **birds**. Even Downtown in Stanley Park you'll be able to see birds such as bald eagles, swans and great blue heron. The park also has a heron rookery just outside the Vancouver Aquarium.

The city's key birdwatching spot is the **George C. Reifel Migratory Bird Sanctuary** (daily 9am–4pm; $4; ☏604/946-6980, ⓦwww .reifelbirdsanctuary.com), 300 hectares (850 acres) of natural marshes and managed wetland at 5191 Robertson Rd, Westham Island, 35km south of Vancouver on the southern shore at the entrance to the Fraser River delta. It attracts some 1.5 million migratory birds annually, with over 268 species spotted here year round, most notably the vast wintering flocks of lesser snow geese from Wrangle Island above the Arctic Circle. The so-called Fraser-Skagit flock numbers anything between 30,000 and 60,000, depending on the success of nesting in the Arctic. Some winter on the Fraser, others on the nearby Skagit Estuary in Washington State. In spring, the most common visitors are millions of Western sandpipers, but this is also a good time to see fish-eating birds of prey (including ospreys), which follow migrating salmon up the Fraser. Low dikes serve as walkways (3km in total) around the reserve and are wheelchair accessible, while in the west of the reserve there is a two-storey observation tower on the foreshore. Some walkways are edged with trees, offering habitats for forest birds and roost sites for birds of prey such as owls, eagles and various hawks. Note that the sanctuary holds a Snow Goose Festival in the first weekend of November to celebrate the arrival of the eponymous birds, which generally stay in the region until around mid-December.

Elsewhere, you stand a good chance of seeing herons in the rookeries in Stanley and Pacific Spirit parks (there are generally nesting herons right by the Vancouver Aquarium). In winter you'll almost certainly see bald eagles at Brackendale near Squamish en route for Whistler (see p.252). In January 1994 some 3700 eagles were officially counted here, the largest number ever recorded in North America.

Canoeing and kayaking

There are several places to **canoe** or **kayak** – or learn to do either – in and around Vancouver: **False Creek** (nearest to Downtown, and a good place for beginners); **English Bay** – but *not* the Lions Gate Bridge, where the currents are strong and dangerous; **Deer Lake** in East Vancouver; and **Indian Arm** – a striking finger-shaped inlet and fjord flanked by 1200-metre mountains on the North Shore. For the last, rent a canoe or kayak at Deep Cove in North Vancouver (see below) and head either to Cates Park to the south or Jug Island, Combe Park or Belcarra Regional Park across the inlet.

For **rentals**, **tours and lessons** contact Ocean West Expeditions (April–mid-May Mon–Fri 10am–7pm, Sat & Sun 9am–sunset, mid-May–Sept daily 9am–sunset, Oct Mon–Fri 10am–sunset, Sat & Sun 9am–sunset; ☎604/898-4980 or 1-800/660-0051, ⓦwww.ocean-west.com), based at the southern end of Denman Street just outside Stanley Park at the English Bay Bathhouse, English Bay, 1750 Beach Ave. Rental rates are $28 for two hours ($38 for a double kayak), $40 for four hours ($48) and $60 ($70) for the day. A three-hour Introduction to Sea Kayaking course (currently Mon, Tues & Thurs at 6pm and Sat & Sun at 9am) costs $60 plus GST.

Just across the water on Granville Island, and with similar rates, lessons and tours of False Creek and beyond, is Ecomarine Ocean Kayak at 1668 Duranleau St (☎1/888-425-2925 or 689-7575, ⓦwww.ecomarine.com). It also has an office at the Jericho Sailing Centre at 1300 Discovery St on Jericho Beach.

Over in North Vancouver, Deep Cove Canoe & Kayak (April–Oct; ☎604/929-2268, ⓦwww.deepcovekayak.com) is located 30 minutes from Downtown in a pretty waterside community on the shores of Indian Arm at 2156 Banbury Rd. This is an excellent outfit, and offers hourly, daily and multi-day rentals, kayak and canoe schools with lessons for all abilities (and special children's classes), as well as guided tours (including women-only tours) and private trips. The 18km fjord that is Indian Arm offers tremendous scenery and sheltered waters, while Deep Cove has plenty of cafés, restaurants, hiking trails and so forth once you come off the water. Rentals in peak season (June 27–Sept 1) for single kayaks start from $28 ($38 double) midweek for two hours and $14 ($20 double) for each extra hour. Day rates are $54 ($78 double). Rates are a few dollars more at weekends, a few dollars less in low season. Overnight and multi-day rentals are also available. A range of boats is available, including broad and very stable craft for beginners.

Further afield still at Bowen Island, west across the water from Horseshoe Bay in West Van, contact Bowen Island Sea Kayaking, Bowen Island (T 604/947-9266 or 1/800-60 KAYAK, W www.bowenislandkayaking.com), where rental rates are $30 for three hours in a single plastic boat ($40 for fibreglass); $40 for five hours ($50) and $50 all day ($60). Add $10 or $20 to these rates for double kayaks. Guided tours include three-hour trips near the island (daily in summer 1–4pm; $50); a sunset paddle (daily in summer 6–9pm, $50); full-moon trips (call for dates; $50); and three-day trips around Howe Sound (3–4 yearly; $375). Bowen Island is easily reached by ferry.

Climbing

Close to the city, there's the chance to **climb** at Juniper Point in Lighthouse Park (see p.126), on the cliffs and crags overlooking Indian Arm in Deep Cove, and on some of the mountains above North Van. Alternatively, you can climb indoors at Cliffhanger Indoor Rock Climbing Centre, 106 W 1st Ave at Manitoba (T 604/874-2400, W www.cliffhanger.bc.ca), and at the Edge Climbing Centre, Suite 2, 1485 Welch St, North Vancouver, off Capilano Rd near Marine Drive (T 604/984-9080, W www.edgeclimbing.com). However, the best climbing in the Vancouver vicinity is at Squamish (see p.252). For much more on climbing locally and in the rest of BC, contact the

Vancouver Alpine Club, West 37th Ave and Oak St (325-4044, W www.clubtread.com), or visit W www.out-there.com which has an extraordinary number climbing-related links. Also good is W www.bivouac.com, which also carries hiking information.

Fishing

Key places for **fishing** are **Burrard Inlet** (open all year); **Howe Sound** and **Horseshoe Bay** – the last is the best place for salmon and one of the most popular **fishing** areas on the coast: there are marinas at Fishermen's Cove, Sunset Beach, Lions Bay and Whytecliff; **Sunshine Coast**, especially between Secret Cove and Egmont and near Pender Harbour; the Fraser River; North Vancouver, notably the Seymour River, Lynn Creek and Capilano River (for salmon in late summer and early autumn); and Buntzen Lake and Harrison Lakes east of the city.

If you want to fish at points around the city, you'll need nonresident saltwater or freshwater **licences**. Freshwater **licences** cost around $15 a day ($30 for eight days); saltwater licences $8 ($20 for three days, $35 for five days). They can be obtained from tackle shops around the city, most of which carry current regulations for fishing. For more on fishing around the city and in BC generally, visit W www.fisheries.gov.bc.ca. The *Vancouver Sun* also carries a daily fishing report detailing which fish are in season and where they can be fished.

Good **tackle shops** include Hanson's Fishing Outfitters, 102-580 Hornby St (T 604/684-8988, W www.hansons-outfitters.com), and Granville Island Boat Rentals, 1696 Duranleau St, Granville Island (T 604/682-6287), and Bonnie Lee Fishing Charters, at 1676 Duranleau St on the dock at the entrance to Granville Island (T 604/290-7447, www.bonnielee.com); many of the charter companies below will also be able to help.

The **months to visit** if you're planning a fishing trip are April and May, when the chinook (or king) salmon run at the mouth of the Fraser River and Howe Sound, or August, when millions of sockeye salmon run up the coast. Charters generally run by the half-day, day or week, and are available through numerous operators (see below). There are also plenty of companies who run seaplane and helicopter trips to remote lakes and rivers for fly-in fishing trips. Full details are available from the infocentre (see p.23).

Charter companies to contact include Bites-On Salmon, 300-1128 Hornby St (⊤1-877/688-2483, www.bites-on.com); Bonnie Lee Fishing Charters (see above); Sewell's Landing, 6695 Nelson Ave, West Vancouver (⊤604/921-3474, www.sewellsmarina.com); and Vancouver Sportfish Center, 1525 Coal Harbour Quay (⊤604/689-7108, www.sportfishcenter.com).

Finally, if you're a fishing fan, don't miss the **fishing museum** on Granville Island (see p.87).

see p.23
see p.87

Golf

There are more than a dozen **golf courses** within an hour's drive of Downtown Vancouver, and more than seventy between Whistler to the north and Hope to the east. Reckon on **green fees** of about $45 to play most courses. The closest public course to Downtown is the par-71 University Golf Club, 5185 University Blvd at UBC (⊤604/224-1818). It's situated near the eastern entrance to the campus where West 10th Ave meets Blanca St. For details of other public courses, contact the Vancouver Board of Parks and Recreation (⊤604/257-8400, www.city. vancouver.bc.ca/parks). One of the most popular is Langara

at 6706 Alberta St, due south of Queen Elizabeth Park near 49th and Cambie (⊤604/713-1816), but you'll need to book around five days in advance to be sure of a round.

Around 5km east, and almost equally popular, is Fraserview, 7800 Vivian Drive (⊤604/257-6923), which has a park setting with rolling hills and mature trees. Furry Creek in Lions Bay (⊤604/922-9576, www.furrycreek.com) lies among the mountain forests and woods of Howe Sound and has won the accolade of BC's "Most Scenic Golf Course". At a pinch, there's always the pitch-and-putt courses at Stanley Park, Ambleside Park and Queen Elizabeth Park.

The Vancouver Open, part of the US PGA tour, is held over the Labour Day weekend at the Northview Golf & Country Club, 6857-168th St, Surrey (⊤604/574-0324 or 576-4653, www.northviewgolf.com). The two courses here were designed by Arnold Palmer.

Hiking

Hiking opportunities beyond Vancouver's boundaries to the north and east in the Coast and Interior mountains of BC are almost unlimited. Closer to Downtown, most of the best trails are in the parks above North Vancouver – see the hiking and trail features in Chapter 7 for details of recommended hikes. Bear in mind that they are often in wilderness or near-wilderness areas, and you should therefore have suitable **equipment and clothing**, and be prepared for sudden changes of weather. There are trails to suit all levels of fitness – and if you don't fancy doing things alone you can contact the infocentre for details about hiring a **guide**.

The best **urban trails** include: Burnaby Mountain, with its good views of Burrard Inlet and Indian Arm; Pacific Spirit Regional Park, which has quiet walks and forest trails; Richmond Dyke and its windswept trails on the Fraser River and Strait of Georgia; and the most obvious and convenient, Stanley Park and its Seawall.

For **creek and shoreline walks** consider the Lighthouse Park, a great spot for sunsets, sea cliffs and old-growth forest (see p.126) and the Lynn and Capilano canyons (see p.119). For something longer, plump for the **Baden–Powell Trail**, a forty-kilometre hike from Horseshoe Bay on Howe Sound to Deep Cove on Indian Arm and Cates Park on the Dollarton Hwy. It links several of the area's best trails, and can be joined – among other places – at Grouse Mountain, where you can follow a popular leg of the trail to Mount Seymour (start early and allow a full day). If you have a car, then head out to **Pitt Lake**, about an hour east of the city: it's North America's largest tidal freshwater lake and has lots of pretty trails.

Ice-skating

If you can't – or don't – **skate** in Vancouver in winter you're in a pretty small minority. Rinks open from about November to mid-March/early April at Robson Square under Robson St between Howe and Hornby (free) and at the West End Community Centre, 870 Denman St (☎604/257-8333), where you can rent skates for a few dollars. If you want to skate where the pros skate, trek out to the eight-rink Ice Sports Centre at 6501 Sprott in Burnaby (☎604/291-0626), the practice facility for the Vancouver Canucks hockey team. It's open year-round, but you'll need to call to check on opening hours for the public. Lessons and rentals are available.

In-line skating

The Seawall in Stanley Park is the obvious choice for **in-line skaters**:

watch out though for cyclists who also share the Seawall. There are plenty of places to hire skates near the park (see p.76).

Stanley Park aside, the route most favoured by skaters is the shared cycleway on and around Granville Island and False Creek: start at the bottom of Denman Street and Beach Avenue and head east. If you're a confident skater, there's a designated – but occasionally steep and difficult – eleven-kilometre route known as the Mainline in North Vancouver in the Seymour Demonstration Forest.

While **skating is banned on pavements** across the city, the police appear to turn a blind eye to transgressors most of the time.

Rafting

You won't find much **whitewater rafting** in Vancouver's immediate vicinity, but in the mountains nearby are some of the finest stretches of white water on the continent. Relatively gentle rafting experiences are available in and around Squamish and Whistler (see p.252, 254); for more variety and more exciting trips you need to head to the Interior Mountains. Several Vancouver-based companies organize trips, notably Canadian Outback Adventure, 100-657 Marine Drive, West Vancouver (☎604/921-7250, ⓦwww .canadianoutback.com) and Hyak Wilderness Adventures, 8507 Glenwood Close, Burnaby (☎734-8622, ⓦwww.hyak.com). Out of town, contact Chilliwack River Rafting Adventures, 49704 Chilliwack Lake Rd, Chilliwack (☎604/824-0334).

Typical of the trips offered by these companies is the one-day package from Reo Rafting (☎1/800-736-7238, ⓦwww.reorafting.com). Around $115 buys you a transfer out to the river, in this case the Nahatlatch about two and half hours' drive from the city, and then four or five hours on the river with breakfast, lunch and all specialist gear and clothing including. This and other companies also offer multi-day trips.

Sailing

Great possibilities for sailing trips can be found in the Gulf Islands between Vancouver and Vancouver Island. If you're not so sure of your abilities, you can hire a skipper for half- or full-day sailing (around $150 for a half-day) around English Bay: for details, enquire at the following charter companies. Experienced sailors can choose from a large range of dinghies and other sailing boats from numerous operators in and around the city.

Boat charter companies include Paradise Yacht Charters, 1253 Johnson St (☎604/816-5274, ⓦwww.trueman.org); Vancouver Yacht Charters, 750 Pacific Blvd (☎604/682-2070, ⓦwww.boatcharters.net); and Westin Bayshore Yacht Charters, 1610 W Georgia St (☎604/691-6936, ⓦwww.westinbayshoreyachts.com).

Scuba diving

Around Vancouver most people **dive** in Howe Sound and Indian Arm: the water is cold (6°C) – you'll need a six-millimetre neoprene wetsuit – and it's worth going out with an experienced local diver for your first dives. Hiring an instructor will cost from $65 a dive, while a place on a weekend dive boat will cost from $75. Tremendous diving is available, however, outside the city around the Gulf Islands and near Powell River (see p.249).

More specific places to dive include West Van's **Whytecliff Park** off Marine Drive, which has a special Marine Protected Area (the best diving here is between Oct and April); **Lighthouse Park**, a great spot but accessible only to better intermediate and advanced divers; and **Porteau Cove** on Hwy 99 (24km

north of Horseshoe Bay), a popular place with a protected provincial marine park, campsite, boat launch, showers, old minesweeper and an artificial reef made from sunken hulls.

Most **dive stores** will rent out all gear by the day, as well as organizing occasional weekend and night dives. You'll need proof of diving certification for all gear and air. Good places to start are the Diving Locker in Kitsilano at 2745 W 4th Ave (☎604/736-2681) and Rowlands Reef Scuba Shop on Granville Island at 1512 Duranleau St (☎604/669-3483). Rentals cost about $50 a day.

Skiing and snowboarding

If you want a few hours' boarding or downhill or cross-country skiing close to the city, then Vancouver has three hills less than thirty-minutes' drive from Downtown. Serious skiers, snowboarders and other winter-sports enthusiasts, however, head for the big-name resorts outside Vancouver such as Whistler (see p.254) or the less-exalted runs of Mount Baker 120km away in the United States. For more on the parks below and access to them, see Chapter 7.

Grouse Mountain lies about 12km from the city centre in North Vancouver, a twenty-minute drive from Downtown. The Grouse Mountain Ski Resort, 6400 Nancy Greene Way, North Vancouver (☎604/984-0661, ⓦwww.grousemountain.com, snow reports ☎604/986-6262), has lift tickets for adults good for a day's skiing that cost $20 on weekdays, $25 at weekends.

Mount Seymour is located in Mount Seymour Provincial Park about 16km north of Vancouver. The Mount Seymour Ski Resort, 1700 Mount Seymour Rd, North Vancouver (☎604/986-2261, snow reports ☎604/986-3999), has all-day lift passes that cost $18 for adults on weekdays, $26 at weekends. The area has a vertical drop of 365m and a base elevation of 1010m, making this the highest of Vancouver's resorts.

Cypress Bowl, 1610 Mount Seymour St, North Vancouver (℡604/926-5612, snow reports ℡604/419-7669) is 16km from Downtown and offers decent downhill skiing and snowboarding, and the closest cross-country skiing to Vancouver. Lift passes for a day's skiing cost $35, $15 for cross-country skiing. Half-day, multi-day and night passes are also available. The area has the longest vertical drop of the resorts near the city – 533m – and a base elevation of 980m.

Swimming

Water temperatures at Vancouver's sandy beaches rarely achieve a summer peak much above 21°C (70°F). Seven of these beaches are patrolled by lifeguards from mid-May to mid-September (Second Beach, Third Beach, English Bay Beach, Kitsilano Beach, Jericho Beach, Locarno Beach and Spanish Banks Beach). See box, p.92, for more on the city's beaches.

There are two major outdoor pools, both of them near beaches. The closest to Downtown is the **Second Beach Pool**, Second Beach, Stanley Park (mid-May to mid-June Mon–Fri noon–8.45pm, Sat–Sun 10am–8.45pm; mid-June to mid-Sept daily 10am–8.45pm; $4; ℡604/257-8371), an enormous freshwater pool beside the Seawall that has lifeguards, a handful of small waterslides and a playground.

The second major outdoor pool is the modern **Kitsilano Pool** at Cornwall Avenue and Yew Street on Kitsilano Beach (mid-May to mid-June Mon–Fri noon–8.45pm, Sat–Sun 10am–8.45pm; mid-June to mid-Sept Mon–Fri 7am–8.45pm, Sat–Sun 10am–8.45pm; $4; ℡604/731-0011), another gargantuan pool, though this one is saltwater

and heated to around 25°C (77°F) in high summer.

One of the best central **indoor pools** is the Olympic-size 50-metre pool at the **UBC Aquatic Centre**, 1050 Beach Ave at the foot of Thurlow Street (call for hours; $4; ℡604/665-3424). The **YWCA Fitness Centre**, 535 Hornby St near Dunsmuir (call for hours; day–pass $11; ℡604/895-5777) has another excellent and very central pool, but it's only 25 metres long.

Tennis

Vancouver's very popular 180 public tennis courts can be used on a first-come, first-served basis for a maximum of an hour per session between 8am and dusk. All the courts are free and can't be booked, with the exception of six of the seventeen courts by the Beach Avenue entrance to Stanley Park; reservations are taken between mid-May and Labour Day weekend (early Sept) for a nominal fee (call ℡604/257-8489).

Other central courts are in Stanley Park by Lost Lagoon at the foot of Robson; Kitsilano Beach Park; behind the Jericho Sailing Centre at Jericho Beach Park; Queen Elizabeth Park at 33rd Avenue and Cambie Street; False Creek Community Centre on Granville Island; and the UBC Tennis Club at the UBC campus (6184 Thunderbird Blvd at East Mall; indoor courts can be booked in advance on ℡604/822-2505).

If you don't have a racquet handy, you can rent one at Bayshore Bicycle and Rollerblade Rental, 745 Denman St (℡604/688-2453) for around $10 a day.

Windsurfing

If you want to windsurf for a morning or so, then you can have lessons and rent (or buy) boards, wetsuits, life-jackets and other equipment at Jericho Beach at Windsure Windsurfing School, 1300 Discovery

St (☎604/224-0615) or Windsurfer at Denman Street and Beach Avenue at English Bay Beach (☎604/685-7245). Note that you can windsurf off Jericho and English Bay beaches (see p.92), but not at the mouth of False Creek between Granville Street and Burrard Street bridges near Granville Island.

Serious windsurfers should head for Squamish on the way to Whistler (see p.252).

Spectator sports

None of the Vancouver teams that take part in North America's leading sports – baseball, ice hockey and football – can really be said to make the grade in the big-time leagues. This is true even in the sports where the city fields teams in the cross-border leagues with the United States, such as the National Hockey League (NHL); the **Vancouver Canucks** rarely do more than put on a respectable showing in the NHL. This said, all the city's teams have a passionate following, something that is especially true of the Canucks, but also of the **Vancouver Canadians** baseball team and the **BC Lions** football team.

This means **tickets** for many events sell quickly, especially those that involve major visiting teams or one-off events such as the **Vancouver Indy**. Even so, you can usually find a seat somewhere right up to the start of the game. Tickets for many events can be obtained from the visitor centre (see p.23), from the box offices listed below, or from one of the forty or so branches of Ticketmaster dotted around the Greater Vancouver area. You can buy tickets with a credit card over the phone from Ticketmaster by calling ☎604/280-4444. **Information** on forthcoming games can be obtained from Ticketmaster's Sports Line (☎604/280-4400, ⊛www.ticketmaster.com), stadium box offices, the visitor centre or local newspapers such as the *Vancouver Sun*.

Baseball

The **Vancouver Canadians** (☎604/872-5232, ⊛www.canadiansbaseball.com) play in the Northwest League at the charming 7500-seat Nat Bailey Stadium on the east side of Queen Elizabeth Park (see p.98) at 4601 Ontario St and West 29th Avenue. To reach the stadium, take bus #3 south on Main Street to West 30th Avenue and walk one block west. The season runs from April to September and there are afternoon and evening games. **Tickets** can usually be bought at the door, however, and cost around $7 for general admission, $12 for a box and $10 for reserved admission.

Car racing

Vancouver's big car racing event is the CART Indy Series **Molson Indy** (☎604/684-4639 or ⊛www.molsonindy.com for information; ☎604/280-4639 for tickets). It's held over the Labour Day weekend (early Sept) in the streets around False Creek and BC Place Stadium and attracts upwards of 350,000 spectators. Pacific Boulevard's normal fifty-kilometre-per-hour speed limit is upped to 300km per hour for the duration of the race, which follows 103 laps of a 2.7-kilometre circuit. The final main race is held on the Sunday. You'll be lucky to pick up a grandstand seat ticket, but plenty of general tickets are usually available on any of the three days. Prices start at around $20, depending on the day.

Football

Canadian football is slightly different from its American cousin. In Canadian football there are three downs instead of four, the field is longer and wider, there are twelve players instead of eleven, and a point (known as a rouge) is gained for a missed field goal. The game is exciting but comes a poor second to American football in commercial terms and in the calibre of players it can attract – the money and real talent head to the United States.

Canadian teams play in the Canadian Football League (CFL). Vancouver's representatives are the **BC Lions** (☎604/589-ROAR, ⓦwww.bclions.com), who play at the 60,000-seat BC Place Stadium at 777 Pacific Blvd S at the foot of Robson and Beatty streets. The season runs from June to late October and tickets cost from about $25 to $50. The best approach to the stadium is to take the SkyTrain (see p.29) to Stadium Station.

For visitors from outside North America, an ice hockey game is probably the most exciting sport to choose if they just want one taste of live sport during their stay. In ice hockey Canada ranks among the world's best, though in the **Canucks** (☎604/899-4625, ⓦwww.canucks.com) Vancouver has a team which doesn't always reach the heights of rivals such as the Edmonton Oilers and Calgary Flames. The Canucks play at General Motors Place Stadium – known colloquially as "The Garage" – at 800 Griffiths Way close to Beatty Street and Pacific Boulevard (☎604/899-7469, event hotline ☎604/899-7444). They draw big crowds in a season that runs from October to mid-April. Ticket prices range from around $30 to $100.

△ Vancouver affords numerous skiing opportunities

17

Festival and events

Whatever time of year you visit Vancouver, a festival or annual event of some description is probably being held somewhere in the city. While we've listed the major ones below, you can learn more about these as well as various one-off events and shows by contacting Tourism Vancouver (ⓣ604/683-2000, ⓦwww.tourismvancouver.com, or pick up *The Vancouver Book*, an annually updated listing of festivals and general information available free from the tourist infocentre (see p.23). Other listings can be found by visiting ⓦwww.foundlocally.com/vancouver or ⓦwww.bcpassport.com/festivals.

January

Polar Bear Swim New Year's Day Every year since 1819 hardy locals jump into the icy waters at English Bay Beach in a mass swim. In 1920, the event was formalized as the New Year's Day Polar Bear Swim. In a good year, some two thousand people take the plunge, though not all manage the "required" 90-metre swim to a special buoy. In 2003, there were 1200 participants, including the 91-year-old Ivy Granstrom. Most sensible people – and crowds can number over 10,000 – come simply to stand and watch, but if you take the plunge, bear in mind that temperatures range from 3 to 8°C. ⓣ604/665-3424.

Annual Bald Eagle Count first Sunday of the month At 9am at the Brackendale Art Gallery, people come to watch the annual count of the huge numbers of bald eagles that gather to gorge on the salmon near Brackendale en route for Whistler (see p.252). In 1994, the record year, volunteers counted 3700 eagles. ⓣ604/898-3333.

International Chinese New Year Festival The precise dates of the Chinese New Year depend on the lunar calendar – it's held sometime between late January and early February – but whenever it occurs you can rely on some fifteen days of festivities in Chinatown and around the city. There's a Dragon Parade (Sun afternoon), music, dancing, storytelling, art exhibitions and lots of fireworks. ⓣ604/687-6021, ⓦwww.bcchinesenewyear.com/newyear. There are similar events in the Chinese communities of Victoria and Burnaby ⓣ604/273-1655, ⓦwww.sunbritefestival.com.

February

Vancouver International Boat Show over five days near the start of the month This is western Canada's largest and oldest boat show. It features the latest in power and sail vessels, accessories, electronics, fishing gear and sports, fishing and sailing lodges. The show takes place in the BC Place Stadium. ⓣ604/294-1313, ⓦwww.sportsmensshows.com.

April

Vancouver Playhouse International Wine Festival near the start of the month One of North America's largest annual wine festivals allows you to sample over six hundred wines from 125 wineries around the world at the Vancouver Convention and Exhibition Centre and leading hotels and restaurants throughout Greater Vancouver.

The event has been running since 1979, when it was launched to help provide funds for the Vancouver Playhouse Theatre Company, and has grown in stature each year – 17,300 people attended the 48 events during the 2003 festival. ☏604/873-3311, ⊚www.playhousewinefest.com.

Baisakhi Day Parade mid-month This vibrant parade, which celebrates the Sikh Indian New Year, takes place on and around Ross Street off Marine Drive in North Vancouver. ☏604/324-2010.

Vancouver Sun Run third weekend of the month The Sun Run is one of the world's largest ten-kilometre runs – in past years it has attracted over 17,000 runners. You can run (or walk) the scenic route through Downtown, starting and finishing at BC Place Stadium, where there are refreshments and entertainment. ☏604/689-9441, ⊚www.sunrun.com.

May

Vancouver International Marathon first Sunday of the month Canada's largest marathon attracts over six thousand runners and takes you from BC Place Stadium and along False Creek to Stanley Park and then Kitsilano. ☏604/872-2928, ⊚www.adidasvanmarathon.bc.ca.

The New Play Festival on Granville Island first week of the month This week-long celebration of the best of new Canadian theatre involves many workshop sessions and some of the city's best actors, actresses and directors. ⊚www.playwrightstheatre.com.

New Music West Festival second weekend of the month An international festival of new pop and rock music, with lots of events, seminars and special music and band nights at various of the city's clubs. ☏604/684-9338, ⊚www.newmusicwest.com.

Cloverdale Rodeo and Exhibition third weekend of the month Some of the top male and female stars of the North American professional rodeo circuit compete in bull-riding and other rodeo events at the Cloverdale Rodeo and Exhibition Fairgrounds in Surrey. ☏604/576-9461, ⊚www.cloverdalerodeo.com.

Hyack Festival third weekend of the month New Westminster is the setting for this popular festival, usually held on the long weekend. It includes a family day, May Day celebrations, fireworks, parade and an antique fair. ⊚www.hyack.bc.ca.

International Children's Festival towards the end of the month or early June Music, theatre, dance and puppetry from around the world. Staged in Vanier Park over about a week, the event is attended by upwards of 70,000 people. For more, see p.191. ☏604/708-5655, ⊚www.vancouverchildrensfestival .com.

June

VanDusen Flower and Garden Show first week of the month The city's premier garden festival held in the botanic garden (see p.99) will appeal to anyone with green fingers. The show features some two hundred stands devoted to everything from flowers and shrubs to gargoyles and garden gnomes. ☏604/878-9274, ⊚www.vandusengarden.org.

Bard on the Beach Shakespeare Festival from the second Tuesday of the month until last week of September This is a popular and long-established theatre festival in which Shakespeare plays are performed in a five-hundred-seat tent on the beach in Vanier Park overlooking English Bay. Two plays are usually performed each year. ☏604/739-0559, ⊚www.bardonthebeach.org.

Dragon Boat Festival third weekend of the month A weekend of boat races on False Creek involving some 150 teams and two thousand international competitors. Other events include a wide range of family-oriented cabaret and other stage shows. ☏604/688-2382, ⊚www.canadadragonboat.com.

Du Maurier International Jazz Festival from the third Friday of the month, for ten days One of Vancouver's major festivals, this jazz-and-blues event brings together some of the world's biggest names in jazz, who perform at some 25 venues around the city – from nightclubs to outdoor stages on Grouse Mountain and in the Dr Sun Yat-Sen Garden. The event, which draws around eight hundred musicians, includes a two-day Mardi Gras-style street festival in Gastown. ☏604/872-5200, ⊚www .coastaljazz.ca.

National Aboriginal Day Community Celebrations the 21st Part of a nationwide celebration of First Nation or aboriginal culture. Many of Vancouver's events take place at the Vancouver Aboriginal Friendship Centre, 1607 E Hasting at Commerical Drive. ☎604/251-4844.

July

Canada Day the 1st Canada celebrates its confederation, a national holiday with festivities, including big fireworks displays, that are held around the city. The special focus is on Canada Place (fireworks start at 10pm), Granville Island and Grouse Mountain. Canada Place ☎604/666-8477, ⓦwww.canadaplace.com; Granville Island ☎604/666-5784, ⓦwww.granvilleisland. bc.ca.

Dancing on the Edge early to mid-month The city's major dance festival brings together leading dance companies from across North America for around ten days. Most performances are staged at the Firehall Arts Centre, 280 E Cordova St. ☎604/689-0926, ⓦwww.dancingontheedge.org.

Theatre Under the Stars from the middle of the month to the middle of August. Two amateur city theatre groups perform two major productions outdoors in the Stanley Park Malkin Bowl. ☎604/687-0174, ⓦwww .tuts.bc.ca.

Vancouver Folk Festival third weekend of the month One of Vancouver's biggest and most respected festivals, this event attracts around 30,000 to Jericho Beach Park. Some 100 performances are given, local and international singers, songwriters and storytellers performing on seven different stages, with shows throughout the day and evening. There's also a special Little Folks Festival for children. Tickets start at about $40 (on the gate) for a Friday ticket ($55 on Sat or Sun) and $120 (bought in advance) for the weekend. ☎604/602-9798 or 1-800-985-8363, ⓦwww.thefestival.bc.ca.

Vancouver International Comedy Festival towards the end of the month Local and international comedians perform at Granville Island and other venues for ten days. ☎604/683-0883, ⓦwww.comedyfest.com.

Festival Vancouver second half of the month or first half of August One of the city's newest music festivals, this is an ambitious seventeen-day event held across several venues. Canadian and international musicians perform orchestral, choral, world music, jazz and opera in around eighty concerts. ☎604/688-1152, ⓦwww.festivalvancouver.bc.ca.

HSBC Power Smart Celebration of Light towards the end of the month or early August Three different countries every year compete in a spectacular fireworks competition – the world's largest – on English Bay, usually over four nights. Each night features a show by a single country; the three come together on the fourth night to lay on a majestic joint spectacle that attracts upwards of 500,000 people to the city's West End. ☎604/783-4304, ⓦwww.celebration-of-light.com.

Caribbean Days Festival towards the end of the month A two-day celebration of Caribbean art, music and culture organized by the Trinidad and Tobago Cultural Society of British Columbia held in Waterfront Park, North Vancouver. It's the largest cultural event of its kind in the province. ☎604/515-2400, ⓦwww.ttcsbc.com/cdf.

Vancouver Early Music Festival from the end of the month to early August The University of British Columbia (UBC) School of Music organizes this celebration of medieval, baroque and other early music. Performances are held over about three weeks at the UBC Recital Hall, 6361 Memorial Rd. ☎604/732-1610, ⓦwww.earlymusic.bc.ca.

Vancouver Chamber Music Festival end of the month The Vancouver Recital Society has been running this two-week festival since 1986. Events are broadcast on national radio and held in the park-like campus of Crofton House School in Vanier Park. This may sound low-key, but it's considered one of the finest events of its kind in Canada, bringing together many of the most talented classical musicians from Canada and abroad. ☎604/602-0363, ⓦwww.vanrecital.com.

August

Powell Street Festival first weekend of the month A celebration of Japanese and Japanese-Canadian culture, this festival provides an eclectic mixture of parades, food, workshops, music and other entertainment, often drawing leading exponents of Japanese culture from around the world. ☎604/739-9388, ⓦwww.powellfestival.shinnova.com.

Harmony Arts Festival beginning of the month
North Shore artists are showcased in this two-week event, with numerous exhibitions, free events, demonstrations, concerts, markets and workshops. ☎604/925-7268, ☒www.harmonyarts.net.
Abbotsford Air Show second weekend of the month Plane enthusiasts reckon this is one of the world's best air shows. The event is held at Abbotsford airport, 56km southeast of Vancouver. ☎604/852-8511, ☒www.abbotsfordairshow.com.
Vancouver Pride Parade towards the beginning of the month Events vary from year to year, but there's usually a fancy-dress parade on and around Denman St and plenty of celebrations in the city's gay and lesbian clubs and pubs. ☎604/737-7433, ☒www.vanpride.org.
Wooden Boat Festival last weekend of the month Boat owners and enthusiasts gather on the west dock at Granville Island to show off and admire wooden boats of all kinds. ☎604/666-5784, ☒www.granvilleisland.bc.ca.

September

Molson Indy Vancouver Labour Day weekend Indy racing comes to Vancouver for a weekend of very fast cars around False Creek and Yaletown. The racing attracts around 500,000 spectators. For more, see p.204. ☎604/280-4639, ☒www.molsonindy.com.
Vancouver Fringe Theatre Festival mid-month A highly popular event dating from 1985 in which over one hundred theatre, dance and comedy groups from around the world put on five hundred shows at various indoor and outdoor venues around the city. The event usually lasts for between ten and fourteen days. There are two ways to purchase tickets: on the day at venues or through the box office on ☎604/257-0366. Further information ☎604/257-0350, ☒www.vancouverfringe.com.
Vancouver International Film Festival from the end of the month to mid-October
North America's third largest film festival presents up to 500 screenings of 300 new films, revivals and retrospectives from some fifty countries. It runs for around seventeen days, and events take place in cinemas around the city. The festival is popular – upwards of 114,000 people attend.

☎604/685-0260, ☒www.viff.org.
Moon Festival This outdoor Chinese mid-autumn festival takes place on the 15th day of the 8th month of the Chinese calendar, which means it varies from year to year depending on the lunar cycle sometime in late September or early October. The festival is staged at the Dr Sun Yat-Sen Garden (see p.69) and involves music, moon cakes, storytelling and a lantern parade. ☎604/662-3207.

October

International Writers & Readers Festival third week of the month Around sixty national and international literary stars and new writers give readings and workshops on Granville Island and other locations around Vancouver and BC. The festival attracts some big-hitters – Martin Amis, Margaret Atwood, Peter Carey, John Irving, P D James, Alice Munro, Frank McCourt and J K Rowling are some of the past speakers. ☎604/681-6330, ☒www.writersfest.bc.ca.
Vancouver Snow Show end of the month BC Place Stadium hosts Canada's winter-sports show. This is a place to pick up cheap clothes and equipment as companies unload old stock and members of the public buy gear to raise money for charity. ☎604/878-0754, ☒www.skiandboardshow.com.

November

Remembrance Day Nov 11th Armistice Day – marking the moment hostilities ceased in World War I – is the day when all Canada, in common with many countries, remembers soldiers who died in the war. In Vancouver a twenty-one-gun salute is fired from Deadman's Island in Stanley Park at noon, and vintage aircraft fly over the park and Canada Place.
VanDusen Market and Festival of Light late November and early December This popular and high-quality craft and gift market is held in the VanDusen Botanical Garden (see p.99). (☎604/878-9274). Throughout December the Festival of Light sees the gardens illuminated by over 20,000 lights.

Christmas Carol Ship Parade three weeks leading up to Christmas. This is one of Vancouver's more magical events, in which a flotilla of decorated and illuminated boats of all descriptions cruises around the harbour on different nights. People on board sing carols or broadcast taped Christmas music. ☎604/878-8999.

Directory

Airlines Air Canada (☎604/688-5515, 1-888/247-2262 or 1-800/661-3936, ✆www.aircanada.ca); American Airlines (☎604/222-2532 or 1-800/433-7300, ✆www.aa.com); Baxter: float-plane services to Victoria's Inner Harbour (☎604/688-5136, ✆www.baxterair.com); British Airways (☎604/270-8131 or 1-800/247-9297, ✆www.ba.com); Continental (☎1-800/525-0280, ✆www.continental.com); Delta (☎1-800/241-4141, ✆www.delta.com); Harbour Air Seaplanes: services to Victoria Inner Harbour (☎604/274-1277 or 1-800/665-0212, ✆www.harbour-air.com); Helijet Airways: helicopter service to Victoria (☎604/273-1414 or 1-800/665-4354, ✆www.helijet.com); KLM (☎604/303-3666); United (☎1-800/241-6522, ✆www.ual.com); West Coast Air: seaplane services to Victoria and Gulf Islands (☎604/688-9115, 606-6888 or 1-800/347-2222, ✆www.westcoastair.com); Whistler Air: direct flights to Whistler from Vancouver Harbour Air Terminal by *Pan Pacific Hotel* (☎604/932-6615 or 1-888/806-2299).

Airport tax All passengers departing from Vancouver have to pay departure tax, or an "airport-improvement fee" before leaving. This tax is $5 for flights within British Columbia, $10 for flights within Canada and the US, and $15 for overseas flights. Cash and credit cards are accepted.

American Express Park Place Building, 666 Burrard St, enter at Hornby and Dunsmuir (☎604/669-2813 or 1-800/772-4473), and is open Mon–Fri 8.30am–5.30pm, Sat 10am–4pm.

Area code The area code for the greater Vancouver area is ☎604.

BC Parks ☎604/924-2200, ✆www.gov.bc.ca/bcparks.

Bike rental Bayshore Bicycles & Rollerblade Rentals, 745 Denman St (☎604/688-2453) and 1610 W Georgia St at Cardero St and the Westin Bayshore Hotel (☎604/689-5071); Harbour Air, Harbour Air Terminal at the waterfront one block west of Canada Place and the foot of Burrard St (☎604/688-1277) – also rents blades and motorcycles; Spokes, 1798 Georgia at Denman (☎604/688-5141, ✆www.vancouverbikerental.com).

Bookshops Chapters, 788 Robson St (☎604/682-4066, ✆www.chapters.ca), is a colossal bookshop (also with good music department) at the heart of Downtown. International Travel Maps, 552 Seymour St (☎604/687-3320, ✆www.itmb.com), is adequate for maps, guides and travel.

Buses Airporter (☎604/946-8866 or 1-800/668-3141, ✆www.yvrairporter.com) for shuttle from Vancouver Airport to bus depot and Downtown; BC Transit for city buses, SeaBus and SkyTrain (☎604/953-3333, ✆www.translink.bc.ca); Greyhound (☎604/662-3222 or 1-800/661-8747, ✆www.greyhound.ca) for BC, Alberta, Yukon and long-haul destinations including Seattle and the US; Malaspina Coach Lines (☎1-877/227-8287) for the Sunshine Coast, Powell River, Whistler, Pemberton and Nanaimo on Vancouver Island; Pacific Coach Lines (☎604/662-8074 or 1-800/661-1725, ✆www.pacificcoach.com) for Victoria, Vancouver Island; Perimeter (☎604/266-5386 or ☎604/905-0041, ✆www.perimeterbus.com) for services between Whistler and Vancouver Airport; Quick Shuttle (☎604/940-4428 or 1-800/665-2122, ✆www.quickcoach.com) for Bellingham Airport, downtown Seattle and SeaTac Airport.

Car rental Budget, airport, 501 W Georgia St and 1705 Burrard St (☎604/668-7000 or 1-800/268-8900 in Canada, 1-800/527-

0700 in US, ⓦwww.bc.budget.com); Hertz, 1128 Seymour St (ⓣ604/688-2411 or 1-800/263-0600, ⓦwww.hertz.com); Lo-Cost, 1835 Marine Drive (ⓣ604/986-1266, ⓦwwwlocost.com); National (ⓣ1-800/227-7368), airport (ⓣ604/207-3730) and 1130 W Georgia at Thurlow (ⓣ604/609-7150, ⓦwww.nationalcar.com); Rent-a-Wreck, 1349 Hornby St (ⓣ604/688-0001, ⓦwww.rentawreckvancouver.com).

Consulates Australia, 1225-Suite 888 Dunsmuir St (ⓣ604/684-1177); Ireland, 1400-100 W Pender St (ⓣ604/683-8440); New Zealand, 1200-Suite 888 Dunsmuir (ⓣ604/684-7388); UK, 800-1111 Melville St (ⓣ604/683-4421); US, 1095 W Pender (ⓣ604/685-4311).

Currency Exchange Custom House Currency, Unit 60-200 Granville St (ⓣ604/608-1763, ⓦwww.customhouse.com); International Securities Exchange, 1169 Robson St near Thurlow (ⓣ604/683-9666); QuickEx 300-609 West Hastings (ⓣ604/683-6789, ⓦwwwquickex.ca); Travelex-Thomas Cook, Suite 130, 999 Canada Place (ⓣ604/641-1229); Vancouver Bullion & Currency Exchange, 402 Hornby St (ⓣ604/685-1008, ⓦwww.vbc.ca).

Dentists For your nearest dentists, call the College of Dental Surgeons for a referral (ⓣ604/736-3621). Drop-in dentist, Dentacare (Mon–Fri 8am–5pm only; ⓣ604/669-6700), is in the lower level of the Bentall Centre at 1055 Dunsmuir and Burrard.

Directory enquiries ⓣ411.

Doctors The College of Physicians can provide names of three doctors near you (ⓣ604/733-7758). Drop-in service at Bentall Centre Rexall Drugstore, Suite 400, Bental 4, 1055 Dunsmuir (ⓣ604/684-8204, ⓦwww.rexall.ca); Ultima Vancouver Airport Medical Clinic, Vancouver International Airport, Domestic Terminal (ⓣ604/207-6900, ⓦwww.ultimamedical.ca); Vancouver Mediclinics (ⓣ604/683-8138, ⓦwww.medicentre.ca), also in the Bentall Centre (Mon–Fri 8am–4.30pm); see above.

Electricity Canada uses 110-volt, 60-cycle electricity, which means that travellers from the US should find that their appliances work without a hitch, but Europeans and others will need an adapter.

Emergency services (police, fire and ambulance) ⓣ911.

Gay and lesbian switchboard Touch-tone guide (ⓣ604/684-XTRA).

Hospitals Emergency Room, St Paul's Hospital, 1081 Burrard Street (ⓣ682-2344). Vancouver General Hospital, 855 W.12th Avenue (ⓣ604/874-4111) or British Columbia's Children's Hospital, 4480 Oak St. (ⓣ604/875-2345).

Laundries Davie Laundromat, 1061 Davie St (ⓣ604/682-2717); Scotty's One Hour Cleaners, 834 Thurlow near Robson (ⓣ604/685-7732).

Left luggage At Pacific Central Station ($2 per 24hr).

Liquor laws The legal drinking age in British Columbia is 19.

Lost property BC Transit (ⓣ604/682-7887); West Vancouver Transit (ⓣ604/985-7777); police (ⓣ604/717-2726); airport (ⓣ604/276-6104).

Maps Geological Survey of Canada, 101-605 Robson near Richards (Mon–Fri 8.30am–4.30pm; ⓣ604/666-0529). Superb source of official survey maps, including *all* 1:50,000 maps of BC and Yukon.

Optician Opticana Eyewear, 455 Granville St (ⓣ604/685-1031, ⓦwww.opticana.ca).

Parking Main Downtown garages are at The Bay (entrance on Richards near Dunsmuir), Robson Square (on Smithe and Howe), and the Pacific Centre (on Howe and Dunsmuir) – all are expensive and fill up quickly. A better idea might be to leave your car at the free Park'n'Ride in New Westminster (off Hwy 1).

Pharmacies Shopper's Drug Mart, 1125 Davie and Thurlow (ⓣ604/669-2424), is open 24hr and has five other outlets open Mon–Sat 9am–midnight, Sun 9am–9pm. Carson Midnite Drug Store, 6517 Main at 49th, is open daily until midnight.

Police Non-emergency 24-hr (ⓣ604/717-3321). RCMP (ⓣ604/264-3111); Vancouver City Police (ⓣ604/665-3535).

Post office Main office at 349 W Georgia and Homer (Mon–Fri 8am–5.30pm; ⓣ604/662-5722). Post-office information (ⓣ1-800/267-1177).

Student cards Most places will accept a school ID for student discounts; an ISIC card, however, is the most widely recognized and accepted card of all.

Tax Provincial Sales Tax (PST) is 7.5 percent on most goods and services, rising to eight percent on hotel bills and ten percent in restaurants and bars; this is supplemented by the nationwide **Goods and Services Tax** (GST), a seven percent levy equivalent to VAT in Europe.

Taxis Black Top (☎604/731-1111 or 681-2181); Vancouver Taxi (☎604/255-5111 or 604/874-5111); Yellow Cab (☎604/681-3311 or 604/681-1111).

Temperature S Vancouver averages 55–70°F (13–21°C) in the summer months, and 33–42°F (1–6°C) in the winter.

Time zones Vancouver runs on Pacific Time, or eight hours behind G.M.T.

Tipping 15 percent is generally expected.

Tourist information Vancouver Tourist infocentre 200 Burrard St (☎604/683-2000, ⊛www.tourismvancouver.com). BC Tourism/Hello BC (☎1-800/435-5622, ⊛www.hellobc.com). Granville Island, 1398 Cartwright St, Granville Island (☎604/666-5784, ⊛www.granvilleisland.com).

Train enquiries VIA Rail (☎604/669-3050 or toll-free in Canada only ☎1-800/561-8630, 1-800/561-3949 in the US, ⊛www.viarail,ca); Amtrak (☎1-800/872-7245, ⊛www.amtrak.com); Rocky Mountain Railtours (☎604/606-7200 or 1-800/665-7245) for expensive rail tours through the Rockies.

Weather information ☎604/664-9010.

Out of the City

Out of the City

19

Victoria

British Columbia's provincial capital **Victoria** is the region's second city, after Vancouver. It's a popular excursion from Vancouver, and though it's possible to come here for the day – especially if you take a seaplane from Vancouver's harbour – you'd be far better advised to stay overnight and give the city the two or so days it deserves.

This said, Victoria has a lot to live up to. Leading US travel magazine *Condé Nast Traveler* has voted it one of the world's top-ten cities to visit, and world number one for ambience and environment. Moreover, it was not named after a queen and an era for nothing. Much of the waterfront area has an undeniably quaint and likeable English feel – "Brighton Pavilion with the Himalayas for a backdrop", remarked Rudyard Kipling – and Victoria has more British-born residents than anywhere in Canada. However, its tourist potential is exploited chiefly by American visitors, served up with lashings of fake Victoriana and chintzy commercialism, and ersatz echoes of empire at every turn.

Despite the seasonal influx, and the sometimes atrociously tacky attractions designed to part tourists from their money, it's a small, relaxed and pleasantly sophisticated place, worth lingering in if only for its inspirational museum. It also offers plenty of pubs, restaurants (and the odd club) and serves as a base for a range of outdoor activities and slightly more far-flung attractions. Chief of these is whale-watching, with a plethora of companies on hand (see box, p.232) to take you out to the teeming waters around the city.

As a final lure, the weather here – though often damp – is extremely mild: Victoria's meteorological station has the distinction of being the only one in Canada to record a winter in which the temperature never fell below freezing.

Some history

Victoria's site was originally inhabited by **Salish natives**, and in particular by the **Lekwammen**, who had a string of some ten villages in the area. Here they cultivated camas bulbs – vital to their diet and trade – and applied their advanced salmon-fishing methods to the shoals of migrating salmon in net-strung reefs offshore. At the time, the region must have been idyllic. **Captain George Vancouver**, who was mapping the North American coast and apparently mindless of the aboriginal presence, described his feelings on first glimpsing this part of Vancouver Island: "The serenity of the climate, the innumerable pleasing landscapes, and the abundant fertility that nature puts forth, require only to be enriched by the industry of man with villages, mansions, cottages and other buildings, to render it the most lovely country that can be imagined."

The first step in this process began in 1842 when Victoria received some of its earliest **white visitors**, notably Hudson's Bay Company representative **James Douglas,** who disembarked at present-day Clover Point during a

△ Victoria's Inner Harbour

search for a new local headquarters for the company. One look at the natural harbour and its surroundings was enough: this, he declared, was a "perfect Eden", a feeling only reinforced by the friendliness of the indigenous population, who helped him build Fort Camouson, named after an important aboriginal landmark (the name was later changed to Fort Victoria to honour the British queen). The indigenous peoples from up and down the island settled near the fort, attracted by the new trading opportunities it offered. Soon they were joined by British pioneers, brought in to settle the land by a Bay subsidiary, the Puget Sound Agricultural Company, which quickly built several large company farms to accommodate settlers. In time, the harbour became the busiest West Coast port north of San Francisco and a major base for the British navy's Pacific fleet, a role it now fulfils for the bulk of Canada's navy.

Boom time came in the 1850s following the mainland **gold strikes**, when Victoria's port became an essential stopoff and supplies depot for prospectors heading across the water and into the interior. Military and bureaucratic personnel moved in to ensure order, bringing the morals and manners of Victorian England with them. Alongside, there grew a rumbustuous shantytown of shops, bars and brothels, one bar run by "Gassy" Jack Leighton (see box, p.63), who unwittingly was soon to become one of Vancouver's founders.

Though the gold-rush bubble soon burst, Victoria carried on as a military, economic and political centre, becoming the capital of the newly created British Columbia in 1866 – years before the founding of Vancouver. Its new status was underlined when the Canadian Pacific Railway built the redoubtable **Empress Hotel** in 1908 in place of a proposed railway link that never came into being. Victoria's planned role as Canada's western rail terminus was surrendered to Vancouver, and with it any chance of realistic growth or industrial development. These days, the town survives quite well almost entirely on the backs of tourists (four million a year), the civil-service bureaucracy and – shades of the home country – retirees in search of a mild-weathered retreat. Its population today is around 350,000, almost exactly double what it was just thirty years ago.

Getting to Victoria

There are three ways to reach Victoria – by **bus and ferry**, by **car and ferry**, or by **air**. Most people travelling under their own steam from Vancouver use the first means, which is a simple matter of buying an all-inclusive throughticket from Vancouver's bus terminal (see p.26) to Victoria's bus depot. By far the quickest approach, however, is to take a seaplane from Vancouver's port: this approach takes just 25 minutes – as opposed to 3hr 30min by bus and ferry – and drops you right in Victoria's Inner Harbour; however, it works out around three times as expensive.

You can also reach Victoria directly from Vancouver Airport by inclusive coach and ferry arrangements: ask for details at the bus desk in international arrivals of Pacific Coach Lines bus services (7 daily; $36 single, $71 round-trip). Journey time is about 3hr 30min.

The telephone code for Victoria is ☎250.

However, if you intend to visit Victoria before Vancouver, and are flying, then it usually only costs a little more to fly direct to the city from further afield, so it's not usually worth flying to Vancouver and then taking the bus-ferry option to save money.

By bus and ferry from Vancouver

If you're without your own transport, the most painless way to Victoria from Vancouver is to buy a **Pacific Coach Lines** (☎604/662-8074 or 1-800/661-1725, ⓦwww.pacificcoach.com) ticket at the Vancouver bus terminal at 1150 Station St, which takes you, inclusive of the ferry crossing and journeys to and from ferry terminals at both ends, to Victoria's central bus station at 700 Douglas St. Buses leave hourly in the summer, every two hours in the winter: total journey time is about 3 hours 30min and a single ticket costs $29 ($56 round-trip). No bookings are necessary: overflow passengers are simply put on another coach. Be sure to keep your ticket stub for reboarding the bus after the crossing.

By car and ferry from Vancouver

BC Ferries operates four routes to Vancouver Island across the Georgia Strait from mainland British Columbia (☎1-888/223-3779 from anywhere in BC; otherwise ☎604/444-2890 or 250/386-3431, ⓦwww.bcferries.com). Reservations are essential in summer if you want to avoid long waits. The route used by most Vancouver-Victoria passengers is the Tsawwassen–Swartz Bay connection, also the route used by Pacific Coach Lines' buses. Ferries ply the route almost continuously from 7am to 10pm (sixteen sailings daily in summer, minimum of eight daily in winter). Tickets for people with cars cost $34.75 at weekends (noon Fri to last sailing on Sun) and $32.75 on weekdays in high season from late June to early Sept ($31.50/29.75 in shoulder season from mid-March to mid-June and early Sept to Oct); tickets for bicyclists cost $2.50 year-round. Fares do not include driver or passenger fares, which are $10 per person daily in peak season and $9.50 daily in the shoulder season.

By air

Flying into Victoria from Vancouver airport is an expensive option. Open round-trip fares from Vancouver typically run to around $150, excursion fares (tickets have restrictions) around $100. If you are going to fly, however, it's more fun and more direct to fly from Vancouver harbour to Victoria harbour by helicopter or float plane: Harbour Air and West Coast Air fly from the Tradewinds Marina just west of Canada Place in Vancouver (see p.49 for details) for a one-way price of $99. Helijet Airways (☎604/273-1414) flies from the helipad to the east or from Vancouver Airport for $140 one way, less if you book in advance.

Arrival, information and city transport

Victoria International Airport (☎250/953-7500, ⓦwww.cyyj.ca or
ⓦwww.victoriaairport.com) is 26km north of downtown on Hwy 17 near the
Sidney ferry terminal. Hwy 17 runs south and takes you to the city outskirts
where it becomes Douglas St, which runs to the heart of downtown. The Akal
Airporter shuttle bus heads downtown (where it stops at major hotels) every
half-hour between about 4.30am and 1am; a single fare for the 45-minute
journey is $13 (☎250/386-2525, 386-2526 or 1-877/386-2525,
ⓦwww.akalairporter.travel.bc.ca). They can also arrange pick-ups to the airport. Otherwise contact Harbour Air (☎250/384-2215 or 1-800/665-0212,
ⓦwww.harbour-air.com) or West Coast Air (☎250/388-4521 or 1-800/347-
2222, ⓦwww.westcoastair.com), which operate efficient and quick float planes
between Vancouver's port and Victoria's downtown Inner Harbour: both companies share terminals in both cities ($99 single; planes leave about every hour;
crossing time is 35 minutes). Helijet Airways (☎604/273-1414, ⓦwww.helijet
.com) flies from Vancouver airport or a terminal east of Canada Place in downtown to Victoria's Inner Harbour from $140 single.

The **bus terminal** is downtown at 700 Douglas St and Belleville Street, close
to the Royal British Columbia Museum. Pacific Coach Lines' buses from
Vancouver or Vancouver airport will drop you here, and it is the base for
onward connections on Vancouver Island provided by Laidlaw Coach Lines
(☎250/385-4411, ⓦwww.grayline.ca/victoria).

Victoria's busy **infocentre** is at 812 Wharf St, in front of the *Empress Hotel* on
the harbour (daily: May–Sept 8.30am–6.30pm; Oct–April 9am–5pm;
☎250/953-2033, for accommodation reservations 1-800/663-3883,
ⓦwww.tourismvictoria.com). The staff can help you book whale-watching and
other tours (see box, p.232), and provide a huge range of general information.

City transport

The most enjoyable means of transport are the tiny Inner Harbour **ferries** that
run around the harbour. Stops include Fisherman's Wharf, Ocean Pointe
Resort and West Bay Marina, but they're worth taking just for the ride: try an
evening mini-cruise around the harbour (buy tickets – from $3 - on ferries in
the Inner Harbour or book at the infocentre). You're unlikely to need to take
a local **bus** if you stick to the downtown area, but if you do venture out, most
services run from the corner of Douglas and Yates streets. The fare within the
large central zone is $1.75 – tickets and the DayPass ($5.50) are sold at the
infocentre, 7-Eleven stores and other marked outlets, or you can pay on board
if you have the exact fare. For 24-hour recorded information on city transport,
call the Busline (☎250/382-6161, lost property ☎250/995-5637,
ⓦwww.bctransit.com).

Accommodation

Victoria fills up quickly in the summer, and most of its budget **accommodation** is well known and heavily patronized. Top-price hotels cluster around the
Inner Harbour area; **hostels** and more downmarket alternatives are scattered
all over, though the largest concentration of cheap **hotels** and **motels** is

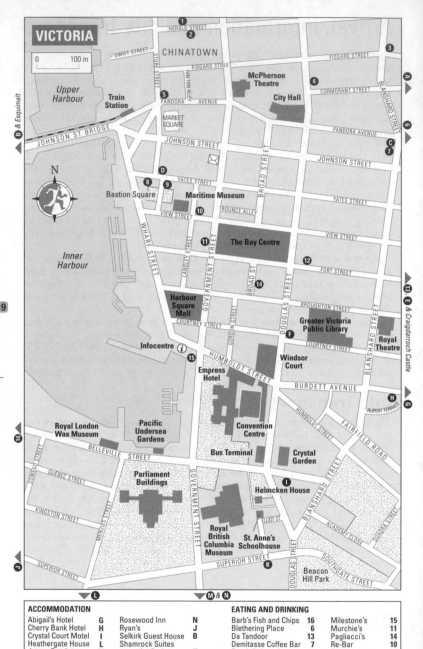

VICTORIA

Upper Harbour

B & Esquimalt

CHINATOWN

Train Station

McPherson Theatre

City Hall

Inner Harbour

Bastion Square

Maritime Museum

The Bay Centre

Harbour Square Mall

Greater Victoria Public Library

Royal Theatre

Infocentre

Empress Hotel

Windsor Court

Royal London Wax Museum

Pacific Undersea Gardens

Convention Centre

Bus Terminal

Crystal Garden

Parliament Buildings

Helmcken House

Royal British Columbia Museum

St. Anne's Schoolhouse

Beacon Hill Park

E & Craigdarroch Castle

around the Gorge Road and Douglas Street areas northwest of downtown. Reservations are virtually obligatory in all categories, though the infocentre's accommodation service will root out a room if you're stuck (☎1–800/663–3883 in North America, ☎250/953–2033 from outside North America). They are more than likely to offer you **B&B** accommodation, of which the town has a vast selection, though prices for many are surprisingly high; many owners of the more far-flung places will pick you up from downtown.

Victoria's commercial **campsites** are full to bursting in summer, with most space given over to RVs. Few of these are convenient for downtown – given that you'll have to travel, you might as well head for one of the more scenic provincial park sites. Most are on the Trans-Canada Highway to the north, or on Hwy 14 east of Victoria.

Hotels and motels

Abigail's Hotel 960 McClure St ☎250/388-5363 or 1-800/561-6565, ⓕ 388-7787, ⓦwww.abigailshotel.com. A very classy, small hotel in a fine building with log fires, voluminous duvets, Jacuzzis and a good breakfast. If you want to treat yourself, this is the place. Situated on the corner of Quadra St, a block east of Blanshard St and within easy walking distance of the city centre. All rooms are nonsmoking. ❽/❼

Cherry Bank Hotel 825 Burdett Ave ☎250/385-5380 or 1-800/998-6688, ⓕ383-0949, ⓦwww.bctravel.com/cherrybankhotel. Reservations are essential at this deservedly popular and pleasantly eccentric (note the rotating mermaid on the roof) 26-room budget hotel, which has excellent rooms and breakfast included. First choice at this price. ❸

Crystal Court Motel 701 Belleville St ☎250/ 84-0551, ⓕ384-5125, ⓦwww.crystalcourtmotel.supersites.ca. This is a large, functional and fairly priced motel well located just one block from the Inner Harbour, though it fronts a fairly busy road. ❹

James Bay Inn 270 Government St at Toronto St ☎250/384-7151 or 1-800/836-2649, ⓕ385-2311, ⓦwww.jamesbayinn.bc.ca. This 45-room hotel vies with the *Cherry Bank* as Victoria's best reasonably priced option, though rates have climbed in the last couple of years.

The Edwardian building was the home of painter Emily Carr. Simple rooms at varying prices, with a restaurant and pub in the basement. Two blocks south of the Parliament Buildings. ❻

Rosewood Inn 595 Michigan St near Government St ☎250/384-6644 or 1-866/986-2222, ⓕ384-6117, ⓦwww.rosewoodvictoria.com. A comfortable and smart, small hotel located a couple of blocks south of the Royal BC Museum. ❻/❼

Shamrock Suites on the Park 675 Superior St at Douglas ☎250/385-8768 or 1-800/294-5544, ⓕ385-1837. The *Shamrock* lies a block from the Royal BC Museums close to Beacon Hill Park. It has just sixteen units, upgraded from simple motel status to "suites" following a renovation in 2002. Prices have gone up, but the studios and one-bedroom suites are roomy and come with kitchenettes at no extra cost: some rooms have park views. A continental breakfast is included in the rates between July and September. ❺

Strathcona Hotel 919 Douglas St ☎250/ 383-7137 or 1-800/663-7476, ⓕ383-6893, ⓦwww.strathconahotel.com. Large, modern hotel where rooms include baths and TVs. Note that there's a British-style pub and restaurant downstairs with booming live and DJ music that may not be to all tastes. ❹

Bed and breakfasts

Heathergate House 122 Simcoe St ☎250/383-0068 or 1-888/683-0068, ⓕ383-4320, ⓦwww.heathergatebb.com. This small B&B offers three rooms plus a separate two-bed cottage within walking distance of the Inner Harbour and the sights. All rooms are en suite. There's a private floor for guests with

a lounge and TV room. ❺

Prior House 620 St Charles St ☎250/592-8847 or 1-877/924-3300, ⓕ592-8223, ⓦwww.prior-house.com. This very smart five-room B&B was once the home of Victoria's lieutenant governor – ask for his suite, complete with bathroom with chandelier. About 2.5km east of downtown in the smart Rockland area, so it's better if you have transport. ❼

Ryan's 224 Superior St ☎ 250/389-0012 or 1-877/389-0012, ⓕ 389-2857, ⓦ www.ryansbb.com. A very pretty 1892 heritage building south of the Royal BC Museum and a five-minute walk to downtown; all seven rooms are nicely decorated and have private bathrooms. ❼

Selkirk Guest House 934 Selkirk Ave ☎ 250/389-1213 or 1/800/974-6638, ⓦ www.selkirkguesthouse.com. Fine historic

waterfront home dating from 1909 northwest of the Inner Harbour: take bus #14 from Douglas St (to within two blocks) or cross the Johnston Bridge and follow the water past Bay St and Banfield Park. Then take Arcadia, a right turn from Craigflower Rd to Selkirk Ave. It's well placed for bike and walking trails (it's on the Galloping Goose Trail) and you can rent boats and canoes. Dorm places cost $20 and there's a choice of four other good double rooms $75–90 with breakfast at $5. ❻

University residences and hostels

Ocean Island Backpacker's Inn 791 Pandora Ave at Blanshard St ☎ 250/385-1788 or 1-888/888-4180, ⓦ www.oceanisland.com. A good, reasonably central location in the northeast corner of downtown. Facilities include private and shared rooms, Internet access, a music room with instruments, no curfew, free morning coffee, laundry room, free bike storage, linen and towels provided and limited parking at $4 a day. The restored 1893 heritage building has a wide variety of dorms and rooms (singles and doubles with and without bathroom) on a sliding scale depending on the time of year or the day of the week (more on Fri and Sat) and whether you have a HI card. The following prices are Fri and Sat rates and assume you do not have a card (subtract $1-3 if you do): dorm beds cost $17.75 from mid-Oct to mid-March up to $23 in July and Aug. Private doubles cost from $40 to $55. Weekly and monthly rates are available on dorms and rooms.

Turtle Refuge Hostel 1608 Quadra St at corner of Pandora ☎ 250/386-4471, ⓔ turtlerefuge@hotmail.com. Central residential home with 25 dorm beds, two doubles and two four-bed family rooms. There's a communal kitchen, laundry, no curfew, parking, luggage storage and free morning

coffee. Dorm beds cost $13 ($12 Nov–April), doubles $40 ($30) plus $10 for each extra person.

University of Victoria corner of Sinclair and Finnerty Rd ☎ 250/721-8395, ⓕ 721-8930, ⓦ www.hfcs.uvic.ca. Good, if plain rooms (single or double) on the university campus are available May to September when not required for students or conferences. Shared bathroom, laundry and kitchen facilities. Good-value four-room suites with bathroom, kitchen and living room are also available. For a small extra fee guests have access to the university pool and other sports facilities. It is a half-hour car or bus (#4 or #14) ride to downtown. Singles $44 (with breakfast), doubles $55.

Victoria Youth Hostel (HI) 516 Yates and Wharf sts. Mon–Thurs 7.30am to midnight, Fri–Sun 7am–2am; ☎ 250/385-4511 or 1-888/ 883-0099, ⓕ 385-3232, ⓦ www.hihostels.ca. Large, modern, welcoming and extremely well-run place just a few blocks north of the Inner Harbour. The bunk rooms, though, can be noisy: the reception, rather ominously, sells earplugs. The notice boards are packed with useful information on the city. Members $16–20 nonmembers $17–24. A handful of private doubles are available at $38 for members, $48 for nonmembers.

Campsites

Fort Victoria RV and Park Campground 340 Island Hwy 1A ☎ 250/479-8112, ⓕ 479-5806, ⓦ www.fortvicrv.com. Closest site to downtown, located 6km north of Victoria off the Trans-Canada Hwy. Take bus #14 (for Craigflower) from the city centre: it stops right by the gate. Large 300-pitch site

mainly for RVs but with a few tent sites; free hot showers. $29 per two persons.

Goldstream Provincial Park 2930 Trans-Canada Hwy ☎ 604/689-9025 or 1-800/689-9025, ⓦ www.discovercamping.ca. Bus #50 from Douglas St from downtown. Although 20km north of the city on Hwy 1, this site is set in old-growth forests of cedar and Douglas fir and is Victoria's best camping option. Flush toilets and free hot showers, with plenty of hiking, swimming and fishing opportunities. $22 per site.

Thetis Lake 1938 Trans-Canada Hwy at 1938 West Park Lane ℡ 250/478-3845,

Ⓔ thetislake@shaw.ca. Runs a close second to *Goldstream Provincial Park*'s campsites for the pleasantness of its setting, and is only 10km north of downtown. Family-oriented, with 147 sites, as well as laundry and coin-operated showers. $16 per two persons.

The city

The Victoria that's worth bothering with is very small: almost everything worth seeing, as well as the best shops and restaurants, is within walking distance of the **Inner Harbour** area and the Old Town district behind it. On summer evenings this area is alive with strollers and buskers, and a pleasure to wander as the sun drops over the water. Foremost among the daytime diversions are the **Royal British Columbia Museum** and the **Empress Hotel**. Most of the other trumpeted attractions are dreadful, and many charge entry fees out of all proportion to what's on show. If you're tempted by the Royal London Wax Museum, the Pacific Undersea Gardens, Miniature World, English Village, Anne Hathaway's Thatched Cottage or any of Victoria's other dubious commercial propositions, details are available from the infocentre. Outside the Inner Harbour, Victoria has a scattering of minor attractions that don't fit into any logical tour of the city – and at any rate are only quick-stop diversions – the most compelling of which is Craigdarroch Castle. You might drop by the only moderately diverting **Maritime Museum** and think about a trip to the celebrated **Butchart Gardens**, some way out of town, but easily accessible by public transport or regular all-inclusive tours from the bus terminal. If you're around for a couple of days you should also find time to walk around **Beacon Hill Park**, a few minutes' walk from downtown to the south.

The Royal British Columbia Museum

The **Royal British Columbia Museum,** at 675 Belleville St (daily 9am–5pm. National Geographic IMAX Theatre: daily 9am–8pm; museum $11, IMAX Theatre $9.75, combined ticket $16.25, IMAX double feature $15; museum ℡ 250/356-7226 or 1-888/447-7977, Ⓦ www.rbcm.gov.bc.ca), is a short stroll along the waterfront from the infocentre. Founded in 1886, it is arguably the best museum in Canada, and regularly rated, by visitors and travel-magazine polls, as one of North America's top ten. All conceivable aspects of the province are examined, but the aboriginal peoples section is probably the definitive collection of a much-covered genre, while the **natural-history displays** – huge re-creations of natural habitats, complete with sights, sounds and smells – are mind-boggling in scope and imagination. Allow at least two trips to take it all in.

Victoria's beaches

The best of the area's **beaches** are well out of town, around three or four miles on Hwy 14 and Hwy 1, but for idling by the sea drop down to the pebble shore along the southern edge of Beacon Hill Park. For some local swimming, the best option by far is **Willows Beach** on the Esplanade in Oak Bay, 2km east of Victoria; take bus #1 to Beach and Dalhousie Road. Other good stretches of sand can be found on Dallas Road and at Island View Beach.

From the first thing you see as you enter the display area – a huge stuffed mammoth – you can tell that thought, wit and a lot of money have gone into the museum. Much of the cash must have been sunk into its most popular display, the **Open Ocean**, a self-contained, in-depth look at the sea and the deep-level ocean. Groups of ten are admitted into a series of tunnels, dark rooms, lifts and mock-ups of submarines at thirty-minute intervals. You take a time-coded ticket and wait your turn, so either arrive early or reckon on seeing the rest of the museum first. Though rather heavy-handed in its "we're-all-part-of-the-cosmic-soup" message, it's still an object lesson in presentation and state-of-the-art museum dynamics. It's also designed to be dark and enclosed, and signs wisely warn you to stay out if you suffer even a twinge of claustrophobia.

The first floor

The first floor features full-scale reconstructions of some of the many natural habitats found in British Columbia. The idea of re-creating shorelines, coastal rainforests and Fraser Delta landscapes may sound far-fetched, yet all are incredibly realistic, down to dripping water and cool, dank atmospheres. Audiovisual displays and a tumult of information accompany the exhibits (the beaver film is worth hunting down), most of which focus on the province's 25,600km of coastline, a side of British Columbia usually overlooked in favour of its interior forests and mountains.

The second floor

Upstairs on the second floor is the mother of all the tiny museums of bric-a-brac and pioneer memorabilia in BC. Arranged eccentrically from the present day backwards, it explores every aspect of the province's **social history** over two centuries in nitpicking detail. Prominently featured are part of an early twentieth-century town, complete with cinema and silent films, plus comprehensive displays on logging, mining, the Gold Rush, farming, fishing and lesser domestic details, all the artefacts and accompanying information being presented with impeccable finesse.

The third floor

Up on the mezzanine third floor is a superb collection of **aboriginal peoples' art, culture and history** (see p.267). It's presented in gloomy light against muted wood walls and brown carpet, which creates a solemn atmosphere in keeping with the tragic nature of many of the displays. The collection divides into two epochs – before and after the coming of Europeans – tellingly linked by a single aboriginal carving of a white man, starkly and brilliantly capturing the initial wonder and weirdness of the new arrivals. The whole collection takes a thoughtful and oblique approach, taking you to the point where, in one year, smallpox virtually wiped out a culture that was eight millennia in the making.

A section on land and reservations is left for last – the issues are contentious even today – and even if you're succumbing to museum fatigue, the arrogance and duplicity of the documents on display will shock you. The highlights in this section are many, but try to make a point of seeing the short film *In the Land of the War Canoes* (1914), the **Bighouse** (a facsimile of a meeting hall) and its chants, and the audiovisual display on aboriginal myths and superstition. The **National Geographic Theatre** in the museum plays host to a huge IMAX screen and a changing programme of special-format films. Outside the museum, there's also **Thunderbird Park**, a strip of grass with a handful of totem poles.

Helmcken House and St Anne's Pioneer Schoolhouse

Directly adjacent to the museum, **Helmcken House** (daily May–Oct 10am–5pm, Thurs–Mon 11am–4pm; $5; ☎250/361-0021) stands strangely isolated off Belleville Street. The oldest house in BC still on its original site, it is a predictable heritage offering that showcases the home, furnishings and embroidery talents of the Helmcken family. Built in 1852, it is the oldest surviving home on the island. Dr John Helmcken was Fort Victoria's doctor and local political bigwig (he married the daughter of the governor Sir James Douglas), and his house is a typical monument to stolid Victoria values. Upstairs it contains various attic treasures and some of the good doctor's fearsome-looking medical tools. It's probably only of interest, however, if you've so far managed to avoid any of Canada's many thousands of similar houses. If you do visit, pick up the free guided tapes and hear "voices from history" (actually, those of actors and actresses) that give a more personalized slant on the building: listen, for example, to "Aunt Dolly" as she tells why she left the good doctor's room untouched as a shrine after his death.

Just behind the house there's another old white-wood building, the **St Anne's Pioneer Schoolhouse** (not open to the public) originally purchased by a Bishop Demers for four sisters of the Order of St Anne, who in 1858 took it upon themselves to leave their Québec home to come and teach in Victoria. Built between 1843 and 1858, it's believed to be the oldest building in Victoria still in use.

The Parliament Buildings

One block west of the museum, at 501 Belleville St, stands the huge Victorian pile of the **Parliament Buildings** (daily: June to early Sept 9am–5pm; early Sept to May 9am–4pm; ☎250/387-3046 or 1-800/663-7867 in BC). Old and imposing in the manner of a large and particularly grand British town hall, the buildings are beautifully lit at night by some three hundred tiny bulbs (though locals grumble about the cost). The domed building is fronted by the sea and well-kept gardens – a pleasant enough ensemble, though it doesn't really warrant the manic enthusiasm visited on it by hordes of summer tourists. You're more likely to find yourself taking time out on the front lawns, distinguished by a perky statue of Queen Victoria and a giant sequoia, a gift from the state of California.

Designed by the 25-year-old Francis Rattenbury, who was also responsible for the nearby *Empress Hotel*, the building was completed in 1897, at a cost of $923,000, in time for Queen Victoria's jubilee. Figures from Victoria's grey bureaucratic past are duly celebrated, the main door guarded by statues of Sir James Douglas, who chose the site of the city, and Sir Matthew Baillie Begbie (aka the "Hanging Judge"), responsible for law and order during the heady days of gold fever. Sir George Vancouver keeps an eye on proceedings from the top of the dome.

Free tours (every 20–30min Oct–April, booked tours only the rest of the year Mon–Fri hourly 9am–3pm, plus one public tour at 4pm) start to the right of the main steps and are led by guides who are chirpy and full of anecdotes. Look out for the dagger that killed Captain Cook, and the gold-plated dome, painted with scenes from Canadian history.

Beacon Hill Park

For horticultural enthusiasts who do not have time to make it out to the Butchart Gardens (see p.231), the best greenspace within walking distance of the town centre is **Beacon Hill Park**, south of the Inner Harbour and a few minutes' walk up the road behind the museum. Victoria is sometimes known as the "City of Gardens", and at the right times of the year this park shows why. Victoria's biggest park, it has lots of paths, ponds, big trees and quiet corners, and plenty of views over the Juan de Fuca Strait to the distant Olympic Mountains of Washington State (especially on the park's southern side).

These pretty straits are the focus of some rather bad feeling between Victoria and the US for the city has a dark secret: it dumps raw sewage into the strait, excusing itself by claiming it's quickly broken up by the sea's strong currents. Washington State isn't so sure, and there have been plenty of arguments over the matter and, more to the point for city elders, economically damaging convention boycotts by American companies. Either way, it's pretty bad PR for Victoria and totally at odds with its image.

The gardens in the park are by turns well tended and wonderfully wild and unkempt, a far cry from their earliest days, when it was known by the local Salish as Meeacan, their word for a belly, as the hill was thought to resemble the stomach of large man lying on his back. The park was a favoured retreat of celebrated Victorian artist, Emily Carr. They also claim the world's tallest totem carved from a single tree (at 48m), as well as the "Mile Zero" marker of the Trans-Canada Highway and – that ultimate emblem of Englishness – a cricket pitch. Some of the trees are massive old-growth timbers that you'd normally only see on the island's unlogged west coast.

If you come in spring, you'll catch swaths of daffodils and blue camas flowers, the latter a floral monument to Victoria's earliest aboriginal inhabitants, who cultivated the flower for its edible bulb. Some 30,000 other flowers are planted in the gardens annually.

Crystal Garden

The heavily advertised **Crystal Garden** (daily: mid-March–mid-June & mid-Sept–Oct 9am–6pm; mid-June–mid-Sept 9am–8pm; Nov–mid-March 10am–4.30pm; $9; ☏250/381-1213, ⊛www.bcpcc.com/crystal), behind the bus terminal at 713 Douglas St, was modelled after London's Crystal Palace and, on opening in 1925, claimed to house the "Largest Saltwater Swimming Pool in the British Empire". Much restored, the greenhouse – filled with flora, monkeys and birds – makes for an unaccountably popular tourist spot; only the exterior has any claims to architectural sophistication, and much of its effect is spoilt by the souvenir and other shops on its ground-floor arcade. Once the meeting place of the town's tea-sipping elite, it now plays host to events such as the Jive and Ballroom Dance Club and the People Meeting People Dance. The daytime draws are the conservatory-type tearoom and tropical gardens. Inhumanely enclosed birds, butterflies and monkeys, though, are liable to put you off your scones.

The Empress Hotel

A town is usually desperate when one of its key attractions is a hotel, but in the case of Victoria the **Empress Hotel** is so physically overbearing and plays such a part in the town's tourist appeal that it demands some sort of attention.

You're unlikely to be staying here – rooms are expensive – but it's worth wandering through the huge lobbies and palatial dining areas for a glimpse of well-restored colonial splendour. In a couple of lounges there's a fairly limp "Smart Casual" dress code – no dirty jeans, running shoes, short shorts or backpacks – but elsewhere you can wander freely. If you want to **take tea**, which is why most casual visitors are here, enter the *Tea Lounge* by the hotel's side entrance (the right, or south side): there you can enjoy scones, biscuits, cakes and, of course, tea over six courses but you have to abide by the dress code and be prepared for an enormous outlay.

The hotel's **Crystal Lounge** and its lovely Tiffany-glass dome form the most opulent part of the hotel on view, but the marginally less ornate entrance lounge is *the* place for the charade of afternoon tea, and indulging can be a bit of a laugh. There's also a reasonably priced bar and restaurant downstairs, **Kipling's**, and the attractive **Bengal Lounge**, complete with tiger-skin over the fireplace. Here, you can ask for just tea and scones or have a curry and all the trimmings for about $15. For a bigger treat, take dinner amid the Edwardian splendour of *the Empress Dining Room*.

The Old Town

The oldest part of Victoria lies in the streets north of the Inner Harbour, and focuses on **Bastion Square**, original site of Fort Victoria (of which little remains save a plaque). From here it's a short walk to Market Square, a nice piece of old-town rejuvenation, and the main downtown shopping streets. Bastion Square's former saloons, brothels and warehouses have been spruced up and turned into offices, cafés and galleries. The modest **Maritime Museum** at 28 Bastion Square (daily 9.30am–4.30pm; $6; ☎250/385-4222, Ⓦwww.mmbc.bc.ca) is of interest mainly for the lovely chocolate-and-vanilla-coloured building in which it's housed, the former provincial courthouse. Displays embrace old charts, uniforms, ships' bells, old photographs, lots of models and a new BC Ferries section on the second floor. On the top floor is the restored vice-admiralty courtroom, once the main seat of justice for the entire province. Note the old open elevator built to reach it, commissioned by Chief Justice Davie in 1901, supposedly because he was too fat to manage the stairs.

Two blocks to the north of the square lies the attractive **Market Square**, the old heart of Victoria but now a collection of some 65 speciality shops and cafés around a central courtyard (bounded by Store, Pandora and Johnson streets). This area boomed in 1858 following the gold rush, providing houses, saloons, opium dens, stores and various salacious entertainments for thousands of chancers and would-be immigrants. On the Pandora Avenue side of the area was a ravine, marked by the current sunken courtyard, beyond which lay **Chinatown** (now centred slightly further north on Fisgard St), the oldest on North America's west coast. Here, among other things, 23 factories processed 90,000 pounds of opium a year for what was then a legitimate trade and – until the twentieth century – one of BC's biggest industries.

As for the **shopping streets**, it's worth looking out for E A Morris, at 1110 Government St, a wonderful old cigar and tobacco shop next to *Murchie's* coffee shop (see p.233), and Roger's Chocolates, 913 Government St, whose whopping Victoria creams (among other things), are regularly dispatched to Buckingham Palace for royal consumption.

Emily Carr House

Ten rooms are open to the public at **Emily Carr House** (daily 10am–5pm; $5.35; ☎250/383-5843), two blocks from the Inner Harbour at 207 Government St. This was the early home of British Columbia's best-known artist (see box, p.54), born here during a blizzard in 1871 in the old wooden bed still visible in what would become her bedroom. The building was constructed in 1864, and has been painstakingly restored to its former state with an almost neurotic attention to detail. Fans of the artist may want to pay homage, but will have to visit the Art Gallery of Victoria to see her art; the works on the walls here are copies. Otherwise the appeal here is to see the interior of a typical upper-class Victorian Victoria home.

Craigdarroch Castle

Perched on a hilltop at 1050 Joan Crescent in Rockland, one of Victoria's more prestigious neighbourhoods, **Craigdarroch Castle** (mid-June to early Sept 9am–7pm; early Sept to mid-June 10am–4.30pm; $10; ☎250/592-5323, ⓦwww .craigdarrochcastle.com) was built by Robert Dunsmuir. A caricature of a Victorian politician, strike-breaker, robber baron and coal tycoon, Dunsmuir was the sort of man who could change an entire community's name on a whim (Ladysmith near Nanaimo used to be "Oyster Bay"). He was obliged to put up this gaunt Gothic pastiche to lure his wife away from Scotland, and a further idea of his megalomania is revealed by the fact that he wished to build his pile at the highest point in the city. Only the best was good enough, from the marble, granite and sandstone of the superstructure to the intricately handworked panels of the ceilings over the main hall and staircase. Unfortunately for the dastardly Dunsmuir, he died in 1889, two years after the castle was begun and a year before it was finished. Among the 39 rooms there's the usual clutter of Victoriana and period detail, in particular some impressive woodwork and stained and leaded glass.

To get here by **bus** take the #11-University or #14-University from downtown to the foot of Joan Crescent, two minutes' walk from the castle. If you decide to walk the whole way, allow 45 minutes from the Inner Harbour.

The Art Gallery of Victoria

Near Craigdarroch Castle at 1040 Moss St, just off Fort Street, the **Art Gallery of Greater Victoria** (Mon–Sat 10am–5pm, Thurs till 9pm, Sun 1–5pm; $5; ☎250/384-4101, ⓦwww.aggv.bc.ca) is of only moderate interest unless you're partial to contemporary Canadian paintings and the country's best collection of Japanese art. The building, housed in the 1890 Spencer Mansion, boasts what is claimed to be the only complete Shinto shrine outside Japan. It does, however, have a small permanent collection of Emily Carr's work (see box, p.54) as well as a temporary exhibition, usually interesting, that changes every six weeks.

To get here by **bus**, take the #10-Haultain, #11-Uplands/Beacon Hill or #14-University from downtown.

Point Ellice House and Gardens

The 1861 Victorian-Italianate **Point Ellice House and Gardens** (guided tours mid-May–mid-Sept daily noon–5pm; $5.35; ☎250/387-4697) at 2616 Pleasant St is magnificently re-created but less enticing than Craigdarroch Castle because of its slightly shabby surroundings. These can be overlooked, however, if you make a point of arriving by sea, taking one of the little Harbour

Ferry services to the house (10min) from the Inner Harbour. The restored Victorian-style gardens here are a delight on a summer afternoon. The interior – one of the best of its kind in western Canada – retains its largely Victorian appearance thanks partly to the reduced circumstances of the O'Reilly family, whose genteel slide into relative poverty over several generations (they lived here from 1861 to 1974) meant that many furnishings were simply not replaced. Tea, inevitably, is served on the lawns in the summer: it's a good idea to book ahead.

Bus #14-University will get you here from downtown if you don't fancy the approach by water.

Craigflower Manor and Farmhouse

In its day, **Craigflower Manor and Farmhouse** (May–Oct daily 10am–5pm; $5; ☎250/387-4697) on Admiral's Road about 9km and fifteen minutes' drive from downtown, was among the earliest of Victoria's farming homesteads, marking the town's transition from trading post to permanent community. It was built in a mock-Georgian style in 1856, apparently from timbers salvaged from the first four farmhouses built in the region. Its owner was Kenneth McKenzie, a Hudson's Bay Company bailiff, who recruited fellow Scottish settlers to form a farming community on Portage Inlet. The house was to remind him of the old country, and soon became the foremost social centre in the fledgling village – mainly visited by officers because McKenzie's daughters were virtually the only white women on the island. As with Point Ellice House and Gardens, reservations for tea are recommended.

Take **bus** #14-Craigflower from downtown.

The Butchart Gardens

If you're into things horticultural you'll want to make a trek out to the celebrated and much-hyped **Butchart Gardens**, 22km north of Victoria at 800 Benvenuto Ave, Brentwood Bay on Hwy 17 towards the Swartz Bay ferry terminal (daily: mid-June–Aug 9am–10.30pm, first two weeks of Sept & Dec 9am–9pm; rest of the year 9am–sunset; rates $10.50 in early Jan, then on a sliding scale through the year to $20 between mid-June and Sept; ☎250/652-4422 or 652-5256 for recorded information, ⓦwww.butchartgardens.com). The gardens are renowned among visitors and locals alike for the stunning **firework displays** that usually take place each Saturday evening in July and August. There is also a restaurant and various other commercial enterprises, with musical entertainment well to the fore. The gardens are also illuminated during the late-evening opening hours between mid-June and the end of September.

The gardens were started in 1904 by Jenny Butchart, wife of a mine-owner and pioneer of Portland Cement in Canada and the US, her initial aim being to landscape one of her husband's quarries. The garden now covers fifty breathtaking acres, comprising rose, Japanese and Italian gardens and lots of decorative details. About half a million visitors a year tramp through the foliage, which includes over a million plants and seven hundred different species. At the same time, the amount of space actually given over to gardens may strike you as slightly disproportionate to the space allotted to the car park, gift shop and restaurant.

To get here by public transport take **bus** #75 for "Central Saanich" from downtown. Otherwise, there are regular summer **shuttles** (May–Oct daily, hourly in the morning, half-hourly in the afternoon; ☎250/388-5248) from the main bus terminal, where tickets ($4) are obtainable not from the main ticket office but a separate Gray Lines desk.

The waters around Victoria are not as whale-rich as those around Tofino on the west coast of Vancouver Island, but there's still a very good chance of spotting the creatures. Three pods of orcas (killer whales) live in the seas around southern Vancouver Island, about a hundred creatures in all, so you may see these, though minke are the most common whale spotted, with occasional greys and humpbacks also present. Few outfits offer guaranteed sightings, and many cover themselves by preparing you for the fact that if you don't see whales you stand a good chance of seeing harbour and Dall's porpoises, harbour or elephant seals and California and Steller sea lions.

While there are many outfits to choose from, they offer almost identical trips at the same prices, typically around $60 to 90 for a three-hour outing. There's usually a naturalist, or at least a knowledgeable crew member, to fill you in on what you're seeing (or not). The only real variables are the **boats** used, so you need to decide whether you want rigid-hull cruisers (covered or uncovered), which are more comfortable and sedate (and usually the most expensive at around $90), a catamaran ($75–90), or the high-speed aluminium-hull inflatables known as "zodiacs" ($60–90), which are infinitely more exhilarating, but can offer a fast and sometimes bumpy ride that makes them unsuitable for pregnant women, young children or people with back problems. They won't have toilets on board either.

The two companies below have been around longer than most; the infocentre (p.221) will have details on other options.

Seacoast Expeditions is located across the Inner Harbour at the Boardwalk Level, Ocean Pointe Resort, 45 Songhees Rd (℡250/383-2254 or 1-800/386-1525, Ⓦwww.seacoastexpeditions.com). It's ten-minutes' walk across the Johnson Street bridge or a three-minute harbour ferry crossing to Seacoast: it also has a shuttle-bus pick-up from downtown hotels. Victoria's founding whale-watching company, it's been in the business over a decade and offers one trip daily in April and October, four three-hour trips daily in May, June and September, and five daily in July and August ($79). It also offers a guaranteed sighting deal (May–Aug only) whereby you carry a pager that tells you to turn up at the office for a tour only when whales have been spotted. All trips are in one of the company's three zodiacs.

Five Star Charters at 706 Douglas St (℡250/388-7223 or 1-800/634-9617, Ⓦwww.5starwhales.com) has been in business since 1985 and in the past claimed the highest percentage of whale sightings out of all the tour operators (thanks to spotter boats and a good network of contacts). It runs three daily three-hour trips from mid-April through to September ($79) and two daily two-hour trips from October to mid-April ($60). Trips are in 12-passenger open cruisers or 40-person "Supercat" boats.

Eating, drinking and nightlife

Although clearly in Vancouver's culinary shadow, Victoria still has a plethora of **restaurants**, some extremely good, offering greater variety – and higher prices – than you'll find in most other BC towns. **Pubs** tend to be plastic imitations of their British equivalents, with one or two worthy exceptions, as do the numerous **cafés** that pander to Victoria's self-conscious afternoon-tea ritual. Good snacks and pastry shops abound, while at the other extreme there are budget-busting establishments if you want a one-off treat or a change from the standard Canadian menus that await you on much of the rest of the island.

Nocturnal diversions in Victoria are for the most part tame: highbrow tastes, though, are surprisingly well catered for, and there's a smattering of **bars**, as well as **live music** venues and **clubs** to keep you happy for the limited time you're likely to spend in the city. **Jazz** is particularly popular – for information on the city's jazz underground, contact the Victoria Jazz Society, 250-727 Johnson St (℡250/388-4423, ⓦwww.vicjazz.bc.ca).

Listings appear in the main daily newspaper, the *Times-Colonist*, and in a variety of free magazines (titles change from year to year) you can pick up in shops, cafés and hotels: the latest is the excellent *Monday Magazine* (ⓦwww.mondaymag.com), published every Thursday. **Tickets** for most offerings are available from the city's main performance space, the McPherson Playhouse, 3 Centennial Square, Pandora and Government streets (℡250/386-6121 or 1-888-717-6121, ⓦwww.rmts.bc.ca).

Cafés, tea and snacks

Barb's Fish and Chips 310 St Lawrence St, Fisherman's Wharf, off Kingston St ℡250/384-6515. A much-loved floating shack that offers classic home-cut chips, fish straight off the boat and oyster burgers and chowder to boot: the small bathtub-size ferries from the Inner Harbour drop you close by.

Blethering Place 2250 Oak Bay Ave ℡250/598-1413 or 1-888/598-1413. Along with the *Empress Hotel*, this rather over-rated spot is known as a place to indulge in the tea-taking custom. Scones, cakes and dainty sandwiches are served up against the background of hundreds of toby jugs and royal-family memorabilia.

Demitasse Coffee Bar 320 Blanshard St near Pandora Ave ℡250/386-4442. A popular, elegantly laid-back hole-in-the-wall café with excellent coffee, salads, bagels, lunch-time snacks, and an open fire in season. Recommended.

Dutch Bakery & Coffee Shop 718 Fort St ℡250/385-1052. A Victoria institution serving pastries and chocolate to take away. You can also eat in the popular if plain coffee shop at the back.

Empress Hotel 721 Government St ℡250/348-8111. Try tea in the lobby, with tourists and locals alike on their best behaviour amidst the chintz and potted plants. A strict dress code allows no dirty jeans, anoraks or sportswear.

Murchie's 1110 Government St ℡250/381-5451. This long-established place, with high quality produce, is the best retreat for basic tea, coffee and cakes in the centre of Victoria's shopping streets.

Re-Bar 50 Bastion Square at Langley St ℡250/360-2401. A great place that serves teas, coffees (charcoal-filtered water) and health food at lunch (usually organically grown), but most remarkable for its extraordinary range of fresh-squeezed juices in strange combinations, smoothies, "power tonics" and frighteningly healthy wheatgrass drinks (Astro Turf: a blend of carrot, beetroot, garlic and wheatgrass).

Sally's 714 Cormorant St near Douglas St ℡250/381-1431. Funky little café that's very popular with locals and local office workers despite its location on the northern edge of downtown. Drop by if you're up this way, but don't come specially.

Restaurants

Da Tandoor 1010 Fort St ℡250/384-6333. Tandoori specialist that is, with the *Taj Mahal*, the best of Victoria's half-dozen or so Indian restaurants offering good food and a definitely over-the-top interior.

Earl's 1703 Blanshard St and Fisgard St ℡250/386-4323. You'll find an *Earl's* in many Canadian towns, but the restaurants are none the worse for being part of a chain: good – not fast – food, with a lively, pleasant interior and friendly service.

Herald Street Café 546 Herald St ℡250/381-1441. An excellent and stylish old favourite for Italian food with a northwest twist such as wild Pacific salmon, pesto and Roma tomato relish, and rack of lamb with a rosemary crust and baked garlic mustard cream. Pricey, but good value, along with a relaxed atmosphere and lots of art on the walls. Well worth the walk from the Inner Harbour.

Il Terrazzo 555 Johnson St, Waddington Alley ℡250/361-0028. Smooth, laid-back ambience with lots of red brick and plants and a summer patio that provides the setting for good North American versions of Italian food. With *Pagliacci's* (see below), this is the best place in town for moderately priced Italian food.

Milestone's 812 Wharf St ☎ 250/381-2244. Popular mid-priced place for burgers, pastas, steaks and the like, slap-bang on the Inner Harbour beneath the infocentre, so expect lots of bustle, passing trade and good views.

Pagliacci's 1011 Broad St between Fort and Broughton ☎ 250/386-1662. The best restaurant in Victoria if you want a fast, furious atmosphere, live music, good Italian food and excellent desserts. A rowdy throng begins to queue almost from the moment the doors are open.

Süze 515 Yates St ☎ 250/383-2829. This is a great place for an early or late-evening drink, thanks to its snug, informal and vaguely exotic feel, and to its wonderful broad bar. Its eclectic menu ranges from Asian cuisine to steak, pasta, chicken and seafood, which you can take either at tables up on the tiny mezzanine or in the cozy dining room through the velvet curtains to the right.

Taj Mahal 679 Herald St ☎ 250/383-4662. Housed in a mini Taj Mahal and a bit of a walk from the centre, this restaurant serves good and inexpensive Indian food with chicken, lamb and tandoori specialities.

Bars and pubs

Bartholomew's Bar and Rockefeller Grill Executive House Hotel, 777 Douglas St ☎ 250/388-5111. This is an upbeat pub with a steady diet of local bands. For the same sort of place, try *Steamers,* 570 Yates St, where you'll catch enthusiastic local bands most nights, and most types of music from reggae to Celtic.

Big Bad John's 919 Douglas St ☎ 250/383-7137. Next to the *Strathcona Hotel* this is Victoria's most atmospheric bar by far, with bare boards, a fog of smoke, and authentic old banknotes and IOUs pasted to the walls. It also hosts occasional live bands and singers, usually of a country-music persuasion.

D'Arcy McGee's 1127 Wharf St ☎ 250/380-1322. It was only a matter of time before Victoria acquired an "Irish pub". This one has a prime site on the edge of Bastion Square, offers predictable food and beer, and has excellent occasional live Irish music.

Spinnakers BrewPub 308 Catherine St near Esquimalt Rd ☎ 250/384-6613. Bus #23 to Esquimalt Rd. Thirty-eight beers, including several home-brewed options, a restaurant, live music, occasional tours of the brewery and good harbour views draw a mixed and relaxed clientele.

Swans Brewpub 506 Pandora Ave at Store St ☎ 250/361-3310. This pretty and highly popular hotel-café-brewery, housed in a 1913 warehouse, is the place to watch Victoria's young professionals at play. Several foreign and six home-brewed beers on tap, with the *Neptune* nightclub (see review below) in the basement.

Clubs and live music

Esquimalt Inn 856 Esquimalt Rd ☎ 250/382-7161. A long-established venue with country bands most nights and occasional jam sessions. Take bus #23.

Evolution 502 Discovery St ☎ 250/388-3000. One of Victoria's more interesting clubs and discos, thanks to plenty of techno, rave and alternative sounds.

Hermann's Jazz Club 753 View St ☎ 250/388-9166. Dimly lit club thick with 1950s atmosphere that specializes in Dixieland but has occasional excursions into fusion and blues.

Legends 919 Douglas St ☎ 250/383-7137. The biggest, best and noisiest of the live-music venues, this club occupies the garish, neon-lit basement of the *Strathcona Hotel*. Varied live bands, including the occasional big name, and dancing nightly.

Neptune Soundbar 1605 Store St at Pandora Ave ☎ 250/360-9098. You may well have to queue to join the thirty-something crew who frequent the basement disco of *Swans Brewpub*. 1960s and 1970s classics generally rule as well as current Top 40 fodder, but there's also a sprinkling of hip-hop and more modern offerings.

Festivals in Victoria

Summer brings out the buskers and **free entertainment** in Victoria's people-places – James Bay, Market Square and Beacon Hill Park in particular. Annual highlights include:

TerrifVic Jazz Party, April ☎250/953-2011. A showcase for about a dozen top international bands held over four days.

Jazz Fest, June ☎250/386-6121, ⓦwww.vicjazz.bc.ca. More than a hundred assorted lesser-known bands perform in Market Square.

Canada Day, July 1. Celebration of Canada's national day concentrated in and around the Inner Harbour, and includes fireworks, food, music and other cultural events.

Victoria International Festival, July and August ☎250/736-2119. Victoria's largest general arts jamboree.

Folk Fest, last week of July ☎250/388-4728. Multicultural arts extravaganza.

First People's Festival, early August ☎250/384-3211. A celebration of the cultures of Canada's aboriginal peoples.

Canadian International Dragon Boat Festival, mid-August ☎250/472-2628, ⓦwwwvictoriadragonboat.com. Over 100 international teams take part in dragon-boat races on the Inner Harbour.

Classic Boat Festival, August 30–September 1 ☎250/385-7766. Dozens of wooden antique boats are on display at this festival.

Royal Victoria Marathon, early October ☎250/658-0951, ⓦwww.royalvictoriamarathon.com. Marathon and half-marathon around the city streets and surroundings held on the Canadian Thanksgiving weekend.

Fringe Festival, September ☎250/383-2663. Avant-garde performances of all kinds.

The Great Canadian Beer Festival, second week of November ☎250/952-0360. Selections of beer from some of the province's best micro-breweries can be tasted at the Victoria Conference Centre, 720 Douglas St.

Merrython Fun Run, mid-December ☎250/953-2033. A 10-kilometre run through downtown Victoria.

Listings

American Express 1213 Douglas St (Mon–Fri 8.30am–5pm, Sat 10am–4pm; ☎250/385-8731).

Bike rental Cycle Victoria Rentals, 950 Wharf St (☎250/885-2453 or 1-877/869-0039, ⓦwww.cyclevictoriarentals.com); Harbour Rentals, 811 Wharf St (☎250/995-1661 or 1-877-733-6722), rent a big range of bikes (from $6 an hour, $19 daily) plus five types of scooter (from $12 per hour, $45 daily); also kayaks, rowing boats, motor boats and motor bikes.

Bus information Airporter shuttle bus from Victoria Airport (☎250/386-2525 or 1-877/386-2525, ⓦwww.akalairporter.travel.bc.ca). For services to Vancouver, there's Pacific Coast Lines (☎604/662-8074 in Vancouver or 250/385-4411 at the Victoria bus terminal, ⓦwww.pacificcoach.com); for services on the island, Laidlaw (☎250/385-4411, 388-5248 or 1-800/318-0818, ⓦwww.grayline.ca/victoria). Both operate from the bus terminal at 700 Douglas St and Belleville St, which also has an office for Greyhound (☎250/388-5248 or 1-800/663-8390, ⓦwww.greyhound.com).

Car rental Avis, 62B-1001 Douglas St (☎250/386-8468 or 1-800/879-2847) and Victoria Airport (☎250/656-6033); Budget, 757 Douglas St (☎250/953-5300 or 1-800/268-8900); National, 767 Douglas St (☎250/386-1213 or 1-800/227-7368).

Doctor and dentist Most hotels have a doctor or dentist on call. Otherwise contact Cresta Dental Centre in the Tillicum Street Mall at 3170 Tillicum Rd, Burnside St (☎250/384-7711). The Tillicum Mall Medical

Clinic at the same address (℡250/381-8112) accepts walk-in patients.
Equipment rental Sports Rent, 1950 Government St at Discovery (℡250/385-7368, ⓦwww.sportsrentbc.com). Rents a colossal range of equipment, including bikes, rollerblades, all camping, hiking, climbing and diving gear.
Ferries BC Ferries (℡250/386-3431 or 1-888-223-3779, ⓦwww.bcferries.com); Black Ball Transport (℡250/386-2202 or 360/457-4491 in Port Angeles, ⓦww.northolympic .com/coho); Victoria Clipper (℡250/382-8100, 206/448-5000 or 1-800/888-2535, ⓦwww.victoriaclipper.com); Washington State Ferries (℡250/382-1551 or 1-800/542-7052, ⓦwww.wsdof.wa.gov/ferries).
Hospital Victoria General Hospital, 35 Helmcken Rd (℡250/727-4212).
Post office Main office, 714 Yates St at Douglas (℡250/953-1352, 1-800/267-1177 in Canada). Mon–Fri 8.30am–5pm.
Taxis Blue Bird Cabs (℡382-4235); Empress Cabs (℡250/381-2222); Victoria Taxi (℡250/383-7111).
Train information VIA Rail, 450 Pandora Ave (℡250/383-4324 or 1-800/561-8630 in Canada and 1-800/561-3949 in the US, ⓦwww.viarail.ca).
Weather Victoria Environment Canada Weatherline (℡250/656-3978).

The Gulf Islands

Scattered between Vancouver Island and the mainland lie several hundred tiny islands, most no more than lumps of rock, a few large enough to hold permanent populations and warrant a regular ferry service. Two main clusters are accessible from Victoria: the **Gulf Islands** and the San Juan Islands, both part of the same archipelago, except that the latter group belongs to the United States.

You get a good look at the Gulf Islands on the seaplanes from Vancouver (see p.239) or on the ferry from Tsawwassen – twisting and threading through their coves and channels, the ride sometimes seems even a little too close for comfort. The coastline makes for superb **sailing**, and an armada of small boats criss-crosses between the islands whenever the weather allows. Hikers and campers are well served, and **fishing** is also good – some of the world's biggest salmon having met their doom in the surrounding waters. Indeed, there's an abundance of marine wildlife here featuring sea lions, orcas, seals, bald eagles, herons, cormorants, all of which you stand a good chance of seeing both on the islands and from the inter-island ferries. And while the climate is hardly "Mediterranean" as claimed in the tourist blurbs, it is mild and the vegetation is particularly lush, making the Gulf Islands the dream idyll of many people from Washington State and British Columbia, whether they're artists, writers, pensioners or dropouts from the mainstream. For full details of what they're all up to, grab a copy of the local listings, the *Gulf Islander* (published annually), distributed on the islands and the ferries, or the *Gulf Islands Driftwood*, the islands' newspaper (published every Wednesday).

Have your **accommodation** worked out well in advance in summer. **Campers** should have few problems finding sites, most of which are located in the islands' provincial parks, though at peak times you'll want to arrive before noon to ensure a pitch – there are reservations in some parks. For help with B&Bs, use the *BC Accommodations* guide and the BC tourism phone and website (☎604/435-5622 or 1-800/435-5622, ⓦwww.HelloBC.com), or contact the Victoria infocentre or **specialist agencies** such as the Canadian Gulf Islands B&B Reservation Service (☎1-888/539-2930, ⓦwww.gulfislandsreservations.com).

Getting to the islands

BC Ferries (☎250/386-3431 or 1-800/223-3779, ⓦwww.bcferries.com) sails to five of the Gulf Islands – **Salt Spring**, **Pender**, **Saturna**, **Mayne** and **Galiano** – from Swartz Bay, 33km north of Victoria on Hwy 17. Reckon on at least two crossings to each daily, but be prepared for all boats to be jammed

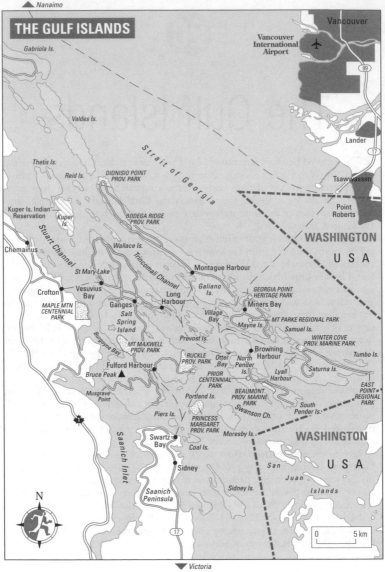

THE GULF ISLANDS

Nanaimo

Gabriola Is.

Vancouver

Vancouver International Airport

99

Valdes Is.

Lander

Thetis Is.

Strait of Georgia

17

Reid Is.

DIONISIO POINT PROV. PARK

Tsawwassen

Kuper Is. Indian Reservation

Kuper Is.

BODEGA RIDGE PROV. PARK

Point Roberts

Chemainus

Stuart Channel

Wallace Is.

WASHINGTON

St Mary Lake

Trincomali Channel

USA

Crofton

Vesuvius Bay

Montague Harbour

Galiano Is.

GEORGIA POINT HERITAGE PARK

MAPLE MTN CENTENNIAL PARK

Ganges

Long Harbour

Miners Bay

Salt Spring Island

Village Bay

MT PARKE REGIONAL PARK

Mayne Is.

Samuel Is.

Prevost Is.

WINTER COVE PROV. MARINE PARK

Burgoyne Bay

MT MAXWELL PROV. PARK

RUCKLE PROV. PARK

Otter Bay

Browning Harbour

Saturna Is.

Tumbo Is.

Fulford Harbour

North Pender Is.

Lyall Harbour

Bruce Peak ▲

PRIOR CENTENNIAL PARK

EAST POINT REGIONAL PARK

Musgrave Point

Portland Is.

BEAUMONT PROV. MARINE PARK

South Pender Is.

Piers Is.

PRINCESS MARGARET PROV. PARK

Swanson Ch.

Moresby Is.

WASHINGTON

Saanich Inlet

Swartz Bay

Coal Is.

USA

Sidney

San

N

Saanich Peninsula

Sidney Is.

Juan

Islands

0   5 km

17

Victoria

solid during the summer. Visit the website or pick up the company's *Gulf Islands* timetable, widely available on boats and in the mainland infocentres, which is invaluable if you aim to exploit the many inter-island connections. All the ferries take cars, bikes and motorbikes, though with a car you'll need to make a **reservation** (☎250/386-3431 or 1-888/223-3779). Bear in mind that there's next to no public transport on the islands, so what few taxis there are can charge more or less what they wish. It only costs around $2 to take bikes on board, and cycling can be a great way to see the islands – most are small (if hilly), with few roads, the majority of them quiet.

A quicker and equally scenic way of approaching some of the islands is to take a float plane. Harbour Air (☎604/274-1277 or 1-800/665-0212, ⓦwww.harbour-air.com) flies from Vancouver (the terminal is just west of Canada Place) to Salt Spring (Ganges Harbour) for $74 one-way.

Salt Spring Island

SALT SPRING (pop. 9500), sometimes spelt Saltspring, is the biggest (at twenty kilometres by ten), most populated and most visited of the islands – its population triples in summer – though if you're without transport think twice about coming here on a day-trip as getting around is pretty tough. It's served by Harbour Air seaplanes from Vancouver (see above) and three ferry terminals: **Fulford Harbour** in the south, from Victoria's Swartz Bay (ten sailings daily, more in summer; 35min; foot passengers $6.25/$6 round-trip, cars $20/$17.25) and **Vesuvius Bay** in the northwest (from Crofton, near Duncan on Vancouver Island; 13 daily; 20min; same fares) provide links to Vancouver Island; **Long Harbour** midway down the east coast connects to points on the BC mainland, notably Tsawwassen, usually via other islands.

The last is also the main terminal for inter-island travel. In the past the Salt Spring Island Bus service has connected the ferry terminals with **Ganges**, the island's main village on the east coast 5km from Long Harbour, but check with the Victoria or local infocentre (see below) for the latest. For more complicated journeys, call up the Silver Shadow Taxi (☎250/537-3030) or rent **a bike** from the Salt Spring Kayaking & Cycling, 2923 Fulford-Ganges Rd, Fulford Harbour (☎250/653-4222, ⓦwww.saltspring.com/sskayak). Rates start at $5 hourly, $25 for 24hrs and $35 for two days. Kayak rentals are $12 hourly ($20 for a double kayak) and $45 daily ($80). If necessary the company will deliver bikes or kayaks to where you are staying on the island for $15. You can also rent a scooter, kayak or car from Salt Spring Island Marina (☎1-800/334-6629, ⓦwww.mobyspub.com), one of several rental places near *Moby's Marine Pub* (☎537-5559) – a very popular local hang-out for drinks, meals and occasional live music in Ganges at 124 Upper Ganges Rd.

The Island

Most enjoyment on Salt Spring, as with the other Gulf Islands, is to be had from sinking back into its laid-back approach to life: grabbing a coffee at a café overlooking the water, browsing galleries, cycling the back roads, hiking the odd easy trail, and so on. If you're here to slum it on a **beach**, the best strips are on the island's more sheltered east side – Beddis Beach in particular, off the Fulford to Ganges road – and at Vesuvius Bay in the northwest and at Drummond Park near Fulford in the south.

Beddis can be visited en route to one of the best parks in the Gulf Islands, the **Ruckle Provincial Park** (always open; free), 486 hectares of lovely forest, field and maritime scenery tucked in the island's southeast corner 10km east of Fulford Harbour. It has 15km–worth of trails, most leaving from trailheads at Beaver Point, the rocky headland that marks the end of the access road – the best path marches north from here along the coast of tiny coves and rocky headlands to Yeo Point. The park also has an outstanding campsite at the end of the access road (see below), but note that there are no reservations - it is first-come, first-served. The island's other main park, **Mount Maxwell Provincial Park, lies** midway up the west coast: its mountain provides a tremendous 588-metre viewpoint of the island-dotted ocean. The park is accessed on Cranberry Rd, which strikes west midway down the island off the main Ganges to Fulford road.

Ganges, close to Long Harbour on the east coast, is armed with a small **infocentre (see below)** and a rapidly proliferating assortment of galleries, tourist shops and holiday homes. Community spirits reach a climax during the annual **Artcraft** (late June to mid-Sept), a summer crafts fair in Ganges' Mahon Hall that displays the talents of the island's many dab-handed creatives. The other main focus for cultural events is ArtSpring, 100 Jackson, Ganges (☎250/537-2102 or 1-866/537-2102, ⓦwww.artspring.ca), a summer festival of the performing arts (July–Aug). Between April and October, head for the Saturday Market (Sat 8.30am–3pm; ⓦwww.saltspringmarket.com) in Ganges' Centennial Park for food and crafts.

Practicalities

Ganges' infocentre, at 121 Lower Ganges Rd (daily 10am–4pm; ☎250/537-5252 or 537-4223, ⓦwww.saltspringtoday.com), is the place to check out the island's relatively plentiful **accommodation**. Otherwise you can choose from the hundred or more (but often rather exorbitant) B&B options (owners can arrange to pick you up from the ferry) or one of the so-called "resorts" dotted round the island – usually a handful of houses with camping, a few rooms to rent and little else. Each of the ferry terminals also has a range of mid-price motels. The best bets in each of three terminals are the twelve-unit *Beachcomber Motel* at 770 Vesuvius Bay Rd at Vesuvius Bay 7km from Ganges (☎250/537-5415 or 1-866/537-5415, ⓕ537-1753, ❹) – some rooms have sea views and some have kitchenettes; the *Harbour House Hotel*, 121 Upper Ganges Rd, Ganges (☎250/537-5571 or 1-

888/799-5571, Ⓔharbourhouse@saltspring.com; ❹), with waterfront dining and some rooms with ocean views; and the 28-unit *Seabreeze Inn* in an attractive park-like setting above Ganges harbour at 101 Bittancourt Rd (☎250/537-4145 or 1-800/434-4112, Ⓦwww.seabreezeinns.com; ❺).

A lot of independent travellers are lured here by the prospect of the lovely official HI-affiliated *Salt Spring Island Hostel*, set amid ten peaceful acres on the eastern side of the island (5km south of Ganges and just over a kilometre from Beddis Beach) at 640 Cusheon Lake Rd (☎250/537-4149; closed Nov–mid-March; check-in 5–8pm). Under your own steam from Victoria, take the #70 Pat Bay Hwy bus ($2.50) to the Swartz Bay ferry terminal. Catch the ferry to Fulford Harbour ($6.25 round-trip) and ask car drivers disembarking the ferry if they're headed past the hostel on Cusheon Lake Road: if they're locals, and en route for Ganges, most say yes. You can choose between dorm rooms in a cedar lodge ($17 for members, $21 for nonmembers), three tepees, two adult and family tree houses (be sure to book these and be prepared to pay around $65) and private family rooms ($40–70) – 35 beds in all. Note, however, that there's no camping, but you can rent bikes and scooters. It's just a short walk to Cusheon Lake to the northwest or the ocean at Beddis Beach to the southeast.

The island's best **campsite** is to be found in Ruckle Provincial Park. The magnificent waterfront 78-pitch site ($14 in summer, $9 in winter; day-use parking $3) is at Beaver Point, and is reached by following Beaver Point Road from the Fulford Harbour ferry terminal (10km).

One of the island's best **places to eat** is *The Vesuvius Inn* (☎250/537-2312) alongside the ferry at 805 Vesuvius Bay Rd, blessed with live music nightly and a great **bar** deck overlooking the harbour where you can eat expensive seafood and the usual range of pastas, chickens and salads. In Ganges, there are numerous **cafés** and coffee shops for high-quality sandwiches: for something more ambitious, try the appealing *Treehouse Café-Restaurant*, 106 Purvis Lane (☎250/537-5379), which serves breakfast, lunch and dinner and has places to sit outside and low-key live (often acoustic) music most nights of the week. For a treat, the place to go is *House Piccolo*, 108 Hereford Ave, Ganges (☎250/537-1844, dinner only), which has won *Wine Spectator* magazine awards for its excellent wine list and serves sublime European and Scandinavian food.

Galiano Island

Long and finger-shaped, **Galiano** (pop. 1040) lies to the northwest of Salt Spring. It is just 27km from north to south and barely five kilometres wide, but it remains one of the more promising and less-developed islands to visit if you want variety and a realistic chance of finding somewhere to stay. There are two ferry terminals: **Sturdies Bay** in the southeast, which takes boats from the mainland (foot passengers $10, cars $36.50), and **Montague Harbour** on the west coast, which handles the Vancouver Island crossings from Swartz Bay (foot passengers $6.50/$6.25, cars $22.25/$19.50). You can also get here with the Gulf Islands Water Taxi (see box opposite) and there are inter-island *BC Ferries* connections (1–4 daily) from Salt Spring via Pender and Mayne. *Go Galiano Island Shuttle* (☎250/539-0202) provides a taxi service.

The **infocentre** is a booth at Sturdies Bay at 2590 Sturdies Bay Rd (July–Aug daily 9am–5/6pm; ☎1-866/539-2233 or 539-2507 off season, Ⓦwww.galianoisland.com). For **bike rentals**, contact *Galiano Bicycle Rental* at 36 Burrill Rd in Sturdies Bay (☎250/539-9906; four hours $23, day $28).

If you're **canoeing**, stick to the calmer waters, cliffs and coves off the west coast. You can rent kayaks or join guided kayak tours at *Galiano Island Kayaking* at the marina at Montague Harbour (☎250/539-2442, ⓦwww.seakayak.ca). **Hikers** can walk almost the entire length of the east coast, or climb Mount Sutil (323m) or Mount Galiano (342m) for views of the mainland mountains. To reach the trailhead for the latter, take Burrill south from the ferry at Sturdies Bay and along Bluff Rd through the forest of Bluffs Park. A left fork, Active Pass Drive, takes you to the trailhead (a total of 5km from the ferry). The locals' favourite **beach** can be found at Coon Bay on the island's northern tip, but there are excellent marine landscapes and beaches elsewhere, notably at **Montague Harbour Provincial Marine Park** (always open; free), 10km from the Sturdies Bay ferry terminal on the west side of the island (and immediately in and around the Montagu Harbour terminal). The park has stretches of shell and pebble foreshore, a café, shop, three-kilometre waterfront trail to Gray Peninsula (though you can easily forge you own foreshore walks) and, more to the point, a glorious provincial campsite ($17 in summer, $9 in winter; 15 walk-in reservable tent sites, and 25 drive-in sites, of which eight are reservable). Booking is essential in summerl.

Practicalities

For a comfortable **stay** in peaceful and elegant surroundings (close to Montague Harbour Provincial Marine Park), try the excellent 12-room *Woodstone Country Inn* (☎250/539-2022 or 1-888/339-2022, ⒺWoodstone@ gulfislands.com; ❺) on Georgeson Bay Road, 4km from the ferry: breakfast and afternoon tea are included in the price. Right at Studies Bay is the very pleasant 10-room *Galiano Inn*, 134 Madronna Drive (☎205/539-3388, ⓦwww.galianoinn.com; ❼), though rates include gourmet breakfast in the downstairs restaurant. For a lovely and romantic stay, head for one of the three rooms at the *Bellhouse Inn*, 29 Farmhouse Rd (☎1-800/970-7464, ⓦwww.bellhouseinn.com; ❻), a historic waterfront farmhouse set in beautiful grounds with sandy beach and great ocean views; breakfast is included in the room rate. A good choice on the island's quieter northern end are the seven log cabins of the *Bodega Resort*, at 120 Monastee Rd off Porlier Pass Drive and Cook Drive (☎250/539-2677, ⓦwww.cedarplace.com/bodega; ❸), complete with kitchens and wood-burning stoves and set in acres of woods and meadows with sea views.

For **food and drink** – and to meet locals – the island's main pub, the *Hummingbird Inn* (☎250/539-5472) is about 2km away from Sturdies Bay at 47 Sturdies Bay Road. Food is reasonable at the *Hummingbird*, likewise at *La Bérengerie*, about the same distance from Montague Harbour on the corner of Montague and Clanton roads (☎250/539-5392), a genteel restaurant with refined French-influenced menu that usually rents three B&B rooms (❸) upstairs.

North and South Pender

The somnolent bridge-linked islands of **North** and **South Pender** occupy just 24 square kilometre and muster about two thousand people between them, many of whom will try to entice you into their studios to buy local arts and crafts. Otherwise you are here to swim, snooze or walk on one of the many tiny **beaches** – there's accessible public ocean at some twenty points around the island. Two of the best are Hamilton Beach near Browning Beach on the east coast of North Pender and Mortimer Spit just south of the bridge that links the two islands. The latter spot is also the place to pick up trails to Mount Norman and Beaumont Provincial Marine Park.

Ferries come to North Pender from Swartz Bay (up to 7 daily; 40min direct or 2hr via Galiano and/Mayne; foot passengers $6.50/$6.25, cars $22.25/$19.50) and Tsawwassen (foot-passenger one-way tickets cost $10/$9.75, less off peak; cars $36.50/$31.50). The **infocentre** booth is just east up the hill from the ferry terminal in **Otter Bay** on the island's west coast at 2332 Otter Bay Rd (daily mid-May to early Sept 9am–6pm; ☎250/629-6541) on North Pender, home to the Otter Bay Marina, where you can rent **bikes** and buy maps for a tour of the islands' rolling, hilly interior.

Accommodation-wise there are a handful of B&Bs, and a small wooded **campsite** at Prior Centennial Provincial Park, 6km south of the Otter Bay ferry terminal (March–Sept; $14). For the only hotel-type rooms, try the 12-room *Inn on Pender Island*, prettily situated in 7.5 acres of wooded country near Prior Park at 4709 Canal Rd, North Pender (☎250/629-3353 or 1-800/550-0172, ⓦwww.innonpender.com; ❹); or the newly refurbished *Poets Cove at Bedwell Harbour*, a plush resort at 9801 Spalding Rd, South Pender (☎250/629-3212 or 1-888/512-7638, ⓦwww.poetscove.com; ❼), which boasts a pool, marina, bistro–pub, restaurant, store, tennis, harbour views, canoe, boat and bike rentals, and a choice of rooms or cabins; or the three fully equipped self-catering cottages 500m sharp left from the ferry at *Arcadia by the Sea*, 1325 MacKinnon Rd, North Pender (☎250/629-3221 or 1-877-470-8439, ⓦwww.arcadiabythesea.com; ❺; mid-April–Oct), with tennis court, outdoor pool and private decks.

Mayne Island

Mayne is the first island to your left (Galiano is on your right) if you're crossing from Tsawwassen to Swartz Bay – which is perhaps as close as you'll get, since it's the quietest and most difficult to reach of the islands served by ferries (one-way tickets from Tsawwassen via Galiano/Montague Harbour in high season cost foot passengers $10, cars cost $36.50). It also has few places to stay, so, as ever in the Gulf Islands, aim to fix up accommodation before you arrive. The island's remoteness may be as good a reason as any for heading out here, however, particularly if you have a bike to explore the quiet country roads that snake over the island's 21 square kilometres. Best of several **beaches** is Bennett Bay, a sheltered strip with warm water and good sand. It's reached by heading east from the island's principal community at Miner's Bay (5min from the ferry terminal at Village Bay on the west coast) to the end of Fernhill Road and then turning left onto Wilks Road. If you want to **walk**, try the 45-minute climb up Mount Parke in the eponymous regional park: it starts near the Fernhill Centre on Montrose Rd.

Village Bay – don't be fooled by the name: there's no village – has a summer-only **infocentre** booth (daily 9am–6pm; no phone, ⓦwww.mayneislandchamber .ca), which should be able to fill you in on the limited (currently seven) but expanding number of **B&B** possibilities – though the island is small enough to explore as a day-trip. Try the *Blue Vista Cottages*, eight fully equipped cabins overlooking Bennett Bay at 563 Arbutus Drive 6km from the ferry terminal (☎250/539-2463 or 1-877/535-2424, ⓦwww.bluevistaresort.com; ❸), with ferry pick-up, handy sandy beach, park–like setting and bike, canoe and kayak rental. The *Tinkerer's B&B* on Miner's Bay at 417 Sunset Place off Georgina Point Road (☎250/539-2280; ❹; April to Oct), 2.4km from the Village Bay ferry terminal, is nicely offbeat: it rents bikes, provides hammocks and offers "demonstrations of medicinal herb and flower gardens". For a real treat, the best **food** around (and excellent if expensive lodgings) is to be found at the waterfront *Oceanwood Country Inn*, 2km south of the ferry at 630 Dinner Bay

Rd (℡250/539-5074, Ⓦwww.oceanwood.com; ❼; March–Nov), which has 12 smart rooms, sauna, oceanfront hot tub and a superb, quiet garden setting. The fixed four-course dinner menu (with choice of two main courses) changes daily, but typical dishes might include sorrel and spinach soup with goat's cheese mousse, Mayne Island lamb and rosemary caramel roasted apples.

Saturna Island

Saturna, to the south, is another **B&B** hideaway. There are daily **ferries** from Swartz Bay on Vancouver Island (2–3 daily; $6.25 round-trip for foot passengers, vehicles $21.50) and from Tsawwassen but only via Mayne. The island boasts some good **beaches**, the best being at Russell Reef and Winter Cove Marine Park (no campsite) on its northwest tip. There's walking, wildlife and good views to the mainland from Mount Warburton Pike (497m) and on Brown Bridge in the southwest of the island.

If Saturna grips you long enough **to stay** over, try the three-room waterfront *Lyall Harbour B&B* (℡250/539-5577 or 1-877/473-9343; ❺), 500m from the ferry at 121 East Point Rd in Saturna Point, home to a shop and modest **infocentre** (May–Sept daily 8am–6pm; no phone, Ⓦwww.saturnatourism .bc.ca). Another relatively large place to stay is the *East Point Resort*, East Point Road (℡250/539-2975; ❺), situated in a park-like setting near a gradually sloping sandy beach; the six cabins are fully equipped and you can choose between one- and two-bedroom units – note that in July and August there's generally a minimum stay of a week (no credit cards). There are no campgrounds and only one or two places to eat, notably the pub-restaurant at the modern, waterfront *Saturna Lodge,* 130 Payne Rd (℡250/539-2254, Ⓦwww.saturna-island.bc.ca; ❻; May–Oct), which also has seven rooms to rent: rates include breakfast.

Whistler and the Sunshine Coast

A part from Victoria and the Southern Gulf Islands, two other major excursions from Vancouver are possible, each of which can easily be extended to embrace longer itineraries out of the city. The first, and less enticing, is the 150-kilometre Sunshine Coast, the only stretch of accessible coastline on mainland British Columbia, and a possible springboard to Vancouver Island: ferries depart from Powell River, the coast's largest town, to Comox on Vancouver Island. Most people on short trips, however, make the run to Powell River and then turn tail for Vancouver – there is no alternative route back to the city and no onward road route after the village of Lund and the end of Hwy 101 beyond Powell River.

The second, and far more tempting trip is the inland route to **Garibaldi Provincial Park**, which contains by far the best scenery and hiking country within striking distance of Vancouver, and the famous world-class ski resort of **Whistler**. The latter is well worth visiting at any time of the year, with winter an obviously busy time and summer almost equally popular, thanks to the area's many outdoor activities. En route to Whistler you'll pass through **Squamish**, nothing to rave over scenically, but rapidly emerging as one of North America's premier destinations for windsurfing, climbing and – in season – eagle-watching.

The Sunshine Coast

A mild-weathered stretch of sandy beaches, rugged headlands and quiet lagoons running northwest of Vancouver, the **Sunshine Coast** receives heavy promotion – and heavy tourist traffic as a result – though in truth its reputation is considerably overstated and the scenic rewards are slim compared to the grandeur of the BC interior. Even as a taste of the province's mountain scenery it leaves much to be desired, and the best that can be said of the region is that in summer it offers some of western Canada's best diving, boating and fishing. If you are just coming out for the day, the best parts of the trip are the various **ferry crossings** en route: the first is from Horseshoe Bay at the western extreme of West Vancouver to Langdale and Gibsons Landing, where you pick up Highway 101 for the 79-kilometre run along the coast to Earl's Cove, and the beautiful (and slightly longer) crossing to Saltery Bay, where the boat pro-

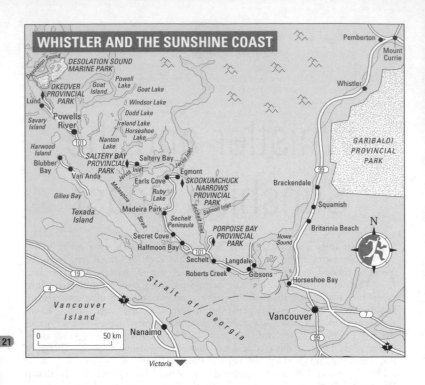

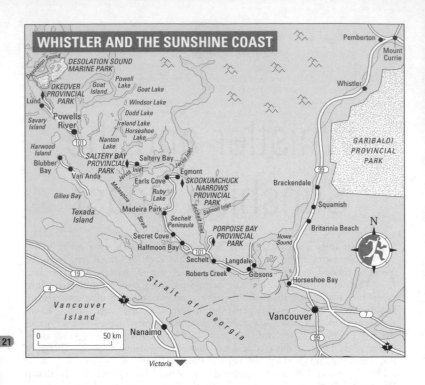

vides views of some fine maritime landscapes. The road then continues 35km to Powell River before coming to an abrupt conclusion 23km later at the village of Lund.

Highway 101

Highway 101 runs almost the length of the coast from Gibsons Landing, often known simply as Gibsons, which is just 5km from the ferry terminal at Langdale for boats coming from **Horseshoe Bay** at the end of Marine Drive and the western edge of West Vancouver. You can reach the ferry terminal here from the city by taking bus #250 or the #257 express westbound from points on West Georgia Street downtown. Given that the coast is hardly worth full-scale exploration by car, and that the two ferry crossings provide two of the trip's highlights, you might consider saving the price of a rental and going by **bus**; it's perfectly feasible to get to **Powell River** in a day. Malaspina Coachlines (☎604/485-5030 or 1-888/227-8287) runs two buses daily to Powell River, at 8.30am and 6.30pm (5hr; $37.50 one way). Returns leave at 8.30am and 2.30pm. Bus tickets include the price of the ferry crossings en route.

Gibsons to Powell River

Soon reached and well signposted from North and West Vancouver, **Horseshoe Bay** is the departure point for the first of the Hwy 101 **ferry** crossings, a half-hour to 40-minute passage through the islands of fjord-like

Howe Sound. There are regular sailings year-round, and tickets cost $8.25 for adults and $28.75 for cars: bikes cost $2.50; all tickets cost a little less outside the late-June to early September peak period. Note that each ticket is valid for one Horseshoe Bay-Langdale (return), Earl's Cove-Saltery Bay (return) or single journeys on both the Horseshoe Bay-Langdale and Earl's Cove-Saltery Bay crossings. Ferries also ply from here to Nanaimo on Vancouver Island, with hourly sailings in summer and every other hour off-season. Tickets cost $10 per adult and $34.75 for cars (less off season and less for cars year-round outside weekends). For information on either of these services, contact BC Ferries in Vancouver (☎604/669-1211, 250/386-3431 or 1/888-223-3779, ⓦwww.bcferries.com), or pick up a timetable from the Vancouver infocentre.

Gibsons, the terminal on the other side of Howe Sound, is spread widely over a wooded hillside – the nicest area is around the busy marina and public wharf, a better bet if you're pausing than Upper Gibsons a little further down the highway, which is little more than a busy strip. If you have time to kill, check out the town's two modest museums: the **Sunshine Coast Maritime Museum** on Molly's Lane (June–Aug Tues–Sat 10.30am–4pm; free) and the **Elphinstone Pioneer Museum** at 716 Winn Rd (May–Sept Thurs–Sat 10.30am–4.30pm; free), which contain predictable displays of maritime and frontier memorabilia. For more on the town and details of local trails, beaches and swimming areas, visit the **infocentre** at 1177 Stewart Rd (daily 9am–6pm; ☎604/886-2325, ⓦwww.gibsonschamber.com).

Further west on Hwy 101 is Pender Harbour, a string of small coastal communities of which **Madeira Park** is the most substantial; whales occasionally pass this section of coast – which, sadly, is the source of many of the whales in the world's aquariums – but the main draws are fishing and boating. **Earl's Cove** is nothing but the departure ramp of the second ferry hop – a longer crossing (45min) that again offers fantastic views, including an immense waterfall that drops off a "Lost World"-type plateau into the sea.

From Jervis Bay, the opposite landing stage, it's a couple of kilometres up the road to the best of all the provincial parks in this region, **Saltery Bay Provincial Park**. Everything here is discreetly hidden in the trees between the road and the coast, and the campsite ($12) – beautifully situated – is connected by short trails to a couple of swimming beaches. Further along on the main road, various **campsites** give onto the sea, notably the big *Oceanside Resort Motel* site which also has 11 cabins, 7km short of Powell River, which sits on a superb piece of shoreline (☎604/485-2435 or 1-888/889-2435, ⓦwww.oceansidepark.com; sites $16 per two persons; ❸).

Powell River and beyond

Given its seafront location, **Powell River** has its scenic side, but like many a BC town its unfocused sprawl and nearby sawmill slightly dampen the overall appeal. If you're catching the **ferry** to Courtenay on Vancouver Island (4 daily; 75min), you might not see the town site, as the terminal is 2km to the east at Westview, and some of the **buses** from Vancouver are timed to coincide with the boats; if your bus doesn't connect, you can either walk from the town centre or bus terminal or call a taxi (☎604/483-3666). The local **infocentre** (daily 9am–5pm; ☎604/485-4701 or 1/877-817-8669, ⓦwww.discoverpowellriver .com), which is immediately at the end of the wooden ferry pier at 4690 Marine Ave, can supply a visitors' map showing the many trails leading inland from the coast hereabouts; they can also advise on boat trips on Powell Lake, immediately inland, and tours to Desolation Sound further up the coast. The

△ Shannon Falls

most central of several **campsites** is the 81-site *Willingdon Beach Municipal Campground* on the seafront off Marine Avenue at 6910 Duncan St (T604/485-2242; $15–20).

The northern end-point of Hwy 101 – which, incidentally, starts in Mexico City, making it one of North America's longest continuous routes – is the hamlet of **Lund**, 28km up the coast from Powell River. **Desolation Sound Marine Provincial Park**, about 10km north of Lund, offers some of Canada's best boating and scuba diving, plus fishing, canoeing and kayaking. There's no road access to the park, but a number of outfitters in Powell River run tours to it and can hire all the equipment you could possibly need – try Westview Live Bait Ltd, 4527 Marine Ave, for **canoes**; Coulter's Diving, 4557 Willingdon Ave, for **scuba gear**; and Spokes, 4710 Marine Drive, for **bicycles**. The more modest **Okeover Provincial Park**, immediately north of Lund, has an unserviced campsite ($14).

The Sea to Sky Highway

A fancy name for Hwy 99 between North Vancouver and Whistler, the **Sea to Sky Highway** has a slightly better reputation than it deserves, mainly because Vancouver's weekend hordes need to reassure themselves of the grandeur of the scenery at their doorstep. It undoubtedly scores in its early coastal stretch, where the road clings perilously to an almost sheer cliff and mountains come dramatically into view on both sides of Howe Sound. Views here are better than along the Sunshine Coast, though plenty of campsites, motels and minor roadside distractions fill the route until the mountains of the Coast Range rear up beyond **Squamish** for the rest of the way to Whistler.

If you've a **car** you're better off driving the highway only as far as **Garibaldi Provincial Park** – the section between Pemberton and Lillooet, the Duffy Lake Road, is very slow going and often impassable in winter, though the drive is a stunner, with wonderful views of lakes and glaciers. Regular buses (see "Perimeter bus" details on p.252) connect Vancouver and Whistler (some continue to Pemberton), which you can easily manage as a day-trip (it's 2hr 30min one-way to Whistler from Vancouver by bus).

Britannia Beach

Road and rail lines meet with some squalor at tiny **Britannia Beach**, 53km from Vancouver, whose **BC Museum of Mining** is the first reason to take time out from admiring the views (early May to early Sept daily 9am–4.30pm; $12.95; T604/688-8735, Wwww.bcmuseumofmining.org). Centring around what was, in the 1930s, the largest producer of copper in the British Empire – 56 million tons of ore were extracted here before the mine closed in 1974 – the museum is housed in a huge, derelict-looking building on the hillside and is chock-full of hands-on displays, original working machinery, a 235-ton monster mine truck and archive photographs. You can also take guided underground tours (every 30min) around about 350m of the mine's galleries on small electric trains. And if parts of the complex look familiar it's because the mine has been used as a location in *The X-Files* and numerous other films and TV programmes.

Continuing north you pass several small coastal reserves, the most striking of which is **Shannon Falls Provincial Park**, 7km from Britannia Beach, signed right off the road and worth a stop for its spectacular 335-metre **waterfall**. Six times the height of Niagara, you can see it from the road, but it's only five min-utes' walk to the viewing area at the base, where the proximity of the road, plus a campsite and diner, detract a touch.

Squamish

The sea views and coastal drama end 11km beyond Britannia Beach at **SQUAMISH**, whose houses spread out over a flat plain amidst warehouses, logging waste and old machinery. However, if you want to climb, windsurf or mountain bike, there's nowhere better in the region to do so. At a glance, all the town has by way of fame is the vast granite rock overshadowing it, "The Stawamus Chief", which looms into view to the east just beyond Shannon Falls and is claimed to be the world's "second-biggest free-standing rock" (after Gibraltar, apparently). The town rates as one of Canada's top − if not *the* top − spot for **rock climbing**. Around 200,000 climbers from around the world come here annually, swarming to more than four hundred routes covering the 625-metre monolith: the University Wall and its culmination, the Dance Platform, is rated Canada's toughest climb.

The rock is sacred to the local Squamish, whose ancient tribal name − which means "place where the wind blows" − gives a clue as to the town's second big activity: **windsurfing**. There are strong, consistent winds to suit all abilities, but the water is cold, so a wet suit's a good idea (there are rental outlets around town). Most people head for the artificial **Squamish Spit**, a dyke separating the waters of the Howe Sound from the Squamish River. The area is run by the Squamish Windsurfing Society (small fee; ☎604/926-WIND or 892-2235) and is 3km from town.

Rounding out Squamish's outdoor activities is the tremendous **mountain biking** terrain − there are 63 trails in the area ranging from gnarly single-track trails to readily accessible deactivated forestry roads. The best areas are the Valley Cliff Trails (stream-bed, single-track and woodland trails); Mamquam Forest Service roads (active logging roads with fine views of the Mamquam Glacier); the Cat Lake and Brohm Lake trails; and the Alice Lake trails, which include an abandoned railway for an easy ride.

The town has one more unexpected treat, for the Squamish River, and the tiny hamlet of Brackendale in particular (10km to the north on Hwy 99), which is the world's best place to see **bald-eagles**. In winter around 2000 eagles congregate here, attracted by the migrating salmon. The best places to see them are the so-called Eagle Run just south of the centre of Brackendale, and on the river in the Brackendale Eagles Provincial Park.

If you want to base yourself locally while seeing the eagles, contact the Sunwolf Outdoor Centre (☎604/898-1537, ⓦwww.sunwolf.net), signposted off Hwy 1 − take a left onto Squamish Valley Road at the Alice Lake junction 2km past Brackendale, continue for 4km and the centre is on the right. It has ten great three-person cabins on the shore of the Cheakamus River for $90; some have kitchens for an extra $10. To see the eagles from a raft costs $89 per person, including light lunch; a raft trip plus cabin accommodation costs $124 per person, if two share a cabin.

Practicalities

Most of the relevant parts of the town are concentrated on Cleveland Avenue, off Hwy 99, including the **infocentre** (May–Sept daily 9am–5pm; Oct–April Mon–Fri 9am–5pm, Sat & Sun 10am–2pm; ☎604/892-9244, ⓦwww.squamishchamber.bc.ca), a big supermarket and the most central

accommodation if you're not at the hostel (see below), the *August Jack Motor Inn* opposite the infocentre (☎604/892-3504; ❸). Alternatively, the *Garibaldi Budget Inn*, 38012-3rd Ave (☎604/892-5204; ❷), is excellent value. The superlative *Squamish Hostel* on Buckley Avenue (☎ 604/892-9240 or 1-800/449-8614, ⓦwww.hostels.com/squamish; ❶) is clean and friendly, with a kitchen, common room and 18 beds including two private rooms. To get here, turn left off Hwy 99 (heading north) onto Cleveland Avenue (look for the *McDonald's*) and then right on Buckley at the first set of lights: the hostel is on the right just past Carson Street and the high school. Beds are $15 a night (three nights cost $40) and private rooms are $30. The owners are set to open a larger 60-bed hostel nearby at Mamquam Blind Channel on Hwy 99.

If you're looking into **renting equipment**, Vertical Reality Sports Centre at 38154 2nd Ave (☎604/892-8248) rents climbing shoes ($10 a day) and mountain bikes ($15–40 a day), whilst Slipstream Rock & Ice (☎604/898-4891 or 1-800/616-1325, ⓦwww.slipstreamadventures.com) offers rock- and ice-climbing guiding and instruction. Most of their tours are for two days and start from about $160 and they teach all abilities. For **mountain bike hire**, contact Tantalus (☎604/898-2588), by the Greyhound depot at 40446 Government Rd, or Corsa Cycles (☎604/892-3331, ⓦwww.corsacycles.com) at Hunter Place: rates for both start at about $20 for a half-day hire. If you are here to climb, there are several **guides**, available from bookstores in Vancouver as well as the climbing shops in Squamish: Kevin McLane is the author of several books, including *The Climbers' Guide to Squamish* (Elaho, $34.95).

Garibaldi Provincial Park

After about 5km, the road north of Squamish enters the classic river, mountain and forest country of the BC interior. The journey thereafter up to Whistler is a joy, with only the march of electricity pylons to take the edge off an idyllic drive.

Unless you're skiing, **Garibaldi Provincial Park** is the main incentive for heading this way. It's a huge and unspoilt area that combines all the usual breathtaking ingredients of lakes, rivers, forests, glaciers and the peaks of the Coast Mountains (Wedge Mountain, at 2891m, is the park's highest point). Four rough roads access the park from points along the highway between Squamish and Whistler, but you'll need transport to reach the trailheads at the end of them. Other than camping, the only accommodation close to the park is at Whistler.

There are five main areas with trails, of which the **Black Tusk/Garibaldi Lake** region is the most popular and probably most beautiful, thanks to its high-mountain views. Further trails fan out from Garibaldi Lake, including one to the huge basalt outcrop of **Black Tusk** (2316m), a rare opportunity to reach an alpine summit without any rock climbing. The other hiking areas from south to north are **Diamond Head**, **Cheakamus Lake**, **Singing Pass** and **Wedgemount Lake**. Outside these small, defined areas, however, the park is untrammelled wilderness. For more **information**, including good advice on trails, visit ⓦwww.garibaldipark.com or pick the dedicated BC Parks pamphlet from infocentres in Vancouver and elsewhere, whose information can also be accessed at ⓦwww.gov.bc.ca/bcparks.

Whistler

WHISTLER, 56km beyond Squamish, is Canada's finest four-season resort, and frequently ranks among most people's world top-five winter ski resorts. Skiing and snowboarding are clearly the main activities, but all manner of other winter sports are possible and in summer the lifts keep running to provide supreme highline hiking and other outdoor activities (not to mention North America's finest summer skiing). It is a busy place, be warned – over two million lift tickets are sold here every winter, more than at any other North American resort. Fortunately it also has one of the continent's largest ski areas, so the crowds are spread thinly over the resort's 200-plus trails and 12 Alpine bowls.

The resort consists of two adjacent but separate mountains – **Whistler** (2182m) and **Blackcomb** (2284m) – each with their own extensive lift and chair systems (but a joint ticket scheme). The mountains can be accessed from a total of five bases, including lift systems to both mountains from the resort's heart, the purpose-built and largely pedestrianized **Whistler Village**, the tight-clustered focus of many hotels, shops, restaurants and après-ski activity. Around this core are two other "village" complexes, **Upper Village Blackcomb** about a kilometre to the northeast and the recently completed Village North about 700m to the north. Around 6km to the south of Whistler Village is **Whistler Creekside** (also with a gondola and lift base), which has typically been a cheaper alternative but is now undergoing a $50 million redevelopment that will see its accommodation and local services duplicating those of its famous neighbour.

Arrival, information and getting around

There are several ways of **getting to** Whistler. If you're driving from Vancouver, allow about two and a bit hours for the 125-kilometre run on the highway – the road was only completed as recently as 1965: before that the area was little visited. Perimeter (℡604/266-5386 or 1-877-317-7788, ⓦ www.perimeterbus.com) runs a shuttle **bus** from Vancouver airport and various Vancouver hotels to Whistler. Reservations are required for the service (May–Nov 7 daily, 3 of which are express services and do not stop at Vancouver hotels – there are 8 southbound departures including 3 express runs; Dec–April 11 daily, including 5 express services; 2hr 30min–3hr; $58 plus tax one-way). Note that winter schedules can be affected by bad weather on the Sea to Sky highway.

Maverick/Greyhound (℡604/662-8051 in Vancouver, ℡604/932-5031 in Whistler or 1-800/661-TRIP from anywhere in North America, ⓦ www.greyhound.ca) runs six daily bus services from Vancouver's bus depot (see p.26) to the Village (2hr 30min; $21.50 one-way) via Britannia Beach, Whistler Creek and other stops. In winter (Dec–April) Greyhound's ski express leaves Vancouver at 6.30am and goes nonstop to Whistler arriving at 8.30am.

Faster still is a helicopter with Helijet (℡604/273-1414, ⓦ www.helijet.com), which costs $147 one-way from Vancouver Airport (2 daily; 45min) or the terminal at Coal Harbour in downtown Vancouver (2 daily; 30min).

If you're staying in or near the Village, then you won't really need **local transport**, but WAVE (℡604/932-4040) runs a free shuttle bus service around Whistler Village, Village North and Upper Village as well as buses to Whistler Creek and other destinations ($1.50 flat fare, five-day pass $5). Buses have racks for skis and bikes. If you need taxis to get around locally, try Sea-to-Sky Taxi (☎604/932-3333), Whistler Taxi (☎604/938-3333) or Airport Limousine Service (☎1/800-278-8742 or 604/273-1331).

Information

For recorded **information** on Whistler-Blackcomb call ☎1-800/766-0449 (☎604/664-5614 from Vancouver or ☎604/932-3434 from Whistler, ⓦwww.whistler-blackcomb.com). Tourism Whistler (☎604/932-3928) is another source of information, though they cater towards the top end of the market; they also run the Whistler Activity and Information Centre, in the green-roofed Conference Centre near the Village Square (daily 9am–5pm; ☎604/932-2394 or 1-800-WHISTLER, ⓦwww.tourismwhistler.com). Whistler Creek is home to the more down-to-earth and friendly **Chamber of Commerce**, 2097 Lake Placid Rd (daily 9am–5pm, longer hours in summer; ☎604/932-5528, ⓦwww.whistlerchamberofcommerce.com). This office can assist with general information, tickets for events and last-minute accommodation. **Information kiosks** open daily 9am to 5pm between May and early September at several points, including the main bus stop and the Village Gate Boulevard at the entrance to Whistler Village.

Accommodation

If you're here in summer and not on a package tour, all local **accommodation** can be booked through the excellent Whistler Central Reservations (☎604/664-5625 or 1-800/944-7853, ⓦwww.tourismwhistler.com or ⓦwww.mywhistler.com). In winter, reservations for those not on a package tour should be made well in advance, as many hotels have a thirty-day cancellation window and may insist on a minimum of three days' stay; prices are highest at this time, too.

To do Whistler in style, the top resort **hotel** is the $75-million *Fairmont Chateau Whistler* on Blackcomb Way (☎604/938-8000; ⓦwww.fairmont.com; ❾). Then come the spanking all-suite *Westin Resort & Spa* (☎604/905-5000 or 1-888/634-5577, ⓦwww.westinwhistler.com; ❾) with ski-in, ski-out facilities and the *Pan Pacific Lodge* (☎604/905-2999 or 1-888/905-9995, ⓦwww.panpacific.com; ❾).

At the other end of the scale is the 32-bed **youth hostel** 7km from the Village right on the shores of Alta Lake at 5678 Alta Lake Rd, one of the nicest hostels in BC (☎604/932-5492, ⓦwww.hihostels.ca; beds for members $19.50, non-members $23.50), a signposted fifty-minute walk from Whistler Creek or ten-minute drive to the village centre; local buses (☎604/932-4020) leave the gondola base in the Village four times a day for the hostel 15min; $1.50). As it's popular year-round, reserve ahead. Check-in is between 4 and 10pm.

The *Shoestring Lodge*, with an often rowdy adjacent pub, is an equally popular alternative. It has private rooms with small bathrooms – aim to be as far from the bar as possible – as well as dorms and is a ten-minute walk north of Whistler Village on Nancy Greene Drive (☎604/932-3338; ❸). Other good choices which won't break the bank are the *Fireside Lodge*, 2117 Nordic Drive (☎604/932-4545; ❷) at Nordic Estates, 3km south of the village, and the *Whistler Resort and Club*, 2129 Lake Placid Rd on the southern edge of Nita Lake 3km south of the village (☎604/932-2343, ⓦwww.rainbowretreats.com; ❸). An equal distance north of the village is the pricier *Edgewater Lodge*, set in lovely forested grounds at 8841 Hwy 99 (☎604/932-0688, ⓦwww.edgewater-lodge.com; ❻).

The **skiing and snowboarding season** for Whistler and Blackcomb begins in late November, weather permitting. The yearly average snowfall is a whopping ten metres (for **snow conditions** call ☏604/932-4211 in Whistler or ☏604/687-7507 from Vancouver). Blackcomb closes at the end of April, while Whistler stays open until early June. Then the mountains switch places, as Whistler closes and Blackcomb reopens in early June for glacier skiing and snowboarding (lift passes for summer skiing cost $42 a day for adults), staying open until late July. The lifts are open daily 8.30am–3pm, and until 4pm after January.

Lift tickets give you full use of both Whistler and Blackcomb mountains, and it will take days for even the most advanced skier or snowboarder to cover all the terrain. Tickets are available from the lift base in Whistler Village, but the queues can be horrendous. Instead, plan ahead and purchase your tickets online from ⓦwww.whistler.net. Your hotel can often set you up with tickets if you prebook far enough in advance. **Prices** increase in peak season – over Christmas and New Year and from mid-February to mid-March – and lift tickets are subject to a seven-percent tax. Regular/peak season tickets are $65/69 for adults. You can save money by purchasing your lift pass before the end of September or, if you plan to ski regularly at Whistler, by purchasing an **Express Card**. These cost $79 for adults, $67 for youths and $39 for seniors, and are valid all season – scan it each time you ski and it automatically charges your credit card. Your first day skiing is free and then you pay a discounted rate of $35–53 depending on the season; call ☏1-800/766-0449 for more details.

Intermediate and expert skiers can join the **free tours** of the mountains that leave at 10.30am and 1pm daily. The Whistler All-Mountain tour departs from the Guest Satisfaction Centre at the top of the Whistler Village gondola. The Blackcomb All-Mountain tour meets at the Mountain Tour Centre, top of the Solar Coaster Express, or at the *Glacier Creek Lodge*. To explore Blackcomb's glaciers join the tour at the *Glacier Creek Lodge*, weather permitting.

Best of the **campsites** is the *Riverside RV Resort and Campground* (☏604/905-5533 or 1-877/905-5533, ⓦwww.whistlercamping.com), 1.8km north of Whistler Village at 8018 Mons Rd, which has 14 five-person log cabins for $125–205 and 107 RV/tent sites for $25 per two persons in winter, $30 in summer.

Whistler Village

WHISTLER VILLAGE is the key to the resort, a rather characterless and pastel-shaded conglomeration of hotels, restaurants, mountain-gear shops and more loud people in fluorescent clothes than are healthy in one place at the same time. Whistler's name is said to derive either from the distinctive shriek of the marmot (a small and rather chubby mammal), or else the sound of the wind whistling through Singing Pass up in the mountains. Whatever its origins, huge amounts of money have been invested in the area since the resort opened in 1980, and the investments have paid off well; the resort's services, lifts and general overall polish are almost faultless, and those of its nearby satellites are not far behind.

Whistler Mountain

Winter-sports enthusiasts can argue long and late over the relative merits of **WHISTLER MOUNTAIN** and its rival, Blackcomb Mountain, both accessed from Whistler Village's lifts. Both are great mountains, and both offer top-notch skiing and boarding, as evidenced by world-class events like the Snowboard FIS World Cup in December and the World Ski and Snowboard Festival in April – both held on Whistler. Each mountain has its own distinctive character, and traditionally Whistler has been seen as the more homely of the two mountains, somewhere you can ski or board for days on end and never have to retrace your steps.

The ski area is 3657 acres and there are over a hundred marked **trails** and seven major bowls. The breakdown of terrain is twenty percent beginner, fifty-five percent intermediate and twenty-five percent expert. **Lifts** include two high-speed gondolas, six high-speed quads, two triple and one double chairlift, and five surface lifts. Snowboarders are blessed with a half-pipe and park. Total vertical drop is 1530m and the longest run is 11km.

Blackcomb Mountain

BLACKCOMB MOUNTAIN, the "Mile-High Mountain", is a ski area laden with superlatives: the most modern resort in Canada, North America's finest summer skiing (on Horstman Glacier), the continent's longest unbroken fall-line skiing and the longest *and* second longest lift-serviced vertical falls in North America (1609m and 1530m).

Blackcomb is slightly smaller than Whistler, at 3341 acres, and has a similar breakdown of **terrain** (fifteen percent beginner, fifty-five percent intermediate and thirty percent expert). **Lifts** are one high-speed gondola, six express quads, three triple chairlifts, and seven surface lifts. There are over a hundred marked trails, two glaciers and five bowls along with two half-pipes and a park for snowboarders. Even if you're not skiing, come up here (summer or winter) on the ski lifts to walk, enjoy the **view** from the top of the mountain, or to eat in the restaurants like *Rendezvous* or *Glacier Creek*.

Eating and drinking

When it comes to **food and drink**, Whistler Village and its satellites are loaded with cafés and around a hundred restaurants, though none really have an "address" as such. These can come and go at an alarming rate, but one top-rated restaurant of long standing is *Araxi's Restaurant and Antipasto Bar* in Village Square (☏604/932-4540), which serves up expensive West Coast-style food and inventive pasta dishes – try the amazing mussels in chilli, vermouth and lemongrass followed by a perfect crème brûlée for dessert. Equally fine, the *Rim Rock Café & Oyster Bar* at 2117 Whistler Rd (☏604/932-5565) is excellent for seafood. Other more down-to-earth places to try are *Trattoria di Umberto* (☏604/932-5858) in the *Mountainside Lodge*, beside the *Pan Pacific*, for a cozy Italian meal; *Black's Dining Room* (☏604/932-6408) in Mountain Square for pizza and pasta and a snug bar, *Black's Pub*, upstairs; the simple *Amsterdam Café* (☏604/932-8334) for reliable pub food; and *Citta's Bistro* (☏604/932-4177), a modern American-style bistro.

Nightlife

Winter or summer, Whistler enjoys a lot of **nightlife** and après-ski activity, with visitors being bolstered by the large seasonal workforce. For relative peace and quiet, hit any of the smartish bars in the *Fairmont Chateau Whistler* hotel. Just off Whistler Mountain, the après-ski haunt is the sports-crazy *Longhorn*

Whistler offers a wealth of outdoor activities in addition to skiing and snowboarding. You can ride the ski lifts up onto both mountains for tremendous views and easy access to high-altitude **walking** trails (July to early Sept daily 10am–8pm; early Sept to late Sept daily 10am–5pm, late Sept to mid-Oct Sat & Sun 10am–5pm; adults $23, youth and seniors $19). **Mountain bikers** can also take bikes up and ride down, for an additional $4 charge for the bike. You must have a helmet and the bike undergoes a safety inspection.

Pick up the sheet of biking and hiking trails from the infocentres (see p.253), or better yet buy the 1:50,000 *Whistler and Garibaldi Region* **map**. The two most popular day walks are the **Rainbow Falls** and **Singing Pass** trails (both five to six hours). Other good choices are the four-kilometre trail to Cheakamus Lake or any of the high-alpine hikes accessed from the Upper Gondola station (1837m) on Whistler Mountain or the Seventh Heaven lift on Blackcomb. Among the eight walks from Whistler Mountain gondola station, consider the **Glacier Trail** (2.5km round trip; 85m ascent; 1hr) for views of the snow and ice in Glacier Bowl. The slightly more challenging **Little Whistler Trail** (3.8km round trip; 265m ascent; 1hr 30min–2hr) takes you to the summit of Little Whistler Peak (2115m) and gives grand views of Black Tusk in Garibaldi Provincial Park. Remember to time your hike to get back to the gondola station for the last ride down (times vary according to season).

If the high-level hiking seems too daunting (it shouldn't be – the trails are good and less than 4km, save the Musical Bumps trail at 19km) – then there are plenty of trails (some surfaced) for bikers, walkers and in-line skaters around the Village. The **Valley Trail** system starts on the west side of Hwy 99 by the Whistler Park Golf Course and takes you through parks, golf courses and peaceful residential areas: the 30km of trails on and around **Lost Lake**, entered by the northern end of the Day Skier car park at Blackcomb Mountain, wend through cedar forest and past lakes and creeks; the eponymous lake is just over a kilometre from the main trailhead. There are also numerous operators offering guided walks and bike rides to suit all abilities, as well as **rental outlets** for bikes, blades and other equipment around the Village.

Between May and September, Whistler River Adventures (☎604/932-3532, ⊛www.whistlerriver.com; from $75 for one-hour cruise to $135 for six-hour trip) has **jet boating** on the Green River to below the Nairn Falls, with a good chance of spotting wildlife such as moose and bears. It also has rafting trips from $65 for two-hour trips and $140 for full-day tours: beginners are taken to the Green River, while experts can plump for the Class-IV thrills of the Elaho or Squamish River rapids.

You can **play tennis** at several public courts, or ask at the visitor centre for details of hotels which allow players to use their courts and provide racket rental (from $10 an hour); or play squash or **swim** at the Meadow Park Sports Centre (☎604/938-7275).

The area has four great **golf** courses, including one designed by Jack Nicklaus. Despite a recent upgrade, the Whistler Golf Club course remains the cheapest to play, ranging from $70 to $150 (☎1-800/376-1777 or 604/932-4544), while the others, including Nicklaus North (☎604/938-9898), cost from about $125 to $205. After any of these activities there are umpteen **spas** for massage, mud baths and treatments that soothe all aches and pains – try Whistler Body Wrap (☎604/932-4710) next to *The Keg in the Village* (at 210 St Andrew's House), or - for utter luxury - the top-of-the-range spa at the *Fairmont Chateau Whistler* (☎604/938-2086).

Snowshoe rental and tours are available to get you across some of the safer snowfields in summer. For **snowshoe tours** for novices contact Outdoor Adventures (☎604/932-0647, ⊛www.adventureswhistler.com; from $39 for 90 minutes) or Whistler Cross Country Ski & Hike (☎604/932-7711 or 1-888/771-2382, ⊛www.whistlerhikingcentre.com).

If you want some **cross-country skiing**, the best spots are the 22km of groomed trails around Lost Lake and the *Chateau Whistler* golf course, all easily accessible from Whistler Village.

Saloon and Grill (☎604/932-5999) in the Village at the base of the gondolas, while the lively beer-heavy *Merlin's* (☎604/938-7700) in the *Blackcomb Lodge* performs the same function for Blackcomb. As evening draws on, make for the *Dubh Linn Gate* Irish pub, 4320 Sundial Crescent (☎604/905-4047), or *Buffalo Bill's Bar & Grill* (☎604/932-6613) across from the Whistler gondola at the *Timberline Lodge*, a thirty-something bar/club with comedy nights, hypnosis shows, video screens, a huge dancefloor and live music.

A younger set, snowboarding hipsters among them, make for **clubs** in both the Village and North Village. These include *Tommy Africa's*, aka *Tommy's* (☎604/932-6090); the musically adventurous *Maxx Fish* (☎604/932-1904), home to hip-hop and house DJs; and the lively *Moe Joe's* (☎604/935-1152), where locals hang out to catch DJs and live music.

Contexts

Contexts

A brief history of Vancouver

The following account provides a brief overview of Vancouver's history, from centuries of slow – or no – development to its relatively rapid rise in the last 130-plus years. For further reading on the city's background, check out the books listed on p.269.

Beginnings and early inhabitants

The area's **first inhabitants** probably arrived some 10,000 years ago, Asiatic peoples who crossed a land bridge which then existed across the present-day Bering Straits. From here they drifted southwards, evolving eventually into a variety of geographically distinct and culturally advanced peoples.

On the banks of the Fraser, the river which flows into the Pacific south of modern-day Vancouver, the ancient indigenous population was known as the **Stó:lo**, or "People of the River", a grouping of the Tsawwassen, Musqueam and another twenty or so peoples who probably consolidated their presence on Vancouver's Burrard Inlet around 3000 BC.

A highly developed people, the Stó:lo were skilled carpenters, canoe-makers and artists, although little in modern Vancouver – outside the city's museums – pays anything but lip service to their existence. They lived off the bounty of the sea and river – rich in salmon, shellfish, sturgeon and the like – and led more sedentary lives than the mostly nomadic peoples of the North American interior. They also hunted for deer, elk, bears and other animals, and gathered berries, fruit, roots and the *wapato*, a tuber that grew along the banks of the Fraser.

By about the eighteenth century, the area's indigenous groups lived in parts of what would become Greater Vancouver. Richmond and the Fraser delta were home to the Tsawwassen – the name now given to the city's principal ferry terminal. New Westminster was the preserve of the Kwantlen, while much of North Vancouver belonged to the Tsleil'waututh. The Squamish lived in villages on Howe Sound, Stanley Park, Jericho Beach, Kitsilano and North and West Vancouver. Other key areas in the modern city, like Locarno Beach and the North Shore east of the Capilano River, were largely occupied by the Coast Salish, who in turn divided into smaller tribes such as the Cowichan, Nanaimo and Saanich.

The first Europeans

Probably the first European to see the British Columbian coast was the British explorer **Sir Francis Drake** during a round-the-world voyage in 1579. The first recorded landing – at Nootka Sound on Vancouver Island – was made in 1778 by another Briton, **Sir James Cook**, during a voyage that took him up the Pacific coast from Oregon to Alaska. Ignorant of the area's true geography, Cook mistook Vancouver Island for the North American mainland. Mistaken or not, the mariner succeeded in sparking immediate British interest in the region.

The next fifteen years saw a variety of British, Spanish and French contacts with the area, all of which were prompted by the search for gold, new territory and improved trade routes, in particular the elusive Northwest Passage, the sea route across the roof of the American continent (see p.96). The Spanish dispatched three expeditions to the region between 1774 and 1779, and it may be that **Juan Perez Hernandez**, captain on one of these missions, dropped anchor off Vancouver Island in 1774. In 1790, another Spaniard, the explorer Manuel Quimper, encountered the Songhees, a Coast Salish people, and apparently attempted to claim their land for Spain. In 1791, yet another Spaniard, **José María Narváez**, a Spanish pilot and surveyor, glimpsed the mouth of the Fraser from his ship, the *Santa Saturnia*. He also sailed into Burrard Inlet, but stopped short of what is today the inner harbour, mistaking Point Grey for a group of islands, which he christened the Islas de Langara.

Britain's interests at the time were represented by **George Vancouver**, a midshipman who had served under Cook in 1774, but who, by 1792, was a captain in command of his own ships, the *Chatham* and *Discovery*. Both vessels were engaged in mapping parts of the North American Pacific coast, a task that saw them shadowed by two Spanish ships under Dionisio Alcalá Galiano, with whom Vancouver pooled information. Vancouver eventually stumbled across the mouth of the Fraser, which he officially claimed for Britain in 1792. After studying the delta from a small boat, however, he deemed it too shallow to be of practical use.

Instead, he rounded a headland to the north, sailing into a deep natural port – the future site of Vancouver – which he named Burrard after one of his crew. He then traded briefly with the Squamish at X'ay'xi, a village on the inlet's forested headland – the future Stanley Park. The Squamish named the spot Whul-whul-Lay-ton, or "place of the white man". Vancouver then met Galiano and sailed on, having spent just a day in the region – scant homage to an area that would be named after him a century later.

Fur traders

What might have become long-running disputes between Britain and Spain over the region were settled in Britain's favour when Spain became domestically embroiled in the aftermath of the French Revolution. Exploration of the coast gave way to the exploration of the Canadian interior, prompted by the search for an easier route to export furs westwards to the Pacific instead of the arduous haul eastwards across the continent. **Alexander Mackenzie** of the North West Company, one of the great fur-trading companies of the day, made the first crossing of North America north of Mexico in 1793. He was followed by two further adventurers, Scottish-born explorers **Simon Fraser** (1776–1862) and **David Thompson**, whose names resonate as sobriquets for rivers, shops, motels and streets in Vancouver and elsewhere in British Columbia.

Fraser uncovered George Vancouver's error with regard to the Fraser River in 1808, when he made an epic 1368-kilometre journey down the river from the Rockies to the sea. With the benefit of hindsight, this was one of the greatest feats in the annals of North American exploration, though Fraser – who had thought he was following the Columbia River – deemed the venture a failure. Nor did he travel the short distance north from the river's mouth to Burrard Inlet – not least because on emerging at the mouth of the river he was chased back upstream by the Musqueam.

In 1827, another fur-trading company, the **Hudson's Bay Company**, established a trading post at Fort Langley on the Fraser 48km from the sea – the area's first permanent European settlement. The post traded as far afield as Hawaii, but by 1839 had been abandoned for a more favourable site 35km upriver, where a reconstructed trading post survives to this day. Neither post, however, attempted to attract permanent homesteaders, the Hudson's Bay Company deciding that the presence of settlers would be detrimental to fur and other trades.

Victoria

The area that would become Vancouver remained a mixture of forest and aboriginal villages for the next twenty years, during which time the historical focus shifted to **Victoria** on Vancouver Island. Victoria received some of its earliest **white visitors** after 1842 when James Douglas, the Hudson Bay Company's chief factor, founded Fort Camouson on the city's present site. The name was later changed to Fort Victoria to honour the British queen (see p.218 for more on Victoria's history).

The fort blossomed, attracting European immigrants, though the new settlement – like much of western Canada – remained a virtual fiefdom of the **Hudson's Bay Company**. The company's monopoly, among other things, antagonized the Americans, and led to a flurry of diplomatic activity that persuaded the British to formalize its claims to the region in order to forestall American expansion. In 1846 the **Oregon Treaty** set the 49th Parallel as the national boundary between the two areas. Vancouver Island, however, which lies partly south of the line, remained wholly British and was officially designated a crown colony in 1849.

Despite the treaty and the involvement of the Crown, The "Bay" still reigned in all but name, and took no interest in promoting immigration; as late as 1855 the island's white population numbered only 774. As for the mainland – and what would become Vancouver – it remained almost unknown except to trappers and the odd prospector.

The gold rush

The event that transformed Victoria and led directly to the creation of Vancouver was the **discovery of gold**, first on the Fraser in 1858 and then in the Cariboo region of British Columbia three years later. Some 30,000 prospectors, many of them old-timers from the California gold rush of 1849, surged to the area, heading first to Victoria to pick up supplies, and then to the mainland for the trip up the Fraser. James Douglas, still Victoria's effective ruler, enlisted the support of the British government to control the influx, half-afraid that the Americans would use it as an excuse to expand territorially to the north. As a precautionary measure Britain declared the mainland north of the 49th Parallel a crown colony, lending it the same status as Vancouver Island.

At the same time, the British government made available a detachment of the Royal Engineers under Colonel Richard Moody to build roads and a military garrison to keep watch on the flood of prospectors. Moody took one look at

Fort Langley and decided its position was ill-suited to the task. Instead, he built a fort at **New Westminster** on the Fraser, now a suburb of southern Vancouver, which was then declared capital of British Columbia. The future downtown area of Vancouver remained no more than a tract of forest on the Burrard Inlet to the north.

All that began to change in 1859, when a trail – today's North Road – was blazed between New Westminster and the Burrard Inlet to provide guaranteed access to an ice-free harbour. In the same year, a British survey ship discovered coal on Burrard Inlet (at a spot still known as Coal Harbour). Another trail – which followed roughly the route of present-day Kingsway – was then cut in 1860 to link New Westminster and False Creek. Most development, however, continued on and around the Fraser, where the first saw mills were established in 1860.

Development of sorts began on the southern shore of **Burrard Inlet** in 1862, when three failed British prospectors – the so-called "Three Greenhorns" – bought 500 acres of land at $1.01 an acre with a view to founding a brickworks. This was a doomed idea, given the amount of timber around, and the project duly failed, as did the trio's attempts to develop the land for housing. Today, the land is occupied by the West End, and includes some of the most expensive real estate in North America.

By 1865 the gold rush was all but dead. A year later, the crown colonies of British Columbia and Vancouver Island were merged under the name **British Columbia**. New Westminster remained its capital. In 1867 the Dominion of Canada was created, a union of many of the British colonies and territories in eastern and central Canada. British Columbia, fearful it might eventually be absorbed by the United States, was brought into the new **Confederation of Canada** in 1871 with the promise of a transcontinental railway. **Port Moody**, a thriving settlement based around a saw mill at the eastern end of the Burrard Inlet, was earmarked as its eastern terminus. The railway, however, would take fifteen years to materialize.

Meanwhile, in 1867, the British entrepreneur Edward Stamp established **Hasting Mill** on the south shore of Burrard Inlet, one of the two seeds from which Vancouver would spring. The other was a tavern established close to the mill by one **"Gassy" Jack Leighton** (see p.63), around which a shanty town quickly developed, the site of which is now occupied by **Gastown**. In 1869, the settlement was incorporated as the town of **Granville**, the sum total of which amounted to six saloons, three hotels and a hardware store. The "town" prospered quietly for the next fifteen years on the back of its timber and modest coal deposits. Port Moody also continued to grow – in 1882 it gained the first electric lights north of San Francisco.

The railway and the Great Fire

By 1884 the long-promised transcontintental **Canadian Pacific Railway** (CPR) was within striking distance of Canada's east coast. Port Moody, however, would not be its terminus. Railway executives discovered the port was too small to handle the large ships that could be expected to dock once the railway was completed. Instead they chose an area 25km closer to the open sea – Granville – a decision that proved to be the turning point in Vancouver's history. The fact that the government granted the company 6000 acres of what everyone knew would become prime real estate was not entirely unconnected with the decision. Nor was the fact that various CPR executives already owned land near Granville.

The extent to which the CPR was influential in local affairs – much as the Hudson's Bay Company had been years earlier – was further illustrated when the company came up with a new name for Granville. The story goes that William Cornelius Van Horne, the CPR's larger-than-life vice-president, was being rowed around along the shore of the future Stanley Park when he decided the railway's terminus needed a more marketable name if visitors, businesses and immigrants were to be attracted to the new city. On April 6, 1886, the town of Granville – population 400 – was duly incorporated as the **City of Vancouver**.

Just three months later, on July 13, the entire "city" burned to the ground, the so-called **Great Fire** consuming Vancouver's 1000 or so wooden buildings in less than 45 minutes. Twenty-eight people were killed and many left homeless. Rebuilding began almost immediately, this time using stone and brick, and by the end of the year, 800 buildings had risen from the flames, many of which can still be seen in Gastown. In the same month, the first CPR train pulled into Port Moody – the track to Vancouver not being complete – and the port of Vancouver received its first shipment: a consignment of tea from China. The next year saw the first CPR train complete the transcontinental journey to Vancouver.

The new city

The arrival of the railway changed everything. Within four years the city's population had soared from 400 to 13,000, and between 1891 and 1901 it grew to 29,000: in 1895 it surpassed that of Victoria for the first time. The CPR continued to shape the new city, developing the port and building swaths of residential housing in what would become the West End, Kitsilano and Shaughnessy Heights. The last was nicknamed "CPR Heaven", and was aimed at the city's new upper class, with the exception of Jews and Asians – the deeds of sale in CPR houses forbade the resale of property to either group. The company also built **Granville Street**, still one of the city's main thoroughfares, and paved Pender and Hastings streets. The port boomed, growing rich on shipments of local timber and vast supplies of wheat from the Canadian interior. So, too, did the population, bolstered by the arrival of **immigrants** from both Asia and Europe, immigration being a feature of the city that has continued, though not without problems, to the present day (see p.68).

Change continued apace. In 1901, the first proper **ferry services** began between Tsawwassen and Sidney on Vancouver Island. In 1908 the University of British Columbia was founded. Six years later, the opening of the Panama Canal – a major boost for the city – provided a quicker route to Europe for ships carrying Canadian wheat. By 1929, Vancouver's population was 80,000, making it Canada's third largest city.

More far-flung areas on the north shore of Burrard Inlet were brought within the city's orbit following the opening of the original Second Narrows Bridge in 1925 (see p.109 for more on the history of the North Shore). The **Lions Gate Bridge** – more convenient for the centre of Downtown – was built in 1938 by the Guinness company, mainly to link its large residential developments in North Vancouver to the burgeoning Downtown peninsula. The first transcontinental air service to Montréal began a year later.

Contemporary Vancouver

Subsequent highlights in the city's twentieth-century history included the 1954 **British Empire Games**, a sporting forerunner of the Commonwealth Games. It was notable for being the first time two runners (Britain's Roger Bannister and the Australian John Landy) ran a mile in under four minutes; it was also the first sporting event broadcast live across North America. Also significant was the founding in 1969 of the organization that would become **Greenpeace**, and the 1986 **Expo '86**, a world-trade fair held to commemorate Vancouver's centenary. The latter event attracted 21 million visitors and considerably heightened Vancouver's profile on the world stage. A similarly high profile was achieved in 1993, when the city hosted the Peace Summit between presidents Clinton and Yeltsin, and again in 1997.

Tourism to the city has benefited from such exposure, and is worth an estimated $4 billion a year and rising. Not that Vancouver, a city with a good economy and one of the five largest ports in the western hemisphere, needs tourism to survive. And while factories and sawmills may occasionally close, the city now has a thriving **TV and movie industry** – launched partly on the back of *The X-Files*, the early series of which were filmed here – and a host of multimedia, software and service industries (see p.172 for more on films and TV production in the city).

Visitors to the city cannot help but notice the knock-on effects of its healthy economy, especially on the southern fringes of Downtown at False Creek, where dozens of high-rise condominiums are rising from formerly derelict railway yards. Nor, however, can they fail to notice the poverty and rundown neighbourhoods east of Downtown on and around Hastings Street, the most obvious blight on contemporary Vancouver. After years of talking but no action, it was the feeling that something needed to be done about this area – among other things – that saw the election of Vancouver's new mayor, **Larry Campbell**, in November 2002.

Campbell had been involved with the BC Coroners' Office for twenty years, and had witnessed firsthand the deadly effects of the area's drug culture and other social problems. During 2003 concerted efforts were made by the police, welfare officers and other agencies to start tackling the issues. Results have been achieved, though at what cost remains to be seen, because representatives of the mostly affluent West End district of Downtown have since begun to complain that the drug dealers and others forced out of the city's eastern margins are now appearing on their own streets, and Davie and Denman in particular.

On a happier note, and a subject that will dominate much of Vancouver life for several years, the city's $34 million bid to stage the **2010 Winter Olympics** was successful in July 2003, defeating bids from Pyeongchang in South Korea and Salzburg in Austria. Not everyone in the city was behind it – a citywide plebiscite in February 2003 voted only 64 percent in favour – but there is little doubt that the successful bid will continue to help improve both Vancouver's infrastructure and economy.

That the city's underlying health is good is reinforced by figures from the 2001 census, which put the population of the Greater Vancouver area at 1,986,965, and the population of the City of Vancouver at 514,008. This represented an increase of 14.3 percent since 1996 in the metropolitan district, making it the fastest-growing such area in Canada (Toronto, by comparison, managed an increase of 9.4 percent). Not bad for a place that just over 130 years ago was little more than a clearing in the wilderness.

Aboriginal cultures

Though few visible traces remain in modern Vancouver, **aboriginal cultures** have played an undeniable role in shaping the progress and development of the area. In particular, of all Canada's aboriginal peoples, the numerous linguistic groups that once inhabited – and in some cases still inhabit – Vancouver, Vancouver Island and parts of the northwest coast of British Columbia have the most sophisticated artistic tradition and the most lavish of ceremonials, a legacy well worth searching out.

Organization and ritual

Traditionally these groups' social organization stemmed from a belief in a mythical time when humans and animals were essentially the same: each tribe was divided into **kin groups** who were linked by a common supernatural animal ancestor and shared the same names, ritual dances, songs and regalia. Seniority within each kin group was held by a rank of chiefs and nobles, who controlled the resources of private property such as house sites, stands of cedar and fishing, gathering and hunting territories.

Such privileges, almost unique among Canadian aboriginal groups, led to the accumulation of private wealth, and thus great emphasis was placed on their inheritance. Central to the power structure was the ceremonial **potlatch**, which was held in the winter village, a seasonal resting place for these otherwise nomadic people, located where the supernatural forces were believed to be most accessible. The potlatch marked every significant occasion from the birth of an heir to the raising of a carved pole, and underscored an individual's right to his or her inherited status. Taking its name from the Chinook word for "gift", the potlatch also had the function of **redistributing wealth**. All the guests at the potlatch acted as witnesses to whatever event or object was being validated, and were repaid for their services with gifts from the host chief. Though these gifts often temporarily bankrupted the host, they heightened his prestige and ensured that he would be repaid in kind at a subsequent potlatch.

The most important element of potlatches was the **masked dances** that re-enacted ancestral encounters with supernatural beings, and were the principal means of perpetuating the history and heritage of each kin group. Created by artists whose innovative ideas were eagerly sought by chiefs in order to impress their guests, the dramatic masks were often elaborate mechanisms that could burst open to reveal the wearer or – like the well-known Cannibal Bird – could produce loud and disconcerting noises.

The **Kwakiutl** produced the most-developed potlatches, featuring highly ranked dances like the *hamatsa* or "**cannibal dance**", whose performers had served a long apprenticeship as participants in less-exalted dances. Before the *hamatsa*, the initiate was sent to the "Cannibal at the North End of the World", a long period of seclusion and instruction in the snowbound woods. On returning to the village he would seem to be in a complete cannibalistic frenzy and would rush around biting members of the audience. These apparent victims were all paid for their role, which usually involved cutting themselves with knives to draw a flow of blood – and the *hamatsa* would burst blood-filled bladders in his mouth to add to the carnage, while relatives shook rattles and sang to tame him. A fantastic finale came with the arrival of the loudly clacking "Cannibal Birds", dancers dressed in long strips of cedar bark and huge masks, of which the most fearsome was the "Cannibal Raven", whose long straight beak could crush a human skull. The *hamatsa* would then return in ceremonial finery completely restored to his human state.

Foreign contact and consequences

As elsewhere in Canada, **European contact** was disastrous for the coastal peoples. The establishment of fur-trading posts in the early nineteenth century led to the abandonment of traditional economic cycles, the loss of their creative skills through reliance on readily available European goods, the debilitation from alcohol and internecine wars. Though most of BC remains nontreaty, lands on Vancouver Island were surrendered to become the "Entire property of the White people forever" in return for small payments – the whole Victoria area was obtained for 371 blankets. Infectious disease, the greatest of all threats, reached its peak with the 1862 smallpox epidemic, which spread from Victoria along the entire coast and far into the interior, killing probably a third of BC's aboriginal population.

In this period of decline, potlatches assumed an increased significance as virtually the only medium of cultural continuity, with rival chiefs asserting their status through ever more extravagant displays – even going as far as to burn slaves who had been captured in battle. Excesses such as these and the newly adopted "whiskey feasts" were seen by the **missionaries** as a confirmation that these peoples were enveloped in the "dark mantle of degrading superstition". With BC's entry into confederation the responsibility for the natives fell to the federal government in faraway Ottawa, much of whose knowledge of the indigenous peoples came from the missionaries – the subsequent **Indian Act**, passed in 1884, prohibited the potlatch ceremony.

For a while the defiant aboriginal groups managed to evade detection by holding potlatches at fishing camps rather than the winter villages, and there were few successful prosecutions until the 1920s. Things came to a head in 1922 with the conviction of 34 Kwakiutl from Alert Bay – all were sentenced to jail terms but a deal was struck whereby all those who surrendered their potlatch regalia were freed. Thirty years later, when potlatching was again legalized, aboriginal pressure began to mount for return of these treasures from the collections into which they had been dispersed, but it took a further twenty years for the federal government to agree to return the goods on condition that they be put on public display. Though the masks totally lose their dramatic emphasis in static exhibitions, many of the more local museums have a dual function as community centres, and as such are vital to the preservation of a dynamic aboriginal culture.

Books

Most of the following books should be readily available in the UK, US or Canada. We have given publishers for each title in the form UK/US publisher, unless the book is published in one country only; o/p means out of print. Note that virtually all the listed books published in the US will be stocked by major Canadian bookshops; we've indicated those books published only in Canada. Books we especially recommend are flagged with the ★ symbol.

Travel, culture and society

Douglas Coupland *City of Glass: Douglas Coupland's Vancouver* (Douglas & McIntyre, Canada). A Vancouver native – and better known for his pop culture treatises like *Generation X* and *Microserfs* – Coupland has put together a slender but rather fey volume that tries hard to be smart about the city's modern society, art and architecture. At least there are plenty of appealing visuals throughout.

Rhodri Windsor Liscombe *The New Spirit: Modern Architecture in Vancouver, 1938–1963* (MIT Press). The architecture examined in this large tome hardly looks modern when set against some of the buildings now going up in the city, but a good buy if you want the full story on the period which gave Vancouver many of its extant buildings.

Alan D. McMillan *Native Peoples and Cultures of Canada* (Orca, US). Comprehensive account of Canada's native groups from prehistory to current issues of self-government and land claims. Well-written, though more an academic textbook than a leisure-time read.

Jan Morris *O Canada: Travels in an Unknown Country* (Robert Hale, o/p/HarperCollins, o/p). Musings from this well-known travel writer after a coast-to-coast Canadian trip.

Dennis Reid *A Concise History of Canadian Painting* (Oxford University Press). Not especially concise, but a thorough trawl through Canada's leading artists, including many you will see in Vancouver's art gallery (see p.53) with bags of biographical detail and lots of black-and-white (and a few colour) illustrations of major works.

History and biography

★ **Pierre Berton** Berton is one of Canada's finest writers, and many of his books touch on subjects with a powerful bearing on the history of Vancouver and Victoria: these include *The Last Spike* (Penguin US), an account of the history and building of the transcontinental railway, and *Flames across the Frontier* (Penguin US), episodes from the often uneasy relationship between Canada and the US.

Paul Kane *Wanderings of an Artist among the Indians of North America* (Dover). Kane, one of Canada's better-known landscape artists, spent two and a half years travelling from Toronto to the Pacific Coast and back in the 1840s. His witty, racy account of his wanderings makes a delightful read.

Robert McDonald *Making Vancouver: 1863–1913* (University of British Columbia Press). A scholarly account of the city during the busiest period in its history.

⭐ **Peter C. Newman** *Caesars of the Wilderness* (Penguin, o/p). Highly acclaimed and readable

account of the rise and fall of the Hudson's Bay Company, including material on the history of the company in and around Vancouver.

Fiction and poetry

Malcolm Lowry *Hear Us O Lord from Heaven thy Dwelling Place* (Carroll & Graf). Lowry spent almost half his writing life (1939–54) in log cabins and beach houses he built for himself around Vancouver. *Hear Us O Lord* is a difficult read to say the least: a fragmentary novella that, amongst other things, describes a disturbing sojourn on Canada's wild Pacific coast.

New Oxford Book of Canadian Short Stories in English (ed. Margaret Atwood & Robert Weaver; OUP). A broad selection which delves beyond the better-known names of Alice Munro and Margaret Atwood, with space being given to diaspora writers. While the intention is to celebrate Canadian writing, some of the works offer a strangely negative view of the country.

⭐ **New Oxford Book of Canadian Verse** (ed. Margaret Atwood; OUP). Canadian poets are

increasingly finding a distinctive voice, but few except this collection's editor have made much impact outside their native country. Atwood's own sharp, witty examinations of nationality and gender are among the best in this anthology.

Oxford Companion to Canadian Literature (OUP, o/p). At almost 900 pages, this is the last word on the subject, though it is more useful as a work of reference than as a primer for the country's literature.

Linda Svendsen *Marine Life* (HarperCollins, Canada/Penguin, US, o/p). Spare and powerful linked stories, most fairly downbeat, set against a Vancouver backdrop.

Vancouver Short Stories (ed. Carole Gerson; University of BC, Canada). Not tons of fiction has come out of Vancouver; this collection of a few choicer bits serves as a good starting point.

Specialist guides

John Acorn & Nancy Baron *Birds of the Pacific Northwest* (Lone Pine Publishing, Canada). A large selection of books is available for birdwatchers in BC, but this provides the best general introduction, with first-rate illustrations. See p.197 for information on birdwatching around Vancouver.

Volker Bodegom *Bicycling Vancouver* (Lone Pine Publishing, Canada). Guide to cycling for pleasure in and around the city.

Victoria Bushnell *Kids' Vancouver: Things to See and Things to Do for Kids of Every Age* (Raincoast Books). A guide that does exactly what it says on the cover.

⭐ **Jean Cousins** *Easy Hiking Around Vancouver: An All-Season Guide* (Greystone Books). Describes 55 hikes with trailheads less than an hour's drive from Vancouver.

Greg Dombowsky *Diver's Guide: Vancouver Island South* (Heritage House, Canada). Handbook to the region's best dive sites.

Teri Lydiard *The British Columbia Bicycling Guide* (Gordon Soules, US). Small but extremely detailed pointer to some tempting routes, backed up with good maps.

Andrea Pistolesi *Vancouver: Sunrise to Sunset* (Bonechi, Canada). Vancouver's bookshops offer a plethora of glossy illustrated titles with photographs of the city; this sumptuous book is the best.

Ian Sheldon *Seashore of British Columbia* (Lone Pine Publishing, Canada). This title is too general for specialists, but provides a good introduction to the mammals, foreshore plants, birds and other aspects of the region's coastal habitats.

Collin Varner and Christine Allen *Gardens of Vancouver* (Raincoast Books). A green-fingered guide to the city's gardens.

Rough Guides

advertiser

stay in touch

roughnews

Rough Guides' FREE full-colour newsletter

News, travel issues, music reviews, readers' letters and the latest dispatches from authors on the road

If you would like to receive roughnews, please send us your name and address:

Rough Guides, 80 Strand, London WC2R 0RL, UK

Rough Guides, 4th Floor, 345 Hudson St, New York NY10014, USA

newslettersubs@roughguides.co.uk

274

...music & reference

277

Also! More than 120 Rough Guide music CDs are available from all good book
and record stores. Listen in at www.worldmusic.net

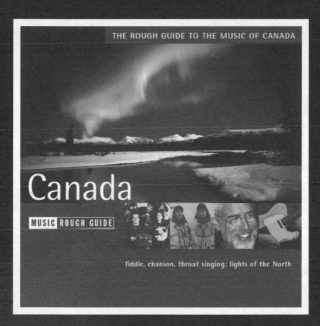
293

Index

and small print

A Rough Guide to Rough Guides

In the summer of 1981, Mark Ellingham, a recent graduate from Bristol University, was travelling round Greece and couldn't find a guidebook that really met his needs. On the one hand there were the student guides, insistent on saving every last cent, and on the other the heavyweight cultural tomes whose authors seemed to have spent more time in a research library than lounging away the afternoon at a taverna or on the beach.

In a bid to avoid getting a job, Mark and a small group of writers set about creating their own guidebook. It was a guide to Greece that aimed to combine a journalistic approach to description with a thoroughly practical approach to travellers' needs – a guide that would incorporate culture, history and contemporary insights with a critical edge, together with up-to-date, value-for-money listings. Back in London, Mark and the team finished their Rough Guide, as they called it, and talked Routledge into publishing the book.

That first *Rough Guide to Greece*, published in 1982, was a student scheme that became a publishing phenomenon. The immediate success of the book – with numerous reprints and a Thomas Cook prize shortlisting – spawned a series that rapidly covered dozens of destinations. Rough Guides had a ready market among low-budget backpackers, but soon also acquired a much broader and older readership that relished Rough Guides' wit and inquisitiveness as much as their enthusiastic, critical approach. Everyone wants value for money, but not at any price.

Rough Guides soon began supplementing the "rougher" information about hostels and low-budget listings with the kind of detail on restaurants and quality hotels that independent-minded visitors on any budget might expect, whether on business in New York or trekking in Thailand.

These days the guides – distributed worldwide by the Penguin group – offer recommendations from shoestring to luxury and cover more than 200 destinations around the globe, including almost every country in the Americas and Europe, more than half of Africa and most of Asia and Australasia. Our ever-growing team of authors and photographers is spread all over the world, particularly in Europe, the USA and Australia.

In 1994, we published the *Rough Guide to World Music* and *Rough Guide to Classical Music*; and a year later the *Rough Guide to the Internet*. All three books have become benchmark titles in their fields – which encouraged us to expand into other areas of publishing, mainly around popular culture. Rough Guides now publish:

- Travel guides to more than 200 worldwide destinations
- Dictionary phrasebooks to 22 major languages
- History guides ranging from Ireland to Islam
- Maps printed on rip-proof and waterproof Polyart™ paper
- Music guides running the gamut from Opera to Elvis
- Restaurant guides to London, New York and San Francisco
- Reference books on topics as diverse as the Weather and Shakespeare
- Sports guides from Formula 1 to Man Utd
- Pop culture books from *Lord of the Rings* to Cult TV
- World Music CDs in association with World Music Network

Visit **www.roughguides.com** to see our latest publications.

SMALL PRINT

Rough Guide Credits

Text editor: Richard Koss
Layout: Helen Prior
Cartography: Ed Wright
Picture research: JJ Luck
Proofreader: David Price

....

Editorial: London Martin Dunford, Kate Berens, Helena Smith, Claire Saunders, Geoff Howard, Ruth Blackmore, Gavin Thomas, Polly Thomas, Richard Lim, Lucy Ratcliffe, Clifton Wilkinson, Alison Murchie, Fran Sandham, Sally Schafer, Alexander Mark Rogers, Karoline Densley, Andy Turner, Ella O'Donnell, Andrew Lockett, Joe Staines, Duncan Clark, Peter Buckley, Matthew Milton; **New York** Andrew Rosenberg, Richard Koss, Yuki Takagaki, Hunter Slaton, Chris Barsanti, Thomas Kohnstamm, Steven Horak
Design & Layout: London Helen Prior, Dan May, Diana Jarvis; **Delhi** Madhulita Mohapatra, Umesh Aggarwal, Ajay Verma
Production: Julia Bovis, John McKay, Sophie Hewat

Cartography: London Maxine Repath, Ed Wright, Katie Lloyd-Jones; **Delhi** Manish Chandra, Rajesh Chhibber, Jai Prakesh Mishra, Ashutosh Bharti, Rajesh Mishra, Animesh Pathak
Cover art direction: Louise Boulton
Picture research: Sharon Martins, Mark Thomas, Jj Luck
Online: New York Jennifer Gold, Cree Lawson, Suzanne Welles; **Delhi** Manik Chauhan, Amarjyoti Dutta, Narender Kumar
Marketing & Publicity: London Richard Trillo, Niki Smith, David Wearn, Chloë Roberts, Demelza Dallow; **New York** Geoff Colquitt, David Wechsler, Megan Kennedy
Finance: Gary Singh
Manager India: Punita Singh
Series editor: Mark Ellingham
PA to Managing Director: Julie Sanderson
Managing Director: Kevin Fitzgerald

Publishing Information

This second edition published April 2004 by **Rough Guides Ltd**, 80 Strand, London WC2R 0RL. 345 Hudson St, 4th Floor, New York, NY 10014, USA.
Distributed by the Penguin Group
Penguin Books Ltd, 80 Strand, London WC2R 0RL
Penguin Putnam, Inc. 375 Hudson Street, NY 10014, USA
Penguin Books Australia Ltd, 487 Maroondah Highway, PO Box 257, Ringwood, Victoria 3134, Australia
Penguin Books Canada Ltd, 10 Alcorn Avenue, Toronto, Ontario, Canada M4V 1E4
Penguin Books (NZ) Ltd, 182–190 Wairau Road, Auckland 10, New Zealand
Typeset in Bembo and Helvetica to an original design by Henry Iles.

Printed in China

© Tim Jepson

288pp includes index
A catalogue record for this book is available from the British Library

ISBN 1-84353-245-X

3 5 7 9 8 6 4 2

Help us update

We've gone to a lot of effort to ensure that the second edition of **The Rough Guide to Vancouver** is accurate and up to date. However, things change – places get "discovered", opening hours are notoriously fickle, restaurants and rooms raise prices or lower standards. If you feel we've got it wrong or left something out, we'd like to know, and if you can remember the address, the price, the time, the phone number, so much the better.

We'll credit all contributions, and send a copy of the next edition (or any other Rough

Guide if you prefer) for the best letters. Everyone who writes to us and isn't already a subscriber will receive a copy of our full-colour thrice-yearly newsletter. Please mark letters: "**Rough Guide Vancouver Update**" and send to: Rough Guides, 80 Strand, London WC2R 0RL, or Rough Guides, 4th Floor, 345 Hudson St, New York, NY 10014. Or send an email to **mail@roughguides.com**

Have your questions answered and tell others about your trip at **www.roughguides.atinfopop.com**

Acknowledgements

The author would like to thank his editor, Richard Koss; Yuki Takagaki; Lucy Hyslop; James and Vicky Ballentyne; Air Canada; Charlotte Fraser and Fairmont Hotels; Claire Griffin and Four Seasons hotels; and Kathleen Eccles.

Readers' letters

Thanks to all the readers who took the trouble to write in with their comments and suggestions (and apologies to anyone whose name we've misspelt or omitted):

Gay Battersby, Sean Connelly, Matthew Ellis, Greg Harper, Sharon Harris, David R. Howe, Tony Francis, Jane King, Kyle Upton, Alan Weeks, Peter W. White, Andrew Young

Photo Credits

Cover credits
Main front Downtown skyline © Getty
small front top picture Science World © Alamy
small front lower picture Canada Place © Alamy
top back picture Chinese Cultural Centre ©Getty
top lower picture Stanley Park © Alamy

Colour introduction
Canoeist near Downtown Vancouver © Richard Cummins/CORBIS
Vancouver Library Square © Picturescolourlibrary.com
Stanley Park Totem Pole © Tourism Vancouver © Tom Ryan
Yaletown Shopping © Tourism Vancouver / Al Harvey
Aerial view of Vancouver © Tourism Vancouver / Colin Jewall
Public library © Richard T. Nowitz/CORBIS
Chinatown Shop © Nick Hanmer
West view © www.vancouverlookout.com
Ben Affleck on set filming 'Paycheck' in Gastown © bigpicturesphoto.com
Lynn Canyon – walks and great outdoors © John Shandy Watson

Things Not To Miss
01. Canada Place and the Harbour Centre buildings on the waterfront at downtown Vancouver © Kevin R. Morris/CORBIS
02. Lonsdale Quay and SeaBus © Tourism Vancouver / Al Harvey
03. Art Deco Marine Building © www.Pbase.ca
04. Emily Carr, Totem Poles, Kitseukla 1912, oil on canvas, Vancouver Art Gallery, Founders Fund, VAG 37.2

05. "Vancouver" houses and high-rise apartment buildings in the district of Yaletown © Gunter Marx
06. Dr Sun Yat-Sen Garden © Nick Hanmer
07. Granville Island Market Deli ©Tourism Vancouver
08. Stanley Park and Vancouver Skyline © Tim Thompson/CORBIS
09. SeaPlane © John Shandy Watson
10. Kitsilano Beach © Tourism Vancouver / Al Harvey
11. "The Raven and the First Men" by Bill Reid (Haida), 1980 Courtesy Museum of Anthropology, Vancouver. © Bill McLennan
12. Grouse Mountain Skyride © "Grouse Mountain Resorts Ltd"
13. Crab Sculpture Outside H.R. MacMillan Planetarium, Vancouver © Gunter Marx Photography/CORBIS
14. Beacon Hill Park, Victoria – view across strait to Washington State © Carollyne Yardley
15. The Butchart Gardens – the Sunken Garden Lake in Spring © "Courtesy of The Butchart Gardens Ltd., Victoria, BC, Canada
16. Woolly Mammoth – largest mammal to have ever roamed BC © Royal British Columbia Museum
17. Whales - Kayakers Viewing a Pod of Orcas © Joel W. Rogers/CORBIS
18. Skiing in the Whistler Mountains © Randy Lincks/Masterfile
19. Pacific Rim Cuisine © CinCin Ristorante, Top Table Restaurant Group
20. Canuks vs. Montreal Canadiens, Markus Naslund scores on Jose Theodore © Jeff Vinnick/Vancouver Canucks

SMALL PRINT

Black and white images

p.56. Downtown © IMAGINA / Atsushi Tsunoda

p.70. Chinatown Night Market © Albert Normandin/Masterfile

p.86. Granville Island © Marilyn Shenton / Alamy

p.95. Bloedel Conservatory © Gunter Marx Photography/CORBIS

p.117. Skiers on Mt. Seymour get a view of downtown Vancouver © Annie Griffiths Belt/CORBIS

p.150. Blue Crabs for Sale © Owen Franken/CORBIS

p.205. Snowshoeing in Mt. Seymour Provincial Park © Gunter Marx Photography/CORBIS

p.218. Empress Hotel, Victoria © Dale Sanders/Masterfile

p.250. Shannon Falls, Squamish © Roy Ooms/Masterfile

SMALL PRINT

Index

map entries are in colour

Map symbols

maps are listed in the index in coloured text

🍁	Trans-Canada Highway
	Provincial highway
	Main road
	Minor road
	Pedestrianized street (town maps)
- - - - -	Footpath
	Railway
– – –	SkyTrain
— —	Ferry route
	River
	Wall
✈	Airport
◆	Point of interest
▲	Mountain peak
⛷	Skiiing area
♟	Museum
🌳	Public gardens

🏛	Monument
☉	Totem pole
★	Bus/shuttle stop
Ⓥ	SkyTrain/subway station
●--●	Cable car & station
▣	Restaurant/café/bar
T	Public convenience
P	Parking
ⓘ	Tourist Infocentre
⊠	Post office
⊞	Hospital
▬	Building
⊞	Church (town maps)
⛳	Golf course
⊤⊥	Cemetery
▒	Park/National park/reserve
▨	Reservation

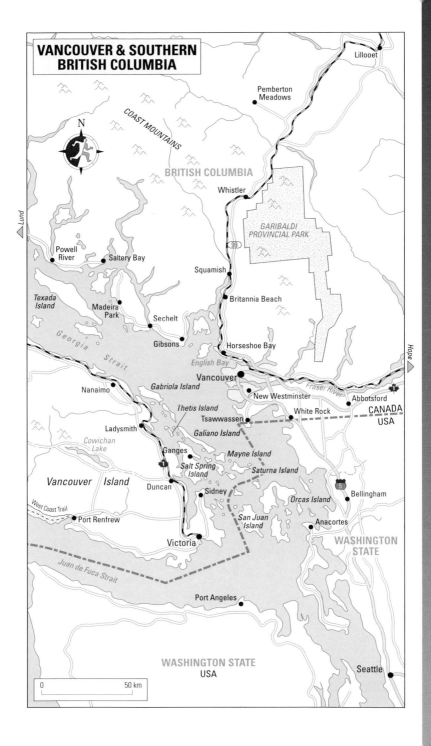

VANCOUVER & SOUTHERN BRITISH COLUMBIA

N

COAST MOUNTAINS

BRITISH COLUMBIA

Lillooet

Pemberton Meadows

Whistler

GARIBALDI PROVINCIAL PARK

99

Lund

Powell River

Saltery Bay

Squamish

Britannia Beach

Texada Island

Madeira Park

Sechelt

Georgia Strait

Gibsons

Horseshoe Bay

English Bay

Vancouver

Hope

Nanaimo

Gabriola Island

New Westminster

Abbotsford

Fraser River

Thetis Island

Tsawwassen

White Rock

CANADA

Ladysmith

Galiano Island

USA

Cowichan Lake

Ganges

Mayne Island

Salt Spring Island

Saturna Island

Vancouver Island

Duncan

Sidney

Bellingham

5

West Coast Trail

Orcas Island

Port Renfrew

San Juan Island

Anacortes

Victoria

WASHINGTON STATE

Juan de Fuca Strait

Port Angeles

WASHINGTON STATE
USA

Seattle

0   50 km

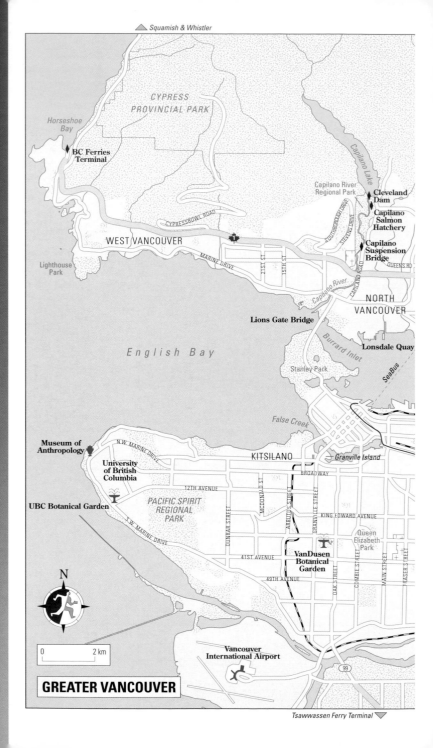

CYPRESS
PROVINCIAL PARK

Horseshoe
Bay

BC Ferries
Terminal

Capilano Lake

Capilano River
Regional Park

Cleveland
Dam

Capilano
Salmon
Hatchery

CYPRESSBOWL ROAD

STEVENS DRIVE

SOUTHBOROUGH DRIVE

WEST VANCOUVER

MARINE DRIVE

21ST ST.

15TH ST.

CAPILANO ROAD

Capilano
Suspension
Bridge

QUEENS RD.

Lighthouse
Park

Capilano River

QUEENS RD.

NORTH
VANCOUVER

Lions Gate Bridge

Burrard Inlet

Lonsdale Quay

English Bay

Stanley Park

SeaBus

False Creek

Museum of
Anthropology

N.W. MARINE DRIVE

KITSILANO

Granville Island

University
of British
Columbia

BROADWAY

12TH AVENUE

DUNBAR STREET

MCDONALD ST.

ABBOTT STREET

GRANVILLE STREET

KING EDWARD AVENUE

UBC Botanical Garden

PACIFIC SPIRIT
REGIONAL
PARK

S.W. MARINE DRIVE

41ST AVENUE

49TH AVENUE

OAK STREET

VanDusen
Botanical
Garden

Queen
Elizabeth
Park

COMBIE STREET

MAIN STREET

FRASER STREET

N

0   2 km

Vancouver
International
Airport

99

GREATER VANCOUVER

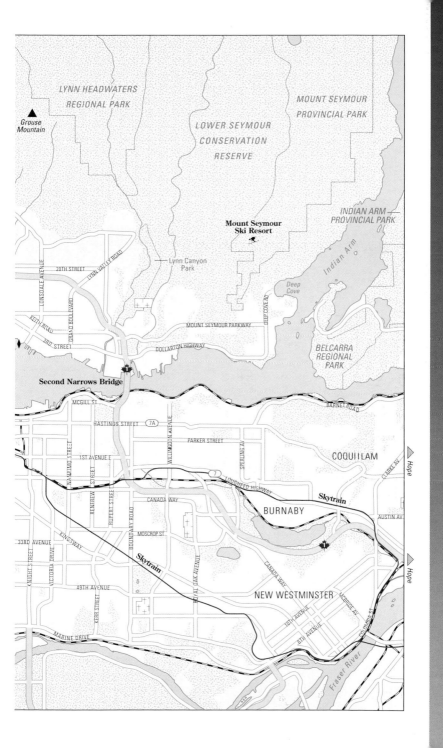

CENTRAL VANCOUVER

Lost Lagoon

Stanley Park

STANLEY PARK DRIVE

LAGOON DRIVE

Devonian Harbour Park

Coal Harbour

Dead Man's Island

PARK LANE

CHILCO STREET

GILFORD STREET

ROBSON STREET

ALBERNI STREET

GEORGIA STREET

HARO STREET

DENMAN STREET

BIDWELL STREET

WEST END

NELSON STREET

BARCLAY STREET

Coal Harbour Park

Coal Harbour

WEST CORDOVA

WEST PENDER STREET

English Bay Beach

DENMAN STREET

COMOX STREET

PENDRELL STREET

DAVIE STREET

CARDERO STREET

NICOLA STREET

BROUGHTON STREET

JERVIS STREET

ALBERNI STREET

MELVILLE STREET

THURLOW STREET

Barclay Square

◆ **Roedde House**

Alexandra Park

NICOLA STREET

BROUGHTON STREET

JERVIS STREET

BURNABY STREET

HARWOOD STREET

BUTE STREET

Nelson Park

BARCLAY STREET

ROBSON STREET

HARO STREET

Christ Church Cathedral

Hotel Vancouver ◆

Vancouver Art Gallery

Robson Square

English Bay

Sunset Beach Park

DAVIE STREET

St Paul's Hospital ✚

Law Courts

NELSON STREET

SMITHE

Vancouver Maritime Museum ◆

Vancouver Museum H.R. MacMillan Space Centre ◆

Gordon Southam Observatory ◆

Vanier Park

THURLOW STREET

BEACH AVENUE

PACIFIC STREET

BURRARD STREET

HELMCKEN STREET

HORNBY STREET

HOWE STREET

Sunset Beach

◆ **Vancouver Aquatic Centre**

GRANVILLE STREET

SEYMOUR STREET

RICHARDS

DAVIE STREET

HOMER

YALETOWN

CHESTNUT STREET

KITSILANO

BURRARD BRIDGE

DURANLEAU

Broker's Bay

GRANVILLE BRIDGE

Granville Island

DRAKE STREET

David Lam Park

ⓘ

| 0 | 250 m |

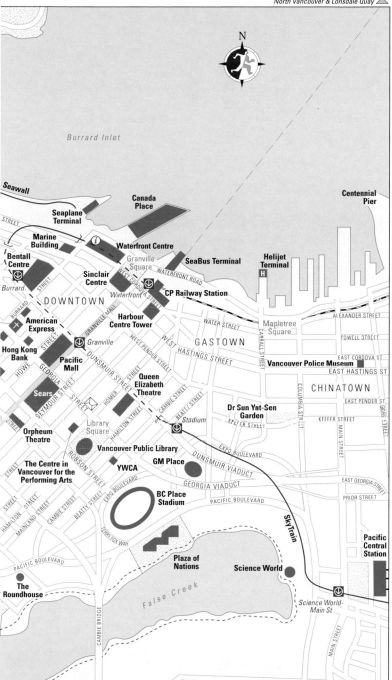

N

Burrard Inlet

Seawall

Canada
Place

Centennial
Pier

STREET

Seaplane
Terminal

Marine
Building

ⓘ Waterfront Centre

Helijet
Terminal
H

Bentall
Centre

Ⓜ

Burrard

Sinclair
Centre

Granville
Square

WATERFRONT ROAD

SeaBus Terminal

WEST CORDOVA STREET

CP Railway Station

Waterfront

Ⓜ

BURRARD STREET

DOWNTOWN

Harbour
Centre Tower

WATER STREET

Mapletree
Square

ALEXANDER STREET

American
Express

GRANVILLE MALL

WEST PENDER STREET

GASTOWN

CARRALL STREET

POWELL STREET

Hong Kong
Bank

Ⓜ *Granville*

WEST HASTINGS STREET

EAST CORDOVA ST

Vancouver Police Museum

HOWE

DUNSMUIR STREET

STREET

EAST HASTINGS ST

Pacific
Mall

GEORGIA STREET

HOMER STREET

Queen
Elizabeth
Theatre

COLUMBIA STREET

CHINATOWN

SEYMOUR STREET

Sears

HAMILTON STREET

CAMBIE STREET

BEATTY STREET

Dr Sun Yat-Sen
Garden

EAST PENDER ST

GORE STREET

STREET

Orpheum
Theatre

Library
Square

Stadium

Ⓜ

KEEFER STREET

KEEFER STREET

MAIN STREET

ROBSON STREET

Vancouver Public Library

EXPO BOULEVARD

The Centre in
Vancouver for the
Performing Arts

YWCA

GM Place

DUNSMUIR VIADUCT

EAST GEORGIA STREET

STREET

GEORGIA VIADUCT

HAMILTON STREET

CAMBIE STREET

BEATTY STREET

EXPO BOULEVARD

BC Place
Stadium

PACIFIC BOULEVARD

MAINLAND STREET

PRIOR STREET

SkyTrain

PACIFIC BOULEVARD

TERRY FOX WAY

Plaza of
Nations

Science World

Pacific
Central
Station

The
Roundhouse

CAMBIE BRIDGE

False Creek

Science World-
Main St

Ⓜ

MAIN STREET

DOWNTOWN & GASTOWN

0   250 m

Burrard Inlet

Canada Place

SeaBus Terminal

COAL HARBOUR ROAD

GASTOWN

Float-Plane Terminal

SkyTrain Terminal

Waterfront Station

Steam Clock

The Landing

WATER STREET

ABBOTT STREET

TROUNCE ALLEY

WEST CORDOVA STREET

Infocentre

SkyTrain

Marine Building

Sinclair Centre

Harbour Centre-The Lookout!

WEST HASTINGS STREET

Chinatown

300

400

Victory Square

DOWNTOWN

WEST HASTINGS STREET

700W

600W

500W

400W

300W

PENDER STREET

WEST PENDER STREET

500

BURRARD STREET

Burrard Station

1000W

900W

800W

Pacific Mall

200W

DUNSMUIR STREET

600

Granville Station

Vancouver Playhouse

Hong Kong Bank of Canada

HOWE STREET

Pacific Mall

The Bay

Queen Elizabeth Theatre

Christ Church Cathedral

RICHARDS STREET

HOMER STREET

GEORGIA STREET

700

Library Square

YWCA

CAMBIE STREET

ALBERNI STREET

Hotel Vancouver

Sears

Ford Centre for the Performing Arts

Vancouver Public Library

Vancouver Art Gallery

GRANVILLE MALL

ROBSON STREET

Robson Square

800

ROBSON STREET

HOMER STREET

HAMILTON STREET

SMITHE STREET

Orpheum Theatre

SMITHE STREET

900

BARCLAY STREET

BURRARD STREET

HORNBY STREET

HOWE STREET

GRANVILLE STREET

SEYMOUR STREET

RICHARDS STREET

Nelson Park

NELSON STREET

NELSON STREET

CAMBIE STREET

1000

COMOX STREET

MAINLAND STREET

YALETOWN

HELMCKEN STREET

1100

HELMCKEN STREET

HAMILTON STREET

DAVIE STREET

DAVIE STREET

N

BURNABY STREET

BURRARD STREET

HORNBY STREET

HOWE STREET

GRANVILLE STREET

SEYMOUR STREET

RICHARDS STREET

HOMER STREET

DRAKE STREET

DRAKE STREET

Granville Island

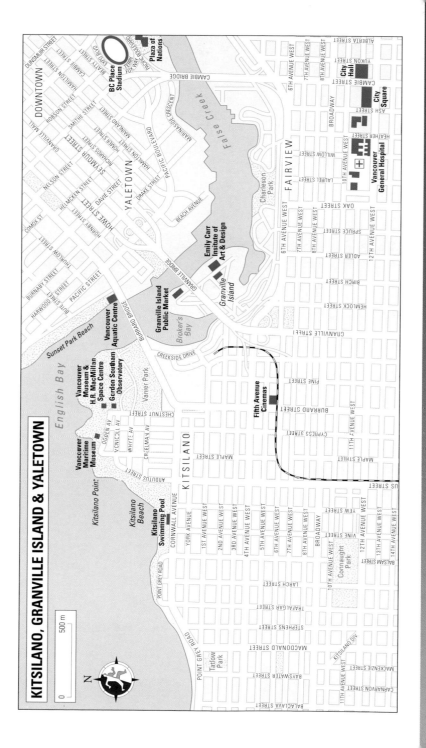

KITSILANO, GRANVILLE ISLAND & YALETOWN

SOUTHERN VANCOUVER

1 km

0

N

Pacific Central Station

Mountain Equipment Co-op

City Hall

City Square

Vancouver General Hospital

Bloedel Conservatory

Queen Elizabeth Park

VanDusen Botanical Gardens

Vancouver Museum
H.R. MacMillan Space Centre
Gordon Southam Observatory
Vancouver Maritime Museum
Kitsilano Point
Kitsilano Beach
Kitsilano Swimming Pool

Granville Island

False Creek

Brocker's Bay

English Bay

FAIRVIEW

Fifth Avenue Cinemas

SHAUGHNESSY

Devonshire Park

Ridge Theatre

ARBUTUS RIDGE

KITSILANO

Hollywood Cinema

POINT GREY

Jericho Beach Park

West Point Grey Park

PACIFIC SPIRIT REGIONAL PARK

Memorial Park West

QUILCHENA

Vanier Park

Charleson Park

Hadden Park

Tatlow Park

McBride Park

Connaught Park

Trafalgar Park

Carnarvon Park

Balaclava Park

Braemar Park

Douglas Park

Hillcrest Park

Midlothian Park

Chaldecott Park

Pacific Boulevard

Street names (selection):

CAROLINA STREET
ST GEORGE STREET
GUELPH ST
BRUNSWICK ST
SCOTIA STREET
QUEBEC STREET
ONTARIO STREET
MANITOBA ST
ALBERTA STREET
YUKON STREET
ASH STREET
WILLOW ST
LAUREL STREET
OAK STREET
SPRUCE STREET
ALDER STREET
BIRCH STREET
HEMLOCK STREET
GRANVILLE STREET
FIR STREET
PINE STREET
MAPLE STREET
CYPRESS STREET
BURRARD STREET
ARBUTUS STREET
YEW STREET
VINE STREET
BALSAM STREET
LARCH STREET
MACDONALD STREET
BAYSWATER STREET
STEPHENS STREET
TRAFALGAR STREET
TRUTCH STREET
BLENHEIM STREET
WATERLOO STREET
COLLINGWOOD STREET
DUNBAR STREET
ALMA STREET
HIGHBURY STREET
WALLACE STREET
CROWN STREET
CAMOSUN STREET
DISCOVERY
COURTENAY
TRIMBLE STREET

N.W. MARINE DRIVE
POINT GREY ROAD
CORNWALL ROAD
BROADWAY
KING EDWARD AVENUE WEST
VALLEY DRIVE
ANGUS DRIVE
NANTON AVENUE
OSLER STREET
SELKIRK STREET
MATTHEWS AVENUE
MARGUERITE STREET
CARTIER
ALEXANDRA STREET
LAURIER AVENUE
WEST BOULEVARD
EAST BOULEVARD
PINE CRESCENT
QUALCHENA
OLIVE CRESCENT
MAPLE CRESCENT
MACKENZIE STREET

2 AVENUE WEST
4 AVENUE WEST
4TH AVENUE WEST
6 AVENUE WEST
8 AVENUE WEST
10 AVENUE WEST
12 AVENUE WEST
16 AVENUE WEST
20 AVENUE WEST
24 AVENUE WEST
28 AVENUE WEST
33 AVENUE WEST
36 AVENUE WEST

MAIN STREET
SOPHIA STREET
PRINCE EDWARD STREET
WALDEN STREET
QUEBEC STREET
ONTARIO STREET
COLUMBIA STREET
TUPPER STREET
CAMBIE STREET
HEATHER STREET
HILLCREST
MIDLOTHIAN AVENUE
33 AVENUE EAST
KINGSWAY

CAMBIE BRIDGE
GRANVILLE BRIDGE
BURRARD BRIDGE

BEATTY STREET
SMITHE ST
NELSON ST
HELMCKEN ST
DAVIE STREET
DRAKE ST
PACIFIC STREET
RICHARDS STREET
HORNBY STREET
ROBSON ST
MAINLAND ST

Jonathan Rogers Park